Ghosts
of Sheridan Circle

Ghosts
of Sheridan Circle

How a Washington Assassination
Brought Pinochet's Terror State to Justice

Alan McPherson

THE UNIVERSITY OF NORTH CAROLINA PRESS

Chapel Hill

This book was published with the assistance of the
Thornton H. Brooks Fund of the University of North Carolina Press.

© 2019 The University of North Carolina Press

All rights reserved

Designed by Jamison Cockerham
Set in Arno, Futura, and Scala Sans
by Tseng Information Systems, Inc.

The University of North Carolina Press has been a member
of the Green Press Initiative since 2003.

Cover photographs: (front, bottom, and back cover) AP Photo/Peter Bregg; (front, top)
Fondo Orlando Letelier, Archivo de la Administración, Santiago, Chile.

LIBRARY OF CONGRESS CATALOGING-IN-PUBLICATION DATA
Names: McPherson, Alan L., author.
Title: Ghosts of Sheridan Circle : how a Washington assassination
   brought Pinochet's terror state to justice / Alan McPherson.
Description: Chapel Hill : University of North Carolina Press, [2019] |
   Includes bibliographical references and index.
Identifiers: LCCN 2019011818 | ISBN 9781469653501 (cloth : alk. paper) |
   ISBN 9781469669298 (pbk : alk. paper) | ISBN 9781469653518 (ebook)
Subjects: LCSH: Letelier, Orlando—Assassination. | Moffitt, Ronni Karpen—
   Assassination. | Assassination—Washington (D.C.)—History—20th century. |
   Assassination—Investigation—United States—History—20th century. | United
   States—Foreign relations—Chile. | Chile—Foreign relations—United States.
Classification: LCC F3101.L47 M39 2019 | DDC 327.7308309/04—dc23
   LC record available at https://lccn.loc.gov/2019011818

To

MICHAEL H. HUNT

(1942–2018)

mentor and friend

CONTENTS

Introduction: Such a Safe City *1*

PART ONE *Assassination*

1. The Center of Each Other's World *11*
2. Himmler of the Andes *23*
3. Kill the Bitch and You Finish the Spawn *29*
4. A Rather Unsavory Past *44*
5. Stand Up with Me *61*
6. Some Misguided Sense of Patriotism *73*
7. Homicide Squad *87*

PART TWO *Investigation*

8. CHILBOM *105*
9. Letelier Diplomacy *117*
10. *Cueca Sola* *147*
11. Events Are Developing at Such a Rapid Pace *164*
12. Prisoners, Survivors, and Judgment Creditors *182*

» PART THREE *Prosecution*

13 Cover-Up *199*

14 The Ghost Who Haunts Our Chile Policy *214*

15 No More Lies Are to Be Told *225*

16 Fight until the End *240*

17 I'm Not Going to Any Jail *249*

18 The Fear Is Over *267*

Epilogue: Intellectual Authors, 1996–2018 *281*

Acknowledgments 297

Notes 299

Bibliography 359

Index 365

A section of illustrations begins on page 125

Ghosts
of Sheridan Circle

INTRODUCTION

Such a Safe City

"Isabel, I have a surprise for you. Have lunch with me."

"Today will be difficult. I have work."

"But you will *love* this surprise," Orlando Letelier insisted. "Come and get me at twelve-thirty and leave your work for the afternoon."[1]

Isabel Letelier acceded. After all, her husband was a charmer. The couple, parents to four teenage boys, had recently reunited after a months-long separation sparked by Orlando's infidelity. "A second honeymoon," Isabel called it.[2]

Besides, there was no time to argue. It was 9 A.M., time for Orlando to go to work at the Institute for Policy Studies (IPS) in Washington, D.C.'s Dupont Circle. He had been at the leftist think tank for nearly two years, using IPS as a platform to undermine General Augusto Pinochet, the iron-fisted dictator who had overthrown the government of President Salvador Allende of Chile. Letelier had been Allende's ambassador to the United States, and then his minister with three portfolios. Now, as a private citizen, he exposed Pinochet's human rights atrocities, incited boycotts, and discouraged investment.

Two of Orlando's colleagues happened to ride with him that day. Michael and Ronni Moffitt, both twenty-five and recently married to each other, had had their car break down the day before. Having become friends with their mentor and his wife, they had enjoyed a late dinner at the Leteliers' and then driven home in Orlando's car. They were back the following morning to pick him up.

The Moffitts waited while Letelier, ever tardy, showered and dressed, skipped breakfast, and rushed out the door. Isabel barely had time to kiss him goodbye. Michael offered to keep driving, but Orlando took the wheel of his 1975 Chevrolet Chevelle Malibu Classic, an unusual muscle car for such a sophisticate. Out of gallantry, Michael opened the front passenger door for Ronni. He plopped himself on the back seat.

That September 21, 1976, was a drizzly, misty morning in the nation's capital. In less than an hour, Orlando and Ronni would be dead. Michael would be traumatized.

"I never learned what the surprise was," Isabel recalled over forty years later.[3]

▶▶ The dust-blue Chevelle took about fifteen minutes to navigate its usual route out of the Leteliers' Bethesda, Maryland, suburb toward IPS. It made its way down River Road into the District of Columbia, south on 46th Street, left on Massachusetts Avenue, past the vice president's home, and through the congested diplomatic neighborhood known as Embassy Row.

Ronni Moffitt, a flute player and music lover, hummed a tune on and off. She and Letelier, who always drove unhurriedly, discussed a science book they had read as children. From behind them Michael sometimes chimed in, read, looked out the window, or admired his new bride's profile. He cracked the window to let Letelier's cigarette smoke escape.

At 9:35, Letelier and the Moffitts passed the new Chilean ambassador's residence, on the edge of Sheridan Circle, a few blocks from IPS and fourteen blocks from the White House. Embassies ringed the posh traffic circle, at the center of which stood the Civil War general Philip Sheridan's statue on horseback.

Unbeknownst to the occupants of the Chevelle, following them was a gray Ford sedan with two men inside, the passenger holding a metallic two-button beeper, the kind on-call doctors used back then, plugged into the Ford's cigarette lighter. As Orlando began to steer into Sheridan Circle, the man pressed one button, and then the other.

Sitting in back, Michael heard a "pssss," like the sound when you "pour water on a hot wire," he later told the FBI. Then "there was a flash in the upper right part of the car, right behind Ronni's head."[4] A momentary silence was then followed by an explosion so thunderous it was heard half a mile away at the State Department. *That's what it feels like when you're electrocuted*, thought Michael.[5] An orange fireball shot up from the floor of the Chevelle. It burned Letelier's left shoulder and singed everyone's hair. Black smoke filled the vehicle, and soot covered its passengers.

The shockwaves held Michael's arms outstretched. They blew off Letelier's door and caved in the roof. "It was as if the entire car were heaved off the ground," Moffitt later said. "Everything was thrown upward, my head struck the roof of the car." The Chevelle shot up into the air and traveled eighty-two feet before crashing into an illegally parked orange Volkswagen. The explosion left shattered glass, twisted metal, torn flesh, and spilled blood in a radius of sixty feet.

Inside the car, said Moffitt, "there was smoke everywhere and intense heat, as if we were in a furnace. Most powerful of all, though, was the overwhelming stench of burned flesh and hair."

"I found myself on my hands and knees in the back. My shoes had been blown off and, initially, I had no physical sensation below my waist. My first instinct was to get out of the car before the gas tank exploded. Somehow, I pulled myself up to a window which had been blown out, and I toppled out of the car. My lungs were burning and I was choking and gasping for air."

Michael kept his eye on Ronni, who stumbled out of the car. "Since she was on her feet, I assumed that she must be all right."

He came around the driver's side and saw Letelier wedged between his seat, the steering column, and the collapsed roof. "Orlando was turned around facing the back of the car. He was leaning back, and his head was rolling back and forth. His eyes were moving a little but he looked unconscious."[6]

Shouting "Orlando, this is Michael, can you hear me?" Moffitt slapped his friend's face. The dazed Letelier muttered something unintelligible. His eyes were blank. His mouth opened and closed, gasping for air. He kept his hands high above him, pawing at nothing. "He tried to put his hand around my neck, but had no strength. Tears ran down his cheeks."[7] "I then tried to lift him out, but it was very difficult since he was surrounded by jagged metal. And I was getting cut trying to lift him."

"After I had moved him slightly, I saw that his lower torso—basically, the whole bottom half of his body—had been blown off." The bomb, placed directly below Letelier's feet, had blasted open the floor of the car and severed his legs just below the hips. The exploding car dragged his lower limbs against the asphalt of the street. His left foot, still in a sock and shoe with bone and pulp sticking out, lay fifteen yards from the crash. Back in the car, "there were gobs of flesh and bloody pieces of seat stuffing everywhere," recalled Moffitt. "A sturdy six-foot man looked like a broken doll."

"Assassins, fascists!" cried Moffitt, consumed by wrath.[8]

Moffitt had not noticed that his wife had stumbled to the grass in front of the Romanian embassy, clutching her throat. Shrapnel had severed her carotid artery, which supplies blood to the neck and head. Blood gurgled out of her mouth, but also down her trachea and into her lungs.

She was drowning in her own blood.

By this time a female doctor, who happened to walk by Sheridan Circle, was reaching into Ronni's throat, trying to plug the artery. "Her belly was swollen and protruding like she was eight months pregnant and blood was gushing out of her mouth—a huge current of blood," recalled Moffitt.

"Save her! Save my sweetheart!" he begged the doctor.[9]

Police were also now on the scene. One officer, misunderstanding, tried to pull the doctor away from Ronni. "By this time I was losing, or had lost, control of myself," said Michael. "I was hysterical, and . . . there was a moment that I thought the police were going to shoot me. I sensed that they mistook me for the criminal, the murderer. I remember thinking that I was going to die."[10] One officer saw Moffitt "running around, very upset. . . . He was yelling words to the effect that the fascists had planted a bomb."[11]

"Somebody help me get Orlando out of here!" Moffitt pleaded, as ambulances screamed to a halt among what was now a crowd of emergency responders and onlookers.[12] Police and paramedics freed Letelier from his seat and tried to stop what blood he had left in his body from spilling out of the stumps that used to be his legs.

Orlando Letelier died before the ambulance reached George Washington Hospital, half a mile away. He bled dry in less than ten minutes, his heart finding no blood left to pump. "Exsanguination," the coroner would mark as the cause of death.[13]

A second ambulance followed with Ronni Moffitt. As he saw the paramedics loading her in, Michael shouted:

"That's my wife! I'm going with her!"

"No, you're not," said a police officer. "You'll just be in the way."

"I want to be with my wife! I was in the car!" pleaded Moffitt, pointing to the charred chassis.

"Yeah, sure," said the officer.

"I *was*!" shouted Moffitt. "Let me go with her!"

"No!" snapped the officer. "You can't help. One of these guys will take you to the hospital."

After the ambulance left, Moffitt, face blackened, shirt torn, screamed up at the Chilean ambassador's residence maybe a hundred feet from the blast: "Fascists! Chilean fascists have done this!"[14] He got into a police cruiser, cursing and crying, and headed for the George Washington Hospital emergency room.

Before Moffitt could see her, the ER doctors tried to revive Ronni. They pounded her chest. They started three IVs. They injected heart stimulants.

They inserted a tracheostomy tube to pump oxygen into her lungs. They sent electric jolts into her. They cut open her chest to get to the heart and lungs.

Meanwhile, Michael was being treated for minor cuts, a fragment of metal having lodged itself in his breast bone. At first, he could not get anything concrete on his wife. "I remember I requested a priest and asked him to help me. I asked the priest to ask God to spare Ronni's life—just for that one small favor, to spare her life. I was filled with anger and horror and a feeling of helplessness."[15]

"They told me Ronni was hurt very badly, but that they were working on her, and it seemed like an eternity." "And they took me in a little room and put me on one of those examining tables and made me lie down." The staff put Moffitt in a green hospital gown and administered tranquilizers to mitigate his shock. Police interviewed him. "There were several people standing around and one of the doctors came over and said, 'Your wife is dead.'"

"It's a trauma that will stay with me for the rest of my life," Moffitt reflected fourteen years later. "Nothing and no one will ever erase those scenes of horror, the moments of almost unbearable desperation: the tragedy of witnessing Orlando's death, with his dismembered legs, a wince of pain on his face that I cannot describe, yet mixed with a certain serenity."

》》 Before he heard of Ronni's or even Letelier's death, Moffitt called IPS to alert Isabel. Receptionist Alyce Wiley heard his voice and began to jest. He cut her off: "Be quiet, Alyce." "I knew something bad had happened," she recalled.[16]

Letelier's secretary then called Isabel. Barely half an hour had passed since her husband and the Moffitts had left her house. "It appears that Orlando had an accident in his car. Go right away to George Washington Hospital."[17]

If there was an accident I hope it wasn't Orlando's fault because he would never forgive himself if he caused bad injury to Michael or Ronni, thought Isabel.[18] She also had a terrible premonition, "a fatal sensation. So I was going to throw on a black jacket. I couldn't. I put on something colorful instead."[19]

When she arrived, "an enormous crowd was at the door of the hospital. I didn't want to think their presence had something to do with me."[20] Strangers pointed. "That's her! That's the widow!" *Oh, they must be talking about something else*, she thought.[21]

"I walked in, nobody told me anything until I went upstairs and heard something about a bomb."[22]

Hospital staff escorted Letelier to a room where Michael Moffitt waited, sitting, his forehead down on his folded arms. "He was crying like a little boy," she recalled. "'They got my baby, too,' he raised his head saying, 'they got my baby.' We embraced. My chest hurt and I felt very weak."

An IPS secretary walked up to her and gave her "a very deep look."

"Orlando?" said Letelier.

The secretary nodded.

"Something serious happened to him?"

Another nod.

"When . . . people told me [Orlando] was dead, I felt my legs might collapse. I had nothing to hold on to. The lack of Orlando caused a pain in my chest. A darkness filled up inside me where he had been."

"Mrs. Letelier, it was not an accident," a hospital administrator told her. "A bomb exploded under your husband's legs." He added that regulations dictated that she could not see Orlando's body. "But I wanted to say goodbye to what was left of him, even if it was just a hand."[23]

The administrator kept telling her to calm down. Isabel countered that she *was* calm. Finally, Ann Barnet, a surgeon and the wife of IPS's Richard Barnet, intervened to let her see Letelier's corpse.[24]

"His body was mangled and disfigured," she remembered years later. "His lower torso was a mass of blood and charred skin. I could see the pain and surprise on his face. It is an image I shall never forget—not even for a moment. The grief and sorrow were overwhelming and immediate, to see my beloved husband's life ended in this manner was more than I could bear."[25] Isabel told a journalist friend that "what most impressed me. . . . was that Orlando, before he died, realized what had happened, his face showed amazement, as if to say, 'They did it, they finally did it.'"[26] She touched him and kissed him.[27]

Moffitt faced more anguish still. "I had to call Ronni's parents. I found a phone and I talked to her mother, Hilda, who began telling jokes. I interrupted her to tell her that Ronni was dead. It was horrible. Then I called my own parents."

He spent the rest of the day with the FBI. "They needed a total debriefing, in painstaking detail. It was grueling. They took me to our home in Potomac for help with possible clues. Bomb sniffing dogs smelled the scent on me and growled. . . . I was not given a moment's rest and did not bathe. My hair was singed and matted and I carried with me the horrible smells and soot of the bombing. I did not wash the entire evening, as if to suffer in some small way what they had suffered."

"That night I went to stay with friends in Georgetown. There was a constant flow of visitors all evening. Congressmen, Senators, diplomats, people from all over Washington came. I was numb and empty. I did not appreciate, even then, the extent to which my life also had been destroyed that day. After people stopped coming, I drank liquor until I fell asleep."

"Everything I was and loved and cared for was destroyed by that bomb."[28]

Fifteen-year-old Juan Pablo Letelier, meanwhile, was between classes at his high school when "they summoned me on the loudspeakers to the principal's office. I couldn't imagine what it could be. Nothing like that had ever happened to me. The principal told me that my aunt Cecilia was going to pick us boys up at school because Orlando had had an accident.... Those were the longest minutes of my life."

An accident, he thought. "I imagined him, like in the movies, with a leg in a cast, his foot up high."[29]

Riding in the car toward the hospital, his brother Francisco, known as "Pancho," heard on the radio vague news about a car bomb with two wounded and one dead. His "very straight-laced" aunt would not tell the boys what had happened. "I could tell that she was having a hard time, that there was something she was not telling us." From down the street from Sheridan Circle, he even saw the emergency vehicles, without knowing they were for his father and Ronni Moffitt.[30]

"I prayed silently that my *papá* would be only among the wounded," said Juan Pablo. "I never imagined anything like this, I never grasped the bomb. We were in such a safe city ... such a safe city."

Another brother, Cristián, was at the University of South Carolina, coincidentally coming out of a World Politics lecture about Cold War détente. A woman came up to him and said, "Are you Cristián Letelier?"

"Yes."

"Your father's just been killed."

He fell back against the wall. "Get away from me!" he told her. "I don't know you."

"No, really, you should call home." He went to the airport and took the first flight to Washington.[31]

When the Letelier boys arrived at the hospital, Isabel hugged them and said, "Yes it's true. But look: Your father has been killed by Pinochet. He sent people to kill him. But in this moment I want you to promise me one thing: You are not to hate. Don't allow hate to enter your heart. If you hate you will be just like them, the criminals."[32] "This affected me deeply," said Juan Pablo. "Only then did I understand that he had died."[33]

▶▶ To this day, the killing of Orlando Letelier and Ronni Moffitt remains the only assassination of a foreign diplomat on U.S. soil. It is also the only state-sponsored assassination ever in Washington, and the most important in U.S. history. "Until Osama bin Laden," assessed one historian, "the Letelier-Moffitt assassinations constituted the most brazen act of international terrorism ever committed in the capital of the United States."[34] It is still the only *state-sponsored* such act, and the only car bomb.

In the fall of 1976, the Letelier-Moffitt assassination was clearly going to create major ripples among several groups.

The FBI agents and others assigned to this case faced a near-unsolvable crime. The bombing left a mess in Sheridan Circle, and the sophistication of crime scene investigation in the 1970s was not what it would be decades later. Apart from Moffitt, there were no witnesses, and no one claimed responsibility. Unlike the Watergate burglary of a few years earlier, no one caught red-handed could be pumped for information. Who could possibly be behind this? Who could have hated a private citizen such as Letelier so much as to provoke a massive international incident? If they lived abroad, how could U.S. justice ever reach them?

The murder of a former foreign official and of a U.S. citizen not only inside U.S. borders but also in the capital set off major diplomatic alarms, as well. The Pinochet government was a Cold War ally of the United States. Had it really dared to assassinate at the heart of the most powerful nation in the world? Did Pinochet know about this? Did he order it, or were there rogue assassins in his government? How would this affect U.S.-Chilean relations?

And the families of Letelier and Moffitt would forever be marked by this tragedy. How were they to live after such devastation? How to hold to account one of the most ruthless, secretive regimes in the world? How to press investigators and the U.S. government not to give up?

Most important for the families, the investigators, the diplomats, and the millions who followed this story, would the case ever produce a full measure of justice?

It took almost two decades to answer these questions. A full exploration of the Letelier assassination has eluded us until now. Yet it would hold implications for Chile, the United States, terrorism, human rights, and the fate of democracy everywhere.

PART ONE

Assassination

1

The Center of Each Other's World

The three-year-old with the orange hair made an impression on the indigenous Mapuche of southern Chile. "*Corilonco, corilonco!*" they shouted in Araucanian. *Head of fire*. The boy from nearby Temuco would earn other nicknames: "Nano," "El Colorado" (the colored one), "El Fanta" for the orange soft drink.[1] He cherished the attention. His uncle recalled him as "a freckled child, redheaded, extraordinarily alive, loving, charming, and talkative. The timidity of the small-town child was not a part of his childhood personality."[2]

It was this boy, Marco Orlando Letelier (luh-TELL-yay) del Solar, who would bleed to death in Sheridan Circle forty-one years later.

And it is halfway through his life that Isabel Margarita Morel Gumucio would fall in love with him, calling him "the center of my world."[3]

>> Isabel was born on January 3, 1932, on the outskirts of Santiago, Chile's capital, 400 miles north of Orlando's natal Temuco. She spent her childhood in the same upper-middle-class home with stable but dissimilar parents.

Isabel described her mother, Victoria "Toto" Gumucio, as "an extraordinary human being, . . . very avant-garde—very forward for her times."[4] The youngest of eleven, this "surprise child" largely evaded her parents' and society's expectations.[5] "Her family was upper middle class, but she spent a lot of time with the working people," mostly farmers and fishermen, recalled Isabel. She was "very different from most of the people in her family" and from most of class-conscious 1930s Chile.

"My mother was very socially minded. Very conscious of social injustice. . . . She just met people and as she liked them, she never questioned them. . . . She would bring these people home, so I saw a great variety of human beings.

And my father was very stern and very serious, and he didn't want anything to do with these strange kinds of people."[6]

At age fifteen, "Toto" was betrothed to a man twice her age, Alfredo Morel, the eldest of six. It seemed to Isabel that her father had always worked for a paper company, becoming its general controller. He was also an avid art collector.[7] "He was the neatest man I ever saw in my life," reflected Isabel. "I never saw him uncombed or without the right shirt, perfectly ironed."[8]

Her father looked away as Toto took up the unusual profession of teaching calisthenics in her home. She also sewed and painted, and she wore shorts when no one else did. Grandson Cristián called Victoria "the Jack LaLanne of Chile. She could walk on her hands and clap!"[9] Though he was "severe" and "old fashioned," Alfredo gave Toto "a lot of room," recalled Francisco, another grandson. "My grandmother was a naturalist. She got caught up in all the health crazes coming through all the Germans that were arriving into Santiago. She soon became a great believer in swimming nude in the ocean, spas.... We walked everywhere at a high brisk pace.... We would rather walk than take the bus.... My mother didn't turn out to be as radical or as revolutionary as my grandmother."[10]

"My father," Isabel recalled, "would have loved to have had a wife who played bridge and canasta with her friends and participated in charities. That would have been his ideal woman. Instead he had this woman that would go out and play tennis" and teach volleyball to fishermen. He devoured newspapers and opposed most of Chile's presidents as crooks, especially the Social Democrats. He did, however, believe in basic freedoms and tolerance.[11]

When Isabel was five, in the midst of a presidential election, a beloved nanny, Carmen Rosa, told the little girl to root for Pedro Aguirre Cerda, the only candidate who cared about the poor. "We have to help the poor," she would tell Isabel, teaching her campaign songs. The revelation shocked her family—but Aguirre won.[12] At her Catholic girls' school, Isabel absorbed from Father Luis Hurtado a sense of mission toward the poor. She loved to sing and play the guitar from a young age and had "a sense of civic participation, but through the Church."[13]

On Saturdays, students worked with poor families in nearby shantytowns. "I saw people with houses made of pressed tin cans ... attached to some two-by-fours. There were no floors, just soil.... They had one bed with no sheets and the whole family slept there.... I remember that every Saturday I brought a kilo of beans or something.... That was something very important in my life, the value in God's eyes that poor people had."

Isabel became the godmother of a shantytown family's newborn. "This is a story I have never told anybody," she later related. Once, a days-long storm raised the riverbed near the family's shack. Its newborn was "in a little wooden crate—an apple crate, and the water took the baby away." "It was terrible. I felt injustice, such tremendous injustice."

Armed with brains and compassion, Isabel Morel was destined for higher education. "I had glasses early because I read too much. I read everything in the house by the time I was twelve or thirteen, including all the books my father forbade me to read." She resisted her father's wishes to go to "finishing school, . . . where you were taught how to run a house, how to do the preserves at the right time, . . . how to serve tea."

She chose instead library science at the university, where she convinced authorities to let her matriculate even though she was only sixteen, under the minimum age. In the afternoons, Morel majored in Spanish literature and also took courses in philosophy, psychology, ethics, "you name it, for five years." She did nothing with her librarian's degree but instead added courses in fine arts, which became her true passion.[14]

>> Orlando Letelier, born three months after Isabel Morel on April 13, 1932, also came from a comfortable and largely apolitical background. His mother, Inés del Solar Rosenberg, the daughter of a German woman and, as one grandson suspected, Jewish, was a volunteer social worker. Her brother recalled her as "a restless poet and avid reader who occasionally submitted articles to magazines and literary publications in Temuco and Santiago." She and her husband formed a rather secular but "united and tradition-conscious family."[15] Don Orlando Letelier Ruiz, the patriarch, operated a print shop and at times a newspaper. He was a member of Chile's Radical Party and a Mason, standing out from the more pedigreed, conservative Leteliers, who had emigrated from France over a century earlier.

When Orlando was three, his parents moved to Santiago. Don Orlando taught his son the causes of poverty in Chile and exposed him to the suffering of the Mapuches, who had been "pacified" just sixty years before Orlando was born.[16] Little Orlando spent his early years in a Montessori school where, like Isabel, he flourished as a freethinker. Also, like Isabel's, Orlando's father "was generally the least flexible in the area of exchange of ideas, opinions, and attitudes. In a way, he still held on to his small-town outlook."[17]

At fourteen, Letelier surprised his parents by asking to enroll in military school — not as a career, he explained, but to imbue himself with self-reliance and discipline.[18] For a while he excelled at academics, marching, and boxing and was appointed cadet officer.

His instinct that a military life was not for him proved right. Once, a teacher instructed students that, if a superior said that black was white, they were to agree. Letelier obtained permission to speak: "I understand that strict discipline is absolutely necessary in military life, but personally I doubt that anyone could convince me that what is white is really black." The teacher punished him for insubordination.[19]

During his fourth year at military school, a drink from a mountain stream resulted in amoebas in Letelier's digestive system, which caused dysentery. The cure burned holes in his stomach. The bleeding ulcers forced him to withdraw from the academy.[20]

>> The ulcers were also fateful for the young couple-to-be. Orlando enrolled in law school and, like many other young Latin Americans, joined a political party. He chose the Liberals but soon found that they were "very reactionary."[21] His uncle described the Liberals as having little "sensibility for the poor and helpless and a wounding and arrogant contempt for those they classified as 'half-breeds,' or the middle class without famous ancestors or well-known surnames."[22]

Letelier and Morel met at a dinner party, she in her second year of university, he in his first of law school. She was not at first as impressed as her sister by this boy everyone called "Nano." "After dinner we went to a disco, and we were eight, and we got into a Volkswagen. Can you imagine eight people in a Volkswagen? We were supposed to sit on the guys' laps, and my sister said, 'I don't sit on the lap of anybody,' and I said 'I couldn't care less' and sat on Orlando's lap." "Orlando was very taken. The next day he called *me*. . . . And he would call me every day after lunch," and soon they met for lunch between classes.[23] He was struck by her beauty, even more so by her singing. He broke up with his girlfriend immediately.[24]

Isabel soon warmed to Nano. "He was full of life. He was a tall redhead, very gentle, but full of life." An extended courtship emerged from shared passions for art, music, and politics. "We were friends for a couple of years. He visited my house. . . . We raised some money together for the university and some of his projects. For the art center at the law school, we wanted to bring theater groups from other schools to the law school, and they needed speakers and things like that."[25] "He sang with a gorgeous voice. He was a super baritone," she recalled in 2017 with a wistful smile.[26]

"Once we had fallen in love," she reminisced, "we had a rare and wonderful combination. We were deeply passionate towards one another, and also we were friends." Orlando "was tall and handsome, and very charismatic. His dynamic way made him capable of accomplishing immense things. He had that unusual combination of being both a peaceful, gentle and loving man, and yet one imbued with relentless energy. People responded to him, liked to be around him, and appreciated his companionship. He was a graceful, elegant man who nonetheless radiated power."[27]

The Letelier name opened social and political doors for Orlando, and he soon grew a circle of close and one day influential friends, such as his future fellow cabinet member José Tohá.[28]

Through law school friends, some from dictator-plagued Venezuela, "I got my political education," Isabel recalled. "It was the first time I had ever really heard about dictatorship and torture, about corporations keeping more than their share, about nationalization of natural resources. Orlando himself was talking about copper belonging to the Chileans. I hadn't realized that it was important that the Chileans own their own copper. That was an awakening." She told Orlando she considered herself on the "Christian left," but she couldn't find a party to join.

"At the end of my second year, we were signing petitions for Pablo Neruda, who had fled the country because he was a communist and they were threatening to put him in jail." Neruda, a celebrated poet, went on to win the Nobel Prize in Literature.[29]

Letelier remembered *his* second year of university as his own awakening. "The truth is that, when I was young, politics mattered little to me, even less so socialism." As he read more and had long discussions with physician and senator Salvador Allende, among others, he grew a social conscience and joined the Socialist Party.[30] Early on in their relationship, he told Isabel that finding out about the extraction of copper, Chile's primary export, by foreign corporations was "a blow to my heart."[31]

"The invasion of Guatemala [in 1954] and the marines in Central America were a big cause célèbre at the university," she added. "We were marching and protesting. At the University of Chile you could not help being aware of politics and American imperialism." University radicalized both of them, with its cocktail of artists, existentialists, and Marxists. But the couple remained largely uninvolved in politics. Rather, they enjoyed those whom Isabel called their "unconventional," "diverse" friends. Accomplished singers and guitarists—Isabel taught Orlando much of what he knew—they fell deeper in love with each other.

As graduation neared, Letelier apprenticed with a lawyer while Morel taught Spanish at Santiago schools. "Finally, I had a salary," said Isabel. "I was so happy to be independent. I worked there until I left Chile. While I was working there, I started a marionette theater" and ran it for three years.[32] Orlando lent his baritone as the dapper prince of the marionettes in Isabel's large, colorful productions. He also performed in Thornton Wilder's *Our Town*.[33]

In 1953, Isabel finished her master's thesis.[34] The following year Orlando finished his own, on copper. "Copper was his obsession," Isabel recalled. "And his hair was copper colored, and when he spoke about copper and natural resources in Chile, he always got very inflamed. I would always say, 'Oh, your head is on fire, Orlando, Your head is burning.'" *Corilonco* lived.

》 In late 1955, Orlando and Isabel married in her childhood home. They were both twenty-three, and she wanted six children "very close in age." A first pregnancy ended in miscarriage, and then another produced a son in 1957 named Cristián. José followed in 1958.

Letelier's first job after university was, logically enough, in Chile's newly created copper department in the Central Bank. One day he announced to Isabel that Allende, the Marxist who was running to be Chile's president, was coming to dinner. Burdened with a newborn and another on the way, Isabel was annoyed: "Why do you have to invite everybody, Orlando?" She failed to remember that her mother used to do the same.

Allende lost the 1958 presidential election, and Letelier's position on the Marxist's economic team spelled personal disaster. Not only was he fired from the copper department, but he was also told, "Do not waste any time trying to find a job with this government. You are not going to find a job from north to south. You are being punished for being a traitor to your class. This is a lesson you should learn now when you are young."

Isabel was twenty-seven and worried. "My third baby," Pancho, "was only five days old. So we had three babies and Orlando couldn't find a job. ... People at the copper department, who had been our friends, now crossed the street rather than say hello to us. ... Some people in my family—we had a large family—didn't show any sympathy."[35]

The Leteliers were resourceful. Three months after Orlando lost his job, in late 1959, he and the family left for Venezuela, where his exiled friends were now back and in power and offered him a position with the Vollmer Group conglomerate doing market studies. Soon after, the governments of the Americas created the Inter-American Development Bank (IDB) in

Washington, and its first president happened to be Letelier's former law professor, Felipe Herrera. He offered Orlando a job.

Just then, Allende showed up at the Leteliers' in Caracas and told them to pack their bags for Cuba to mark the first anniversary of Fidel Castro's revolution. While Castro made an hours-long speech to a million people in the Plaza de la Revolución, Ernesto "Ché" Guevara, then the head of Cuba's Central Bank, first chatted with Orlando. The next day he offered him a job. "Orlando was very enthusiastic. He loved it." On one hand, Cuba had great weather and raising kids there was "easy. They had great doctors." On the other hand, everybody in Cuba was on board with the revolution, whereas in Washington Orlando could act as a counterweight to his bourgeois colleagues at the IDB.[36] At the end of 1960, the Leteliers packed up again.

In Washington, the family spent a busy but politically subdued decade. "Being an international employee those days," according to Isabel, "you had to promise not to be involved in politics in any way." Besides, Letelier's working for a bank that promised to develop and integrate Latin America was a statement in itself. "Those first years were very exciting. They were mystical about the bank.... There was a lot of pride at having Spanish as the language at the bank and all the Americans had to speak Spanish.... It was a time when most of the countries were democracies. It was sort of a golden era in Latin America.... We were dreaming of a Latin American common market, a Latin American parliament, a Latin American cabinet. Very grandiose dreams we had."[37]

The young Chilean economist impressed many with his charm and boundless energy. In his decade at the IDB, he held a variety of positions that offered world travel, especially to Asia. A superior at the IDB called him "daring, but reasonably and intelligently so. He needed to be challenged without himself being challenging. He was not afraid of danger. He was seldom on time, but he always had a good and acceptable reason for being late. His gift for making friends and his cordiality were his best allies."[38]

As of 1960, the CIA kept tabs on Letelier, citing his "reputation as a capable, hard-working individual who earned most of his promotions." It described the economist as "personable, socially pleasant" and his wife as "very active and charming."[39]

What his uncle described as Letelier's "superhuman capacity for work" produced admirers, detractors, and dangers. He once worked so hard that he passed out in his office and had to be admitted to a hospital. The diagnosis: *surménage*, or overwork.[40] He was also hospitalized for ulcers.[41] When Letelier died, the *Washington Post* editorialized that he was "a very brave man, as well as being an extremely arrogant person," citing his "dictatorial managerial style" at the IDB.[42]

The Leteliers' fourth and final son, Juan Pablo, was born in Washington in 1961. "When he was born, Orlando told me, 'There you have your family—love it—take care of it—honor it. That's it.' The six-son family that we envisioned was good for Chile but not for a couple in the United States."[43]

"Orlando was always extremely dedicated to our sons and spent countless hours imparting his special views of life, politics and humanity to them."[44] He inculcated the boys with the discipline he had acquired at the academy. He refused to sign their report cards until their grades were good enough. He'd bounce a quarter off their bed sheets to test their tautness. He taught them to box.[45] When Letelier entered the kitchen he'd say, "*Buenos días*, how are the troops?" "Well, my captain!" the boys would answer. On Saturdays, after breakfast, the captain commanded his troops to study Chilean history and copy readings in Spanish. "I hated those classes," recalled Juan Pablo, the youngest.[46]

Yet Letelier was as loving a father as he was a husband. When he saw his first baby, recalled Isabel, "he was so moved he fainted. It was a miracle." He coached their soccer team. With her and the boys, "Orlando was so powerful and wonderful, such a support, such a rock, he was almighty. He gave advice and fortitude, and even in the worst moments he always said 'we will overcome.'"[47] A psychiatrist who evaluated Isabel in the 1990s observed that her relationship with Orlando "was idyllic. . . . Orlando was the center of her life as she was of his—he was always proud of the sculpting and painting in which she became involved and encouraged her by telling her that her work was 'like magic.'"[48]

Isabel, too, worked outside the home. From 1961 to 1964, at the Department of State's Foreign Service Institute, she taught Spanish to diplomats. She described those as "boring" years filled with teaching basic phrases.[49] By 1965 she moved to Georgetown University.[50]

Three months out of the year she brought her four boys back to Chile, making sure they learned Chilean history and culture and Spanish-language literature. Cristián, José, Francisco, and Juan Pablo grew to be fluent in English and Spanish. They identified with both the United States and Chile.[51]

In 1969, the Leteliers and Orlando's uncle Edmundo purchased a riverside property in Virginia's Shenandoah Valley that they baptized Chile Chico, "Little Chile." Orlando and Edmundo split up the land, and the Leteliers built a cozy rambler on their lot. They converted old chicken coops into stables and Orlando, a gifted rider, gave lessons. They played cards. Isabel beautified the property with flowers and planted a vegetable garden. The family began spending most of their weekends there.[52]

"Wherever we lived, the first thing Orlando did was plant poplar trees," recalled Juan Pablo. Chile Chico was no exception. "It's like my roots were in those trees." The son held forever in his mind the memory of sitting on his father's back in the river, while Orlando taught his sons to swim.[53]

>> At 3 A.M. one day in late 1970, the whole clan at Chile Chico was awakened by Isabel's shouts: "Allende won!"

Their old Chilean friend, the physician-senator and head of a leftist coalition called Popular Unity, had pulled off the feat of winning Chile's presidency while openly Marxist.

Letelier, following the results from Washington, immediately drove out to the Shenandoah Valley, honking his horn as he approached the property. Isabel and he hugged.

"I've decided to resign my post at the IDB—."

Isabel cut him off: "—We're going back to Chile!?"[54]

Not quite. Orlando did fly back, and Isabel began to pack up the house. Upon his return to Washington, however, he announced a change of plans. "How great that you've got everything ready, but the trip will be a bit shorter than planned. Instead of changing countries, we're changing states: from Maryland to Washington!"[55]

Allende had named Orlando, among his most loyal followers, Chile's new ambassador to the United States. In February 1971 the Leteliers moved from the suburb of Bethesda to the ambassador's residence inside the District of Columbia, on Massachusetts Avenue, beginning three tumultuous years that mirrored those in Chile. "My life was that of a normal east coast upper middle class youth," recalled Juan Pablo. "I was a Redskins and Senators fan, was part of the school's basketball team, and spent my summer vacations with my family at Rehoboth or Bethany Beach."[56]

Isabel adjusted to the life of a diplomat's wife. Sherry-soaked breakfasts with other diplomats' wives were not her favorite. "I decided I would also do other things." She offended other Chilean women by inviting Chilean maids to her events. She created the Chile Foundation, which repurposed used U.S. medical equipment and sent it to Chileans, whether on the right or the left. She even volunteered with the Red Cross, dispensing books to the geriatric and bedpans to the drug addicted in Washington hospitals. Such humbling toil didn't bother her. "I never got it in my mind that I was an ambassador's wife."[57] The boys, meanwhile, entered their teen years. They still needed parental guidance but left Isabel time for her own initiatives.[58]

The family still spent weekends at Chile Chico, where Alfie, their English sheepdog, could run free and Isabel and Orlando attended local square dances where they met "nonartificial, real Americans who are not involved in the Washington glitter."[59] The four boys were themselves turning more American—attending Washington schools, hobnobbing with children of high U.S. officials, even joining the White House Easter egg hunt.[60]

Allende's Marxist agenda, however, was on a collision course with Washington's. His very victory showed a democratic path to socialism that challenged U.S. interests, and once in office, he became friendly with Cuba and other communist regimes. Allende also planned to nationalize U.S.-owned copper mines.

In retaliation, the Richard Nixon government, through its CIA and its national security adviser, Henry Kissinger, first tried to prevent Allende's confirmation as president by plotting the kidnapping of the Chilean Army commander in chief who oversaw it. Nixon also told his CIA to "make the economy scream."

When the gambit failed and Allende ascended to the presidency's La Moneda Palace, the Nixon team installed what Allende called the "invisible blockade" with the help of U.S. corporations. The ruthless campaign of propaganda, diplomatic pressure, and economic sabotage, fueled by tens of millions of dollars in CIA funds, aimed to turn Chileans against their president and to foment a military coup.

Letelier, as ambassador, advised his president to avoid confrontation with the United States, which provided half of Chile's industrial supplies and nearly all its military equipment.[61] He was the right man for the job, being, as the CIA assessed in 1971, "a reasonable, mature democrat with a profound belief that Allende would revolutionize the structure of Chile without interfering with fundamental liberties or traditions." Letelier reassured U.S. officials "that there could never be Communist control of Chile because the traditions and emotions of the country were too anti-Communist."[62]

Washington seemed to respond in kind. When Letelier presented his credentials, Nixon claimed to respect Chile's self-determination. Kissinger labeled "nonsense" press reports that the White House sought to confront Chile, and he suggested he might visit the country to improve relations.[63] One U.S. diplomat recalled that most experts on Latin America in his shop "had very good opinions of Letelier. We thought he was a straight shooter and that he was not misleading us or misleading his government about our attitude."[64]

Even Kissinger said of Letelier, "I knew him. I liked him personally."[65]

But the Nixon administration felt tremendous pressure from U.S. businesses. It was also on the warpath against communism. First, it delayed for several months accepting Letelier's appointment as ambassador.[66] In July 1971, Chile nationalized three U.S. copper mines. In October, it announced it would offer no compensation because of "excess profits" over the years.

Retaliation was swift. In mid-August, the president of the U.S. Export-Import Bank, Henry Kearns, called Letelier to his office. Kearns was warm and smiling as he delivered chilling news: the bank would not finance $21 million worth of Boeing jet airliners as long as Chile did not compensate the copper companies.[67] In 1972, another of Letelier's deals fell through, this time to reschedule his country's $300 million debt to U.S. banks.[68] To make matters worse still, secrets about U.S. efforts to keep Allende from the presidency leaked, and the ambassador's residence and chancery were broken into *five* times, while police solved none of the crimes.[69] Two of the burglars, who apparently sought sensitive documents, were also involved in the Watergate break-ins.[70] Letelier took to keeping such documents in a bedroom closet because the CIA also bugged his embassy.[71]

Letelier had begun his ambassadorship in an optimistic, generous mood. Early on, when tight budgets threatened to shut down the embassy's celebrations of Chile's national holiday, he reached into his own pocket to pay the $2,000 bill, a substantial sum at the time. What's more, he invited several opponents of Allende to the party.

Uncle Edmundo questioned why his nephew would pay for partygoers who "are set on destroying your president and his government." "They are Chileans," Letelier answered, showing no anger. "Ideological and partisan differences must disappear on such occasions as this."[72]

By mid-1973, Chile was far from united, reeling instead from economic calamity and rumors of a coup. Letelier was recalled to Santiago on May 22 to become minister of foreign affairs. Back in Santiago, he reflected on his experience in Washington, this time somewhat embittered about the distance between Chileans and Americans: "One realizes that there are two cultural frameworks: For us, making our resources truly ours is legitimate; for them, the right to property is fundamental, they are not familiar with the concept of human solidarity."[73]

On June 28, Isabel and the boys returned to Chile after thirteen years in Washington, D.C. The next day, a coup attempt against Allende failed. But it showed that the military could mobilize quickly against the president.

>> Chileans often called their country the "England of Latin America" for its enduring tradition of representative self-government. Save for a mild dictatorship from 1927 to 1932, peaceful and constitutional rule—though not perfect democracy—had prevailed since the country's independence from Spain.[74]

Now Orlando, with Isabel watching and worrying, spent the rest of the Allende presidency shuffled from one portfolio to the next: two and a half months at Foreign Affairs, two weeks at the Interior, and two and a half weeks at Defense. All were positions where Orlando was in charge of Chile's security—the very thing that was collapsing.

Before the Leteliers returned to Chile, Uncle Edmundo once again questioned his nephew's wisdom. "Do you think it is wise to accept an appointment as part of a government whose days, in my opinion, are numbered?"

Letelier looked at Edmundo in disbelief. "Do you think that I would refuse to return to Chile and help my government? You must be crazy or you don't know me well enough. Only the rats leave the ship when the ship is in danger of sinking, and there will be no sinking. Somehow we will weather the crisis."[75]

2

Himmler of the Andes

The nation of Chile sits on a slim ribbon of land that stretches 2,653 miles from north to south and barely 100 miles wide on average. The northern tip is hot and dry—home to the driest place on earth, the Atacama Desert. The central region is a cornucopia where grapes and other fruit grow as plentifully as around the Mediterranean. The capital of Santiago and the country's largest port city, Valparaíso, anchor this center.

Hours south of Santiago, before one gets to the less habitable tundra, is a temperate and verdant region that covers nearly 350 miles north to south. Blessed with abundant rain, powerful rivers, and beautiful vistas of volcanoes and lakes, the southern region is among the country's prides.

Chile's South is also unusually isolated—by the Andes, the sea, and its own vast expanse. Not for nothing has it remained the home of the indigenous Mapuche, who used the natural insularity of the region to protect themselves from encroaching Spaniards.

Neither was it a coincidence that German immigrants long felt an attraction to the region. In the nineteenth century, perhaps it was its lakes and mountains, akin to those of Bavaria, that attracted 30,000 settlers from the German states.

From the War of the Pacific against Peru and Bolivia in the 1870s and 1880s, Chile emerged victorious but also determined to professionalize its military. A military mission from Prussia shaped up its troops, resulting in the gray uniforms and goose-stepping of the daunting Chilean Army.[1]

Throughout the twentieth century, the mostly fair-skinned, well-to-do Germans of southern Chile, not necessarily Nazis but often sympathizers or descendants, filled the ranks of the far right parties.[2] Their remoteness in the south made them feel untouchable. Often owners of large agroindustrial concerns, they consistently drove parties toward radicalism and violence, waiting for the right conditions for them to consummate an alliance with those in power.³

Chile's far right Germans considered not only that their race was superior to all others but also that they were destined to crush other social systems. In 1932, the global depression led a lawyer named Jorge González von Marées to found the National Socialist Movement of Chile. González preached "fascism . . . as the triumph of great politics, rule by a few superior men from each generation over the mediocrity that characterizes liberalism; it means also the predominance of blood and race over economic materialism and internationalism."⁴

Before World War II, about 5 percent of Chile's population was German. The National Socialists boasted 60,000 members, electing three to the national legislature.⁵ *El nacismo*, the movement was called—Nazism.⁶

War clouds gathered over Europe in the late 1930s. The southern provinces of Chile brimmed with enthusiasm. German Chileans organized into *Ortsgruppen* or local Nazi lodges. They spoke favorably of towns with more than a thousand Germans as "zones of occupation." Children and grandchildren of settlers were deemed German only if they could attest that their blood had not mixed with that of the native race. They pledged allegiance to their local lodge chiefs and, through them, to Adolf Hitler. On May Day, as Nazi Germany celebrated its *Anschluss* of Austria, Chilean Nazis paraded down the streets of major southern towns such as Puerto Montt and Osorno dressed in the brown shirts and armbands of Hitler's shock troops, the SS. Strapped to their belts were revolvers and daggers.

Such displays of fascism stirred fears of "de-Chilenization" and Nazi penetration, which, one Chilean journalist noted, "could bring about lamentable consequences for the country's sovereignty."⁷ On September 5, 1938, the Chilean Nazis attempted a putsch. One group seized the main building of the University of Chile, while the other set up across the street from the presidential palace. The government shelled the main door of the university. Seven dead and thirty-seven wounded Nazis resulted. Soon after, the party's fortunes waned.⁸

After World War II, southern communities became favorite destinations for former Nazi officers fleeing persecution or seeking opportunities. Walter Rauff, a Nazi exterminator, was one. He and his family settled in Chile in 1958, where Rauff managed a king crab cannery in Punta Arenas, among the southernmost towns in the world. He continued to scheme from Chile, from which Germany demanded but never received an extradition. He reportedly advised Chile's feared secret police. When Rauff died in 1984, aging Nazis honored him with chants of "Heil Hitler!"[9]

In the early 1960s, language teacher Franz Pfeiffer Richter revived the National Socialist Party. "We are anti-Communist and anti-Semites," claimed Pfeiffer. "Our movement follows the same rules set by Hitler."[10] "Commander" Pfeiffer also parroted Hitler's uniforms, flags, and salutes. He tried to found the Chilean branch of the Ku Klux Klan and held a contest to crown "Miss Nazi." His magazine? *Swastika*.[11]

Most perverse of all was Paul Schäfer (or Schaefer), a former Nazi corporal who ran a secretive German-themed cult enclave in southern Chile. After World War II Schäfer became a preacher and fled Germany, dogged by accusations of molesting boys at the orphanage he ran. In 1961, he founded the Colony of Dignity, a 34,000-acre compound at the end of a dirt road at the Andean foothills, some 220 miles south of Santiago. Inside its barbed wire walls, the glass-eyed patriarch demanded absolute loyalty of the 350 men, women, and children who lived under his rule, as depicted in the 2015 film *Colonia*. Escapees recalled how they became "real slaves of Schaefer, like robots dedicated only to obey his orders and not displease him." Married couples had to live apart. Children were separated from their parents and sexually abused. No one could leave. Schäfer punished those who strayed with electric shocks, tranquilizers, and protracted isolation.[12] The Colony of Dignity, finally, served as a prison and torture chamber for the military dictatorship during the 1970s.[13]

Throughout, fascism in Chile not only adhered to all of Nazi Germany's tenets — anti-Semitism, anticommunism, state control of the economy, hierarchical leadership, and intense nationalism — but also added its own. A love of all things Spain, a celebration of the traditions of Catholicism, a rejection of empire, and the championing of Latin American unity made this among one of the most potent totalitarianisms in Latin America.[14]

Another difference between the fascists of Germany and those of Chile was that the latter never infiltrated the conservative parties, the government, or the army.

Until 1973.

>> Among the many children who looked on as Nazis in the south marched in celebration in the late 1930s was nine-year-old Juan Manuel Guillermo Contreras Sepúlveda.[15]

The man who would oversee Orlando Letelier's assassination was born in Santiago on May 4, 1929. His family moved to Osorno, almost 600 miles south of the capital, right before the Nazi parades began.

It was also after little Manuel's most traumatic childhood experience. Aged six, he watched while his mother writhed in bed from an unknown ailment. Things got much worse after a nurse dropped by the Contreras household. Careless or hurried, she injected his mother with an air bubble, causing an embolism.

"My children! My children!" Contreras's mother screamed as she convulsed. Manuel, terrified, hid behind a dresser and listened helplessly as she expired. Family members wailed and sobbed. Contreras was silent.

The boy had inherited his mother's strong, domineering temperament. She had also bestowed upon him his nickname—El Mamo, inspired by the toddler's inability to say *mamá*.

His father quickly found another spouse—his own wife's half-sister—who became Contreras's sworn enemy. She never showed him any warmth, he said, in contrast to the affection she showered on his lighter-skinned little brother. While everyone else called him "Mamo," she addressed him with a curt "Juan Manuel." Once grown, Contreras refused to invite his stepmother to his wedding or attend her funeral. His rancor was absolute.[16]

Manuel Contreras was the son, grandson, and great-grandson of military men. His grandfather was decorated in the War of the Pacific.[17] The army was Contreras's fate. His mother had wished for him to avoid the armed forces, a life she deemed of low social standing, with barely a middle-class salary, and too peripatetic. But he would not become the doctor she longed for.

At fifteen, Contreras embraced his move back to Santiago and, like Orlando Letelier, attended a military high school. He now rarely saw his family, even during breaks, since his father's own orders sent him to faraway Arica, along the Peruvian border.[18]

As a young man, El Mamo became obsessed with all things military. He breezed through several Chilean military academies, and then through U.S.-run programs in Fort Belvoir, Virginia, and Fort Benning, Georgia, where he specialized in repressive techniques and antisubversion. For much of his early career he taught military history, strategy, and intelligence at the War Academy in Santiago and then directed the School of Engineers of Tejas Verdes, where he would remain until 1973.[19]

At twenty-three he married María Teresa Valdebenito, known as "Maruja," the daughter of an admiral. They had one son, plus three daughters who all married military men.[20] Contreras's view of marriage was traditional: man as provider, woman as caretaker of children. Eventually he got bored with

Maruja, whom he found unequal to the task of keeping his house and cooking his food.²¹ The marriage was tense and unhappy, the children neglected. Contreras openly carried on a fifteen-year affair with his secretary before leaving his wife. He admitted in his late fifties that "I dedicated myself to my Army and my Fatherland, and my family—unfortunately—remained secondary."²²

The 1960s, when Contreras distinguished himself as a thinker, were tumultuous times in Latin America's military history. Leftist guerrilla groups, inspired by Fidel Castro and Ché Guevara, sprang up in almost every country. Their targets—the rightist armed forces—hit back with a savage vengeance by building up massive apparatuses of repression. The U.S. government taught Latin American military leaders, at its Panama School of the Americas and elsewhere, the logic of the "national security doctrine"— that all political opponents of a regime, even peaceful ones, were tools of the Soviet Union and therefore insurgents deserving persecution. In Chile, the national security doctrine dovetailed with the paranoia and totalitarianism of resurgent fascism. Contreras embodied that marriage.²³

In 1968, El Mamo clarified his ruthless approach to counterrevolution: "Guerrilla war is won only by killing guerrillas and conquering their hideouts with blood and fire, submitting to strict surveillance the population, the base on which the guerrilla feeds."²⁴ Contreras's time in the United States further indoctrinated him to see communists as devils incarnate, and his contacts at the CIA provided him with the manuals of spy agencies from South Korea, Iran, and Brazil.²⁵

As a military leader, Contreras was an enigma. On one hand, he was the best military student of his generation. Brilliant and composed as an instructor, he could also be extroverted, full of anecdotes. He loved chess, seafood—including German food—and good red wine.²⁶ One U.S. intelligence officer described him generously as "mild-mannered and polite. When you talk to him he seems gentle and disarming. He doesn't whistle or bark orders to his subordinates. He's not your typical Chilean officer—who usually puts on a Prussian military manner. He comes across as reasonable and likes intelligent conversation."²⁷

Legend has it that at Fort Benning, in the mid-1960s, Contreras sailed through a simulation exam well under the two hours allotted and that his answers beat those of the school's computer. "In Chile we don't work with computers," sniffed Contreras as he graduated first in his class.²⁸ Such feats built a following among students and younger officers. Many treated his every word as scripture and pledged undying loyalty.²⁹

On the other hand, Contreras appeared physically unimpressive—about 5 feet 8 inches and 185 pounds. More important, he was Machiavellian, egocentric, disorderly, and cruel. He reined in neither his appetites nor his penchant for violence. One military school classmate described Contreras as "a psychopath, with ingredients of sadism, delusions of grandeur and a superiority complex."[30]

Perhaps unwittingly setting him on a fateful path, his teachers rewarded his successful first year at Santiago's Military School by entrusting him with disciplining the next cohort. One cadet recalled one of Contreras's punishments—the "shampoo." "He forced our heads into a toilet bowl and then he pulled the chain." He also rammed the end of a shower hose down the students' mouths and turned on freezing water at full blast, sometimes causing ear damage. The cadet's opinion of Contreras? "Domineering, perverse, explosive, and soulless, to say the least."[31]

So feared and hated was Contreras that there would be twenty-one attempts on his life. During several, he shot back with his own weapon.[32]

He cherished the role of spymaster even when his job did not call for it. As a lieutenant colonel directing a military school, Contreras once was playing dice in its casino with other officers when he stepped away to take a few phone calls. Upon his return he announced, "The captain is in his house with his cronies; the lieutenant is a womanizing bum, and Janito, as always, is with his mistress. One has to know what one's people are doing."

"But how do you do it, my *comandante*?" asked an officer.

"Aaaahh," Contreras smiled mysteriously. He had already taken to keeping tabs on everyone, even allies.[33]

Late in his life, two psychologists, a social worker, and a criminologist gave a balanced, if clinical, assessment of Contreras's personality. "The subject is self-assertive, with leadership ability," they wrote. "He possesses a marked ability for perseverance, to the point of rigidity in the pursuit of the achievement of his objectives. He requires recognition and social reinforcement as a way to renew the high opinion he has of himself." They read Contreras as soldierly, cold, and repressing any feelings of guilt and foisting them upon others. "There is no sign that he is aware of his crimes."[34]

His own son, Manuel Jr., testified to his father's hollowness: "He could be sitting next to you and carelessly spill his coffee on you, and he would not apologize. He's like that, he was born that way and will die that way."[35]

3

Kill the Bitch and You Finish the Spawn

"Pinochet used to carry Orlando's briefcase."[1]

So recalled Isabel Letelier of the man who would later make Manuel Contreras the head of his secret police. Augusto Pinochet was universally thought of as the most loyal officer in Salvador Allende's army high command. When the June 1973 coup attempt failed, Allende elevated him to commander in chief. After the botched coup, Pinochet vowed to shoot its ringleaders. "The blood of generals is repaid with generals," he swore.[2]

Shortly after, Allende appointed Orlando Letelier his minister of defense, and therefore Pinochet's superior. The two saw each other every day, according to Isabel. "[Pinochet] was trying, all the time, to show loyalty in a very exaggerated manner, that made Orlando sort of aware of something wrong and at the same time, he was extremely servile."[3]

"He gives me the creeps," Letelier told his wife.[4] He likened Pinochet to "the man in the barber shop who runs after you with a whisk broom after you've had your hair cut and doesn't stop sweeping at your back until you've given him a tip."[5]

Pinochet's obsequiousness also unnerved Isabel. During her husband's swearing in at the Ministry of Defense, the general sauntered up to her: "¡Ay, señora! What a pleasure to meet you. You are as beautiful as all the other defense ministers' wives. Another beauty—for us," he smarmed. "I can't wait for you to meet my wife. . . . I'm sure you and she will be the closest of friends." "I found him *too much*," she recalled. "A flattering idiot."[6]

Pinochet was also in the habit of bringing presents to the Letelier sons.[7] Their fourteen-year-old, Francisco, had a suspicion when the general came over for dinner. "I can see him now in my father's study," he recalled thirty years later, "the Andes visible in the windows behind him. I remember that he looked strangely disconcerted amid the bookcases and leather backed tomes. Perhaps he was already making plans for the future."

Probably. Thirteen days later, on September 11, 1973, Pinochet seized power. "In the days that followed," Pancho remembered, "we watched jets fly overhead, heard bombs hit, smelled the smoke. Tanks rolled through the streets."[8] A stray bullet almost killed Pancho.[9] Jets and tanks were the tip of a much deadlier spear of a regime that would kill thousands and torture tens of thousands, most of them in the few months left in 1973.

Pinochet's was a philosophy of annihilation: "Kill the bitch and you finish the spawn."[10]

>> Augusto José Ramón Pinochet Ugarte was born a half-generation before the Leteliers and Manuel Contreras, on November 25, 1915, in Valparaíso. Like the Leteliers and the Morels, the Pinochets were longtime French immigrants who had done well in Chile. His father, Augusto Sr., a customs officer at the port, considered himself middle class, but the Pinochets and their six children lived in a three-story house with servants.

Pinochet's path to the military would not be as preordained as that of Contreras. While the blonde boy played in the street at the age of four, a horse-drawn cart ran over his leg. Little Augusto seemed to recover, but two years later his knee swelled up. Doctors concluded he had tuberculosis and suggested amputating the limb. Pinochet's mother refused and prayed. A famous German surgeon diagnosed the swelling quite differently, as benign hydroarthrosis or an accumulation of fluid. The boy was told to lie in the sun, which healed his leg.

Pinochet attended private Catholic schools, where he fenced and boxed. But he remained frail. He also proved a mediocre student. One school kicked him out for being naughty, while another returned grades of 3 out of 7 on seven of the eight tests he took.[11] (In contrast, in second grade Isabel Letelier received ten 7s out of 7 and one 6.)[12] He was raised Catholic, to be sure, but showed little interest in religion and even in politics. As a teen he showed up at a conservative political club. When told to throw rocks and bottles at rallies, he declined. He forever after mistrusted politicians.[13]

At fifteen, like Contreras, Pinochet chose a military career. He was proud of his soldier grandfather who fought in World War I and admiring of the feats of Louis XIV and Napoleon. (He also esteemed Rommel for his strategy but allegedly not for his politics.) Unlike Contreras's, Pinochet's mother, Avelina Ugarte, fully backed his choice—if she did not make it for him. "She was very energetic and very, very authoritarian," said one woman who knew the Pinochet family. "She was his lighthouse, his compass, the finger which pointed out his way to him. She was fixated on military life and Augusto as a result was a soldier. He couldn't have ever contradicted her."

Pinochet eventually married a similar woman. "If I was head of government I'd be much harder than my husband," María Lucía Hiriart once said. "I'd have the whole of Chile under a state of siege."[14] Lucía was always the politician in the couple, while Augusto fancied himself more of a soldier.

Pinochet applied to military school, but, again unlike Contreras, he was judged too scrawny. The "weak lad," as he called himself, reapplied and was turned down again, but the third time, at age seventeen, was the charm. He remained a middling student but became a crack shot and a karate black belt. He graduated as an ensign in 1936 and received a commission in the infantry.[15] He took law and social sciences at the University of Chile, studied abroad in Ecuador, and held several appointments as an instructor in military schools, where he taught Contreras and authored books on geopolitics.[16] He later described his life as consisting "of nothing but discipline and obedience."

Unquestioning subservience he offered as a subordinate, and unquestioning subservience he would demand as a general.

▶▶ "Where can they be holding Pinochet?" Allende asked on September 11, 1973, so sure was he that his army commander in chief could not be involved in the coup targeting him. Pinochet's precise role in the toppling of Allende is still unclear, but within six months he systematically set the other three junta members aside and seized dictatorial control. The Congress, political parties, trade unions, and free media were no more. By 1975, Pinochet was president of the republic, declaring, "I'll die, and my successor as well, but there will be no elections."[17] He had his uniform hat tailored higher than that of other officers and fostered a personality cult that fused fascist authority with Catholic iconography.

Contreras, meanwhile, proved an enthusiastic participant in the coup. On September 10, when his son fretted over an English exam the next day, Contreras looked at him and smiled: "Don't worry. You're not going to school tomorrow."[18]

From his post at Tejas Verdes army base in the port town of San Antonio, he had gathered intelligence on enemies and allies of Allende. At 5 A.M. on the 11th, Contreras already controlled much of the southern coast, from Algarrobo to Topocalma, and he quickly drew up a list of fifteen foreigners who might collaborate with the "extremists" who defended Allende.[19]

Right after the coup, Contreras oversaw the disappearance of thousands. About 150 bodies, many weighed down by sections of railroad track, were tossed from helicopters into lakes or the ocean.[20] El Mamo was quickly making his reputation as one of the monsters of Latin America.

>> Pinochet considered his regime to be saving the country from the scourge of communism. As president, he ended all Allende's nationalizations, returned many businesses and much land to private ownership, and adopted the free market purism of Milton Friedman and the University of Chicago. Like Contreras, he also entertained the fiction that there had been massive human rights violations during the democratic regime of Allende.[21] Shortly after the coup, the military circulated trumped up "revelations" about Plan Z, an alleged conspiracy by Allende's people to massacre military and civil opponents and install a dictatorship. The tale featured secret weapons caches, guerrilla training camps, war clinics and hospitals, and underground tunnels.[22]

The darkest of ironies, Plan Z was essentially "plan A" of the Pinochet regime. In Pinochet's mind, the only appropriate response to opposition was detention, torture, and assassination. The communist guerrillas that threatened his regime, he said, "*must* be tortured. Without torture they don't sing."[23] He extended his philosophy to all who opposed him.

"There is no way to exaggerate the atmosphere of terror that the military imposed on Chile after September 11, 1973," recalled journalist John Dinges, who lived in Santiago. "For days, it was common to see bodies along roadsides or floating in the Mapocho River, which traverses Santiago. City morgue workers filled all available refrigeration units and began to stack bodies in corridors.... Automatic rifle fire could be heard every night for months during the dusk-to-dawn curfew."[24]

>> Years before the coup, when Contreras arrived at military school, one of its lieutenants was Augusto Pinochet. Pinochet taught him strategy, and they found in one another kindred spirits.[25] Pinochet grasped that Contreras was superior to him in intellect and at least equal in cunning and cruelty. They saw eye to eye on the apocalyptic danger of communism and the need for a national security apparatus to crush it.

After his coup, Pinochet plucked Contreras out of his fiefdom at Tejas Verdes and made him the head of the National Intelligence Directorate, established in November 1973 and known as DINA in its Spanish-language acronym. "My father got one order from Pinochet," recalled Manuel Jr.: "to pacify Chile no matter how much it costs."[26]

Every day at 6:30 A.M., Contreras picked up Pinochet at his residence. He then briefed him over breakfast at Pinochet's home or in the Diego Portales building, out of which the dictator ruled for his first years and where the two men rode in Pinochet's armored Mercedes, escorted by a small army of motorcycles. For additional "face time" with the boss, Contreras rigged a closed circuit television in his own office that connected directly to Pinochet's.[27] He also cozied up to Pinochet's children and especially Lucía. She considered Contreras "a family friend," wrote a Pinochet biographer, because he watched over her household.[28]

Contreras himself designed DINA, and a June 1974 decree formalized it. A colonel, Contreras was now director of national intelligence and answered to no general, minister, or judge—only to Pinochet. DINA dominated all other intelligence agencies. Its 9,300 employees could raid homes and jail suspects without charges, and its 20,000–30,000 informants spread fear throughout other Chilean government agencies.[29]

By 1975, DINA had built a twenty-story headquarters befitting its position at the pinnacle of Pinochet's government. Beautiful young secretaries staffed its ornate interiors. Its operatives wore no uniforms, could wear their hair long, and enjoyed the rewards of women, cars, money, and travel abroad.[30]

Its logo featuring an iron glove, DINA disappeared, tortured, and killed with impunity. Over its three-year existence, it was responsible for about 1,200 of the 3,200 executions and 38,000 imprisonments and tortures during Pinochet's seventeen-year dictatorship.[31] "We fight in the shadows so that Chileans can live in the sun" is how Contreras justified the horror. "Whatever action is done for the good of the fatherland is clean."[32]

Some complained of the outsized power wielded by this mere colonel. In 1974, one director of an intelligence school labeled Contreras an arrogant Nazi before his entire student body, and his students came to blows against Contreras loyalists. Pinochet took Contreras's side. He sent into retirement those who questioned the DINA chief.

The associations between DINA and fascism were legion. It was alleged that its employees engaged in rituals harking back to bygone warrior myths: the use of runes, an ancient Germanic alphabet; and the celebration of solstices and equinoxes to revive Nazism. DINA members addressed one another as "pharaohs," "priests," and "slaves," denoting their status within the hierarchy.[33] Contreras even allied with former Nazi Paul Schäfer of Colony of Dignity infamy by using the enclave as a detention and torture center.[34] His son, Manuel Jr., would come to call the fascistic leader of the compound

"Uncle Paul."[35] The U.S. Department of Defense compared DINA to Hitler's Gestapo.[36]

By early 1976, wrote Contreras biographer Manuel Salazar Salvo, the DINA director had reached the apex of his power. His spies were everywhere in Chile and around the world, and few dared whisper his name. "Colonel Contreras felt, in sum, that he had power over life and death, that he was nearly a god in the midst of a war."[37]

▶▶ In October 1973, a month into the Pinochet regime, a unit of army officers traveled through the progressively arid northern countryside, from La Serena to Calama, stopping at one jail after another. In each, they executed political prisoners who had received no trial—at least seventy-three in all met their fate at the hands of this so-called Caravan of Death. Most were savagely tortured beforehand.[38] On the night of October 16, for instance, thirteen prisoners were taken from their cells because their name was on a list. The caravan killed two at the garrison itself. The others were driven in a truck outside of town. As ordered, several got out and were promptly shot to death in the moonlight. Then the caravan officers, reportedly drunk off *pisco*, climbed into the bed of the truck. Unsheathing their crescent-shaped knives called *corvos*, they slashed and stabbed those who had refused to disembark.[39]

In the caravan served Armando Fernández Larios, a baby-faced twenty-four-year-old second lieutenant with small, dark eyes. Born in Washington, D.C., where his father had been an attaché, he had graduated from Chile's military school in 1970. He was later recalled as taking pleasure in tormenting prisoners. A Chilean Army corporal called him "a psychopath and the biggest murderer in Chile. In my regiment he took a soldier from my section and disfigured his face. He tortured him for a week."[40] Fernández later denied taking part in the incident in the truck or in any torture, though he admitted overhearing executions. He also confessed to a part in the assault on the presidential palace on September 11 and later working at the infamous National Stadium that the junta transformed into an enormous prison, torture center, and morgue.[41] By mid-1974, he joined DINA.

In 1976, Fernández would surveil Orlando Letelier.

Apparently "giving the orders" at the stadium was Major Pedro Espinoza Bravo, who would also serve in the Caravan of Death and in subsequent death squads.[42]

Espinoza had a more illustrious career than Fernández, one that began at the same military school that Letelier attended; the two knew each other since Orlando was ahead by two years. Inspired by his military father and the heroics of World War II, Espinoza made officer in 1953, attended the U.S. Army School of the Americas, worked his way up the counterintelligence ladder, and, after showing his mettle as an executioner, settled in as Contreras's chief of operations within DINA.[43]

In 1976, Espinoza would transmit Contreras's order to kill Letelier.

>> At 6:22 A.M. on September 11, 1973, the Leteliers' phone startled Isabel awake. She answered and turned to Orlando: "It's Salvador." Her husband, now minister of defense, had gotten to sleep only three hours earlier, worried about intelligence reports of an imminent coup.

The warnings were accurate. "The navy has revolted," announced President Allende to Letelier. "Six truckloads of navy troops are on the way to Santiago from Valparaíso. The Carabineros are the only units that respond. The other commanders in chief don't answer the phone. Pinochet doesn't answer. Find out what you can."

An admiral from the Ministry of Defense reassured Letelier: "It's some kind of a raid, nothing more."[44] Orlando handed the receiver to Isabel: "Listen to the voice of a traitor," he whispered.[45]

Allende was also skeptical. "Go, Orlando, and take control of the Defense Ministry if you can get there."

Isabel walked with her husband to his car. His bodyguard had called in sick, but his driver was waiting. Isabel took the man by his lapels and nodded toward Orlando, "You take care that nothing happens to him."[46]

At 7:30 A.M., Letelier arrived, unarmed, at his ministry across the street from the Moneda presidential palace. Troops surrounded his building, and officers and some armed civilians wore orange scarves, denoting coup plotters. A guard at the door would not let him pass, but a voice from inside shouted, "Let the Minister in." As soon as he entered, Orlando felt a sharp rifle butt poke his back ribs. His allegedly sick bodyguard held the other end of the rifle.[47] "I saw myself surrounded by ten or twelve highly excited men in army uniforms pointing their submachine guns at me. Pushing me violently, they took me to the ministry's basement. They searched me, took away my necktie and my belt, and threw me against the wall in a small room. I demanded to see a senior officer, but the officer who escorted me said, 'Look, sir, if you insist on this, we'll proceed immediately to execute you.'"

Guards took Letelier to an infantry regiment in southern Santiago and kept him in a small room. Through a crack in the shutters, he spent the night watching people being brought in like he had. Their fate was worse. He heard shots and saw bodies being carried back out. "They must have executed 20 persons there that night," he recalled.

"Just before 5 A.M., I heard voices saying, 'Now it's the turn of the minister.' A half hour later, the door to my room was opened and a sergeant told me to come along. There were six soldiers surrounding me. We walked along the corridor, then down a flight of steps. One of the soldiers was carrying a towel and I realized that it was a blindfold. Immediately, I had the feeling that I was being led away to be executed."

After a superior officer gave an order, "One of the soldiers said to me, 'You're lucky. They won't give it to you, you bastard.'"[48]

Still, Letelier was interrogated, stripped naked, and treated roughly. Much of the time a black sack covered his head, and he was forced to remain standing for days. "I never before imagined what it would be like to be blind. But that experience taught me the terror of losing a basic sense."[49]

Three days into the coup, Letelier was taken, along with three dozen bound and hooded other top Allende officials, by bus to a military air base, and then onto a DC-6 plane for an eight-hour flight. They landed at Punta Arenas, the capital of Chile's southernmost region.

The men were then led across the Strait of Magellan to their final destination: Dawson Island. Orlando had not shaved or changed clothes in four days, nor had he smoked a cigarette—no easy task for a man who inhaled four packs per day. He and the other prisoners were walked through four to five miles of icy wind to the penal colony that Chile operated there.

>> Back in Santiago, Isabel was beside herself with worry. She spent much of September 11 trying to get generals or admirals on the phone to find out what happened to her husband. "My mother was as nervous as a person could be and all the phone calls didn't help any except to get her more jumpy and worried," recalled Juan Pablo, twelve at the time.[50]

At Pinochet's house a servant told Isabel that the general could not be bothered while he ate. She hung up and rang General Gustavo Leigh, who led the air force during the coup.

"He is all right," said Leigh about Orlando. "Don't worry, we have taken measures to guarantee his security."

"But how do I know?" said Isabel.

"I give you my word," responded the general, irritated.

"But General Leigh, my husband's security—"

The general hung up.[51]

The boys, meanwhile, lived harried hours of their own. When that early-morning call came on September 11, "I sprung out of bed and pulled my pants on and sat quietly in my bed," wrote Juan Pablo for a ninth-grade English project. "In the air there was an evil thing which made a person feel unwanted and scared.... Machine gun shots were all about.... Helicopters, airplanes and trucks were all about the city. My mother and family were very strong but I myself felt like crying out loud at times."

From the family's small apartment, the brothers saw flames shooting out of barracks and Hawker Hunter jets circling downtown Santiago. Juan Pablo described the bombing of the Moneda palace as "a sound that I had never in my life heard... as if the world was exploding.... My mother told us not to get too close to the windows just in case."[52] "We believed my father was in the palace at the time," added Francisco.[53]

At around 6 p.m., Letelier finally called home. "I just found out that the President is dead, that a military junta has control over the country, and that many of my *compañeros* are dead. I am being transferred to the Military School—." The line went dead.[54]

The sun mercifully set on September 11. "When I finally got in bed," recalled Juan Pablo, "I just laid there thinking of where my father could be now and tears slowly rolled down my cheeks. I laid in my bed staring at the ceiling looking for the angle where the bullet would have to hit on the ceiling to bounce off and hit and kill me."

On September 12, Isabel received an anonymous phone call. "Orlando is OK," the voice at the other end said, "and he says for you not to move from your house." Before she could say a word, the person hung up, called again later with the same message, and hung up again.[55] Letelier also wrote to her that day to ask for some personal effects and profess his love for her. "I hope that we will all be together again before long."[56]

Four days later, Isabel and Moy Tohá, the wife of José Tohá, Letelier's college friend and fellow cabinet member, showed up at the Ministry of Defense. The next day, they and another worried wife sat in Pinochet's waiting room after having gone through intrusive searches on every floor.[57] After twenty minutes, Pinochet stepped in and began shouting, "For your information, your husbands are being fed well, well cared for, in a secure place with medical attention!" He allowed no one else to speak or stand as he continued to bark at the three women whose husbands had disappeared.

"We watched him in astonishment," Isabel said. He "ranted about Plan Z.... He said, 'It would have been quite different for us if the situation had been reversed, because in this case'—and he made a horrible gesture, drawing his hand across his throat and sticking out his tongue."

Pinochet "went on shouting, but when he saw our determination he allowed us to enter his office." He agreed to let them write to their husbands.[58]

Isabel was placed under house arrest for the next month and a half. "It is a very unpleasant situation," she explained.[59] "You must stay in the house and you cannot go out and there is a guard in the door that checks everybody that comes to visit you and so anybody that comes to visit you is also on a list of dangerous people or of suspicious people."[60] "This ate me up inside," recalled Juan Pablo. "My mother who had never gotten into any politics was being punished for something that she had never done."[61] The family's bank account was frozen. Isabel had no income, so she sold personal belongings to feed her boys.[62] Eventually she did "tedious, technical translation work which no one else wanted [to do]." With no money for heating, "it was so very cold and I sat translating all night long, for it always had to be done in a rush, with many ponchos to keep me warm." With an Orwellian flourish, the military finally informed her she was no longer under Pinochet's "protection" and could step outside.[63] "I stayed in Santiago with the other wives. We'd go see the military officials every day to send food and clothes to our husbands."[64]

Juan Pablo was taken out of high school while his mother was under house arrest. "I never understood why, nor did I understand why they let us return."[65] "The days went on slowly and each day more and more hate grew in me," he recalled. "One night we had to burn more than a hundred books and around sixty posters.... I thought, why were we forced to do this and destroy the ideas they fought for for such a long time[?]"[66]

Chile's armed forces occupied several schools. Francisco stopped attending his and hid it from his mother. "It was a little easier for us than it was for our mother because we were still discovering the world for ourselves at this point. Our mother's world, though, had been completely destroyed."[67]

Only weeks after the coup was Isabel told where Orlando ended up. "Dawson Island, it is a dreadful place. It is a very cold, windy, . . . and because of the cold current, the Humboldt Current. . . . Nobody lives there."[68]

>> Orlando Letelier did live there, for eight months.

Dawson Island was occupied by the Chilean state not for its ease of settlement or its natural resources but so it could claim the land against competitors. There is no other reason to own that bleak, desolate piece of tundra on the 54th parallel.[69] If anyone tried to swim away, say, in October, the frigid water would cause loss of dexterity in five minutes, exhaustion or unconsciousness in half an hour, and death half an hour later. And the wind—

"terrible wind," said Letelier, "with gusts up to 80 miles per hour. It's the Antarctic wind, sometimes blowing stones and pieces of ice into one's face, slashing it."[70] A voyage to the corresponding latitude in the northern hemisphere would place one in Alaska or Siberia.

The concentration camp where Letelier and his fellow political prisoners were kept was reminiscent of Auschwitz, fenced off by a double row of barbed wire and surrounded by guards armed with antiaircraft guns in watchtowers. Letelier lived in an 8-by-15-foot room with seven other men, sleeping in three-tiered bunks with scratchy sheets, if any. To lighten the mood, they christened it El Sheraton.

The U.N. Human Rights Commission called the treatment of the Dawson prisoners "barbaric sadism."[71] "Guards awoke us at 6 A.M. and we were taken in groups of three to the canal to fill our buckets with water for drinking and washing. But, because we were below the other camp, the buckets often came up filled with the excrement of the other prisoners." The prisoners worked twelve hours per day building latrines, reinforcing barbed wire, or cutting firewood. To erect telephone polls in rocky soil, "sometimes we had to dig the postholes with our hands."

"At the very outset, all of us came down with bad colds; we had no warm clothing."[72] Letelier had but a light poncho. They were fed coffee, bread, lentils, and potatoes, but no meat or fruit, partly because supplying Dawson was so arduous. "We developed a generalized condition of malnutrition.... Even the lentils we ate were mixed with pebbles." Letelier lost thirty pounds in his first three months at Dawson. Prison officials eventually added pieces of fat to their diet, but he still lost fifty pounds, dropping his six-foot, broad-shouldered frame to 125 pounds.[73]

The military let Orlando have some clothes his wife sent, but they stole the boots and parka. She also sent onions and oranges. Once she found out he was in Dawson, she sent him skin cream because, back in Washington, Letelier had had a cancerous mole removed from his cheek, and her husband's exposure to wind and sun alarmed her.[74] He began almost all his letters home by noting the almost daily "torrential rain."[75]

Letelier remained stoic, even funny, keeping up his campmates' spirits by teaching English, singing, and playing guitar.[76] "The songs of Letelier—boleros, tangos, and Mexican songs—we would remember them forever," wrote fellow prisoner Sergio Bitar.[77] Letelier was never tortured physically, although he did come back with a broken finger.

He did suffer, like the others, nighttime mock executions—now widely considered psychological torture.[78] Guards would line up the men and pretend they were to be shot. Isabel recalled that Orlando refused to wear a blindfold. "I want to see you," he would tell the guards.[79] "We would be yanked out of bed in the middle of the night," Letelier added, "and forced to stand in the rain. We were thrown to the ground in the mud. Then we were made to run in the rain. Some of us were placed in solitary confinement."[80]

In February 1974, halfway through his stay at Dawson, the International Red Cross found Letelier "to be in a very bad condition," recalled Isabel. "So Orlando was taken to the mainland to a hospital in Puerto Arenas and I requested the military authority's permission to see him and I saw him for 15 minutes."[81]

"I love you," they said.[82] They held hands and embraced as a guard stood eighteen inches from them at all times.[83] Isabel wore a yellow wool blouse, and the look she gave him when departing seared itself in his memory. "Now," he wrote to her, "every time I shut my eyes, there you are, magnificent, strong, with that internal strength of yours, looking at me with those deep eyes that I love so much."[84]

>> "It was madness," Isabel said of her life while Orlando was in prison. "A kaleidoscope. Life turned upside down."[85] She agonized over his deteriorating health and wrote to him every few days. Letelier, trying to remain optimistic, sent letters back every week, and a present for the boys on Easter. For decades afterward, Juan Pablo wore around his neck a stone from Dawson Island carved with "J. P." and "S-26," Orlando's prisoner number. Isabel had a similar necklace.[86]

"I have had in you, my husband, an exceptional man for whom I hold the deepest respect and admiration," she wrote to her Nano, "and I say this without passion, because I also have for you the blindest love, a love that reaches only those at the highest and most resplendent point in the world. You are *everything* to me."[87]

Receiving such letters from home was painful for Letelier. "The fundamental thing at that point was to survive, to resist day by day, and for me, that kind of contact with the outside world, the fact that I could see pictures of my family, was very damaging to me. I thought that it would weaken me psychologically; I had to concentrate on my life as a prisoner."[88]

Within a few months, Isabel had organized prisoners' wives, Las Señoras de Dawson, to free Orlando and his campmates. They turned to international civil society—Amnesty International, the International Red Cross, the International Commission of Jurists—whom she kept abreast of Letelier's condition. Orlando's sister, Fabiola, wrote to lawyers, to the regime, and to U.S. senators.[89] Isabel also hired a lawyer, but he had no more luck than Isabel at freeing Letelier.

Threats dogged her. "They [Chilean authorities] kept telling me that I was going to be punished because I was telling international agencies that my husband was in a concentration camp, that he had lost weight and all of that, so I had been constantly threatened to be taken to a military compound as a prisoner."[90] The regime also considered charging Letelier with treason, so Isabel got her network to praise him for his patriotism. As she wrote to her husband, "If the [Pinochet] government can criticize you for anything, it would be for being *too* 'gringo,' too assiduous and demanding in your work and not sectarian enough."[91]

Friends of the Leteliers also wrote to Senator James Abourezk of South Dakota, who was told by the State Department that "Mrs. Letelier, one of whose children is an American citizen," was "periodically in touch" with the U.S. embassy. "Contrary to your impression," however, "we have no information to indicate that Mr. Letelier has suffered any physical abuse."[92]

One political officer at the embassy, whose sons went to school with some Letelier boys, showed Isabel and her sons a television report, banned in Chile, that included an interview with Orlando. "It was the first time that they had seen him and seen that he was in acceptable condition, since he'd been taken months before. This type of thing was done, and I was proud of it. . . . At the same time, I think, the local government also understood that the United States official policy was essentially to support the military."[93]

In May 1974, with the Southern Hemisphere's winter about to descend on Dawson, Letelier was transferred to the Air Force Academy in Santiago and, a month and a half later, to the Ritoque concentration camp some 100 miles north of Santiago. In both prisons, conditions were somewhat better. The U.S. embassy reported that detainees had access to books, magazines, and television. They could receive packets and send three letters per week—all censored.[94]

But great discomfort and psychological torture were still in store for Orlando. "Are you a homosexual?" he was asked repeatedly. "Do you know that your wife is a whore?"[95] Guards would play loud music all night. Other prisoners were electrocuted, raped, their vaginas stuffed with rats, and Orlando heard or saw those episodes. "I think the worst time I spent during my whole imprisonment was at the Air Force Academy," recalled Orlando.[96]

After the military moved Orlando to Ritoque in late July, his family could visit him twice a month. "It shocked me when I saw him again," recalled Juan Pablo. "He was thin, his hair very short like a prisoner's. He, who had been a superman, was now scrawny and pale."[97] "My father," added Pancho, "shared many stories with his sons, but he always held certain things back, as if to protect us from the intensity of the tortures and deaths he had experienced."[98]

>> The change in detention camps indicated that Isabel Letelier's campaign to pressure the regime was working. Henry Kissinger would later brag that he had brought about Letelier's liberation and then publicly said Orlando, because he did not thank him, "did not know the meaning of either truth or gratitude."[99]

But the historical record shows little to no intervention by the U.S. secretary of state. Those who did intervene included U.S., European, and Latin American academics, former colleagues from the Inter-American Development Bank, and U.S. senators.[100] The decisive intermediary, who responded to Isabel's pleas, was Diego Arria, the governor of Caracas. He was the right-hand man of Venezuelan president Carlos Andrés Pérez and a longtime friend of Orlando, who was godfather to Arria's only daughter.

Arria's stature had risen to the point where, in 1974, *Time* magazine had featured him among a select group of world leaders.[101] Still, he recalled, it was unprecedented for a governor to take on a diplomatic mission.[102] He flew to Santiago on September 10, 1974, and obtained an interview with Pinochet.

The Venezuelan first spoke of a cut-rate sale of his country's oil to Chile. "By the way, of course, this depends upon your freeing Orlando Letelier."

"One thing has absolutely nothing to do with the other," was Pinochet's disingenuous reply. "And I resent greatly that you should bring such a thing up. But independently of the oil deal, I was about to free Orlando Letelier anyway."[103]

Pinochet also insisted that Letelier be banned from political action in Venezuela. "I can't promise that, general," Arria countered. "I know too well Orlando's human and political qualities. Anyway, you cannot force anyone to renounce their freedom of expression, even less their convictions. If Orlando had to choose between the limited liberty you allude to and remaining in prison, there is no doubt he would opt for the latter." Pinochet was "visibly annoyed" but let it go.[104]

"Let him leave Chile and never return!"[105]

Only at 5 P.M. did Letelier hear that he might be released.[106] That evening, he was put in a car and driven under heavy escort to Bustos Street in Santiago, where he knew the Venezuelan embassy stood. He arrived at 11 P.M. and learned that the Pinochet government had issued two decrees. The first liberated him on the grounds that he had never been charged with a crime; the second expelled him from Chile without a passport, merely a safe passage.[107] Before his release, Orlando was told in no uncertain words, "General Pinochet will not and does not tolerate activities against his government."[108] After 364 days in captivity, he was a free man—albeit one without a country.

Isabel saw Orlando for only a few hours. As the sun rose on September 11, 1974, Orlando and Arria walked up the mobile stairs to their Viasa Airlines plane. At the hatch, the pilot stopped Pinochet's accompanying soldiers: "No one boards this plane with weapons. From here on out, I am in charge." It was announced that a former Allende minister and political prisoner was on board, and the passengers cheered.[109] Isabel watched anxiously as the plane taxied to the runway. Only once it was in the air did she breathe a sigh of relief.[110]

By December, the rest of the family had joined Letelier in Caracas, where Arria had gotten him a job in the treasury. The Leteliers' departure added half a dozen Chilean souls to the 100,000 already in exile.

4

A Rather Unsavory Past

On October 6, 1975, Bernardo Leighton and his wife, Ana Fresno, were returning from a shopping trip. They walked arm in arm toward their modest apartment on a cobblestone street a few blocks from Vatican City in Rome. Suddenly, Fresno saw a young, sturdy man heading in their direction across the street. When the couple got to the iron gate to their apartment building, she heard his boots walking toward them.

She heard a first shot, turned around, and saw the man right behind them with a .9 mm Beretta pistol—pointed at her. Another shot rang out, and that bullet pierced her right shoulder. Pain surged through her body. When she fell to the ground, she saw Leighton next to her, his face covered in blood. The boots ran away. A neighbor raced downstairs, where he found the couple lying on the sidewalk, unable to move.

"Is he breathing?" asked Fresno.

"Yes," said the neighbor, who ran to call the police.

The sixty-six-year-old Leighton, a former minister and Christian Democrat and more of a mainstream politician than Orlando Letelier, had followed his party in opposing Pinochet's rule and found himself in exile in the Eternal City. Now, in 1975, he promoted an alliance with Letelier-type socialists—not the sort of gambit that would endear him to the Chilean Right.

The Leightons survived the assassination attempt. The first bullet entered the back of Leighton's head and exited above his ear. He lost some of his hearing and suffered severe brain damage. Fresno, whose own bullet grazed her spinal column, never fully used her legs again.[1]

Pinochet, who likely ordered the hit on Leighton, bemoaned the outcome: "Too bad, the old man doesn't want to die."

The identity of the man in the boots was made clear only years later. The conspiracy, however, was the work of Italy's Stefano Delle Chiaie and his neofascist thugs, admirers of Benito Mussolini. And the mission was coordinated by Michael Townley, an American-Chilean who would, not quite a year later, fabricate and affix the bomb to Letelier's Chevelle.²

》》 The attempt against the Leightons was an informal precursor to Operation Condor. In late 1975, Manuel Contreras and his DINA led counterparts in the Southern Cone in creating Condor, a collaborative scheme among repressive military regimes named after Chile's national bird and dedicated to hunting down leftists throughout the continent.³ "Subversion," Contreras explained, "does not recognize borders nor countries."⁴ If subversives were found abroad, Condor would detain, torture, and kill abroad. This was a first qualitative leap for Chile's masters of repression. During its existence, roughly from 1975 to 1983, Condor killed several hundred people.⁵

Pinochet had allies outside South America, too. Contreras and he were devout Catholics and admirers of Spanish dictator Francisco Franco. When the Spaniard died in 1975, Pinochet flew to Madrid for the funeral and Contreras took a planeful of officers along.⁶ Franco supporters lined up on the avenue from the airport and gave the Chilean's motorcade the stiff-armed fascist salute.⁷

A Uruguayan present at Condor's founding described Contreras as wanting "to eliminate enemies all over the world . . . to eliminate people who were causing harm to our countries, people like Letelier."⁸ This was a second qualitative leap. Contreras and Pinochet were going to kill opponents of the regime not only in allied repressive republics in South America but also in the greatest democracies on Earth. The most prominent of these targets were the scattered leaders of the exile community, Leighton among them.

To some in Washington, this scheme posed no problem. The Richard Nixon administration had ended almost all aid to Chile during Allende's presidency and had covertly sabotaged his economy. While Letelier was ambassador, not only was his embassy broken into a handful of times, but the FBI also bugged it at the CIA's insistence until, in 1972, FBI Director J. Edgar Hoover forced the CIA to end surveillance.⁹ U.S. support for Chile, in contrast, skyrocketed after the Pinochet coup.

Washington learned of the existence of Operation Condor within a month or two of its founding. Rather than discourage it, U.S. officials contributed to its intelligence bank. The U.S. military allowed Condor operatives to use a transmitter located in the Panama Canal Zone.¹⁰ The CIA also helped organize DINA and sent twenty-two operatives to Chile to train officers in disrupting guerrilla cells, sleep deprivation, withholding water, beatings, and shooting other prisoners while a detainee watched in horror.¹¹ Beginning in 1974, the U.S. spy agency, despite knowing that the head of DINA engaged in international assassinations, also enlisted him as an informer and made to him at least one payment of $6,000, this after it had concluded that "Contreras was the principal obstacle to a reasonable human rights policy" in the Pinochet government.[12]

Ray Warren, the head of the Western Hemisphere division at CIA headquarters, got wind of the payments. "I said, 'Oh my god, this guy is going to haunt us,' and cut it off."[13] Still, Contreras flew to Washington twice in 1975 to meet with the CIA's second in command, Vernon Walters.[14]

U.S. knowledge of DINA's international assassinations was spreading among spies and diplomats. "We knew fairly early on that the governments of the Southern Cone countries were planning, or at least talking about, some assassinations abroad in the summer of 1976," recalled the deputy assistant secretary in the Department of State, Hewson Ryan. "Whether there was a direct relationship or not, I don't know. Whether if we had gone in, we might have prevented [the Letelier assassination], I don't know. But we didn't."[15]

Henry Kissinger certainly did not. One month before Letelier was killed, his State Department prepared a memo, signed by Kissinger, that instructed Southern Cone ambassadors to express Washington's "deep concern" over Operation Condor's "plans for the assassination of subversives, politicians and prominent figures both within the national borders of certain Southern Cone countries and abroad."[16] But for one month, none of the ambassadors carried out the order—something rare in diplomacy. The ambassador to Uruguay feared for his life if he wagged his finger at the generals. The envoy to Chile worried that Pinochet "might well take as an insult any inference that he was connected with such assassination plots." They asked for further instructions. Five days before the Letelier assassination, Kissinger ordered "that no further action be taken on this matter."[17]

>> Michael Townley, an operative of Operation Condor who coordinated the attempt on the Leightons, was born in Waterloo, Iowa, on December 9, 1942. His father, Vernon Jay Townley, then an administrator in the U.S. War Department, was stationed at an ordnance plant in Mississippi but sent his wife, Margaret, back to Waterloo to give birth to Michael.

Vernon's frequent transfers marked Townley's childhood. He left the War Department for American Airlines, then to the Ford Motor Company in Detroit, and then to Ford's assembly plant in Santiago.[18] Michael went through grade school in New York and New Jersey, junior high in Michigan, and some high school in Chile and some in Florida.[19] "I had a very pleasant life until I was thirteen or fourteen," Townley once recalled. When he moved to Santiago, "everything changed."[20]

An adviser to a Santiago youth group to which Townley belonged described him as "an awkward, appealing, alienated youth, yearning for affection and a meaningful place in the world. With gentle nurturing he could have become a healer, a builder, a responsible citizen."[21] A friend from a Methodist church group in Chile added, "He demonstrated to me the type of characteristics you associate with a high-achiever, a very personable young man. I would have expected him to have become a lawyer, perhaps an electronics engineer." "Likeable," "sincere," and "genius" is how acquaintances described him.[22]

His parents portrayed their son's childhood as "uneventful. [Michael] apparently did well in school, got along with other children, was part of a family that did things together. Both parents saw their son as a caring, intelligent, and gifted person." Margaret described the household as not very political, but Vernon said Michael "was always probably very anti-Communist in his feelings." The elder Townley was quite conservative, and Michael himself said his anticommunism was "originally created by the values fostered in the American public school system."[23]

Others saw in Michael Townley "a typical Cold War political sociopath."[24] "Harsh and cold," he was called.[25] Sources agreed that Vernon was an absent but still overbearing presence in Michael's tense and unhappy home life. A psychological profile reported "disturbing parental relationships especially a very authoritarian father figure" and "a repressive Catholic environment... in his early school years," giving Townley "the same qualities as that of a delinquent kid":

> He is cold and cunning. His coldness[,] which might have initially been due to an inability to relate or establish close relationships, is also a product of his aggression, which is the manifestation of his need for tension release. Like children with behavioral or learning problems, he is unable to control his impulses[. I]n response to this (and combined with the aggression stimulated by other factors) these people often become unfeeling or unemotional in order to control themselves or cover up their lack of ability to do this. Their approach to people is to intellectualize them; rationalize them. They have taken emotion out of their view of life.

"The other factor worth noting is his academic background," the report continued. "Townley never finished high school and got his diploma through a correspondence course. He has a history of not doing well in school[,] which is most probably a source of his personality problems. He might have been a kid with learning problems, there is a chance that they were actually neurological disorders."[26]

"I am a very unsociable person who does not go out," Townley himself admitted. "I read a great deal of technical information and basically dedicate myself to my work. . . . It is very difficult for me to get involved with or open myself up to people."[27]

>> Inés Callejas, known as Mariana, was not blind to Michael Townley's faults. But she saw the young man charitably, perhaps naively. She described him as "maybe a bit petulant, a bit irresponsible, not a good student, but friendly, eager to please, very sociable and handsome without being vain or arrogant like other boys. . . . He was incapable of any kind of violence. If one of our children needed a spanking, I'd be the one to administer it."[28]

Despite Vernon's strong opposition, Michael and Mariana married in July 1961, when he was merely an eighteen-year-old high school dropout and she, almost ten years his senior, was already a self-described twice "divorced bohemian" mother of three.[29] She would be a close but conflicted partner to Michael through the Letelier assassination.

"The story of Mariana Callejas is a novel, or at least a long story," said well-known Chilean writer Enrique Lafourcade.[30]

Callejas grew up in a small town in the northern Chilean province of Coquimbo, where her father was a low-level magistrate. Unlike Townley, she finished high school, but she dropped out of college. She described herself as "naughty and strong willed" and rejecting her militantly anticommunist, anti-Nazi, anti-Zionist, and anti-Catholic elderly father's authoritarian ways.

In defiance of the anti-everything elder Callejas, Mariana harbored, she said, an "obsession for Causes, the great Causes, something that began when I was a little girl, or maybe it was a congenital defect."[31] She was a precocious child, reading *Crime and Punishment* at the age of eight.[32] At fourteen, she distributed Communist Party pamphlets on street corners. The next year, convinced socialism would cure all of humanity's ills, she joined the Young Communists.[33]

In 1950, at seventeen, she married a Chilean, mostly to escape her household. The ill-considered union was annulled three months later when her husband refused to go with her to Israel.[34] Alone, she boarded a steamer to the infant nation and joined a kibbutz. Her mother understood; her father banished her from the family. In Israel, she married Allan Earnest, an idealistic agricultural student from Cornell University.

Her year on a kibbutz, from which she expected "perfection" and "true socialism," proved a further step in Callejas's life path of disillusionment. When all kibbutz members were forced to declare themselves Israelis or citizens of the world and cut all ties to other countries, she judged the ultimatum "infantile," and she and Earnest came back to Chile. She was nineteen.[35]

In Chile, her father refused to even speak to the young couple. They moved to Earnest's mother's apartment in Washington Heights, Manhattan, but *she* complained of Allan's marriage to a shiksa—who couldn't even speak English! Callejas did learn the language. She began to write and go to the theater in New York. In 1957 the couple moved to Long Island, but Callejas hated playing the housewife and loathed working as a waitress. The marriage dissolved, and she returned to Chile with three children aged eight, four, and three.[36]

Callejas's personality baffled many, in contrast to Townley's rather straightforward portrait. "I am an Aries and Aries people are always complicated," she admitted. She was attractive, with a broad, open face and expressive features. She came across as idealistic and intelligent but also mendacious, narcissistic, and possibly sociopathic. "Callejas is difficult to get a fix on," wrote one journalist who interviewed her several times. "A wistful smile constantly plays across her face even when she discusses calamity or hardship." He continued: "She is a fey woman who seems to move through life as if it were a dream, or a nightmare. It is hard to say whether she is the perfect victim of circumstances or as clever as her conversation indicates she may be."[37]

At a party in Santiago, she danced with Townley. He fell hard for her and courted her aggressively with daily red roses. "I met him when he was seventeen. He looked older, he spoke as an older man, he took charge of situations," she later wrote.[38] Townley was bright, practical, and good with electronics and mechanics. He was also desperate for a family, since he had refused to be uprooted once again when his father was transferred to Caracas. They married after a ten-month courtship. Many friends advised against the union, and none of the parents attended the wedding.

Townley worked at various low-pay jobs—selling encyclopedias, fixing cars and appliances—while they had two children together, Christopher and Brian. In 1964, his father got him a manager's job at Ford's subsidiary in Lima, Peru, but Townley quit after four months. The following year he became a salesman for a mutual fund conglomerate. He could finally afford to move his young family out of Mariana's parents' house.[39]

When rumors circulated about his company's bankruptcy, Townley moved the family again—this time to Miami, where from 1966 to 1970 Townley worked as a truck salesman and then an auto mechanic in Little Havana. He also became more knowledgeable of—and enamored with—electronics.[40]

Callejas, meanwhile, spent her time in Miami working for progressive presidential candidate Eugene McCarthy. Despite being shouted at, spit on, and pelted with tomatoes by Cuban exiles, she also marched against the Vietnam War along with friends from the University of Miami, where she audited courses. But an old pattern reasserted itself: "Soon, I also grew disillusioned of McCarthy and of Cesar Chavez (a Chicano leader). I discovered that most politicians are phonies."[41] Her opposition to the Vietnam War was not out of sympathy for communism—far from it—but, rather, against U.S. imperialism. She also grew to dislike and distrust Miami—her sons' friends, the schools, the drugs, and the Cubans. She missed her mother and her friends from Santiago.[42]

》》 When Allende won the presidency in 1970, Callejas wept from joy for the first time since she could remember. The couple discussed whether they should return to Chile.

"I don't want to live there under Allende," said Townley. "I guess we can't go back."

"We *must* go back," responded Callejas. "I must go back now more than ever."[43]

Before Michael followed months later, Mariana returned to Santiago with the children "because Allende had been elected president and Allende was a communist and I wanted to see what things were going to be like in Chile," she later told a grand jury. She also revealed it as a turning point in Michael's political views.

> Q: Did your husband at that time, in October of 1970, share your political views or your political beliefs?
> A: Not at all. Other than being anticommunist, he had no inclination to any politics at all.
> Q: He had no inclination towards any politics?
> A: No.

Q: Did that change in your husband—that lack of political awareness. Did that change in Michael Townley?
A: Yes, it did.
Q: When or why, if you can recall, did that change in your husband?
A: During Allende's government, Chile was in a state of chaos and one night we saw an old man being beaten up by several policemen and Michael and I tried to rescue him from the policeman [sic] and we couldn't. The man was over 70 years old and he was being very badly beaten up. And at that moment my husband decided to cooperate and to do what he could to bring Allende's government down.[44]

"It seems from his ambivalence in this situation," went Michael's psychological profile, "that he cannot tolerate aggression and yet he is able to inflict it upon others; a paradox. . . . The cop figure and Townley's identification with the old man is an anti-authoritarian action bringing up his conflict with his father."

The profile continued:

[Townley] is anti-U.S., thus rejecting his culture or social identity provided by his father, in its place he [ha]s adopted a Chilean cause, yet because it is not his own (provided by his wife and geographical location) he does not feel the same spiritual and cultural identity with it that would insinuate emotional involvement and attachment. . . . The essence of his marriage reflects that he has not yet resolved his Oedipal problems. . . . Mariana Callejas . . . looks after her husband as a mother would her son. With this in mind it is easy to see that he took on Chilean identity over U.S. and by doing this he removed his father to take on his mother. It all fits into a consistent pattern.[45]

Years later Townley also condemned Salvador Allende for "the bread lines, the lack of products, the negative 60% growth rate, the over 1,000% inflation rate, and finally the breaking of the communality of a nation, the divisions and hatred produced even within families."[46] Townley and Callejas, like many on the right, attacked Allende as a shameless bon vivant who, in the midst of poverty and crisis, reserved for himself the best meats, garments, and scotches that Chile had to offer.[47] Later, Townley claimed that "friends of mine had been arrested and tortured during the Allende regime."[48]

While Michael became decidedly anti-Allende and looked forward to his overthrow, Mariana claimed more ambivalence. Though she had opposed the Vietnam War and Allende, she considered herself against "events" and not ideologies. Then again, she also refused to believe that any coup against Marxism in Chile would lead to a dictatorship.

A leftist friend once warned her, "If the armed forces take over, they will never leave."

"Sure they will," she retorted. "When order is restored, they will call elections."

"Haven't you learned anything from history? Look at all the countries of South America where the armed forces have taken power—"

"Yes, but that's in other countries. We're different. In Chile, the armed forces are dignified, honest. There will never be a dictatorship here. A year or two will be enough."[49]

The Townleys, idealist and naive, sought a political family.

Townley approached U.S. diplomats and spies to offer his services. In Miami, he contacted the CIA station three times in 1970 and 1973, but, as he recalled, its employees "were not really interested in talking to me." In February 1971, the CIA did obtain a green light to discuss Townley becoming an "asset," but it could not find him at the Santiago address he had given.[50] The CIA's version? "He had contact with us. He volunteered things to us. We did not seek him out. We never hired him. He was a walk-in, one of those guys that keeps coming in and wants to play with the big boys. We listened, but we didn't take him on."[51]

Townley also became what one political officer in Santiago called an "embassy barnacle," an expat who hung around the U.S. embassy to check out the action and hopefully glean some secrets and share his own.[52] "Townley persistently made contact with arriving embassy political officers," recalled the ambassador, "and invariably sought some intelligence connection with the embassy." But one embassy officer suggested "keeping him at arms length" because of his "rather unsavory past with crypto-fascist Chilean groups."[53]

By way of explanation, Michael offered that, during a forty-day strike in October 1972, "I was involved with a number of groups, primarily the Patria y Libertad."[54]

>> Those who founded Fatherland and Freedom in April 1971, just as Townley was landing in Santiago, described it initially as a nationalist "civic movement" that dreamed of a society ordered by *gremialismo*, or "guildism."

In this corporatist scheme inspired by Catholic traditionalism and Hispanism, all social groups—professionals, mostly, but also workers, students, women, businesses, churches—would form "intermediary organizations" to mediate between the individual and the state. This inheritance from the Spanish Civil War of the 1930s, spread to the Americas by intellectuals from the Francisco Franco regime, did not reject free enterprise but, rather, bemoaned capitalism's destruction of feudal social relations. It abhorred Marxism. Many on the right saw the fight against Allende as a revival of the Spanish search for "order" out of the chaos of socialism.[55]

Fatherland and Freedom's cofounder, Pablo Rodríguez Grez, emerged as its philosopher, *el ideólogo*. When Allende won, Rodríguez called on any Chileans "not contaminated nor committed to the liberal party system" to replace the "anachronistic liberal political system and preven[t] the establishment of a Marxist state."[56] An attorney who spoke in florid phrases and ample gesticulations, Rodríguez claimed that, under *gremialismo*, no social groups would dominate, not even great corporations. Fatherland and Freedom's plans included redistributing some capital to the workers. The guilds would assure fairness and harmony for the good of the nation and its leader.

On paper, the ideology could seem harmless, but it reeked of fascism or at least of authoritarianism, akin to Franco's Spain or Antonio Salazar's Portugal.[57] Fatherland's second in command, the flamboyant Roberto Thieme, grew up in a Bavarian-themed house, his Nazi-sympathizing father having been caught transmitting intelligence to German submarines hugging the Chilean coast during the war. Thieme later took a commando class at Paul Schäfer's Colony of Dignity. He would fake his death in a plane crash aided by Schäfer.[58]

In practice, Fatherland and Freedom acted even more like fascists. Recruits underwent intelligence checks and indoctrination. They received training in coding and code breaking, weapons handling, explosives, and martial arts (with nunchucks!). Rodríguez would regularly line up his "troops"— who wore black uniforms with white armbands adorned with a swastika-like insignia that united three chain links and resembled a spider—and then "review" them with his right arm crossed against his chest.[59] Hitler's Brown Shirts would have approved. Mainstream conservative parties recognized Fatherland and Freedom as de facto shock troops against Allende, and they sent cadres and funds to sustain it.[60]

Allende's followers called Fatherland and Freedom "a bunch of fascists, paid by the CIA," and they were correct.[61] Rodríguez denied accepting CIA funding, but the truth is that, in fall 1970, Henry Kissinger requested and received $38,000 for covert support of Fatherland and Freedom.[62] Others in the group admitted receiving those funds and added that an extra $5,000 per month filtered in through one of their operatives.[63]

The movement, whose membership reached into the thousands, quickly evolved into a political party and then an armed insurgency. Its mix of upper-class students, riffraff, and a few older hard-line nationalists harassed leftists in their homes, threw rocks at demonstrators, tipped over a bus, and blew up or took over television stations.[64] One of its leaders confessed to 500 terrorist attacks. In April 1972, Rodríguez decreed that "the only solution is a nationalist, military government. The Armed Forces are the saviors of the Constitution."[65] In the failed coup attempt of June 1973, Fatherland and Freedom worked with a tank regiment.[66] Rodríguez fled the country after the so-called *tancazo*, but Fatherland kept up the pressure on Allende with a bombing campaign that brought another explosion just about every sunrise. On August 14, 1973, one bomb took out a high-tension wire and left the entirety of Santiago in the dark. "We are on the edge of a civil war," warned Allende that day.[67]

》》 Though Callejas later downplayed Fatherland's reach, she and Townley embraced its rhetoric and its actions.[68] "The masses are not ready to govern themselves," Michael once intoned. "Democracy leads only to mass government, rule by the herd. Power should be reserved for the qualified few, the intellectuals, the philosopher kings."[69]

But it was Callejas who reached out to Fatherland and Freedom. It struck her as secular and militant enough for her taste, and she was spoiling for a fight. In 1972 she showed up at their headquarters, in blue jeans and a thick jacket, and introduced herself as a writer.

"And how could you help us with our magazine?" wondered Manuel Fuentes, its editor.

"I write short stories and urban narratives."

"But that's of little use to a weekly fighting 'in the trenches.'"

"Well, I think the magazine might need to change its appearance," she said suavely.

"You said your husband is a mechanic, but you didn't tell me his nationality," inquired Fuentes, digging for information.

"He's North American," Callejas volunteered, seeing an entry. "His name is Michael Townley. His father was general manager at Ford in Chile.

In addition to being a mechanic, he knows something about electronics and chemistry. He could also help the Movement in . . . *something*." She said this last word with cryptic pride.[70]

Fuentes was intrigued.

With Townley out of the country, Callejas held workshops in their living room for young Fatherland enthusiasts, including her eldest son. She helped them plan demonstrations and wrote for their publication. The returning Townley, being neither a politician nor a Chilean, resisted her entreaties to join Fatherland.

One day, however, he agreed to model for them a "technically correct" Molotov cocktail.[71] The Chileans also warmed somewhat to this bearded dark-blonde *gringo* who wore jeans and plaid shirts and spoke Spanish well but with a thick American accent. His wife, not so much. One said that "her feline face betrayed her distrust, and though she was slight of build, her attitude was outwardly tough and imposing, which signaled insecurity."[72]

By mid-1972, Townley was fully involved as Fatherland's in-house explosives and electronics expert. He made nitroglycerin out of dynamite. He experimented with TNT. And he kept churning out Molotov cocktails—"like one bakes bread," recalled a Fatherland member. Fatherland's leaders began showing up at his house, in awe of his skills. In turn, Townley went on missions with Fatherland operatives—setting fire to a printing company, blowing up railroad tracks. Callejas usually rode along.[73]

Townley cobbled together a crude radio transmitter and drove it around the trunk of his car to get out the opposition's message, while Callejas edited Rodríguez's radio speeches.[74] She even played the Chilean "Tokyo Rose," launching their first broadcast by intoning, "This is Radio Liberation, this is Radio Liberation. This is the voice of democracy. We salute the Chilean people in its struggle for freedom and against Marxist oppression." She also sang patriotic songs. But Callejas enraged Fatherland leaders when she took it upon herself to emit a press release bragging about their clandestine broadcasts.[75]

Both acted "insolently," according to their Chilean coconspirators. Once, when Townley had them at his house, and with his blue eyes fixed on one of Fatherland's leaders and his right index finger nervously picking at his left thumbnail, he told him, "I think we could easily kill Allende."

"What are you saying? Are you crazy?"

With motherly calm, Callejas filled in the details. She and her husband had spent twenty days casing Allende's movements, figuring out exactly his motorcade's patterns and how it could be assaulted. "At one street corner, there's a sewer lid," finished Townley. "We fill it with 50 or 60 kilograms of dynamite and BOOM!" he raised his arms in a big circle.

Curious, the Chilean asked where the couple would find that much dynamite.

"You're sitting on it," laughed Michael. He used as chairs around his dining room table stools topped with ratty plaid cushions stuffed with dynamite. Townley explained that the dynamite mixture was not yet "ripe" and so could not explode.

The Chilean absolutely forbade them to carry out the "supreme stupidity" they had concocted. *Where does the madness of the Townleys end?* he left their house wondering as Mariana cursed him in the background.

With such episodes multiplying, Rodríguez began referring to Townley and Callejas as "that pair of crazy imbeciles."[76]

In March 1973, when the Allende government tried to scramble Fatherland's transmissions, Townley designed his most dangerous mission to date. He took a Fatherland team to Concepción, a southern city, to disable a jamming device at a TV station. To its surprise, the team found a homeless housepainter squatting in the station, asleep. They pinned him to the floor and hogtied the poor man with rope, chloroform, and tape, and then fulfilled their mission. The man then must have woken up and tried to free himself. He choked to death.[77]

Splattered on the front pages, the tragedy of the squatter made of Townley a wanted man. On orders from Rodríguez, Townley either walked or flew over the Andes to Argentina. From there, penniless, he borrowed money from U.S. relatives and took a plane to Miami. Callejas, having lied to Allende's police that she knew nothing of her husband's whereabouts, joined him two months later and for the remainder of the Allende régime. Now more politicized than during his last stay in Florida, Townley again approached the CIA and befriended Cuban exiles. When Allende fell in September, they popped bottles of champagne in celebration.[78]

"I won't deny that the military coup made us immensely happy," said Callejas.[79] She returned on the first commercial flight allowed to land in Chile after the coup. Townley borrowed a passport from a friend called Kenneth Enyart. The name would become one of his many aliases.[80]

Meanwhile, Fatherland and Freedom disbanded, and many of its leaders joined DINA. Pablo Rodríguez, apparently overcoming his distaste for foreign capital, became a newspaper columnist and apologist for Pinochet's free-market radicalism.[81]

>> In the midst of a turbulent political season, the Townley marriage was fraying at the edges.

"Mike and I never did talk much," recalled Callejas. "He likes TV and I hate it. And this affair has undermined our relations. No matter what we start with we end up speaking of the 'affair.'"[82] By the mid-1970s, "we had been pretty distant, Michael and I, for about two years, and a separation seemed appropriate."[83]

There were, in fact, several affairs. The winter before the coup, Townley was involved with rightwing women who organized pot-and-pan-banging protests against Allende's failing economy. Callejas hated those women.[84] This followed a pattern established on both sides. When Townley had come back to Chile after a brief sojourn in Miami, he found that Callejas was carrying on a relationship. This followed several previous flings, including a more serious one of Townley's in Miami. In early 1971, he had even moved to San Francisco to live with a woman. Callejas flew to the West Coast with the children.[85]

When she learned of her husband's plans to marry his lover, she screamed, "You son-of-a-bitch! Why didn't you tell me? I wouldn't have come!"

Three months later, they resolved to try again.

In April 1973, in the heat of anti-Allende terrorism, Townley asked his lawyer to have his wife followed.[86]

>> A perhaps greater divisive factor in the Townley marriage was its association with DINA.

While Townley and Callejas certainly worked with Fatherland and Freedom, they did not work *for* it or receive salaries from it. DINA was another story altogether. Manuel Contreras's secret police lured the couple into its web of intrigue so deeply that escape became all but impossible.

For a while, DINA saved the couple from destitution and insignificance. In mid-1974, Colonel Pedro Espinoza, DINA's chief of operations, heard of the man who outwitted Allende with his clandestine radio and approached Townley. Under the Marxist president, "I was in charge of the army intelligence unit that was supposed to track you down," divulged Espinoza with a smile. "But we didn't try very hard."[87] The men first had drinks and dinner, and then Espinoza invited Townley to fix some electronic equipment. Finally, he offered the couple a full-time relationship with DINA at $600–800 per month.[88] Callejas understood why DINA chose her husband: "DINA found his knowledge of electronics, English, and purchasing extremely

A Rather Unsavory Past

useful. Add to the fact that as an American he had free access to the United States at any moment without having the need for the hard-to-get visas. My husband, moreover, had qualities that made him especially effective in the intelligence community: a bright mind, an incredible memory, and a fail-safe determination and loyalty."[89]

The Townleys were allowed to live in a large house in the posh Lo Curro district high above Santiago, adorned with three floors, a terrace, and a pool and surrounded by fruit trees and a spectacular view of the snow-capped Andes.[90] One journalist described it as "one of the most beautiful views in Latin America."[91] Back when home values plummeted under Allende, Contreras had bought the property for a song.[92] In it, Townley set up a powerful radio transmitter and outfitted the lower-level laboratory with electronic equipment.

Callejas, meanwhile, fancied herself the Madame de Staël of the Pinochet regime, hosting one of Santiago's most illustrious literary salons. She wrote short stories herself and in 1975 won a major Chilean prize for one of them. Every Thursday night, she'd transform her hillside mansion into a meeting place for Chile's finest to drink, dance, and debate books and poetry until the wee hours. Decades later Mariana recalled those days as "marvelous, intense," exuding "a lot of passion for literature."[93]

Downstairs from the oblivious literati, Chilean intelligence officers tortured regime opponents and manufactured toxic gas in Townley's secret lab. One of the writers visiting Mariana once mistakenly opened a downstairs door and found a room filled with cots, lab equipment, and camouflage fabric. "I went up to the salon and didn't say a word," she recalled. "We left after half an hour and we never went back. We also never told anybody what we had seen."[94] What they might have seen was Spanish-Chilean U.N. diplomat Carmelo Soria getting tortured and killed. "Poor Chile" was all Soria said. "Poor Chile."[95]

In 1978, a reporter asked Callejas how she could have begun working with DINA. "I didn't know what DINA was," she claimed. "To me it was just a profession, a job and we needed one." Her ignorance seems feigned since she never spoke about her husband's job to her friends, who complained of the "brutality" of DINA with "resentment." The DINA operatives she met "have always been gentlemen, and somehow I can't believe that gentlemen do brutal things."

What about the reports of torture and killings? "I can believe part of it, but not all of it; I think perhaps it's been grossly exaggerated.... I never met anybody who had been mistreated by DINA."

"Well some of them obviously wouldn't be around to talk any more, would they?"

"Of course, that's true," Callejas responded sheepishly.

She told the reporter she did "nothing at all" for DINA but right after admitted she went on trips abroad with Townley, used an alias, carried a DINA identification, and was paid as a party secretary.

"But don't you feel ashamed?"

"I know that no harm ever came to anyone through me. . . . And therefore I'm not ashamed."[96]

>> If Callejas's conscience was healthy, her marriage to Townley was anything but. "DINA changed everything between us," she wrote.[97] Once it hired her husband, he was "working long long hours, sometimes till 2 or 3 in the morning, and he was up at 8 o'clock in the morning every single morning, and he made very little money."[98]

"Twice, I almost left him, everything, even my children, who didn't understand and refused to come with me." The first near-separation was when Callejas heard Townley in his office listening to a recording of her on the phone with a writer friend. He had begun bugging her. She burst through the door, and he hurriedly turned off the tape player:

"Too late," she said. "I heard everything. I can't go on living with you here, in this way."

"Where could you go?" he asked cruelly.

She had no money, no job. "I have family. My mother, my siblings." But she felt that no one would support her because she could not reveal her reasons for leaving.

The second time Callejas almost walked was following an ugly dinner the couple hosted for Italian fascist Stefano Delle Chiaie—the man responsible for the Leighton attempt. When the Italian launched into "a rageful, anti-Semitic speech," Callejas, wearing a large Cross of David around her neck, spoke up: "Please do not spout anti-Semitism at my table."[99] Her time in Israel and marriage to Allan Earnest had sensitized her to the plight of Jews. She also thought she had Jewish blood in her heritage.[100]

Delle Chiaie looked at her and smiled: "But this is not your table. It's Andres's," he said, using one of Townley's aliases.

Callejas glared at her husband. Rather than defend her, "he threw me a look of disapproval and went back to his meal."[101]

After a half year in DINA, Townley met Contreras and was sent on assassination missions as part of Operation Condor. One was to Buenos Aires, where he fabricated the car bomb that killed Chilean General Carlos Prats and his wife, Sofia Cuthbert.[102] Another was to Mexico, where he arrived too late at a conference to kill two other opponents of Pinochet. Yet another mission, to Paris to kill two journalists, was called off.[103] Townley liaised with groups also in Spain, Germany, Holland, Belgium, Austria, Luxembourg, and, of course, the United States.[104]

Michael Townley was becoming, as one FBI investigator called him, "the most dangerous man I have ever met."[105]

"At that time, 1976," recalled Callejas, "everything seemed reasonable, even assassination."[106]

5

Stand Up with Me

The killing of Orlando Letelier came at a singular time in U.S. history. According to historian Kenneth Cmiel, the years from 1973 to 1978 were "particularly crucial" to contemporary human rights: "As the Vietnam War wound down, human rights emerged as a new way to approach world politics." The apogee of activism for civil rights in the South and against the war in Southeast Asia had passed. Human rights, along with feminism, environmentalism, and gay liberation, took up that reformist real estate.[1]

Focusing on the natural rights of every human being was not new, but the 1970s saw that effort enjoy a new political potency. A *movement* was born. Atrocities at My Lai and in a number of autocratic countries such as Brazil, Greece, and the Soviet Union awakened a nation and a Congress eager to, in historian Barbara Keys's phrase, reclaim its virtue.[2] By 1977, according to Lars Schoultz, human rights became "the largest, most active, and most visible foreign policy lobbying force in Washington."[3] Nongovernmental organizations such as Amnesty International and Human Rights Watch came into their own and attracted unprecedented funding, staffs, and attention. By the end of the decade, more than 200 groups in the United States worked on human rights. More than fifty lobbied Congress, and about fifteen concentrated on Latin America. These watchdogs did one-of-a-kind reporting on human rights violations, and their indexes, yearbooks, checklists, bulletins, newsletters, and other reports became must reads for journalists and diplomats. They also mastered the techniques of direct-mail fund-raising and perfected grant writing to philanthropic giants such as the Ford Foundation.

Celebrities used their platforms to promote human rights. Folk singer Joan Baez, for instance, spent much of the 1970s singing and speaking for Amnesty International, even on a 1973 taping of the *Tonight Show*.[4] Alongside her toiled Pete Seeger, Jane Fonda, Edward Asner, and many others.

Some activists ended up walking the halls of power. Civil rights icon

Patricia Derian, a founder of the Mississippi Civil Liberties Union, became the first assistant secretary of state for human rights and humanitarian affairs under the Jimmy Carter administration. Mark Schneider, her deputy, had worked for Senator Edward ("Ted") Kennedy of Massachusetts on several U.S.-Latin American issues. As a student at the University of California, Berkeley, he had helped the American Civil Liberties Union and volunteered for the Peace Corps in El Salvador.[5]

Some members of Congress, meanwhile, collaborated with this army of lobbyists — or passed laws under its assault. Like the activists, allies in Congress saw their work as patriotic, a reaffirmation of the best ideals of an America that seemed to have lost its moral compass in Vietnam and Watergate. Representative Don Fraser, Democrat of Minnesota, chaired the first congressional hearings on human rights in 1973.[6] Freshman Representative Tom Harkin of Iowa proved successful at tying foreign aid moneys to the human rights performance of foreign governments. In 1974, at the worst of the Pinochet repression, when bodies floated down rivers, Harkin flew down to Chile with no protection and banged on doors behind which the junta tortured opponents, screaming at the men inside that they would one day be judged.[7] As a Democrat, Harkin often worked alongside Senator Kennedy, at the prime of his powers thinking of running for president against Carter, Gerald Ford, and Ronald Reagan, all of whom he outpolled in 1978.[8] Helping them were, among others, Michael Harrington, Toby Moffett, and George Miller in the House and James Abourezk and George McGovern in the Senate. In 1976, Congress required not only that diplomats report back human rights situations but also that those reports be published. Most of the amendments the human rights network passed remain on the books today.

In just a few years, said one human rights lobbyist, his colleagues' access to the State Department, too, had become real: "This would never have happened five years ago. The same people we deal with now would not have helped us then. They know . . . that we are able to vault above them anytime we want, able to make it unpleasant for them not to cooperate. . . . Now we have very nice professional relationships with these people." In 1976, even Henry Kissinger, up to then resistant to any pro-human rights pressure, admitted to the Organization of American States that "the fundamental rights of humanity" were "one of the most compelling issues of our time."[9]

>> Among the signal events identified by Cmiel as stirring the human rights movement was the Chilean *golpe* of 1973.[10] Historian Joe Renouard argued that the coup "helped transform the varied causes of the early 1970s into

an international movement."[11] The brisk killing, imprisoning, and torture of thousands lent a sense of urgency to the human rights crusade. Pinochet and his cronies' labeling of all opponents as unworthy of rights revolted many in the United States. "Humanitarian values openly challenged the prevailing national security ideology," recalled Schoultz.

To be sure, Chile was the concern of a minority in the United States. When an October 1973 poll asked U.S. citizens if Salvador Allende's overthrow was "good because he was a Marxist, or bad because he was democratically elected," 19 percent said "good" and 31 percent "bad," but fully half had no opinion. The U.S.-based human rights community that focused on Latin America was also disproportionately made up of Latin Americans, often themselves former targets of military regimes.[12]

Still, on Chile, the solidarity groups were plentiful and diverse. Eventually, there were two national groups, maybe three dozen local ones from Boston to Seattle, and several more devoted to specific Chilean issues such as women or political prisoners. Trade unions and students also helped.[13]

In 1974, nongovernmental organizations produced two reports that provided the first evidence of systematic torture under Pinochet.[14] From Amnesty International came the revelation that the regime held 6,000–10,000 political prisoners. "The most common forms of physical torture have been prolonged beatings with truncheons, fists or bags of moist material, electricity to all parts of the body, burning with cigarettes or acid," it elaborated. "Such physical tortures have been accompanied with deprivation of food, drink and sleep." Evidence showed that interrogators used "truth drugs" on their victims.[15]

Thanks to Schneider and Kennedy, among others, the Senate sponsored hearings, resolutions, and laws against Pinochet's abuses.[16] Democrats on Capitol Hill were so focused on the small country that aides warned Kissinger not to "go to the mat on the issue of human rights."[17]

On Chile, Congress's greatest achievement was the 1975 Harkin Amendment to the Foreign Assistance Act of 1961. Human rights activists drafted it and then walked it up Capitol Hill, where Harkin agreed to sponsor it. Its first iteration mandated cutting off aid to any government that grossly violated human rights unless the president determined that such aid would directly benefit the needy. The following year, Kennedy led the adoption of a parallel amendment that directly targeted Chile, marking the first time Congress ended military aid to another government because of human rights.[18] In 1978, one Chilean magazine called Kennedy "the most dangerous foreign adversary" of the Pinochet regime.[19]

In response, Santiago hired five public relations and legal firms to win over hearts and minds. One result was the birth of what might be called Chilean AstroTurf—as opposed to grassroots—media organizations such as the American-Chilean Council meant to "counteract the leftist propaganda campaign against Chile," according to its chair.[20] The council, founded by conservative columnist William F. Buckley and lobbyist Marvin Liebman, received money illegally from the Chilean state—perhaps from DINA itself—and legally from private U.S. citizens. In 1979, the Justice Department shut it down as an unregistered "foreign agent" of Pinochet.[21]

Orlando Letelier was aware of all these forces. Alarmed though he was by the tentacles of Pinochet in Washington, the Chilean assessed in March 1976 that "there are still enough people in the U.S. who wish us well." "It is a mistake to think that it is a monolithic country," he explained. "There are 93 solidarity committees with Chile alone. Important groups of the Democratic Party are also in solidarity with us. The proposal not to furnish Chile with any more weapons, which has just been approved by the Senate, passed with 49 in favor and 31 opposed. This is a considerable majority."[22]

》》 Among those who labored with Letelier out of concern for human dignity were Ronni Karpen Moffitt and Michael Moffitt. Both were in the Chevelle with him on that fateful morning of September 21, 1976.

Ronni Karpen was born on January 10, 1951, in Passaic, New Jersey. Her parents, Murray and Hilda Karpen, worked relentlessly in the deli they owned. They were Orthodox Jews descended from Eastern Europeans who ate kosher and observed Rosh Hashanah and Yom Kippur. Karpen was bat mitzvahed, but otherwise her childhood was mainstream. It was also happy. The family was close, and three cousins lived next door. She jumped rope, played the flute, helped with the family catering business, and had lots of loyal friends. In high school she was a good student and a "joiner": she served on the student council, the yearbook committee, and the student magazine staff. "When there was a drudgy story that nonetheless had to be written," recalled a childhood friend, "everyone would toss it around. Finally Ronni would just sit down and do it."[23]

Family and friends remembered her as a cheerful and giving young woman. "Even as a child," said her mother, "she had such a grace, a gift for happiness that brought joy to everyone around her."[24] Both parents recalled her as "a warm bubbly person who considered everybody her best friend."[25] Her younger brother, also named Michael, remembered her as his protector and mentor. When pounced upon by the middle sibling, "all I had to do was shout Ronni's name. No matter what she was doing, she would drop it, and in a matter of seconds, there she would be, coming to my rescue, yelling 'Supergirl!' and throw my brother off of me." She comforted Michael when he didn't make little league. She babysat him, chauffeured him on his first date, cooked for him, and helped him with a school election.[26]

"Ronni was a woman becoming—becoming the political activist, the leader, the revolutionary," wrote her friend Beverly Fisher.[27] The metamorphosis began at the University of Maryland, where Ronni studied from 1968 to 1972 for a degree in education.[28] These years witnessed dramatic transformations in U.S. society. Ronni went from suffering panty raids by sophomoric boys to dodging police raids as a Vietnam protester. "As her mind expanded and she was made aware of certain inequalities and injustices that existed in our society, she was moved to try to change society," added brother Michael. "My sister was not a theorist, she was a doer, someone willing to wear overalls and build solid change, brick by brick."[29] She traveled down to the capital for May Day and Kent State demonstrations. She set up "learning centers" with a teacher friend to extend education for needy children.[30]

After graduation, Karpen looked for meaningful work. Teaching elementary school for a year in Rockville, Maryland, proved frustrating; typing for a Georgetown insurance company, deadening. In 1974, while Orlando Letelier languished in prison, Karpen found at least part-time fulfillment at Music Carry Out, a program that provided instruments and space to disadvantaged child musicians in the Washington area. She became "one of three people responsible for keeping it going."[31]

Karpen called home every Sunday and went back to New Jersey most holidays.[32] "I lived vicariously through Ronni," her mother Hilda recalled. "She was truly a special person. A remarkable person. All the wonderful things she had done and was doing. To me these were all like dreams come true."[33]

Music Carry Out was originally funded by the Institute for Policy Studies (IPS). Karpen heard they were looking for staff, so she quit her insurance job and devoted herself to IPS while still caring for Music Carry Out.

IPS was the brainchild of Marcus Raskin and Richard Barnet. Both had worked in national security in the John Kennedy administration. They left disillusioned and founded IPS in 1963 to transform ideas into social action. Barnet explained that the Vietnam War "was one of the very formative experiences in both my life and the life of the institute." The war, along with issues such as human rights, helped bridge the gap between socialist radicals and liberal democrats. IPS's dozens of fellows, senior fellows, staff associates, and administrators, "committed to the search for alternatives to imperialism," filled small offices in Washington's Dupont Circle neighborhood—and at the Transnational Institute in Amsterdam starting in 1974.[34] Like many human rights activists, IPS fellows nurtured relationships with more liberal members of Congress. Senator Abourezk would serve on its board of trustees.[35]

At IPS, Ronni Karpen at first was Raskin's assistant and did a bit of everything—typing, filing, minute taking, stuffing envelopes, fund-raising—often the labor behind the mostly male fellows at the institute. "She was a woman, who like many of us, did the work and made things happen, but seldom gets the credit or acclaim," said her friend. "However, she was not easily taken advantage of, and fought to change the ways in which work was distributed. When angry, she was a formidable opponent. She fought passionately for justice, equality."[36] Karpen's smarts and energy were so apparent that IPS's leaders made her fund-raising coordinator.[37]

Michael Moffitt was already at IPS when Karpen came on board. He was born on July 29, 1951, in Binghamton, New York, in a working-class, Irish Catholic family. His father, Paul, was a driver-salesman for a milk company. "I did not have a particularly happy adolescence," recalled Moffitt, without elaborating.[38] However, he did well at a community college, where one teacher described him as "a better than average student, a fine human being, and . . . a big, gentle bear of a person." He graduated at the same time as Karpen with a bachelor's in political science.[39] That graduation spring, he first came to Washington and worked for IPS. He returned to the think tank while also in graduate school at American University.[40]

Moffitt remembered September 11, 1973, the day of the Chilean coup, as "one of Washington's typically beautiful autumn scenes, turned dark." He recalled "thinking that the coup in Chile would somehow be extraordinarily important in my life." He considered Salvador Allende's socialism "perhaps the most tolerant political system in the world."[41]

At IPS, Moffitt focused on how to reform global economics to level the playing field between rich and poor nations. The goal of his "International Economic Order Project," he wrote in a manifesto of sorts, was "to contribute to the development of a more just and equitable international economic system which benefits not only a privileged few, but the great majority of the human race now trapped in sub-human economic and social conditions."[42] His devotion to financial issues stemmed from his passionate nature. A woman who dated him in 1974–75 described Moffitt as "highly involved in politics and a very emotional individual."[43] Another said he "has a tremendous ability to write, a fine memory, and is very intelligent." He was "a devoted Marxist but this is an intellectual commitment and he does not advocate violence."[44]

In early 1975, Moffitt met Karpen. "She had seemed the kind of woman who was always out of reach for a person like myself. She was beautiful and charming. Unlike me, she came from a family that was close and loving, and she possessed a special aura or grace that was thrilling. We met and fell in love. It was like a miracle to me. I could hardly believe my good fortune. Very soon after we began dating, we became engaged and were in each other's company constantly. I was deeply and totally in love the way I had always wanted to be."[45]

On Memorial Day, 1976, Karpen and Moffitt married at her parents' home. The groom borrowed his vows from Chilean poet Pablo Neruda:

Stand up with me.

. . . . . .

And let's go off together
To fight face to face
Against the devil's webs,
Against the system that distributes hunger,
Against organized misery. Let's go.[46]

The newlyweds moved into a creaky, white clapboard five-room farmhouse. "Ronni brought immense joy to my life," recalled Moffitt. "She was popular and energetic. We were a devoted young couple. She began to turn our house into a home. We finished the furniture and painted the rooms. She hung curtains and planted and tended a small flower garden. Just being in her presence made me content." They planned to have children and buy a house. "I loved my wife deeply, admired and respected my employer, and was challenged and excited by my work. I felt I was on top of the world."[47]

>> The Moffitts' direct employer was a newly arrived Chilean exile. "My wife and I loved Orlando Letelier," Michael would later state, "because, like he, we believe that the abominable conditions in which the majority of the human race (especially, but not exclusively in the Third World) are forced to live, is morally outrageous and politically insane. This is the legacy which they and the late President Allende bequeathed to the world and millions of people will never forget it."[48]

One month after Letelier flew from Santiago to Caracas, Richard Barnet of IPS wrote to "Compañero Letelier." Following up on a phone call from

Saul Landau, an IPS fellow, Barnet offered Letelier an associate fellowship paying $10,000 per year, or about $50,000 in 2019, "to work with the Latin American work group and to develop ideas about hemispheric security." Letelier accepted five days later.[49] Working from Washington, he thought, would give him a larger audience than would his current perch in Caracas. By January 1975 the Leteliers had reunited in Venezuela and moved to Washington, though Orlando would return to Caracas intermittently until mid-1976. They soon purchased a house at 5818 Ogden Court in Bethesda, Maryland, a Washington suburb. Son Juan Pablo recalled that the family was "searching for normality; we were a torn, tense family." They had rebuilding to do, and the house made them feel "safe."[50]

When Letelier accepted the IPS position, he informed Barnet that he would be concentrating on Chilean affairs. He immediately regained his boundless energy for working—and networking. This despite Pinochet's henchmen warning him to stay quiet and reminding him that the dictator could mete out punishment "no matter where the violator lives."[51]

Michael Moffitt became Letelier's researcher and executive assistant, while the Chilean rose to the directorship of the Transnational Institute in Amsterdam, with a pay raise to $25,000.[52] Moffitt went to Holland with Letelier. He also organized a trip to Chile by representatives Miller, Moffett, and Harkin and helped in the Harkin-Kennedy ban on arms sales to Chile.[53] His working-class background on his mind, Michael was excited to work with such a sophisticated person. *One day, Orlando will be president of Chile*, he thought.

In writings and in meetings, Moffitt and Letelier argued that Pinochet's true evil was in marrying repression with free market economics. The kind of market purism espoused by Milton Friedman and adopted by Pinochet did not necessarily lead to democracy, they stressed. In Chile's case, it actually reinforced inequalities that made tyranny necessary. "Concentration of wealth is no accident, but a rule," Orlando explained in the *Nation* magazine. "Repression for the majorities and 'economic freedom' for small privileged groups are in Chile two sides of the same coin."[54] Isabel Letelier probably best expressed the argument: "An economy that fattens the rich and leaves the hungry to starve must create a repressive apparatus as its only means of governing."[55]

Orlando and Isabel were somewhat redeemed when Pinochet's free-market reforms crashed in the mid-1970s. Inflation ballooned to 341 percent, the gross national product fell by 12 percent, industry declined by one-fourth, and the foreign debt quadrupled.[56]

No doubt reminding him of his time as ambassador, Letelier once again became a fixture in the Washington elite. He was not rich, though his pay at IPS grew to around $30,000 by 1976 and he was offered a book contract with a $20,000 advance.[57]

He was, however, prominent. He met with top State Department officials.[58] He taught at American University. He lunched with Ted Kennedy, Hubert Humphrey, and George McGovern—this last senator admitting that Letelier "sensitized me to human rights violations in Chile" and convinced him to cut aid.[59] Angela Davis once came to his house.[60] Joan Baez was a friend. Richard Avedon photographed him.

Most important, Letelier became a unifier for Chilean exiles, now numbering in the hundreds of thousands worldwide. He persuaded the centrists from the Christian Democratic Party and the violent radicals from the Revolutionary Left Movement to drop most of their disputes. He also brought into discussions the church, the socialists, and the communists.[61] "The magic of Orlando," recalled the director of the Washington Office on Latin America, "was that he could associate with all people opposed to the Pinochet dictatorship."[62] Along with Bernardo Leighton and Carlos Prats, who would also be targeted by DINA, Letelier was seen as one of the three who could organize a government in exile, even though that was never his intention and the anti-Pinochet forces remained atomized. Still, Letelier could bring people together, was in Washington, and spoke English well.[63] He organized financial aid for exiles. "We became his troops, and he became our leader," recalled Juan Gabriel Valdés, then a student activist doing graduate work at Princeton University.[64] Though he had no passport, Letelier obtained an H4 visa from the United States that allowed him to leave and return.

His greatest victories as a lobbyist against Pinochet came in Holland. After four trips to the European country, he convinced its dockworkers' federation to boycott the handling of Chilean goods and won the cancellation of a planned $62.5 million mining investment by the Stevin Group, one that would have made of Holland the single largest foreign investor in Chile. Letelier also may have helped block credits to Chile at the World Bank and the Inter-American Development Bank, his former employer.[65]

Isabel, meanwhile, mostly sculpted and painted. "I was under [Orlando's] visa and my status did not allow me to work in this country. I set up a nonprofit organization, the Chile Committee for Human Rights, and I worked without pay in it. Also, with a group of artists, I started a collective project: 'The Touchstone Gallery.' I resumed my art and had successful showings of my sculptures."[66] She was in her forties now, with flecks of gray in her raven hair, and lines in her face from the trauma of the last few years. Still, with her luminous green eyes, she remained attractive, down-to-earth, sensitive, determined, and the toast of many a Washington dinner party.

>> Behind the activism and activities, a rift divided Orlando and Isabel. As soon as the Leteliers were reunited in Caracas in late 1974 to early 1975, "I felt something, sensed something," said Isabel.

"He confessed that he had an affair, but said it was not important. He told me that he hoped I would understand. I told him that I did understand. Then I looked him straight in the eye and said, 'I hope *you* also could understand [if I cheated].' And he looked at me in horror and shouted, 'Never!'"[67]

Orlando's lover was a Venezuelan, Sagrario Pérez-Soto. Intelligent, tall, beautiful, stylish, and blessed with long dark hair, she was related to the wife of Diego Arria, who had secured Letelier's release. She was also a millionaire with her own bodyguards. He called her "Queen."[68]

Why would Letelier undertake an affair right after a painful year-long separation from his wife in concentration camps? First, he said, he was alone in Venezuela for the first three months and felt intensely lonely.

Second, the end of the year in prison and its constant fear of dying "created in me a situation of self-exaltation.... I was convinced that I had acted very well, that I had been very generous, that I had been very strong; that after having lived through all that, now nothing could touch me, nothing could hurt me." He considered his affair to be "concessions" to Pérez-Soto.[69]

Third and conversely, he also felt he needed the ego boost. "For a man who has felt extreme deprivation, can you realize what it is like to all of a sudden have everything offered to you?" Letelier explained. "While I was secretly wondering at night who I really was, this woman came along and told me I was wonderful."[70]

The affair grew "serious to the point of divorce," Isabel later divulged to the FBI.[71] In early 1975, her husband assured her, "It's nothing important. It's already over." By mid-year, however, Isabel found out that the relationship with the Venezuelan continued.[72] Letelier would meet with Pérez-Soto in Washington, New York, London, Paris, Amsterdam, Mexico, and elsewhere.[73] Michael Moffitt, who sometimes tagged along on these official trips, deduced what was going on and described the relationship as "very intimate."[74]

Letelier had had a fling before, but this one was more serious, and his wife was not going to let him off easy.

"Oh yeah? We're going to get separated now?" she told him angrily. "I want you to sit down with your sons and tell them what the hell's going on."

Letelier, not naturally given to parenting, called his four teenagers into his office and sat them down. "You guys, you know, sometimes, when people have been together for a long time, they might have issues, and your mother and I, we're kind of experiencing a time when we feel it might be better for *all* of us . . . to get our space." He avoided mentioning a lover or an affair.

A few days later, Francisco came home late, showing sings of drinking and smoking pot. "Hey! Come back into this room!" his mother grilled him. "I want to check you out. Why are your eyes so red?"

"God, you're just such a henpecking mom!" the teen retorted. "Would you chill out? No wonder Dad doesn't want to live with you any more!"

"That really triggered her," he recalled. "Your dad's got a girlfriend! I figured it out from his phone records," she explained. From then on, Francisco's anger turned toward his father.[75]

In January 1976, Letelier asked for a divorce so he could marry Pérez-Soto.[76] "I've become like a crazy man," he confided to a friend. "I can't help myself; I'm in love. I feel torn apart inside because I also love Isabel, and God knows we have been through so much together and she is the most marvelous person in the world."[77] In February, he moved into an efficiency apartment near Dupont Circle.

The separation was not complete. Two or three times per week, Orlando and Isabel would have lunch or go to the movies. For Isabel, life as a single parent proved trying: she juggled alone the problems of four teenage boys. On his end, Orlando did not know how to cook, clean, or shop for himself. "He survived concentration camp, but never learned to scramble an egg," said Isabel with evident satisfaction. In the spring, they reconciled fully, and in July Isabel let him move back into the Ogden Court house.[78]

After his assassination, investigators found in Letelier's briefcase three cassette tapes of an Orlando monologue explaining to Pérez-Soto his reasons for calling off the affair. "You are, really, psychologically ill. But what is this sickness?" he asked, after just telling her of his deep love for her. He portrayed her as irrational and inscrutable, calling her self-centered, spoiled, and "capricious." "I decided that the important thing was to arrange my life," he concluded, "and not continue to permit all this to interfere with my work, etc."[79]

After the affair, things seemed to return to normal. Work took up most everyone's time. During Sunday breakfasts and dinners Letelier would be-rate his teenage boys for their long hair. Family gatherings continued at Chile Chico. When Orlando would swim in the ocean, his tall, lithe body luxuriated in "how wonderful freedom is."[80]

The summer of 1976 "was *the* first time I felt that I was beginning to have a different, a more adult relationship with my father; a friend to friend relation," recalled Juan Pablo. "I was just getting to know my father."[81]

6

Some Misguided Sense of Patriotism

Sometime in the fall of 1964, brothers Guillermo and Ignacio Novo walked into an Eighth Avenue army-navy store in New York City's Times Square. For $35 they purchased a World War II German bazooka, 3.46 inches in diameter. They took the near-obsolete rocket launcher either to Ignacio's on West 50th Street or to Guillermo's across the river in North Bergen, New Jersey. There, they sawed off over two of its five feet of tubing. They made of it, as the papers later wrote, "a sort of mortar with a clock-like timing device." Separately, they bought a rocket from an Italian mafioso in Brooklyn who owned a gun store.

On December 11, the Novos, with their partner Julio Cesar Pérez y Pérez, took their modified weapon to the docks on 48th Avenue in Long Island and set it up next to the Adam Metal Supply plant. While Ignacio and Julio looked on, Guillermo aimed the tube at a twenty-degree angle, dropped the shell in, and, with a *whoosh!*, fired it across the East River—right at the United Nations.

Had Guillermo angled the bazooka lower, the shell might have traveled 1,300 yards and crashed into the U.N. Secretariat, shattering glass and concrete and possibly killing many of the 5,000 people in the building. Instead, it arched high and plunged into the water 200 yards from the shore, sending a twenty-foot geyser into the air.

The men, all three Cuban Americans, were aiming for Ché Guevara. The Argentine physician-turned-revolutionary, right-hand man of Fidel Castro, and Cuban minister of industry was at that moment addressing the General Assembly. In the Assembly's hall, the audience heard the detonation. Windows were rattled. El Ché was not: he said the incident "gave added flavor to his speech."[1] As if to add extra spice, right before Ché's address a woman darted out of a picket line in front of the building with a seven-inch knife and tried to force her way into the building, saying she wanted to kill Guevara. After the blast a group of terrorists associated with the Novos burst into the hall, but U.N. guards disarmed them.[2]

Whether the Novos missed the building on purpose was, as District Attorney Frank O'Connor said at the time, "a matter of conjecture." The bombers told Stanley Ross, editor of a Spanish-language weekly in New York, that "they could have hit the United Nations headquarters but purposely didn't."[3] "It was only a symbolic act," Ignacio later told a reporter, "to rob Che of news headlines."[4] Or perhaps the Novos lied to conceal their embarrassment at having misfired.

In any case, the Novos and Pérez fled the scene and, a few days later, were in Ross's office. The editor advised the Cubans to surrender. They were not helping the anti-Castro cause, he explained. The police quickly found and interrogated the three but released them for lack of evidence. "Surveillance and investigation of them continued," according to Chief of Detectives Philip Walsh. Ross and his staff met with the Cubans five times in eight days, finally relaying to police that they "were desirous of surrendering."[5] Another possibility is that Pérez egged them into surrendering or turned them in. The FBI later identified him as working for the CIA.[6]

The men were charged with two felonies — endangering life maliciously and attempting to damage a building — and with one misdemeanor, conspiracy. They could have earned fifty-three years in prison each. Instead, the officers who arrested them either failed to read them their rights or interrogated them without a lawyer present. Whatever the failure in procedure, all charges were dropped. They were free to go.[7]

"In a period when Hispanics were seen by many Americans as intrinsically funny, an accent joke," writer Joan Didion later observed, "this incident was generally treated tolerantly, a comic footnote to the news."[8]

Terrorist attacks by the Novo brothers were no laughing matter, however. Before the U.N. job they raided the Cuban Consulate in New York, and the FBI suspected Guillermo of bombing the *María Teresa*, a ship docked in Montreal and bound for Cuba with food and powdered milk.[9] Later, in 1967, after denying involvement in another bombing in Montreal, the Novos were arrested when police found three blocks of explosives, three blasting caps, and two eighteen-inch links of primer cord in Ignacio's shoe store. Each was sentenced to one to three years in prison, but their sentence was suspended and each was placed on two years' probation and given a $250 fine.[10] In 1968, Ignacio defended the bombings of tourist offices that did business in Cuba. He also talked of executing "representatives of the Cuban government outside of Cuba." The following year, the FBI heard Guillermo plotting to bomb Cuba's consulate and trade commission building in Montreal, and he was charged with violating the Neutrality Act. In 1973, Guillermo spent six months in prison for planning to blow up a Cuban ship anchored in that Canadian city. By 1976, they and dozens of other Cuban Americans had been involved in hundreds of additional attempts or plots to bomb and assassinate, including with the help of the mafia.[11]

That year, too, the Novos and three more Cuban Americans would shuttle Michael Townley around the East Coast while he studied the movements of Orlando Letelier. Two of them detonated the fatal car bomb.

>> District Attorney O'Connor labeled the motive of the bazooka bombers "some misguided sense of patriotism."[12]

The Novos loved Cuba—or hated Castro—so ardently that it drove them to terrorism. Ignacio was born in 1938, and Guillermo followed a year and a day later. Ignacio Sr., nicknamed "Pipo," had migrated with his wife from Majorca, Spain, and sold cosmetics for Max Factor & Co. in Havana. When the boys were thirteen and fourteen, Pipo died when overheating boilers at a shoe mucilage factory next door exploded. The boys watched their house burn to the ground, their father inside. In 1954 their mother emigrated with her five children, following a brother who had moved to New York. Guillermo became a U.S. citizen and studied chemistry. He worked as a lab supervisor in a New Jersey chemical outfit until 1968, when the American Chemists Association expelled him for his conviction for explosives possession.[13] He and Ignacio then occasionally sold used cars.[14] At his Chevrolet dealership in Union City, New Jersey, everyone knew Guillermo as "Bill."[15]

From the New York area, the Novos monitored what they saw as the corruption of the Castro revolution of 1959. "I thought it would be good for Cuba," said Guillermo of its buoyant early months. But he turned bitter when *castristas* seized the conservative daily *Diario de la Marina*. "They were expropriating people's businesses.... People struggle and you get there and take their business. Forget the 'revolution is for the people' slogan."[16]

In time, Guillermo became the better known of the brothers. And the tougher. Once, to prove his mettle, he drove his car at high speed into a brick wall.[17]

Other anti-Castro Cuban exiles who helped kill Letelier and Ronni Moffitt came to terrorism by way of CIA training. Unlike the Novo brothers, Alvin Ross, who helped assemble the Letelier bomb, took part in the failed

1961 CIA-backed invasion of Cuba at the Bay of Pigs and was then imprisoned in Cuba and ransomed back to the United States.[18] Ross was seven years older than Guillermo Novo and lost his blackjack dealer gig when the Castro revolution closed the casinos. He fled. In the United States, he also sold used cars. One journalist described him as "a gracious, neatly groomed man with shiny black hair and gray sideburns." A tic on his round face caused his right cheek to flutter, and his eyes and head often moved, giving him a slightly mad air.[19] He once boasted of firing a bazooka at Castro's motorcade.[20]

José Dionisio Suárez, meanwhile, drove the gray sedan behind Letelier on that fateful morning. He was born in 1939. Raised by patriotic parents, as a teenager he joined Castro's rebels in the Sierra Maestra, was twice wounded, and made lieutenant.[21] Like Guillermo Novo, Suárez admired the regime during its first year, while he worked as an executioner for Castroist *comandante* Húber Matos and rose to colonel.[22] But when communists began taking over top spots and jailed Matos for denouncing them, Suárez was also arrested—for an "anti-Castro statement"—and spent a year in prison. In 1961, he pulled off a near-impossible feat and escaped Santiago's Morro Castle prison by scaling its walls. He hopped on a boat to Miami, where, following the pattern, he sold used cars. He received CIA training and planned to liberate Cuba as a squad leader with the Bay of Pigs brigade, but, reported the FBI, he "missed a connection and was late arriving in Miami, missing the invasion entirely."[23] Despite his suave ways and leadership of the exile community, Suárez's intensity and detestation of Castro never abated, and he joined several commando raids. He earned the monikers "the Brush" and "Pool of Blood" for plying his trade as an executioner. Five days before the Letelier explosion, Suárez was believed to have taken part in the bombing of a Soviet ship, the *Ivan Shepetkov*, in Port Elizabeth, New Jersey.[24] All the while, he presented himself as an urbane community leader. His wife founded the Head Start program in Puerto Rico.

The last Letelier assassin to flee the Castro revolution was Virgilio Paz, who pushed the button that set off the bomb at Sheridan Circle. The Castro Revolution had expelled his father from the Cuban army, he complained. In 1966, with Paz only fifteen, the family moved to Spain, and then found itself in Mexico en route to the United States when the father caught pneumonia and died.[25] Paz blamed Castro. He moved to New York City as a permanent resident alien. He worked as a clerk, a truck driver—and a car salesman. The FBI noted his "extremely neat and dapper appearance, and . . . expensive woven leather brown shoes. Paz loves the social scene and attractive women.

Assassination

He prefers to drink Chevas [sic] Regal, and water, and occasionally smokes Cuban made cigars." Usually armed with a Walther PPK .380, Paz was known to carry two or more weapons at a time, some "possibly secreted in [a] hollowed out book."[26]

In 1961, the Novos joined the Cuban Nationalist Movement (CNM), founded two years earlier in a basement on New York's 46th Street in response to the hardening of communist rule in Cuba.[27] Its founder was Felipe Rivero, whose aristocratic family, not incidentally, had owned the shuttered *Diario de la Marina*.[28] The three other Letelier coconspirators—Ross, Suárez, and Paz—later came aboard CNM's governing council.[29]

》 The CNM was only one of the many U.S.-based groups opposing Castro. The members of Omega 7, Alpha 66, the Brigade 2506 Association, the 30th of November Movement, the Martí Insurrectional Movement, the Insurrectional Movement for Revolutionary Recovery, Operation Eagle, the Secret Cuban Government, Cuban Action, the Cuban National Liberation Front, Young Cuba, and doubtless others found a haven in a southern Florida and northeastern New Jersey awash in anti-Castro intrigue.

In the 1960s and early 1970s, about one-third of Dade County's population was of Cuban descent. Miami itself was over half Cuban by 1975.[30] Didion described the metropolis in those days as "not exactly an American city as American cities have until recently been understood but a tropical capital: long on rumor, short on memory, over built on the chimera of runaway money and referring not to New York or Boston or Los Angeles or Atlanta but to Caracas and Mexico, to Havana and to Bogotá and to Paris and Madrid."[31]

"The majority of these Cubans are strictly anti-Castro politically," explained the Miami FBI. "Anti-Castro organizations who are engaged in strictly political actions against Cuba and other communist countries are considered freedom fighters, and enjoy considerable prestige."[32]

In 1962, while at the Orange Bowl in Miami's Little Havana, President John Kennedy had waved the banner of the 2506 Brigade—the commandos who had floundered at the Bay of Pigs—and promised "that this flag will be returned to this brigade in a free Havana."[33] Kennedy also set up JM/WAVE on the campus of the University of Miami. It became the largest CIA station in the world, its 300 U.S. employees monopolizing anti-Castro activities with a budget of $50 million.[34] At one point, the CIA had up to 6,000 Cuban exiles on its payroll. Many planned to assassinate Castro. Others bombed sugar mills or attacked fishing boats on the island.[35]

Some Misguided Sense of Patriotism

By the late 1960s, however, Washington had completely abandoned the idea of invading Cuba. JM/WAVE ceased to exist in 1968, and the CIA cut loose hundreds of exiles. In 1973, the United States penned an antihijacking agreement with Havana, easing tensions further. Even Henry Kissinger, in 1974, toyed with normalizing relations with the communist regime. By 1975, six Latin American nations and four former British colonies in the Americas had renewed diplomatic relations with Cuba, and the Organization of American States had lifted its sanctions against the regime.[36] On March 4, Ted Kennedy introduced in the Senate a bill to terminate the U.S. trade embargo against Cuba. Fifty-three percent of U.S. citizens were in favor of diplomatic and economic relations with the island.[37]

Cuban Americans seethed at this turnabout, especially as hundreds of their compatriots lingered in Castro's prisons.[38] CIA recruits such as Orlando Bosch, Orlando García, Ricardo Morales, and Luis Posada Carriles angrily turned against the agency. Bosch took credit for killing "CIA stooges."[39] "I felt betrayed by the Kennedy administration and by the CIA," he recalled. "They held out a dream to us and then let us down."[40]

》》 Exiles' bitterness had an outlet: violence. "If we are alone, absolutely alone," proclaimed exile leader José Miró Cardona, "there is only one route left to follow. Violence? Yes, violence. We are obliged to do so."[41]

"You can knock them off the payroll," bemoaned one CIA case officer about Cuban Americans, "but you can't take back what you taught them to do."[42] Hundreds of exiles had received training in weapons, intelligence, and explosives.[43] Some took that expertise into Latin American intelligence services. Others helped with the Watergate burglary.[44] Most continued to harass the Castro regime.

Saul Landau from IPS gave perhaps one of the most devastating descriptions of the Cuban terrorists: "All creatures of U.S. policy, these madmen, some with Hitler photos on their walls or 'Cuba Uber Alles' banners hanging from their balconies, have run wild in the hemisphere. They sell used cars or shoes by day, and murder and bomb by day and night."[45]

Extremists' meager budgets narrowed their choices, however. "If we had the means," Bosch declared to the press, "Cuba would burn from one end to the other."[46] But they could never afford a Bay of Pigs–style commando operation to Cuba, not to mention that U.S. authorities were likely to detect it and seize its assets. So the militants resorted to small-scale terrorism — "a small boat here, an embassy there," explained Ignacio Novo.[47] Exiles also produced publications, community programs, college protests, and agitprop. For funding, they turned to mainstream organizations that represented the 500,000 exiles of Miami and their 8,000 businesses to raise funds through memberships to social clubs, dances, and raffles.[48] Some wealthy émigré doctors shared their fortunes "so as to feel part of the anti-Castro movement."[49] Many terrorists turned to dealing drugs, mostly cocaine.

"War throughout the Roads of the World," their new motto, announced an expanded theater of operations. The concept, pioneered by CNM's Felipe Rivero in 1964, perhaps first practiced at the Novos' bazooka assault and fully adopted a decade later, meant that exiles would hit targets outside Cuba.

Soon, bombs exploded in New York, Montreal, Miami, Lima, Mexico City, Mérida, Kingston, Madrid, London, and Paris. "Bursts of machinegun fire and shrapnel will make it clear to Castro's servants that there are no borders to stop the actions of liberty-loving men," went one exile manifesto.[50] As Ignacio Novo admitted to a journalist, "We have hit them in Japan, in Europe, in South America, in Canada, and in the United States. We have hurt his [Castro's] economy, we have damaged his economic interests outside of the United States, we have damaged his property. That's about all we can do."

"How have you hit him?" asked the journalist.

"There have been ships blown up, Cuban property blown up, Cuban trade missions blown up. . . . That kind of action. Political attempts against his representatives outside of the island."

"Assassination of Cuban Ambassadors and/or agents?"

"Right. We can't have a dialogue with them, they won't allow any opposition, so the only door that we have open is through the use of violence."[51]

Numbers told the story of the globalization of the Cuban counterrevolution. In the 1960s, exile terrorists struck in Cuba 731 times versus 156 in the United States. In the 1970s, the numbers reversed, to 16 versus 279. Between 1974 and 1976, the most intense phase, U.S. authorities tied 202 major bombings in 23 countries — one every five days, on average, and 113 of them in the United States — to Cuban exiles.[52] By another count, over 200 bombs rocked Miami alone in those same years, with thirteen blasting in a single, petrifying forty-eight-hour period.[53] The FBI was said to be calling Miami the "terrorist capital" of the United States.[54]

Of the world, actually. In 1974, Cuban exiles accounted for 45 percent of all terrorist bombings *on the planet.*[55]

The FBI investigated, but no one was talking. "The community is hesitant to cooperate with the police and federal agencies," agents wrote. "They do not want to become involved and feel more strongly about the Cuban cause than what they consider technical violations of the U.S. law."[56] As Igna-

Some Misguided Sense of Patriotism

cio Novo explained, "we feel no obligation to obey the laws of any country that robs us of our right of belligerence." Like Novo, most Cuban exiles considered themselves warriors, not terrorists, and they targeted buildings and representatives of the Castro government rather than innocent bystanders.[57]

Terror spread anyway. Businesses that shipped packages or sent tourists to Cuba were under constant threat. Movie theaters had to think twice before showing a Cuban production. Employees of the Cuban government at the United Nations and at Cuba's embassies throughout the world lived in fear. The next envelope or package they opened could be their last.

Car bombs eventually became popular with exiles, "most likely because you can do it with a timer, you don't have to be there," explained Ignacio Novo. "It's not the same as if you would walk up to me with a gun and shoot me, you know . . . somebody might see you from a second story building somewhere. But if you do it with a car, then you do not have to be there. You can detonate it electronically or by a timing device."[58]

Even the relatively mainstream 2506 Brigade joined this underground. Leaders sued the Kennedy Library for the return of the brigade's flag and, at the same time, gave their "Freedom Award" to Augusto Pinochet. In 1976, the group's elections ushered in a new, radical leadership that called for using terrorism as a tactic.[59] They would eventually help cover legal fees for Letelier's assassins.[60]

"There's only one part of the United States now that's literally exporting terrorism," concluded the Justice Department, "and that's south Florida."[61]

》》 New Jersey was soon to share that distinction.

In 1967, the Jersey-based Novo brothers took over the leadership of the "Northern Zone" or "Zone II" CNM ("Zone I" was Cuba; Miami was "Zone III."). An exile publication, *El Nacionalista*, predicted that the group would become more violent and more radical as a consequence. Ignacio soon admitted to a Spanish-language paper in 1968 that the exiles "were disgusted with the policy toward Cuba and that their disappointment was shown by their actions."[62] The Novos were considered loose cannons even among exile militants.[63]

For many in New Jersey, however, they were heroes.

Bergenline Avenue, a forty-block commercial artery of shops and bodegas, ten minutes by bus from Manhattan's Port Authority, ran north from around the Jersey side of the Holland Tunnel through Weehawken, Union City, and West New York. The area had long been a refuge for immigrants:

first the English and the Dutch, then Swiss and Germans, then Armenians and Syrians, and later Italians and Jews. By the early twentieth century, many worked in the embroidery industry.[64] In the 1960s, observed a journalist, "the Cubans swallowed Bergenline Avenue and made it theirs." By the 1970s, there were a quarter of a million Cubans in the New York-New Jersey area, the second largest concentration after Miami. In 1977, in Union City, nicknamed "Little Havana on the Hudson," Cubans accounted for 54 percent of the 70,000-strong population.[65] In neighboring West New York, the Cubans had grown from 0.1 percent of population in 1960 to 51.1 percent a decade later. Like most Latin Americans, the Jersey Cubans kept their homes, businesses, and sidewalks swept at all times. Coffee shops sold dark Cuban espresso. Graffiti read *La Lucha Sigue*, "the struggle continues." Most houses, cars, and windows sported some Cuban sticker or sign. Many of the over thirty exile groups in New Jersey gathered to do little more than sip cold drinks and spout fiery speeches against Fidel and Ché.[66] Tabloids around Union City had titles such as *War*, *Struggle*, and the *Nationalist*.[67]

In a mordant appraisal, an FBI agent described the strip: "It is nearly impossible to get lost in this area as it was geographically constructed for a person of minor intelligence." "A perfect example of the use of the word 'seedy' is in describing Union City," he continued. "'Tacky' is another appropriate term. It gives one the impression that the whole town was constructed using the same WWII Depression-colored brick that someone must have gotten discount from a brick-business closeout sale. This has only been updated by the use of pastel colored aluminum siding." Madonnas, Jesuses, and prayer boxes adorned most lawns. Furniture stores on Bergenline hawked gaudy plaster and porcelain statues of sad-eyed puppies and dancing couples. The avenue featured only one bookstore, stocked with some classics and a large collection of Cuban history tomes, trashy Spanish-language novels alongside political tracts by Lenin, Marx, Engels, Mao, and Nazi literature, Ku Klux Klan histories, and some anti-Semitic books. "And yet it is a very safe kind of seediness," continued the agent. "I walked around U.C. at all hours of the day and night and never felt threatened. I almost felt as if there was a Big Daddy/Godfather watching out from above making sure that the streets were free of trouble."[68]

Just off Bergenline, the Cuban Nationalist Movement operated out of a two-story gray brick building with black-painted windows. On its door was its shield, an outline of the island of Cuba above a lighting bolt. A woman who studied with some CNM members in the early 1960s recalled how "they were very strange. They used to give each other military decorations for something like hitting somebody over the head in a bar."⁶⁹ The group's motto, "Cuba Before All," not only recalled Nazi Germany's *Deutschland über Alles* but also betrayed its absence of loyalty to the U.S. government.

Its pamphlets outlined an ideology centered on a syndicalist capitalism akin to those of Mussolini, Hitler, Franco — and Chile's Fatherland and Freedom. "I am an extremist in my nationalism," Ignacio Novo later explained. "I support a working democracy in a syndicalist-federal state, similar to corporatism. I support all political creeds — except for Marxism."⁷⁰ Other CNM members explained that, in a "corporate" system, voters would be represented through their professional "syndicates," which would choose legislative bodies. An executive "triumvirate" would also emerge through the syndicates. Such a system, according to them, would eliminate class conflict.⁷¹ In meetings, CNM members dressed in uniforms similar to the Green Berets. One Cuban member of a more mainstream organization dismissed the CNM as "rightwing extremists and fascists."⁷²

José Suárez penned an opinion piece in New Jersey's *El Caimán* that laid out his motives for waging war on his adopted nation. He fumed over "fifteen years of failures" and the "sissy attitudes" of "some leaders of America," who had signed a pact "with the enemy not only of Cuba but of all humanity." He rejected "peaceful coexistence."⁷³

Socially, CNM members were conservative. They expressed dismay that other Cuban exiles failed to teach Spanish and Cuban history and culture to their children. Second-generation Cuban immigrants, they felt, proved bereft of spirituality and escaped through materialism and marijuana.⁷⁴

The CNM and other exile groups raised money by extorting New Jersey shopkeepers. The FBI reported that "businessmen" in Union City "established a network which would collect money in the form of 'taxes' from all segments of the Cuban community who were able to contribute and then divide the money between the various groups they supported. The businessmen would not necessarily sanction or direct specific anti-Castro activities; however, their ability to provide financial support probably gave them, at a minimum, indirect control over the various groups." The bureau suggested that such extortion netted $100,000 per year.⁷⁵ Some owners did give enthusiastically, and some helped direct the groups' missions. Alvin Ross talked of "a board of advisers that we keep secret — doctors, engineers, economists, philosophers, professors from university, and these are the people who give us ideas."⁷⁶

More prosaically, an old Cuban man outside a shop explained the process: "*Los nacionalistas* come and demand pay money. If no give, they smash in window. This window smash three times," he pointed.

"These papers," he added of their publications, "just propaganda."

Were people scared? "Yes, people scared."[77]

Some anti-Castro publications received other funds, sometimes tens of thousands of dollars per year, through official advertisements from the city government. Julia Valdivia, officially an assistant to Union City's mayor but known as "the lady mayor," backed the Novo brothers. She called Guillermo "a friend, and I respected his opinions. He believed in what he was doing, and I respected what he did."[78] The Reverend Sun Myung Moon's ultraconservative Unification Church also sponsored the CNM. Virgilio Paz and José Suárez allegedly did business with Colombian drug cartels.[79]

>> When the September 11 coup occurred in Chile in 1973, the Cubans of Miami and New Jersey rejoiced.[80] Fatherland and Freedom leaders toured the United States to defend the overthrow and recruit Cuban exiles in defense of Pinochet.[81] Some historians argue that the most militant among them grew more fascistic at knowing that the Pinochet regime shared their deep-seated hatred of communism.[82] CNM's Felipe Rivero admitted that exiles longed to curry favor with Santiago's new leaders. "Chile was our fair-haired boy, a favorite of the Cuban exile community. If we had gotten them to say we [CNM] were the best, we would have been the new leaders of the Cuban exile movement, a slap in the face to our rivals within the community."[83]

Guillermo Novo operated out of in Chile from December 1974 to February 1975, while the Leteliers moved their family from Caracas to Washington.[84] Orlando Bosch and José Suárez joined him, and they made a deal with DINA's Manuel Contreras: CNM members would get training in return for participating in covert DINA missions abroad.[85] Bosch recalled making "a lot of effort" while in South America, including killing Cubans in Buenos Aires.[86] The Cuban exiles were being folded into Operation Condor.

>> Michael and Mariana Townley first met with CNM members while on a trip to the United States in early 1975. DINA's Pedro Espinoza was made liaison to the Cubans, and he ordered Townley to connect with Rivero in Miami. Rivero, in turn, instructed Townley to go north to New Jersey and talk to Guillermo Novo.[87]

Townley drove up to New Jersey and had dinner with Guillermo and Suárez. He found them "very talkative."[88] But they were also "exceedingly suspicious and exceedingly security conscious. I think that they were more worried that I was possibly a CIA agent trying to penetrate their organization than I was worried about their security towards DINA at that moment."

They chatted, and the Townleys retired to a nearby motel. "The next morning Dionisio Suarez showed up with Guillermo Novo and with a third Cuban," Townley recalled. They "burst into the motel room after [Michael Townley] responded to their knock at the door," reported the FBI, "and they were all heavily armed with what appeared to be .45 caliber automatic weapons." Townley continued: "They held my wife and I at gunpoint, and searched all of our belongings, went through a briefcase, luggage, took everything apart and were looking for assurances that we were not CIA persons."[89]

"You are CIA!" Guillermo Novo accused them angrily. "You are trying to make us believe you are DINA, but you are CIA!"

"I can't take any more of this!" Mariana Callejas shouted, getting up. "If you are going to do something, then do it! But stop clowning around! You people probably believe that *chair* works for the CIA!"

"You have spirit," Novo admitted. "But you have no idea how much the Cubans have suffered because they trusted the CIA."

"That's right, and I don't care!" said Callejas. "We are DINA and we have a job to do. If you are going to kill us, like the Communists want to, then go ahead and do it. I have lived long enough."[90]

Townley finally cooled heads, as he recounted. "I made contact with the one person that I had previously been in contact telephonically with at the Chilean Military Mission, who supported my story."[91]

The Cubans, however, had also grown suspicious of the Pinochet regime. First, when Guillermo Novo, Suárez, and Bosch arrived in Chile in 1974, DINA took the trio into custody, blindfolded them, and subjected them to "intensive interrogation" for forty-eight hours before releasing them.[92] Then, in early 1976, CNM ally Rolando Otero was mistreated in Santiago and then handcuffed in Miami by the FBI. "This has been a terrible blow to our fighting exiles, who up to now have been considered ideological allies against the common enemy," Guillermo wrote to the consul general for Chile in New York.[93] Townley later assessed that 98 percent of his early conversations with the Cubans concerned Chile's treatment of Otero and Bosch.[94]

So, when the Cubans held Townley and Callejas at gunpoint in that Miami motel room, Townley sympathized with the CNM's shoddy treatment by Santiago and reassured them that DINA's goals overlapped with those of the "War throughout the Roads of the World." Eventually, Guillermo shrugged and said, "Sometimes you have to lose; sometimes you must be confident and lose."[95] He opted to trust Townley.

The partnership began. Townley obtained from the Cubans C-4 explosives, two pistols, several blasting caps, a roll of detonating cord, and a pager modified to detonate for his and Callejas's 1975 trip to a conference in Mexico to assassinate two former Allende officials. (Orlando Letelier attended the meeting, but he was not a target.) The couple bought a used camper, drove 4,000 miles to Mexico, but somehow arrived too late and turned around, the mission in shambles.[96]

Throughout, Callejas was ambivalent about their new associates. "I happen to respect those idealists, crazy as it might seem," she told the BBC. "They fight for what they think is right, and they're willing to do anything to stop Communism from coming to—to the world." But, as with the Italian fascists, she hated the anti-Semitism of the Miami "charlatans."[97]

She once described a dinner to which she and Townley were invited. The Cubans "were elegantly dressed and [their women] had on many jewels. They looked down on Mike and me, who as usual were decked out in old blue jeans and T-shirts."

A Cuban sat face to face with them: "What do you think about the World Jewish Conspiracy?"

"I beg your pardon, the what?" said Callejas.

"The Jewish Conspiracy. It's going to destroy the world if we don't fight it. Before we do anything else, we must destroy the Jews."

"It seems to me that you have gotten sidetracked on purpose," she told him. "Fidel is too difficult a target, so you have chosen the perennial target, the Jews. Naturally, it is easier to fight the Jews than the Cubans."[98]

Callejas also found the Cubans unsophisticated and overly demonstrative. One journalist for the Chilean weekly *Qué Pasa* once described them in a flurry of stereotypes: "The Cubans are a loquacious people, passionate, spirited, forceful in its gestures and expressions, a people somewhat anarchic and accustomed to a rather violent rhythm of life."[99] Callejas, seeming to concur, once threw Virgilio Paz, a declared fascist, out of her house. She had tired not only of his anti-Semitism but also of his cigar smoke and of his habit of "spitting all the time and inhaling his boogers."[100]

>> Still, the DINA-Cuban exile relationship blossomed, with Cubans taking part in missions around the world. In October 1975, Michael Townley arranged for the CNM to take credit for the assassination attempt on Bernardo

Leighton and his wife. The CNM had nothing to do with the incident in Rome, but Townley was trying to elevate its stature as a partner of Pinochet's. He fed Virgilio Paz secret information about the hit to make the Cuban's boasts credible.[101]

Then, DINA turned its attention to Orlando Letelier.

7

Homicide Squad

Around when Orlando Letelier began working alongside Ronni Karpen and Michael Moffitt at the Institute for Policy Studies (IPS), the Pinochet government began a smear campaign against the Chilean. Newspaper articles accused him of having arranged, during Allende's regime, a plane full of arms to land in Chile only to be "exposed" as a CIA operation and thus fortify the shaky regime.[1] Another supposed shipment of weapons had gone to former Allende bodyguards in exchange for terrorist acts.[2] Other rumors floated that Letelier was preparing to blow up a LAN-Chile plane, that he bossed around Ted Kennedy, that he paid thousands of dollars for a dog, that he owned an expensive house, and that he had starred in a pornographic film.[3] Pinochet imagined Letelier "as the generalissimo of this immense, worldwide army," said friend Saul Landau mockingly.[4]

None of it was true. (One arms shipment *had* occurred: as ambassador, Letelier had sent two rifles to his president, an avid hunter.)[5] But the Pinochet government had long ago stopped dealing in facts. Ideology overran it. Its opponents around the world had to be eliminated.

>> It was in Chile that Cuban exile leader Orlando Bosch first heard of the other Orlando: "Chilean officials told me many times when I lived there that they wanted him dead."[6]

In 1976, Bosch left for the Dominican Republic, at the time under the autocratic rule of Joaquín Balaguer. "The Dominican government let me stay in the country and organize actions," Bosch recalled fondly. "I wasn't going to church every day," he understated. "We were conspiring there. Planning bombings and killings. . . . People were coming in and going out. I was plotting with them. Secretly, of course."

One secret soon to leak was a June 1976 two-day meeting of twenty men representing Cuban exile organizations in the Dominican mountain city of Bonao. Felipe Rivero of the Cuban Nationalist Movement (CNM) was there.⁷ Attendees created an umbrella organization, baptized it the Coordinator of United Revolutionary Organizations (CORU in Spanish), and made Bosch their spokesperson. Bosch advised that they set aside their differences and graduate from bombing embassies and police stations to hijacking airliners. In the eleven months that followed, CORU was responsible for over fifty bombings in Miami, New York, Panama, Mexico, and Argentina.⁸

The CIA allegedly approved of the Bonao meeting—some say it even prompted it—and wanted CORU to "punish" Fidel Castro for his intervention in Angola, where the U.S. spy agency was funding Apartheid South Africa's own intervention on the anticommunist side.⁹

The Bonao attendees also allegedly brought up a particular thorn in the side of the Pinochet regime: Orlando Letelier. Manuel Contreras would later cite the Bonao targeting of Letelier as proof that the Cubans had come to this decision on their own.

》 The truth was that DINA's director ordered Michael Townley to kill Letelier, and it may even have been the Chilean government that instigated the unification of the Cubans at Bonao.¹⁰ As Orlando Bosch recalled, the Cubans "discussed Orlando Letelier at [the Bonao] meeting, and the fact that [Letelier's] campaign [to discredit the junta abroad] was bothering some of our friends in Chile."¹¹

Letelier was a long-standing problem for Contreras. In August 1975, almost a year before Bonao, the Chilean spy chief wrote to a Brazilian general of his concern "for the possible triumph of the Democratic Party in the next U.S. presidential election." Democrats' support for Letelier, he specified, "could, in the future, seriously influence the stability of the 'Southern Cone' of our hemisphere."¹² The message was that the hit must take place before the November 1976 elections.

Michael Townley first got his Letelier instructions, he recalled, in late June or early July 1976, when Armando Fernández, one of the alleged torturers in the 1973 Caravan of Death, called him. Townley sensed that Fernández "was extremely secretive." Without going into specifics, Fernández told Townley that "Pedrito"—Colonel Pedro Espinoza, DINA's chief of operations—sought a meeting.

One early morning, Townley trudged out to near the high school in Santiago that Townley and the Letelier boys had attended and brought a thermos of coffee, which he shared with Espinoza. The DINA man asked if Townley could take another Condor job abroad. Townley hesitated. He had spent "a majority of 1975 outside Chile on DINA missions and I felt I was neglecting my family." Mariana Callejas, who had just given birth to their son on June 6, was about to undergo a hysterectomy—not exactly a sign that the couple's brittle relationship was on the mend. The timing was less than optimal.[13]

Still, Townley agreed to a second meeting with Espinoza, who arrived in civilian clothes, six blocks from the Townleys' Lo Curro home, in a rust-colored Chevy Nova. Fernández tagged along but stayed in the vehicle while Espinoza and Townley talked privately outside of it. Espinoza got to the matter at hand: DINA needed someone for an urgent operation abroad.

"Elimination?"

"Yes. This one is in the United States," Espinoza said. The target: Orlando Letelier. "Do you think you can get those Cubans you worked with before to pull it off for us? I don't have to tell you that this operation is of the highest priority. My orders are from Mamo," he added, using Contreras's nickname.

Townley again complained of the poor timing and warned of the Cubans' lingering anger at the Pinochet regime. "When?" he inquired.

"The time frame will be September," said Espinoza, "as usual." Authors John Dinges and Saul Landau described September as "Chile's springtime, the patriotic month, the month of the birth of the nation in 1810 under the sword of Bernardo O'Higgins, Chile's George Washington; the month of Pinochet's 1973 coup, of the 1974 assassination of General Carlos Prats, of the 1975 shooting of Bernardo Leighton."

"I will carry out the mission if given a specific order," Townley vowed.[14]

The talk turned to methods. They could use a Chilean woman to lure Orlando to a local hotel and poison him. A second scenario was a mugging gone awry—something few would see as out of the ordinary in a big American city.[15] Other possibilities, said Espinoza, included "an automobile accident, a suicide, something like that."

"You should make his death seem accidental," ordered Espinoza, and then added two fateful words: "if possible."[16]

That was the opening Townley used to bring up his expertise—explosives. Waiting for him in New Jersey was a Fanon-Courier pager that could remote detonate a bomb. In addition, an explosion would avoid direct contact with Letelier. It was also a sure killer. Townley apparently never contemplated that a bomb, unlike other methods, would guarantee a major international investigation. When he suggested a car bomb, Espinoza foolishly agreed, perhaps overlooking that, if you entrust a killing to a bomb maker, he will kill by making a bomb. "Bottom line," said Espinoza. "Letelier must be eliminated." This was DINA's first error.

Espinoza added "that Letelier should be alone when the assassination took place," as Townley himself phrased it. But Townley would also fail on this count—error number two.

According to Townley, Espinoza also instructed that he and Fernández "were to commit the actual assassination and that Cuban exiles were to be used as backup assistance or in whatever manner it was deemed necessary." Fernández should have no contact with the Cubans. Later, however, Espinoza changed his mind and told Townley that the *Cubans* were to kill Letelier; Townley's only job was to hire them.[17] In the end, Townley would have the Cubans involved from day one and even get them to detonate the bomb. This third error would prove key to investigators.

The conversation over, Townley climbed back into his own vehicle. Despite all the problems he foresaw and failed to foresee, he was exhilarated to be trusted with a major DINA priority.

Callejas, not so much. When Townley walked in and told her to repack his suitcase, she was crestfallen.[18] "I don't like it," she told him. "I could have been determined and stubborn (I usually am) and threatened him with abandonment or indifference," she later wrote. "But I didn't do it, although I knew by the fugitive look of his blue eyes, by his evasive answers, that this one was a mission that he did not quite fully understand, an order that he would have questioned, had he ever questioned orders."[19]

>> One of Townley's orders was to travel to Paraguay with Armando Fernández and there obtain Paraguayan passports under false names and then apply for entry visas for the United States. Already for two decades the fiefdom of dictator Alfredo Stroessner, Paraguay was a reliable partner in Operation Condor, and it would happily mask the identity of Pinochet's men, no questions asked. In July, the two men adopted the respective aliases of "Juan Williams Rose" and "Alejandro Romeral Jara" and traveled from Santiago to Asunción.

The mission was so urgent and crucial to Santiago that, while Townley and Fernández were in Paraguay, Pinochet himself called Stroessner to urge that the paperwork be sped up as an "urgent favor."[20] He lied that the pair were Chilean Army officers going to New York to investigate irregularities in the Chilean copper state agency, CODELCO.

Getting fake Paraguayan documents was easy. The "Williams" and "Romeral" passports were two among the 35 percent of passports granted to Chileans between 1975 and 1977 that proved forgeries.[21]

Trickier was to get U.S. visas. Trying to cut through red tape, Stroessner's chief of protocol and "fixer," Conrado Pappalardo, called U.S. Ambassador to Paraguay George Landau for the favor.

Born in Vienna, Landau had become a U.S. citizen as a soldier during World War II and thereafter grew intensely patriotic. He had made colonel in U.S. Army intelligence, and then worked in Colombia as the general manager of an automobile plant. In 1957, he entered the Foreign Service, with Montevideo, Uruguay, as his first posting. He also served in Franco's Spain, where he defended the dictator. By the mid-1970s, however, he described himself as "personally highly committed to the cause of human rights."[22] As an ambassador, he retained a hint of an Austrian accent and carried himself with an aristocratic panache. He was formal, tough, and thorough, not your typical backslapping U.S. diplomat.

The Paraguayan, Pappalardo, told Ambassador Landau that the two Chileans who needed visas were going to Washington to meet Vernon Walters, the CIA's deputy director. Landau questioned what he considered "a violation of regulations."[23] Pappalardo said he was just asking as a courtesy and that the Chileans would go to the United States no matter what. Besides, Paraguay had just done the CIA a huge favor by releasing one of its agents, accused of plotting to overthrow Stroessner.[24] Landau caved and instructed that the visas be issued.

I smell a rat, Landau thought after hanging up. He cabled Walters in Washington, asking whether Williams and Romeral really had an appointment at CIA headquarters. The response came back on August 4: not only did Walters have no appointment, but he had also retired from the CIA in early July. CIA director and future president George H. W. Bush wanted nothing more to do with DINA, but he failed to inform the embassy of his agency's previously cozy relationship with Contreras.[25] Landau then checked with colleagues at the State Department. Void those visas, they urged.[26] It took Landau six weeks and ten phone calls to Pappalardo to get the visas canceled.[27] Townley and Fernández, it turned out, grew alarmed by Landau's hesitations and never used the visas.

Yet they had left a paper trail—visa applications, visas, and fake passports. When the Paraguayans returned the applications, they first tore out the photographs of Townley and Fernández that went with them.

Out of an abundance of caution, however, Landau had previously made copies of the photos and filed them away, thinking nothing more of it. Those copies would prove a critical clue in the future.

▶▶ The visa gambit had failed, but Fernández still landed in the United States on August 26 to surveil Orlando Letelier. The countdown to September 21 began.

With Fernández was a woman who pretended to be his wife, served as his cover, and might be able to seduce Letelier. DINA had introduced him to "Liliana Walker" ten days earlier, in Santiago. "Walker" was tall, thin, white, blonde, and blue eyed, with fine features on a round face. To many she presented a cold, distant demeanor.

Luisa Mónica Lagos Aguirre described herself as having a "fickle character, which switches often from joy to sadness, impulsive, somewhat frivolous, very affected by my Zodiac sign, easily impassioned. In terms of lifestyle, I enjoy life's luxuries, those well above my means, regardless of what I must do to acquire what I so ardently desire." She made a point of giving her measurements: 36–23–35.[28]

Lagos was from Santiago, where her father owned a small shoe repair shop. She majored in business but spoke no foreign language. In 1973, at age twenty, she sold black market goods, smoked weed with friends — almost all Allende supporters — but stayed out of politics. After the Pinochet coup, money grew scarce for Lagos, and the easy life she was used to vanished.

She joined a group of models and appeared in newspapers and magazines. She also led a four-girl dance group that performed on television and in hotel ballrooms, backing a band called Onda Brava featuring singer Charly Walker, whom she described as similar to Michael Jackson. He became Lagos's boyfriend. She would later adopt his surname as her nom de guerre.[29]

At a party, she met a military officer who offered her a job as an *acompañante* or escort. She accepted but soon grew to hate her superior's "ultraviolent personality." Still, she enjoyed the $3,500 pesos she earned from just accompanying important men to official functions. Sometimes she would collect information for additional "tips." Some clients showered her with gifts.

By late 1975 to early 1976, describing herself as young and naive, Mónica Lagos met Patricio or "Pato" Walker, "the only man I ever loved." Walker was a musician and, it was rumored, a former guerrilla for Chile's Revolutionary Left Movement. For over a year, Lagos and Walker cohabitated. He hated DINA, and it returned the favor by detaining him, but Lagos convinced DINA operatives that her lover had left behind his political life and was not worth "disappearing." Until the Letelier assassination, Pato remained ignorant of Mónica's work for DINA. Still, Lagos's family forever blamed him for all her troubles.

During a conference of the Organization of American States in Santiago, attended by Henry Kissinger among others, Lagos first began to work as a prostitute. She yearned to maintain her lavish lifestyle, had to support some family members, and feared losing Walker, who, despite coming from an aristocratic family of ministers and ambassadors, earned nothing as a musician. She joined Santiago's biggest bordello, owned and operated by the military, namely, "that degenerate faggot [Pedro] Espinoza," as she called the man who ordered Townley to Washington. She was one of two or three sex workers who doubled as DINA agents, plying their trade out of military-owned apartments. At the Organization of American States conference, her mission was to befriend delegates and extract from them information on Chile. She also recruited other "agent-girls," including her sister Diana. One of their goals was "to link *señor* Kissinger to a scandal." Kissinger got wind of his invitation to a prostitution party and made sure to avoid it.

Lagos did get close to Espinoza, "attracting him," she explained enigmatically, "by generating female obligations on my part toward him." He repaid her with "economic benefits," personal security, and "great respect." Nevertheless, she found Espinoza "very strange. I think that his being the son of a sub-officer diminished him into permanent delusions of grandeur and exhibitionism." Espinoza suffered from "a tremendous instability" due to his wife's emotional withdrawal from their marriage.

The many clients Lagos met as a sex worker only sharpened Espinoza's sense of "inferiority and insecurity." On the surface, he accepted her profession, yet around his friends he longed to show her off and have her, a much younger woman, idolize him.

In late July to early August 1976, Espinoza informed Lagos that her next mission would net her more money than ever and elevate her status within DINA. Details came in drips. On August 24, she learned that she would be going to the United States. She would interact only with Chileans and Cubans and so would not need English. In early September, she was told she would accompany a male agent under a fake passport. Her mission resulted from "her proven ability to attract philanderers." She was to command Orlando Letelier's attention and learn his habits.

Soon after, Espinoza introduced Lagos to Armando Fernández, informing both that they were to act as a couple. An act is all it would be, he reminded Fernández coldly. "I warn you that I will be informed of everything you do. If you lay a finger on her, I'll kill you."[30]

Still, a role-play with "Liliana Walker" intrigued Fernández, and on the flight from Chile he hoped she would have sex with him since they were to share hotel rooms in Washington.³¹ Lagos, meanwhile, noted that Fernández had an unusually chummy relationship with the LAN-Chile airline crew. He was also a heavy drinker. "He struck me as very infantile, with an exaggerated sense of loyalty and obedience to General Contreras."

Once they landed, Lagos apparently met Letelier, either in New York or Washington. "He was objectively attractive, manly, and gave the impression of a great gentleman. We spoke little, however, apart from a few elegant flirtations. After excusing himself, he left, apparently to attend to his work and because of his preoccupations with a Venezuelan woman." She learned nothing other than the make and model of his car.³²

Fernández and Lagos did little work in the Washington area, largely because Letelier was traveling. Fernández was born there in 1949, while his father was Chile's air force attaché. He visited his sister and her U.S. husband in Centerville, Virginia.³³

Later, "Fernández tried to seduce me," recalled Mónica Lagos, "but as part of a long-term strategy. He told me he could not understand a man like Espinoza, who sent a woman he loved to take part in a crime. It was then I learned that the mission was to assassinate Orlando Letelier." She tried in vain to learn more. Fernández shut her out of the mission completely in an effort to protect her. It was then she appreciated him as "a perfect military man, who above all obeyed orders."³⁴

Michael Townley, told by Espinoza on September 7 to join up with the "couple," deplaned at Kennedy International Airport in New York two days later with a Chilean passport bearing yet another alias, Hans Petersen. He carried in one pocket bomb parts that he slipped through U.S. customs. In the other pocket was a bottle of an organophosphorus compound with which the Nazis had experimented and that he made from a microwave oven and gas cylinder in his home laboratory. Its scientific name was isopropylmethylphosophonofluoridate; its common name: sarin gas. Even though the colorless, odorless liquid nerve agent was among the most dangerous on Earth, Townley casually considered it as a method of killing Letelier and carried it onto a LAN-Chile aircraft in a Chanel No. 5 perfume bottle. Had it spilled in flight, the muscles of everyone on board — including the pilots — would have been paralyzed and they would have died in minutes.³⁵ Today, sarin is generally considered a weapon of mass destruction. Its production and stockpiling are outlawed.

Still at the airport, Townley met with Fernández. "Liliana Walker" was there, but Fernández did not introduce her. Townley found her "extremely well-dressed and well-groomed and ... carrying a fashion magazine. My initial impression was favorable since she seemed to be a world apart from her and Captain Fernandez's mission."[36] Fernández limited himself to imparting to Townley the little surveillance intelligence he had gathered. Townley rented an Avis car and drove to the New Jersey apartment of Virgilio Paz, his closest associate among the Cubans.

"What's up?" asked Paz.

"Orders," Townley answered. "I need you to arrange a meeting for me with Guillermo as soon as possible. This is something heavy."

"No problem. But you are not the most popular man around here with the Cubans, you know. This may not be the right time."

"I know," said Townley.

"Is it in Europe?" asked Paz.

"No," says Townley. "Here. In Washington."

Paz barely raised an eyebrow. "Who?"

"One of Allende's cabinet ministers," said Townley. "A guy named Letelier."[37]

On September 10, at the Bottom of the Barrel restaurant in Union City, Townley met with Guillermo Novo — a "very sharp dresser," as he recalled — and José Suárez.[38] Townley made his pitch: Letelier, a Marxist, was forming a government in exile, or so DINA suspected. He must be killed, and quickly. The Cubans were at first reluctant, but they seemed agreeable as long as Townley himself took part.

>> Driving through Manhattan that same day, the eve of the third anniversary of the Chilean coup, Townley glanced at a poster and stepped on the brakes. The poster announced a benefit concert in the city that very night in support of Chilean human rights organizations where Joan Baez, Pete Seeger, and a Chilean band were to perform. Incredibly, Letelier was to speak at the event. Michael got out of his car, stared at the poster, and then tore it down. He thought about attending but then decided against it, fearing that a Chilean in the audience might recognize him.[39]

Isabel Letelier accompanied her husband to Manhattan, where he was also to meet with a potential publisher. Before the concert, at the door of the Algonquin Hotel where the Leteliers were staying, reporters met them and asked Orlando if he had heard the news.

"No, what?" he said.

The Pinochet government had just stripped him of his Chilean citizenship in retaliation for, as its decree stated, "carrying out in foreign lands a publicity campaign aimed at bringing about the political, economic and cultural isolation of Chile." By this the junta meant Letelier's defeat of the planned Dutch investment in Chile. His "ignoble and disloyal attitude," the decree continued, "made him deserving of the maximum ... moral sanction contemplated by our juridical order ... the loss of Chilean nationality."[40] When Isabel read the document, signed by the entire Chilean cabinet, she became sick.[41]

"Orlando almost died," she recalled. "The decree was a tremendous blow. If they had aimed to hurt him, they succeeded!"[42]

His despair turning to anger, Letelier sat down at a desk at the Algonquin and rewrote his speech for that evening.

Seventy-five hundred sympathizers of Chile showed up at the Felt Forum at Madison Square Garden that night. With Isabel looking on in a resplendent white lace dress, Letelier's job was to introduce Baez. In so doing, he invoked those killed by the Chilean government and celebrated the growing solidarity movement and isolation of Pinochet. "We will never rest until we achieve the overthrow of the fascist regime in Chile," he vowed.[43]

In the middle of his address, he paused. Then, incensed, he slowly announced, "Today Pinochet has signed a decree in which it is said that I am deprived of my nationality. . . . But this action makes me feel more Chilean than ever!"

His voice rose as he went on: "I was born a Chilean, I am a Chilean, and I will die a Chilean. They, the fascists, were born traitors, live as traitors, and will be remembered forever as fascist traitors!"[44] The audience roared its approval.[45]

After the concert, Letelier sent a letter to the *New York Times* contextualizing the Santiago decree as only one of that government's many human rights violations. "Behind it one sees the logic of a totalitarian mentality, that it projects itself from within a system based on terror and vengeance."

"When democracy is re-established along with the human rights that have been usurped by the dictators," he promised, "no one will be in any doubt about the nationality of the Chileans who are in power today."[46]

>> Orlando and, perhaps more so, Isabel were not unaware of the increasingly threatening atmosphere surrounding him. Over their entire stay in Washington, they received anonymous threats, usually by phone and in Spanish. An assistant at IPS, Lillian Montecina, said Letelier told her "of receiving threats against his life about twice a month." "It usually came at odd hours (at his office) or at home," she added.[47]

In January 1975, having just settled in Washington, Isabel received a phone call: "Are you the wife of Orlando Letelier?" the Spanish voice asked.

"Yes."

"Ha, ha! No, you are his widow!" it said and hung up.[48]

In April 1976, someone spat at Orlando over the phone, "We're going to get you!"[49]

"You are going to pay because of all these things that you are doing against the Chilean government," aides from the Chilean mission told him to his face while at the United Nations lounge. "You traitor! You motherfucking traitor!" one screamed at him.[50]

Another time, two Chilean friends warned Letelier that they saw someone following him.[51] One houseguest discovered a man in the Letelier house rifling through his papers. At IPS, the Chilean once walked to his car only to find the door wide open.[52] One or two days before his murder, his car keys disappeared and he found his headlights blinking. "We had this strange feeling that something wrong was happening," recalled a friend who helped him look for his keys. "We were very paranoid." But Letelier refused to call the police.[53]

Isabel often received letters addressed to her husband that arrived crumpled or not in their original envelopes. She suspected CIA or FBI mail interference and never reported it.[54] One letter, written in blood-red ink, described exactly how the senders were to kill the couple and their children.[55] "Unless you get out of politics, we are going to kill you," said another letter.[56]

Letelier often feared assassination, for instance, after the Rome attempt on the Leightons. He said he repeatedly requested FBI protection but was turned down; the FBI's Washington, D.C., field office denied this.[57]

Standing with him at Chile Chico, his uncle once asked Orlando, "Would not this be a good time to give yourself entirely to your wife and children, to look after the peace of mind of your parents and all the other relatives who suffered so much?"

Letelier looked at him, put his hand on his shoulder, and said, "All those are matters of great concern to me; it keeps me awake nights. But I have a higher cause to serve: that of thousands of men, women, and children who have suffered and will continue to suffer the misery, degradation, and cruelty which characterizes the tyranny which now controls Chile. I am the first political prisoner who has been freed. I enjoy the privilege of having been rescued by the miracle which other men who love and respect freedom made possible."

"And your life, your security?"

"My life," said Letelier, "is a price which I will gladly pay."[58]

Isabel was equally bothered by her husband's dismissals. "If I'm going to be afraid of anything, I won't do a thing," he told her.[59] Besides, he told his aunt, "If they are threatening me, I must be doing something very well."[60]

Eventually, the couple resolved never again to discuss the harassment. They would tear up the letters, hang up the phones.[61] On September 20, 1976, Michael Moffitt offered to act as Letelier's bodyguard, but the Chilean refused. Letelier took no precautions, fearing they would paralyze his work. The Leteliers were also just making ends meet and could not afford a bodyguard.[62]

Deep down, Letelier believed he could not be killed in the U.S. capital. "While I'm here in Washington," he told a friend, "I'm safe. Nobody is so demented as to kill me here."[63]

》 He was not, and with Townley in the United States, even less so.

On September 12, Townley as "Hans Petersen" booked a room at the Château Renaissance motel in North Bergen, New Jersey. Joining him were seven CNM members. After serving his guests whiskey and rum, Townley outlined DINA's deal: if the Cubans helped assassinate Letelier, DINA would continue to help Cuban fugitives seeking shelter and allow them to use a DINA farm in southern Chile for training purposes. The CNM's stature among Cuban exiles would continue to climb due to their partnership with Pinochet.[64]

Shortly after the Château Renaissance meeting, Guillermo Novo met with Townley in Paz's car:

"Okay, we'll do it. But we have a condition."

"What's that?" asked Townley.

"You have to participate," said Novo. "You have to go down to Washington yourself. We want a signal that this will be a more equal partnership."

"That is contrary to my orders," Townley said.

"I thought your orders were to get the job done."

"They are," said Townley. "But I'm not supposed to go to Washington."

"That's what we don't like," Novo said with a smile. "So you better try to get your orders changed. Because if you leave now, it's not going down. It's that simple."

Townley sighed. "Okay, if that's the way it is," he said, "I think it will be all right." But Townley had his own condition. "If I have to go down there, it's got to be a bomb."

"Why is that?" said Paz.

"Because that way I can help you follow him and help you build the device," said Townley, "but I can still follow my orders not to be there when you set it off."[65]

The Cubans did not ask for money, nor was it offered.

On the fifteenth, in Union City, Guillermo and Suárez handed Townley and Paz a plastic bag. In it were a detonating cord, a small piece of C-4 putty, and TNT. Paz had already handed over the Fanon-Courier detonating pager that Michael had built months earlier.[66] The Cubans dubbed it *El Pianito* (the little piano) because of its keys.[67]

On September 16, Paz and Townley drove from New Jersey to the District of Columbia and checked into a Holiday Inn in northeast Washington. Using a LAN-Chile pilot friend, Townley had gotten Callejas to send him a new set of false papers as "Kenneth Enyart."

The next day, Paz and Townley began to tail Letelier. They waited at a Roy Rogers restaurant on River Road, blocks from the Leteliers' home on Ogden Court and on his way to work. They got lucky. Letelier's Chevelle cruised by, and they followed.

Safe in the knowledge that they had nailed down his morning schedule, they went shopping. In a few hours, they had a list of innocent-seeming items: eight-inch square aluminum baking pans, cookie sheets, black electric tape, and rubber gloves.[68]

On September 18, Novo, Suárez, and Alvin Ross joined Paz and Townley, who had bought the final items on their list from Radio Shack: wire cutters, needle-nose pliers, a soldering iron, slide switches, and a level switch. Suárez added a blasting cap. Townley later recalled that it was only that day when the coconspirators finally settled on a bomb versus another means of assassination.[69] Still that day, Paz, Suárez, and Townley built the bomb in Townley's Regency Congress hotel room. The job consisted largely of fitting the C-4 putty or "plastique" into the baking pan between chunks of TNT.

September 18 also happened to be Chilean Independence Day. Letelier had just returned from New York, and Isabel threw a party at their house. For the fifty or so Chilean exiles in attendance, the fiesta was a slice of home—jugs of red wine, empanadas, and a dance-and-guitar-and-song *cueca* performance by Isabel and Orlando. The pleasure of the festivities contrasted with the pain of recalling dead and disappeared friends and compatriots, and specifically with the throbbing in Letelier's left middle finger, a reminder of Dawson Island.[70]

A few hours after the party, shortly after midnight on September 19,

Townley and the two Cubans set off to install the bomb. "During the ride to Letelier's house," Townley recalled, "I was informed by Paz and Suárez that they expected me to place the device on the car as they wished to have a DINA agent, namely myself, directly tied to the placing of the device."[71] "Our movement wants the hand of Chile very close to the act," Paz explained. "You put it on. We will set it off. That seems like a fair partnership to us."[72] Townley was less than thrilled at having to disobey yet another of Espinoza's orders, but what could he do?

Townley found the Leteliers' car parked in their driveway, nose in. He hid the baking pan under his shirt, scurried to the car, and lay down under the driver's side.

"I had a very hard time fixing the device," Townley recalled.[73] Almost as soon as he began to tape the pan to the A-frame, he heard footsteps. He froze, tried not to breathe. The footsteps faded. Then he almost ran out of tape, trying to secure the pan. Then a car approached, its radio on. Again Townley froze, and then began to panic as he realized the car was a police cruiser. From the corner of his eye, he saw its tires. Sweating profusely, he held his breath and considered running.[74]

The cruiser turned the corner and sped away. Townley exhaled. He made sure again that the slide switch on the bomb was on, secured it with still more tape, and left.[75] Located right below the driver's seat, the explosives would concentrate their blast directly toward the legs.

Townley rejoined the Cubans and reminded them to detonate the explosives whenever Letelier was alone. He also advised they detonate the bomb in a park, where no bystanders would be injured or killed. They either did not listen or did not care.[76]

Townley then called his wife, who had stayed in Santiago. He told her, using code, to inform DINA that the bomb was now in place.

Townley then began to build his alibi. He drove north to Westchester County, New York, and spent the afternoon with his sister and her family, eating a chicken dinner. Then he drove to the airport and slipped the I-94 immigration form of "Hans Petersen" into a stack from passengers checking in for an Iberia flight to Spain. According to records, therefore, the man who flew from Chile ten days earlier had left before the bomb was to go off.[77]

Then Townley flew to Miami and visited his parents in Boca Raton.

On September 20, the Cubans were to set off the bomb, but the device malfunctioned. The CNM had to remove it, correct the malfunction, and affix it anew to Letelier's car. Had it worked the first time, the Moffitts would not have been on board.[78]

>> On the evening of September 20, the Moffitts happened to join the Leteliers for dinner at their home. The two couples drank red wine. Isabel complimented Ronni on her new hairdo. Ronni was excited about a new promotion at IPS. Orlando later commented on how much the young Moffitts were in love with each other—and also with Chile.[79]

The only sour note was when Letelier brought up the recent decree. "I've heard that in Santiago there was a long discussion: Some wanted to kill me and others wanted to take away my citizenship," he said. Seeing the Moffitts' shock, he sought to assuage them. "This September, it is not my turn, I will not be the victim. Since my punishment is to take my citizenship, I have won another year of life!"[80]

The following morning, as Letelier and the Moffitts drove toward IPS, no one noticed the gray sedan pulling out of the Roy Rogers parking lot and following them toward Sheridan Circle.

Virgilio Paz had his finger on the two buttons of *El Pianito* plugged into the cigarette lighter.[81]

>> Mónica Lagos had already returned to her life with Pato Walker and, after September 21, confessed to him she had been part of the assassination squad. "I hurt him deeply, especially by linking the name Walker to the assassination of Letelier, who to him was a leftist but a moderate." She forever recalled Espinoza, who sent her on this mission, as "one of the most cowardly, bitter, and degenerate people I have ever known."[82]

On September 21, after the bombing, Townley called Ignacio Novo in Florida. Novo told him that "something has happened in the District of Columbia." The two met and Townley briefed him on the mission. His conscience stirred somewhat upon hearing that Ronni Moffitt was in the car and died.[83]

None of the Cubans shared his remorse. Neither did Callejas. "I can't tell a lie, it hardly made any difference to me. People are assassinated every single day, and Letelier to me was just somebody else assassinated."[84]

On September 23, Townley flew back to Chile. The next day, he informed Pedro Espinoza that the mission had been a success. His superior "conveyed his satisfaction by smiling."[85]

PART TWO

Investigation

»

8

CHILBOM

Immediate reactions to the bombing in Sheridan Circle were inauspicious for those who would investigate it. To be sure, the Letelier-Moffitt assassination made the front page of all major newspapers, and Letelier's U.S. friends sounded the alarm. Senator Ted Kennedy called the act "political terrorism." Senator James Abourezk interpreted it as "the tyranny" of Pinochet extending to the United States. And Senator Hubert Humphrey, Democrat of Minnesota, introduced a Senate resolution calling for "thorough investigation of the circumstances surrounding the bombing."[1]

However, early guesses from mainstream U.S. observers tended toward absolving the Chilean regime. The editors of the *New York Times* concluded that "it is hard to believe that even as ham-handed a regime as Chile's junta would order the murder of so eminent an opponent as Mr. Letelier in the capital of the United States."[2] The *Washington Post* suggested that Chile's Revolutionary Left Movement might be guilty.[3]

Many in the U.S. government also doubted Santiago's guilt. A week after the assassination, the Defense Intelligence Agency assessed that "the reach of DINA—cited as responsible—almost certainly (80 percent) does not extend to the United States."[4] In the House, John Ashbrook, Republican of Ohio, blocked a resolution by Connecticut Democrat Toby Moffett to condemn unanimously Letelier's murder.[5] Jack Devine, a former U.S. spy in Chile, recalled the situation as one "where conventional wisdom and rationality sometimes gets in the way of intelligence." It was "almost incomprehensible" to nearly everyone in the intelligence community that Pinochet would do something so "outlandish." The National Security Council, writing the day of the assassination, admitted that "right wing Chileans are the obvious candidates. But they seem to be *too* obvious."[6]

Most ominously, in early October *Newsweek* ran a short item claiming that the CIA had studied FBI files and had "concluded that the Chilean secret police were not involved in the death of Orlando Letelier. . . . The agency reached its decision because the bomb was too crude to be the work of experts and because the murder, coming while Chile's rulers were wooing U.S. support, could only damage the Santiago regime."[7] The Institute for Policy Studies found out that the *Newsweek* reporter who filed the story "did not talk to anyone at CIA or anyone from FBI." He admitted the story could have come from Chile. Added the Washington bureau chief, "The point is that the item came from places that can't be identified."[8] On October 12, some intelligence officials continued telling the press that the FBI and CIA "had virtually ruled out the idea that Mr. Letelier was killed by agents of the Chilean military junta."[9]

》》 At the Justice Department Earl Silbert, U.S. attorney for the District of Columbia, ventured the opinion that "the assassination was an obvious terrorist act that would be practically impossible to solve."[10] Even in a nonprofessional bombing, the chances of an arrest were less than one in ten. And supposing that the case were solved, the FBI, under the jurisdiction of the Department of Justice, might not want to prosecute for fear of exposing informants.

The man in charge of proving them wrong was Eugene Propper, the assistant U.S. attorney who would lead the investigation. Propper was born in the Bronx, a few months before his father died in the subway on his way to work in Manhattan's garment district. After the tragedy, his mother had no choice but to go to work in the family's belt business. Young Gene, now in Long Island, attended the private Yeshiva Central, half of whose instruction was in Hebrew. When he was twelve, his mother married a scoutmaster, and Gene found himself with a stepbrother of the same age who made straight A's easily while Propper struggled. Yet he was determined and tough — a fighter, sometimes literally at school, taking on bigger boys.

After college in Amherst, Massachusetts, in 1969 he enrolled in the University of Minnesota law school. With the Vietnam War raging, Propper took a preinduction physical. After he unluckily passed, he took on his first "case" — his own, when he claimed to suffer from a severe knee injury from skiing. It worked — he got his results annulled and kept his files in a folder he labeled "The Kid vs. U.S. Army."

When Propper was just twenty-one, a physician informed him that a rare blood disease would kill him in "four to six months." Propper rejected the fatal diagnosis. He went from doctor to doctor until one told him he merely harbored a nonlethal virus. "Well, that's what I have," decided Propper. He was right.

In September 1976, Propper was twenty-nine, tall, slender, and bearded, but more neatly than most men of his generation. He rode motorcycles. At the Justice Department he had been a prosecutor for five years, working more than fifty felonies and winning guilty verdicts in all but one. In those years, he had earned a reputation as relentless and intelligent, irreverent and sarcastic. He had also just moved to the Major Crimes Division. He was not especially political, marrying mainstream liberal views on race and civil liberties tinged with soft anticommunism. At the U.S. Attorney's Office, Propper had paid his dues and was planning a transition to private practice, where the money was better.[11]

Right after September 21, he sat in the cafeteria of the federal courthouse in Washington. "I remember sitting at lunch with a very good friend of mine, who was also an assistant U.S. attorney, saying, 'I wonder who's going to get that case,'" Propper said in 2016, referring to the Letelier assassination. "'That's not going to be any fun.' And when the U.S. attorney spoke to me about it, he said, 'Look, we've never had a case like this. We may never solve it no matter what you do. Give it your best shot.'"[12] Propper had a hunch. He knew nothing of Chile, spoke no Spanish, and had never prosecuted a political case, but this might be a fascinating coda before jumping ship into the private sector. *I'm gonna solve this sucker*, he vowed to himself.[13]

Helping Propper was Lawrence Barcella, another lawyer and deputy head of Major Crimes at the Justice Department. Born and raised in Washington, D.C., Barcella had attended Dartmouth and then Vanderbilt Law School. Like Propper, he had mostly handled local felonies such as drug cases. (Washington is the only jurisdiction in the country where the U.S. attorney is responsible for prosecuting local crimes.) He had jumped into a major sting operation in which FBI agents posed as criminals, leading to the bureau's "Abscam" case of pretending to bribe members of Congress.[14] His hair glistening, Barcella was known in the office as a charming romantic.

At the FBI's New York Division worked special agent Lawrence Wack. He had grown up in Willingboro, New Jersey, where his father labored at a war matériel plant. At age twelve Larry met an FBI clerk who dated his sister, and he became obsessed with the bureau. He wrote Director J. Edgar Hoover for a fingerprinting kit, which he received along with instructions on becoming an agent. Right after graduating high school in 1967, at just sixteen, Wack snagged a clerk's job at FBI headquarters in Washington while taking nighttime criminology courses at American University.

Wack walked with a swagger after he graduated from the FBI academy, talking out of the side of his mouth, flashing his holstered pistol, and drinking with informants. That attitude—and a mustache—compensated for his blue eyes, blond hair, and smooth, boyish features. When assigned the Letelier-Moffitt case, he had been working in the New York office's Bomb and Terrorism Squad for only half a year.[15]

Another key investigator in the United States was Carter Cornick, from the Terrorist Section of the FBI's Bomb Unit. A conservative thirty-eight-year-old ex-marine and graduate of the University of Virginia, Cornick was clean-cut, clean-shaven, genteel, and proud to have learned the ropes under Hoover. He joked that his family had stopped reading newspapers after they ran photos of "pinkos" such as Eleanor Roosevelt back in the 1930s.[16] Isabel Letelier would remember him fondly as a dedicated agent but "super conservative."[17] In 1976, Cornick had just landed in the Washington field office from Puerto Rico, and he spoke Spanish. FBI agents from Florida and the New Jersey/New York area also worked the Letelier case.

In South America, the FBI had Robert Scherrer, posing as the legal attaché at the Buenos Aires U.S. embassy. Like Propper, Scherrer was a tenacious New Yorker. Born and bred in Brooklyn, he grew up in a lower-middle-class family, inheriting the strictness of his German father and the red hair and short stature from his mother's Irish side. He was a bosun's mate in the U.S. Navy. The FBI recruited him at eighteen and sent him to Fordham University for a law degree.[18]

Cornick judged Scherrer to be "too damn bright to be an FBI agent." He had become obsessed with Latin America, learning perfect Spanish. He gained the access to repressive regimes that most human rights activists—not to mention the CIA—only dreamed of. From his perch in Buenos Aires, he surveyed his territory from Argentina to Paraguay, Uruguay, Bolivia, and Chile. In most Operation Condor countries, therefore, he liaised with police and intelligence. He tried to locate "disappeareds" in Argentina on behalf of relatives. By 1976, he had been in the area for six years, and he knew Manuel Contreras personally.[19] "He was used to being with monsters," recalled Isabel.[20]

Scherrer became indispensable to the investigation. None of the others knew much about Latin America, international investigations, or diplomacy. Propper even had to learn that "legat"—Scherrer's job title—was a common contraction of "legal attaché."[21] One week after the assassination, Scherrer explained the details of Operation Condor and hinted that Letelier may have been a target of Condor's new focus on extrahemispheric assassinations.[22]

Because of the international implications of the case, Propper and his team quickly took it over from the District of Columbia police, claiming authority deriving from the U.S. Code, which defines former ambassadors and foreign ministers as "internationally protected person[s]." The FBI also designated the Letelier-Moffitt investigation as a "Bureau Special," meaning that all information relating to the case received top priority handling. In all, seventy-five to one hundred agents worked on solving the murders.[23] It easily became the highest-profile case in the country.

Their administrative code word for the case: CHILBOM, fusing "Chile" and "bomb."

Interactions with George H. W. Bush's CIA dismayed Justice Department officials. Bush, the CIA's director at the time, balked at helping because, one, his agency was banned from collecting information in the United States, and, two, asking questions of South American intelligence agencies might burn bridges. The CIA also seemed to want to bury its collaboration with the Chilean Right. When Propper approached the agency, some warned him, "What the hell are you doing? You can't be pulling that shit up again."[24] Bush also failed to inform Propper that he and Deputy Director Vernon Walters, a few weeks prior to the bombing, had learned about Chile's efforts to sneak "Juan Williams" and "Alejandro Romeral" into the country.[25] Two days after the assassination, the CIA even wrote a memo to Bush speculating that "if [the] Chilean Gov[ernmen]t did order Letelier's killing, it may have hired Cuban thugs to do it."[26]

>> In the early afternoon of October 6, two weeks after the Sheridan Circle bombing, Cubana Airlines Flight 455 lifted off from Seawell Airport, Barbados, on its way to Jamaica. Two men had placed time bombs on the plane during a previous flight and then had flown off to Trinidad and Tobago. "The truck has left with a full load," one of them reported to Orlando Bosch, who had just been arrested in Venezuela on a separate charge.[27]

Eleven minutes after takeoff, a first bomb burst, rocking one of the rear lavatories of the DC-8 and destroying the control cables. A second bomb blew a hole through the aircraft and sparked a fire.[28] "We have an explosion aboard—we are descending immediately!" the pilot radioed the control tower. "We have fire on board! We are requesting immediate landing! We have a total emergency!" The pilot, looking out the window of his spiraling craft, saw the beach on one side and the sea on the other. To save the tourists on the beach, he chose to plunge into the Caribbean. Seventy-three people died. Among them were fifty-seven Cubans, including all twenty-four members of the national fencing team. There were no survivors.[29]

The bombers, two Venezuelans, got in a cab, and the driver overheard them talking and laughing about the explosion.[30] Within hours, Trinidad and Tobago arrested them. One was connected to Cuban exile Luis Posada Carriles. The other had again called Bosch to report that "a bus with 73 dogs went off a cliff and all got killed."[31]

The Cubana Airlines bombing, horrific though it was, produced the first useful clue for Propper and his CHILBOM team. Their examination of the wreckage of the Chevelle and the autopsies of Letelier and Moffitt had yielded little of value. The FBI was also conducting thousands of interviews and eliminating hundreds of false leads, laying to rest theories about killers with a personal motive — say, a jilted lover — or about the extreme left's targeting of the moderate socialist Letelier.[32]

The priority now shifted to interview Bosch in his Venezuelan prison, but neither Propper's team nor major U.S. journalists could get access.[33] As freelance journalist Blake Fleetwood recounted, however, one morning at 8 A.M., he simply lined up at the prison gates with family members visiting prisoners, handed over his passport, and walked in. Once inside, to his surprise, he found himself free to roam about. Guards had even searched his briefcase, presumably saw the tape recorder in it, and handed it back to him. Fleetwood asked a prisoner where he could find Bosch. "You're in the wrong place altogether," the man answered. "I'll take you to him."[34]

"How did you get in here?" Bosch wondered in amazement when Fleetwood found him in a sunlit courtyard. Fleetwood told him, and the terrorist ushered him into his cell, which he shared with Posada and which he had outfitted with a television and "fresh 'designer' sheets."

"Would you like a cigar?" said Posada. "America may have an embargo against Cuban cigars, but we don't."[35]

The two Cubans confessed to the airliner bombing among many others, and added that the CIA had helped lock them up in Caracas. Most important, Bosch divulged that Guillermo and Ignacio Novo carried out the Letelier-Moffitt bombing on behalf of Chile's DINA.[36]

Fleetwood knew he had a major scoop. He called Propper, who could not believe his ears. "Sit tight, I'll get back to you," he instructed the journalist. He called back. "The CIA told the secret police, the Venezuelan secret police, everything. They are out to get you. You are in great danger."

Fleetwood asked if he should go to the U.S. embassy in Caracas. No, said Propper. "I have no power down there. You are on your own."[37]

Fleetwood somehow made it back to the United States, let Propper copy his tapes, and published his interview with Bosch. Venezuela's *El Nacional* also spread the news that the Novos were involved. Scherrer already suspected that DINA may have hired Cuban Americans.[38]

By October 12, the FBI was publicly celebrating this "most promising lead" and giving the press details about Bosch.[39] Bosch himself had boasted publicly, at a Caracas fund-raising dinner before his arrest, that "our organization has come out of the Letelier job looking good."[40]

The following week, the Department of Justice subpoenaed both Novo brothers and José Suárez to appear before a grand jury. Suárez's name came up because he was tied to the bombing of the Russian ship five days before the Letelier assassination, as well as an attempt to bomb the New York Academy of Music on July 24 because it had booked artists from Castro's Cuba. The FBI also served Guillermo's wife, Magaly.[41]

Then another door opened. On October 29, the State Department called to discuss "something that might be useful in the Letelier investigation." Over the summer, two Chileans called Juan Williams and Alejandro Romeral — State did not know these were aliases — tried to enter the United States via the Paraguay gambit. The State Department also forwarded the physical descriptions and photos. Cornick checked them against various immigration lists: no matches.[42] Still, investigators were hearing chatter about Cubans meeting with a tall, blond, blue-eyed Chilean in his early thirties. The description fit this "Juan Williams" fellow.[43]

These hopeful developments contrasted with chilling threats against family and investigators, which would prove a constant during the Letelier investigations. On October 4, an unknown male called Orlando Letelier's aunt, María del Solar. "María, María, María," he said condescendingly, "talking to the FBI won't help you; your legs will be spread in W[ashington]DC like Orlando's." Then he hung up.[44]

In early November Larry Wack's fiancé, Elizabeth Ryden, a flight attendant about to join her crew, was standing in Kennedy Airport, rifling through her purse for her key to an American Airlines office. Suddenly, a man grabbed her arm and yanked her around.

"You tell your little friend Larry Wack to keep his fucking nose out of Chile's business. Or you won't be so pretty anymore!" he said. "Boom! Boom! You know what I mean?"

"Y-yes, I know what you mean," she stammered, terrified.

He stared at her for a moment and then melted back into the crowd. Ryden fell to the floor, screaming for help. When she calmed down, she wrote down the man's description and threat. American Airlines refused to let her on its aircraft, fearing she might attract a terrorist attack.

When Wack told his colleagues, Carter Cornick thought about the implications. Since Wack had been interviewing Cubans in New Jersey, Cornick deduced that those who threatened Wack's fiancée not only displayed sophisticated intelligence capabilities but also were probably *Cubans* who nevertheless warned Wack to stop investigating *Chile*. A few days later, the FBI came across a letter by Guillermo Novo complaining to a Chilean consul general about Santiago's shabby treatment of the exiles.[45] The Cuba-Chile connection theory started to make sense.

By November, the Justice Department now entertained only two main theories — that Letelier and Moffitt were killed either by Chile's government or by Cuba's exiles. A third implied theory, reinforced by the Ryden threat, was that both groups were coconspirators.

》》 The year 1977 would prove a rollercoaster for Propper and his team, their hopes heightened and then dashed repeatedly.

Propper and Cornick continued to subpoena Cuban exiles to the grand jury, sworn in by the U.S. District Court for the District of Columbia on February 7.[46] Investigators offered immunity to José Suárez and Alvin Ross in exchange for their testimony, but both refused. When he was questioned, Suárez just sat there and smiled instead of answering. While both were guilty of contempt of court, Propper chose to jail only Suárez, in what the *Los Angeles Times* called "one of the nation's most unpleasant" prisons. But he let Ross walk in hopes that other Cuban Americans would suspect Ross of having cooperated.[47] It did not work.

Ignacio Novo answered 104 of the grand jury's questions and walked out dismissing it as a "fishing expedition."[48]

Guillermo Novo, who had ordered the others to keep their mouths shut, appeared unfazed by his summonses. When one journalist found Novo at his car dealership and asked him about being investigated, Novo snapped at him. "And so what? Let them investigate. From Washington they already sent me two appearance requests for testimony to a congressional commission. That didn't worry me. They make a big noise and then they quiet down."

"Are you going to deny your participation in terrorist activities?"

"I have never thought of doing that. But why are you staring at me? Do you think terrorists have fangs sticking out, hair standing on end, and blood on their hands?"

Novo demanded an ID from the journalist and from his name concluded that he was Russian. When the man left, Novo ran after him and pinned him against the wall. "His hands shook from rage or fear, his eyes filled with blood, his face distorted," wrote the journalist. "All the pretense rapidly fell away. The forced appearance (he used) for his job flew away. In front of me stood a new Guillermo Novo. Choking with malice and rage he threatened, 'Tell your people that no mercy will be given. I will strike again. I will never give up.'"[49]

On March 29, Propper himself received a direct threat. Alone at his desk in the early morning, he answered his phone.

"Is Mr. Propper here?" asked a raspy voice.

"Speaking."

"If you don't get your ass off our case, you're gonna be in deep shit like Letelier," said the voice.

"Who's this?" said a flustered Propper, but he just heard a click.

In April 1977, Guillermo Novo showed up at the grand jury but refused to answer any questions. Propper expressed the team's frustration: "We don't know a fucking thing. We still don't even know what the bomb was made of!"[50] Two months later, Novo failed to appear at a hearing on his possible parole violation for going to Chile.[51]

"This case was not made in the grand jury," one of the prosecutors concluded of the proceedings.[52]

Scherrer, meanwhile, as liaison to South American intelligence officers, interviewed Manuel Contreras. All Contreras offered was "confidential information" that Michael Moffitt probably killed Letelier since Ronni was one of Letelier's lovers. "Why else would a man sit in the back seat while a woman sat in the front?" he asked of the Chevelle's seating arrangements on September 21. "Michael Moffitt was a cuckold." Contreras also suggested that Letelier's affair with Sagrario Pérez-Soto might have gotten him killed—though he never dared to accuse Isabel.[53] (Cornick and Wack interviewed the Venezuelan lover but found no link to the murder.)

Six months after the assassination, with so many avenues leading nowhere, the Department of Justice began to despair. Officials divulged to journalists that they had leads but no evidence. The *Washington Post's* Bob Woodward of Watergate fame reported in April that authorities were seeking "a former CIA explosives maker," Edwin P. Wilson, who allegedly sought to recruit Cubans, but Wilson turned out to be unrelated to Letelier.[54] "There is no solution in sight," one investigator told the *Washington Star* that same month. "Probably the only way we'll ever break this case is if an informer gives us what we need to make an arrest."[55]

>> On July 8, 1977, the FBI caught that lucky break. At 2 A.M., Larry Wack's phone rang. On the other end was Ricardo Canete, a thirty-five-year-old Cuban exile who claimed to have cofounded the Cuban Nationalist Movement (CNM) but then limited himself to small-time forgery and counterfeiting when he found the group's violence distasteful. Canete was under the mistaken impression that the FBI was sitting on prosecutable evidence against him, so he ratted on his fellow exiles.[56] In May, Canete had met with Wack about a conspiracy by the CNM to assassinate Propper, Attorney General Griffin Bell, and U.S. Attorney for New York Robert Fisk.[57] According to Canete, Ignacio Novo threatened that, if the grand jury sent his brother Guillermo to prison, "it's war" between the CNM and the Justice Department. And if Washington normalized relations with Castro's Cuba, "then the bodies are going to be all over."[58]

At the same meeting, Wack had asked about the Novos assassinating Orlando Letelier. "You think Iggie and his brother are capable of something like that?"

"Sure they are," Canete had answered. "They've been working up to it over the years."

Now, in the middle of the night, at the other end of the line, Canete sounded panicked. "Larry, I gotta talk to you! I'm sorry, but I gotta talk to somebody, and you're the only one who can help." He was panting.

"What's the matter?" Wack asked. "You sound like you've just seen a ghost or something."

"I wish I'd seen a fucking ghost," said Canete. "I wish to God that's what it was. Shit."

"Go ahead," said Wack. "Tell me. Nobody's gonna be on the line at this hour of the night."

"I never thought it would get this heavy, I swear to God," said Canete. "But I was with Alvin tonight, and he told me he built the bomb that blew Letelier away."

Wack snapped to attention "What? Don't fuck with me about something like that! Hold on," he interjected, "start over, I'm going to record this."

Canete told him that, just a few hours prior, he had had a conversation with "Al," meaning Alvin Ross. After they met at Ross's Ford dealership, Canete noticed a briefcase in Ross's car containing two manila folders marked "Orlando Letelier" and "Chile."

As Canete was forging some IDs for the Cubans, he bragged about his craft.

"I'm pretty good at my work, too," countered Ross, and launched into his own brag about making bombs, even one out of a coffeepot.

"Yeah, Al. Sure," said Canete.

Ross's characteristic loquacity then betrayed him. "I'm not kidding. The latest bomb I built did a job on a Commie named Letelier. You heard of that?"

Canete was "about to blow up" inside but kept his cool and said, "Cut it out, Alvin, will you? Can't you see I'm working?"

"I'm telling you."

"Sure, Alvin," Canete humored him. "How'd you do it?"

Alvin looked around, and then lowered his voice. "I always use the C-4 plastic, 'cause it's easier to mold. On the Letelier bomb, I used two timing devices, a clock and an acid backup. Just to make sure."

By now, Canete was sweating but also curious for more. "All right, Alvin. I'm fucking impressed. But anybody can build a bomb, I hear. That was a car bomb, right? Did you have the balls to put the bomb under the car?"

Ross took the bait. "Well, I could have done it, but I didn't handle that part. The Shrimp Man took care of that. He and his partner." By this Ross meant Virgilio Paz and Suárez, who had reinstalled the bomb after Michael Townley's installation proved a dud.

Wack stopped Canete during this tale. "Holy shit. Holy shit, I can't believe it." He secured a commitment from Canete to take a lie detector test. When Wack told Cornick, Cornick was equally bowled over. "That's the first real evidence we've had in the whole damn case."[59] The next week, Canete passed his polygraph. Paz would later confirm to Canete that "we did Letelier," with Ross nodding next to him. "We know it and they know it, but let them try and prove it."[60]

Canete's comments while under the lie detector included the assessment that the photo of "Juan Williams" bore a "fair resemblance" to an unknown covert Chilean who was in touch with the exiles. Canete had seen Michael Townley but did not know his identity. And in his confession to Canete, Ross also mentioned the participation of "the colonel," a Chilean — an allusion possibly to Townley or to Pedro Espinoza or Manuel Contreras — but, again, the man went unnamed. "The significance of this identification cannot be under estimated," reported the FBI, "as it is the first time anyone provided an identity for the blonde haired, blue eyed, English speaking Chilean."[61]

Also in July, Propper finally secured an interview with Rolando Otero, a close associate of the CNM. He got the terrorist talking about his days in Chile, in 1975, when Chilean officers interrogated him. Then Otero described one DINA agent as tall, thin, with blonde hair and blue eyes, and speaking Spanish "with a North American accent." He even offered that a photo of "Juan Williams" looked like the blonde man. Propper kept calm, but the revelation confirmed what he had heard from another informant—that "Juan Williams" might be an American.

"A momentous development," Scherrer called this from South America. He searched Chilean records—the National Identity Cabinet, the Defense Ministry—but found no matches for Williams or Romeral. Scherrer also inspected 1,500 individual cards of U.S. citizens registered in Chile, also in vain.[62] "Williams" was now the elusive focus of the investigation.

In August, the Chilean government confirmed that CNM members had been in Chile but claimed, to no one's surprise, that it found no connection between itself and the Letelier assassination.[63] Propper complained to Robert Pastor of Jimmy Carter's National Security Council that "the information we received [from the Chilean government] was superficial, incomplete, and failed to answer any of the important questions we asked. Their response evidenced a lack of good faith and a definite unwillingness to supply us with anything of value." Propper was now convinced that exiles had committed the crime with support from DINA, but he had no hard evidence.[64]

In September, Ricardo Canete disappeared, and it looked like Guillermo Novo had gone underground. Attending a rally in Union City, Ross told an interviewer that "Novo is a hero to the Cuban people in Union City, New Jersey, and that the Cuban people will hide him as long as necessary." Despite promising leads, what the *Washington Post* called "one of the most complicated investigations since Watergate" was now stalled.[65]

》 And thus the matter remained for half a year more.

In January 1978, Guillermo Novo along with Paz and Ross contacted Michael Townley to demand $25,000 in cash as a loan to relocate because the investigation into the Letelier assassination "was getting hot for them." This was the first and only time they asked for compensation. Townley went to Contreras. "They can send their families to Chile," Contreras responded, "but they are not getting any money from me."[66]

Propper grew convinced that the solution to the case resided in Chile and that the U.S. government had to push Santiago harder.

9

Letelier Diplomacy

"If they can do this and get away with it under the nose of the CIA and the FBI," said president-elect Jimmy Carter in November 1976 of the Letelier-Moffitt assassination, "then no president can govern."[1] Carter understood what Michael Townley, Guillermo Novo, and Manuel Contreras did not — that such a brazen attack on a Chilean dissident on U.S. soil was unacceptable to the U.S. policy-making apparatus, whether Republican or Democrat. It infringed upon U.S. state sovereignty and made the United States look unable to police its own borders. It brought the Cold War far too close to home and made it seem out of control. The killing at Sheridan Circle became what one historian called "the final nail in the coffin of the U.S.-Chile relationship."[2]

Although the Justice Department and FBI were in charge of the investigation, the diplomats also mattered greatly in the Letelier-Moffitt quest for justice. Only they could apply enough pressure on the Pinochet government to collaborate with Gene Propper's team. Their vision for the future of U.S.-Chile relations would be crucial. Robert Steven, a Chile Desk officer at the State Department, was among a growing group who believed that "we were not against the Chilean government, we were not against what the military had done. We were against the abuse of it and the terrorism that had been performed in its name."[3]

》 Luckily for Isabel Letelier and the many others who sought justice, Carter was far more focused on human rights than his predecessors, Richard Nixon and Gerald Ford. Henry Kissinger no longer could muffle those who cared, such as when he scribbled on a cable by U.S. Ambassador to Chile David Popper that suggested paying attention to human rights, "Tell Popper to knock off the God damn social sciences lectures."[4] Carter, in contrast, spoke of rights as the moral core of his foreign policy. During a campaign debate, the former Georgia governor even needled President Ford about his neglect of Chilean political prisoners.[5]

Still, a robust diplomatic response to the Letelier assassination was not foreordained. On September 21, 1976, Gerald Ford's State Department expressed "its gravest concern" over the Letelier bombing, but most of its employees doubted that Chile had anything to do with it.[6] "We have never had any indication that DINA was in any way operational in U.S. territory," wrote Ambassador Popper on that day, "and it is difficult for us to believe that even its rather fanatical leaders would expose themselves to the consequences of being implicated in a terrorist act in Washington."[7] Also, why strip Letelier of his nationality right before killing him? The CIA enjoyed "what amounted to a veto" over the State Department's reporting of human rights abuses, according to Steven, by making it nearly impossible to send that information back to Washington. Even Foggy Bottom was reluctant to "rattle the cage," recalled Steven. His own assistant secretary's intermediary "called me in and said, 'Bob, we really think that we should let Justice take the lead in this.' The signal was very, very clear: Lay off."[8]

But others felt sure that only Pinochet's government would be so bloodthirsty. Still on September 21, someone burst into the office of one of the State Department's Latin American bureau's officials, proclaiming, "DINA killed Letelier!"[9]

One thing was sure, recalled one diplomat: "Everyone in the Justice Department and in the State Department wanted to catch and punish the people who were responsible for this killing in Washington."[10] Steven, who probably most helped Isabel Letelier, confirmed how the killing of her husband "was very much a provocation, a challenge, a slap in the face to us.... [We were] also outraged that they thought they could get away with this sort of thing in Washington DC.... I suspect that more than half of my hours in those two years that I was on the desk were devoted to the Letelier case."[11] The deputy chief of mission in Santiago agreed that "most of the diplomacy of those years" qualified as "Letelier diplomacy."[12]

>> Most Chilean officials, meanwhile, remained unaware that their own government had ordered the hit. Manuel Trucco, Pinochet's ambassador in Washington, lived on the very circle where Letelier and Moffitt were killed. On September 21, he got up at 9:30, later than usual because he was headed to the airport and not to work. It was a few minutes before Letelier turned into Sheridan Circle. From his shower, Trucco heard the blast under the Chevelle. "Something's happened!" he yelled, looking out the window.[13] He

looked for his wife but could not find her. Finally, he made his way outside, where she and their maid were observing the wreckage. Trucco heard from passersby that somebody "threw a bomb," so he went back inside, oblivious to the possibility that his own government was involved. When later questioned, he flatly denied that DINA operated abroad or had personnel in the embassy staff.[14]

Pinochet's government, while it denounced the killing and called for a U.S. investigation, also claimed it was being framed, that *it* was the victim. "This kind of act only affects the Chilean government," posited the Ministry of Foreign Relations, "as part of the propaganda campaign of the Soviet Union against us." It noted that all terror attacks against Chileans overlapped with the U.N. General Assembly and therefore seemed attempts to call its attention.[15]

Chilean newspapers offered still more conjecture. *La Tercera* predicted that "ultraleftist terrorism" would accuse "fascist agents" and pin the blame on Pinochet, linking Letelier's loss of citizenship to his death.[16] *El Mercurio* alleged that Letelier and the Moffitts were headed for the Chilean embassy with a bomb when the explosion took place. Ambassador Trucco peddled a similar story, adding that Letelier was "no worry to me" because he lived on "an island of Marxism, and an island that has no impact in the US." Besides, added the press, if Santiago wanted Letelier dead, why not kill him while it had him in prison?[17]

>> In early 1977, however, Contreras had a rude awakening. Because of the increasing press coverage of the killing, Pinochet disbanded DINA and replaced it with the National Information Center, or CNI in its Spanish-language acronym. The CNI's authority was much lessened, as were Contreras's power and budget. Pinochet's decision apparently divided even his family. His wife, Lucía Hiriart, visited Contreras at his home to comfort him, and she left her husband for two weeks in protest. She returned only after Augusto prevailed on a bishop to mediate for the couple.[18]

Regardless, no more would Contreras be able to spread terror throughout Chile.

>> Diplomatic efforts to advance the Letelier-Moffitt case, meanwhile, moved as slowly as did Gene Propper's investigation.

In mid-1977, President Carter met with the Venezuelan president, who stated that he had "good reports but no proof" that Cubans sent by DINA killed Letelier.[19]

In September, Pinochet traveled to Washington along with twenty-three other Latin American heads of state for the signing of the Panama Canal treaties, a signal achievement for Carter. Alongside him were Manuel Contreras and about thirty security personnel, and allegations of Contreras's involvement in the Letelier-Moffitt affair had just surfaced.[20]

At a breakfast where the dictator appeared before the U.S. press for the first time since Sheridan Circle, Jeremiah O'Leary of the *Washington Star* sat by his side. "Mr. President, I have to ask this: did anyone in the Chilean government or the Chilean military have anything to do with planning or carrying out the Letelier assassination?"[21]

Pinochet looked gravely at O'Leary and placed his thumb and forefinger over his lips in a sign of the cross: "I am a Christian, not an assassin. I can swear that nobody in the Chilean government ever planned such a thing."[22]

Later, in the Oval Office with Pinochet, Carter brought up human rights and his determination to get to the bottom of the Letelier crime. Pinochet nodded and promised cooperation.[23]

None of this evasive courtesy pleased Michael Moffitt, who along with Isabel Letelier had been demanding their own meeting with Carter. "If Carter is serious about human rights, why doesn't he welcome Isabel and me, just like he's welcoming Pinochet?" he asked at a press conference.[24]

A few days after Pinochet returned to Santiago, Carter announced his new ambassador to Chile—none other than George Landau, who had handled the Williams-Romeral fake passports in Paraguay in the summer of 1976. Robert Steven recalled Landau as "a very principled man" who "was at least as outraged as I was at what had been done in this country."[25]

The U.S. government certainly had tools at its disposal to lord over Chile. Among other kinds of support, the Ford administration had supported $60 million in World Bank loans to the small country, and Carter could take that support away.[26]

But Landau had to be careful in approaching the Chileans: too little pressure, and they would ignore or sandbag him; too much, and their pride would be wounded and they would refuse to help. U.S. diplomats, along with Propper, also could not give the Pinochet government too much information, say, on "Williams" and "Romeral," lest Santiago decide to "scrub" the evidence. Diplomats reported that Chilean counterparts were "genuinely shocked" when confronted with accusations or evidence of their government's complicity. Besides, they added, Letelier was "a deserving target," so why even investigate this?[27]

Then, U.S. diplomats suffered an unforeseen setback.

›› On October 22, 1977, Guillermo Osorio headed to the Diego Portales building, the seat of Pinochet's power, for a diplomatic reception to honor visiting Peruvian military authorities. Osorio, a civilian career officer, was Chile's director of protocol and also DINA's man inside the Ministry of Foreign Relations. Among his tasks was the processing of passports, and in August 1976 he had issued official Chilean passports to "Williams" and "Romeral" and signed a request to the U.S. embassy that both be granted diplomatic A-2 visas. Osorio might therefore know the duo's true identity, thought U.S. diplomats.[28]

At the reception, more than a year after the Sheridan Circle blast, Osorio drank a few red wines. Suddenly, across the room, he saw Manuel Contreras standing and smiling at him. With the head of the CNI was Colonel Enrique Valdés Puga, the number two man at the Foreign Ministry. As Contreras and Valdés walked toward him, Osorio looked nervous. They took him to Contreras's car and then to another reception at the Military Club to celebrate two officers' promotions and Osorio's own nomination as the next ambassador to Austria.[29]

Shortly after 2 P.M., Valdés and Contreras drove Osorio back to his own house. Osorio's brother Renato found it "odd" that such important men would curry such favor with a subordinate.[30] Soon after, Osorio's wife, Mary Rose, walked in, crossing paths with Contreras. She had lunch alone with her husband. Here her story began to differ from others'. Mary Rose claimed the meal "was peaceful and pleasant" while their maid reported that "there was a serious argument." Whatever the case, Osorio excused himself to go "lie down for a while." According to Mary Rose, he did so alone.

According to Renato, Mary Rose joined him. At one point, Mary Rose leaned over and thought Guillermo was asleep. At 3:30 P.M., a single gunshot startled her awake.

The maid rushed upstairs.

"Don't come in!" yelled Mary Rose from behind the bedroom door. When she opened it, Osorio had a gun in his hand and a bullet hole in his forehead.

Mary Rose recalled that she ran up the stairs along with the maid.

Rather than phone the police, she called relatives and Valdés. Not until 6 P.M. did a doctor arrive on the scene. Around the same time walked in General Carlos Forestier, one of Pinochet's toughest enforcers, to take command. He ordered that no autopsy be carried out, even though Chilean law required one for any violent death. To circumvent this law, Forestier instructed that the death certificate should note "heart attack" as the cause of death. The investigating judge, a "pusillanimous sort," according to Renato, went along.[31] It was rumored among some that Forestier was having an affair with Mary Rose and that Osorio walked in on them—in which case his death would have had nothing to do with Letelier.[32]

The Osorio family pestered the Supreme Court about the gaping hole in Osorio's forehead—not typically a side effect of a heart attack. One month after his death, the court ordered the body exhumed and autopsied. As a result, a new official cause of death emerged—suicide.[33] *But why would Guillermo kill himself?* thought Mary Rose and Renato. Guillermo was in good spirits on October 22. He was thrilled to be elevated to an ambassadorship. He had just bought a house. These were not behaviors of a man in despair.[34]

When it was revealed that the bullet had entered Osorio's skull from behind and below, rumors circulated of a "crime of passion."[35] Mary Rose did not advance a theory, at least not publicly. Renato, meanwhile, speculated that Mary Rose cooperated with a third party to kill her husband: they had gotten him drunk and drugged, and then someone came in, put a gun in Guillermo's hand, and pulled the trigger.[36]

Whatever the truth, Osorio's untimely death meant that U.S. investigators had lost a potential key witness.

>> The odds of catching Letelier's killers got even worse on January 4, 1978, when Pinochet held a plebiscite to fortify his regime. The U.N. General Assembly had passed a resolution, cosponsored by the Carter administration, condemning Chile for human rights violations. In response, Pinochet put to Chileans the following loaded question, which they had to answer "Yes" or "No": "Given the international aggression against the government of our country, I support President Pinochet in his defense of the dignity of Chile, and I confirm again the legitimacy of the Government of the Republic in its sovereign head of the institutionalization process in the country." All but the most diehard opponents of Pinochet supported such wording. The "Yes" side swept 78.6 percent of the votes.

Helping to shore up Pinochet's political fortunes was Chile's improving economy. Since Allende's days, and after some rough years, inflation was down and the gross national product was rising.[37] In early May, the U.S. Agriculture Department approved $38 million in credits to Chilean farmers and ranchers. Countering accusations that such aid violated the Carter administration's policy on human rights, diplomats explained that the credits might in fact be "encouraging political developments" such as collaboration on the Letelier case. Senator Ted Kennedy would have none of it. He accused the executive of giving "back door" funding to a murderous regime.[38]

As if to vindicate Pinochet's free market purism, its economic guru, Milton Friedman, had won the 1976 Nobel Prize in Economic Sciences.

By May 1978, too, Pinochet had receded as a target for human rights watchers. He lifted a state of siege in the country, granted some prisoners amnesty, placed civilians in his cabinet, and sped up plans for a new constitution. However, many noted, the machinery of repression stayed mostly untouched. A state of emergency was still in effect, hundreds were still "disappeared," and dissents, trade unions, and most political parties remained either banned or severely restricted.[39]

》》 In the middle of this uncertainty, Gene Propper attempted a risky gambit. Frustrated by the inaction of Chile and the tight lips of Cuban Americans, he hit upon the idea of petitioning Santiago with letters rogatory — a formal request from one country's court to another's for judicial assistance. When someone wishes to issue a summons internationally, for instance, or to obtain evidence from another country, letters rogatory are the chosen instrument.

In early February, Propper and his superior, Earl Silbert, signed the request for letters rogatory and forwarded it to the State Department. There, a U.S. district judge, along with Attorney General Griffin Bell and Secretary of State Cyrus Vance, signed the official letters. The judge's cover letter explained that the crime against Letelier was punishable under U.S. Code 1116(a), which protected foreign officials, and that District of Columbia Code 2401 defined Moffitt's death as murder in the first degree. The U.S. government, it continued, had identified two Chilean military men, Juan Williams Rose and Alejandro Romeral Jara, as entering the country before the crime. "It is therefore requested," wrote the judge, "that you cause each of these men to appear in Court to answer under oath the written questions which are attached to this request." Fifty-five questions accompanied the document, in addition to the demand that Propper be in Chile during questioning.[40]

On February 17, Deputy Secretary of State Warren Christopher summoned Chilean Ambassador Jorge Cauas to his office, handed him the letters rogatory, and stressed their "utmost importance."[41] Cauas acted coolly, pledging the full cooperation of his government. At the same time, in Santiago, Ambassador Landau handed the same documents to Foreign Minister Patricio Carvajal.

When Christopher confronted Cauas, the Chilean asked that all contacts in the case be kept secret. "Not possible," answered Christopher. "This one is going public." Propper had the cover letter bearing the names of the two mystery men unsealed, meaning it would be filed as a public document in U.S. district court. Reporters could uncover it—especially when prompted by the Justice Department—and start asking questions of the government in Chile.[42] The list of questions, meanwhile, was attached to the photographs of the two Chileans and kept sealed. Propper kept the questions secret also to keep the public guessing as to how much investigators knew—and did not know.

On February 22, the news of the letters rogatory hit the front pages of the *Washington Post* and the *Washington Star* and ran on NBC, CBS, and ABS television news. It was the first public acknowledgment that Washington was focused on Chile in the seventeen-month-old Letelier case. Santiago's immediate response was not to respond. Journalists, meanwhile, went to the addresses given for "Williams" and "Romeral," but one did not exist and the other did not yield anyone with those names. Officials at the civil registry said the last name "Romeral Jara" could not be found. All three branches of the military declared having no members with those names.[43]

Propper and the diplomats had one ace left up their sleeve: they had kept secret the photos of "Williams" and "Romeral." What if they played it?

Orlando Letelier's Chevelle in Sheridan Circle after the car bomb, September 21, 1976.
AP Photo/Peter Bregg.

Orlando Letelier, *left*, and Isabel Morel, *right*, playing guitar while part of a university cultural group in the early 1950s. They may not have been dating yet.
Fondo Orlando Letelier, Archivo de la Administración, Santiago, Chile.

Isabel and Orlando on their wedding day.
Fondo Orlando Letelier, Archivo de la Administración, Santiago, Chile.

Letelier in Cuba, 1960.
Fondo Orlando Letelier, Archivo de la Administración, Santiago, Chile.

Letelier as ambassador to the United States, early 1971.
Fondo Orlando Letelier, Archivo de la Administración, Santiago, Chile.

Letelier arrested outside the Ministry of Defense, Santiago, on September 11, 1973.
Fondo Orlando Letelier, Archivo de la Administración, Santiago, Chile.

Letelier with Diego Arria, *right*, on September 11, 1974, after both left Chile for Venezuela. Letelier's finger is healing from having been broken at Dawson Island.
Fondo Orlando Letelier, Archivo de la Administración, Santiago, Chile.

Michael Townley and Ines (Mariana) Callejas de Townley, undated but very likely before Townley's arrest in 1978.
MCT/Tribune News Service/Getty Images.

Ronni Moffitt.
Fondo Orlando Letelier, Archivo de la Administración, Santiago, Chile.

Police investigating the bazooka used by Cuban Americans to target the United Nations buildings in the background.
Herald-Tribune-UPI.

José Suárez, with paper in his shirt pocket, as a bearded revolutionary in 1959 Cuba. Comandante Húber Matos is to his left. The two would soon be jailed, and Suárez would escape.
Used by permission of Dr. Antonio Rafael de la Cova.

George Landau, ambassador to Chile from 1977 to 1982.
Photograph of George W. Landau, 1980, Hernán Cubillos Sallato Papers, box 5, folder 12, Hoover Institution Archives, Stanford, California.

Poster for a benefit concert where Orlando Letelier made a passionate speech.
He had just been stripped of his Chilean nationality. Michael Townley was in Manhattan and saw the poster. He assassinated Letelier eleven days later.
Fondo Orlando Letelier, Archivo de la Administración, Santiago, Chile.

Assistant U.S. Attorney Eugene Propper, *center*,
likely while investigating in Chile in 1978 or 1979.
Used by permission of Archivo CENFOTO-UDP, Fondo Diario La Nación.

The Letelier-Moffitt memorial, five days after the assassination. *Left to right:* Michael Moffitt, Hortensia Allende (Salvador's widow), and Isabel Letelier. *Fondo Orlando Letelier, Archivo de la Administración, Santiago, Chile.*

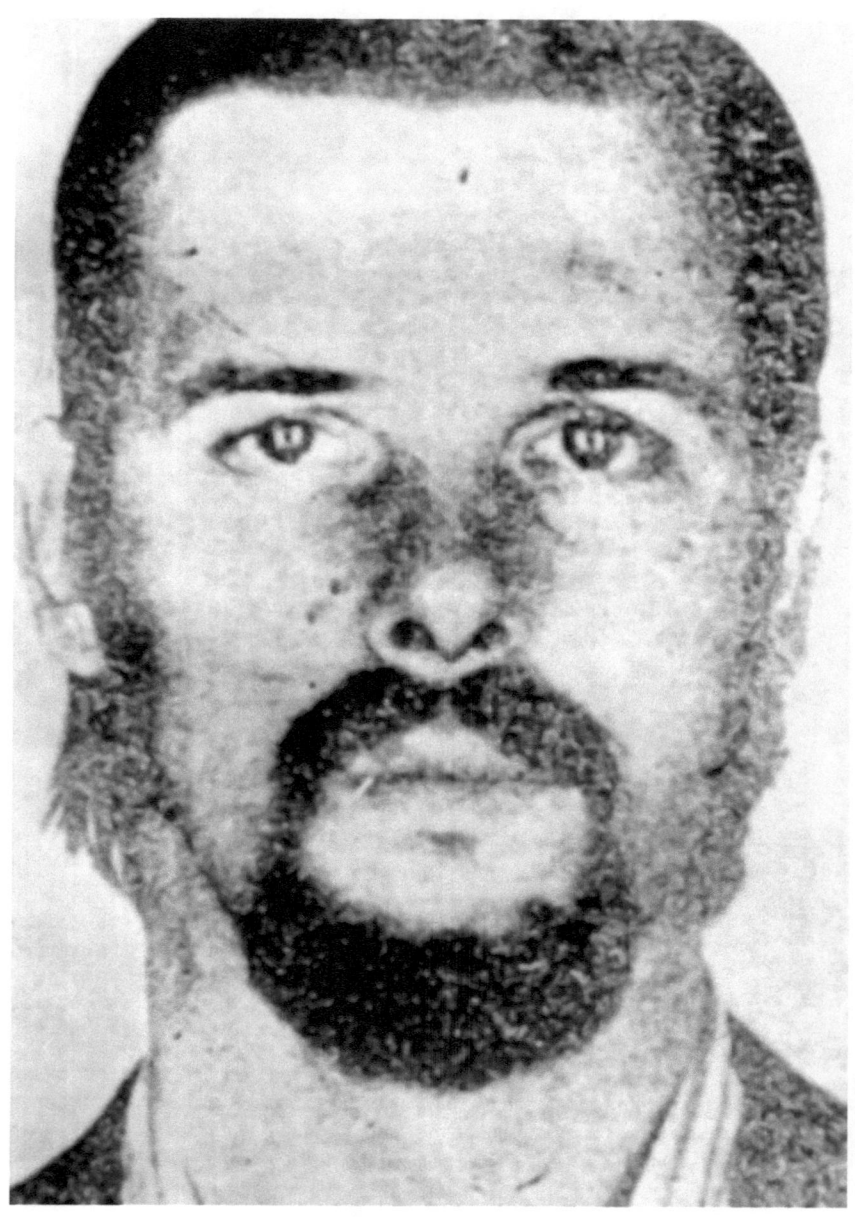

Michael Townley's nameless passport photo, a crucial clue for U.S. investigators.
AP Photo.

Isabel Letelier with the commemorative plaque installed on Sheridan Circle.
Fondo Orlando Letelier, Archivo de la Administración, Santiago, Chile.

Isabel Letelier and Michael Moffitt with Edward Kennedy, May 5, 1978. The senator from Massachusetts, along with others in Congress, helped form a human rights lobbying community that put pressure on the U.S. government over the Letelier case. *AP Photo/Charles Harrity.*

Virgilio Paz's mugshot, April 23, 1991. The FBI arrested Paz as a result of the television program *America's Most Wanted*. AP Photo/FBI.

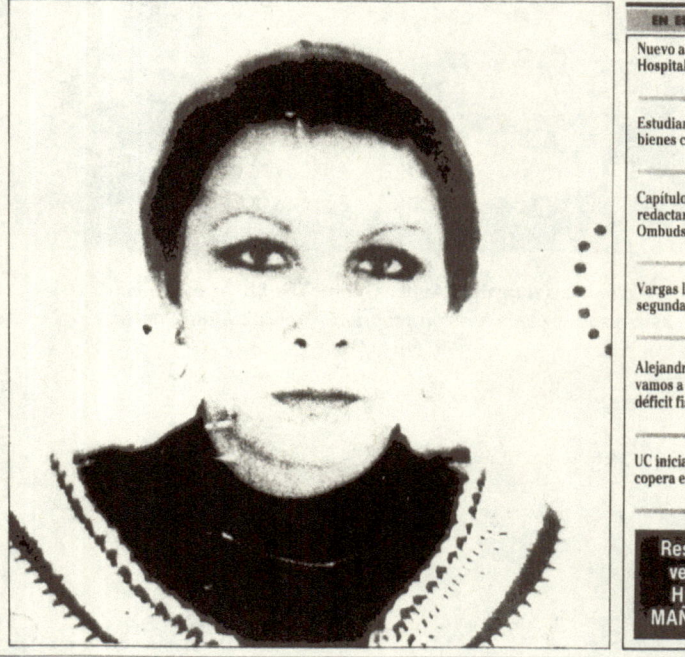

"I am Liliana Walker." On April 17, 1990, Santiago's *La Época* broke the news of the true identity of the woman who helped surveil Letelier. Mónica Lagos's testimony helped reopen the criminal case against Contreras and Espinoza.

Fabiola Letelier, Orlando's sister and a lead lawyer for the family's case in Chile. *Wikimedia Commons.*

Manuel Contreras, *left*, the former head of DINA, Pinochet's secret police, in 1992; and Pedro Espinoza, his chief of operations, in an undated photo. Espinoza, following orders from Contreras, entrusted Michael Townley with the mission to assassinate Orlando Letelier. *Cris Bouroncle/AFP/Getty Images.*

Chileans peacefully calling for the Chilean Supreme Court to ratify the lower court's sentencing of Contreras and Espinoza, April 27, 1995.
Cris Bouroncle/AFP/Getty Images.

Francisco, Cristián, and Juan Pablo Letelier, three of Orlando and Isabel's four sons, and Cristián's daughter Nicolette, five, during the dedication of a statue of their father in Washington, February 25, 2018.
Evelyn Hockstein/The Washington Post/Getty Images.

10

Cueca Sola

The *cueca* is Chile's national dance. It features a man and a woman, dressed in traditional clothing, circling each other in a controlled courtship. When Chile's husbands, fathers, and sons began to disappear under the Pinochet regime, the women left behind danced the cueca with their photographs to underscore their anguish and devotion.

They called this expression of loneliness the *cueca sola*. It signified the new reality of Isabel Letelier's life.

>> The memorials that followed the assassination first made plain the political chasm into which Letelier would be thrust — and the importance of her leadership. In contrast to the caution among the U.S. and Chilean press and governments, supporters of Orlando, Ronni Moffitt, and the Institute for Policy Studies (IPS) made their point of view unequivocal. Mere minutes after the assassination, friends and colleagues at IPS congregated in front of the residence of Pinochet's ambassador in Washington, Manuel Trucco, on Sheridan Circle and shouted "Pinochet, assassin!"[1] In the evening, hundreds gathered in front of the Leteliers' house on Ogden Court. Joan Baez was there, devoting four hours to singing Orlando's favorite songs.[2] "It was a supremely devastating, dark day," recalled son Francisco. Soon after he woke up with survivor's guilt.[3]

On September 22, Letelier received her husband's autopsy report, copied it, and mailed out copies to seventeen of Chile's military leaders, including Pinochet.[4]

The Chile Legislative Center, working for human rights in the country, circulated a flyer calling for a 5 P.M. rally in Dupont Circle and for U.S. citizens to denounce U.S. support for the Pinochet regime. "The terror we create and support abroad has come home to haunt us," it declared.[5] The socialist *Daily World* went even further, claiming the killing was "the work of U.S.

imperialism. If the hand that planted the bomb was Chilean, the money that crossed that hand came from the U.S."[6] In Dupont Circle that afternoon, friends voiced their sorrow and rage.[7]

Meanwhile, the just-widowed Letelier was busy with logistics. She had to deal with Gawler's Funeral Home on Wisconsin Avenue where Orlando's body lay. She received phone calls and telegrams from around the world. She arbitrated the differences among her friends and colleagues over the memorial service. Never did she cry.[8]

The funeral for Letelier and Moffitt came five days after the assassination, on Sunday, September 26. On that gray autumn day, 2,500 well-wishers — some said 5,000 — walked the mile from Sheridan Circle to St. Matthew's Roman Catholic Cathedral for a high requiem mass. It was the largest anti-Pinochet gathering ever in Washington, D.C. Leading the black-armband-clad mourners were Letelier and her four sons, along with Michael Moffitt and Ronni's two brothers. Hortensia Allende, the Chilean president's widow, stood by Isabel's side. Joining the procession were Senators George McGovern and James Abourezk, former Senator Eugene McCarthy, and Representatives George Miller, Tom Harkin, Peter Stark, and John Brademas. Some carried large photos of Letelier and Moffitt. Others hoisted a banner declaring, "Orlando Lives in the Heart of the People." In Sheridan Circle, marchers raised their fist in anger at the ambassador's home. When some noted a man with a camera, they feared a DINA agent and hid their faces with pink cardboard masks. "Chile Sí, Junta No!" they shouted.[9]

The anger and shouting abruptly stopped as Isabel approached the spot where the Chevelle had come to rest and where a memorial would eventually commemorate the event. She placed a rose and a carnation on the sidewalk, and Michael Moffitt put his arms around her.[10]

At the cathedral, only 500 could enter, and only after the FBI's bomb-sniffing dogs vetted them. The remaining 2,000 stayed outside.[11] In addition to the members of Congress, representatives of more than thirty-five embassies and several prominent Chilean exiles attended. The Jimmy Carter campaign sent delegates, as did the Communist Party of the United States.[12]

Bishop James Rausch began the service by bemoaning "the senseless violence of terror."[13] In his own speech, Senator McGovern echoed Carter's fears about the repercussions of a Washington assassination: "If Orlando Letelier must die at the age of forty-five and dear Ronni Moffitt must die at the age of twenty-five because of the unbridled power of madmen, then there is no security for any of us."[14] He pledged the "most persistent investigation" to find the killers. Hortensia Allende urged the "churches, the press, the workers' organizations, the Congress" in the United States and elsewhere to "intensify their activity in solidarity with the people of Chile."

"I am finding it difficult to get along without my wife," Moffitt quietly told the assembled. "She died in the tradition of a great long list of North American heroes," he said, "the kind of heroes you don't hear much about in the Bicentennial year. Those are the heroes who died organizing the first labor unions in the United States. Those were the heroes who died on the highways and the streets of Mississippi and Alabama organizing the civil rights marches. Those are the heroes who died in attacks organizing the farmworkers in California."

"If the purpose of the junta and its henchmen is to silence the voice that speaks for a free Chile and for freedom-loving people everywhere," he concluded, "they have not silenced that voice, they have multiplied it a hundredfold!"[15]

Then Joan Baez sang "Gracias a la Vida." The classic Chilean song, with its refrain, "Thanks to life, which has given me so much," finally brought Isabel to tears.[16]

Around the world, smaller memorials took place. About 700 gathered at the United Nations, with signs reading "Chile Will Be Free," "Down with the Fascist Junta," and "Vengeance for Letelier." In Quebec City, the capital of a province that would welcome thousands of exiles, seventy demonstrated in front of the U.S. consulate demanding an investigation.[17] In early October, several Church groups and nongovernmental organizations pooled their resources to sponsor a service at the Roman Catholic Church of St. Paul the Apostle on New York's West 59th Street.[18]

The Ford administration stayed away from the memorials. But after the St. Matthew's event, the Department of State brought it up to a counterterror working group. It called the speakers "impressive" and noted the vigorous calls for "a full investigation."[19]

The issue of where Letelier was to be buried came up the very day of his death. While still at George Washington Hospital, someone asked his widow if she had any choice but to bury Orlando in Washington, or should he be buried in Chile, even if he was no longer a Chilean citizen? "I don't know," she sighed. "My first thought was that Orlando would have wanted to be buried in Chilean soil. But I don't know."[20]

While she was still at the hospital, the presidents of Venezuela and Mexico, who happened to be meeting in Caracas, offered to bury her husband's body.[21] Isabel chose Venezuela, the land that had twice harbored her family and was closer to Chile.[22] Three days after St. Matthew's, she and

Orlando's body landed at the Caracas airport. Hundreds met them. Along the route to the Cemetery del Este, crowds lined the streets. President Carlos Andrés Pérez and his cabinet expressed their personal condolences to Isabel.[23] Of her husband's resting place, she reported, "It is a very beautiful site, on a hillside overlooking Caracas. He's resting there — in the middle of the road between Washington and Santiago — until the day when we have a free Chile."[24]

>> The assassination hit IPS hard. Letelier and Moffitt were some of its hardest-working and most beloved employees, and their sudden and spectacular death stunned many.

Saul Landau, a close friend and colleague, learned about the bombing from his wife, Rebecca. "She called me and said she'd just witnessed the most horrible accident in her life, pieces of clothes, blood, car parts everywhere in the street. A minute later we learned it was Orlando. There was hysteria at the IPS." While leaders Marcus Raskin and Richard Barnet went to the hospital to meet Isabel, Landau was left in charge. "I had no idea what to do, so I said 'Lock the doors.'"[25]

The office mourned that day. Many cried, others received messages of condolences, and others still worked the phones and planned a press conference.[26]

Staffed as it was with counterculture and antiestablishment types, IPS was long suspicious of the U.S. government, and especially the FBI. In 1974, the think tank had filed a multimillion-dollar suit that, as Landau wrote, "charged the bureau with illegally placing informants inside IPS, tapping its phones, opening its mail, and keeping its fellows under surveillance over the years 1968–1972. In addition, the IPS brief accused the FBI of systemically rifling its garbage and on one occasion reconstructing from discarded typewriter ribbons a letter written by one of its fellows. The FBI admitted to a House Investigating Committee in 1975 that it had placed 62 informants in IPS. The suit was still pending in September 1976."[27]

At around 2 P.M., four and a half hours after the Chevelle blew up, FBI agents with guns and dogs came barreling down the hallways of Letelier and Moffitt's colleagues, searching their offices. Landau countered by taking out of Letelier's files anything that could compromise the anti-Pinochet forces in or out of Chile.[28] All employees refused to be interviewed unless an IPS lawyer was present. The institute's Robert Borosage threatened to sick radical lawyers on the FBI.[29]

The inquiring agents knew nothing about Chile. When they asked who IPS staffers thought was responsible, they were told "DINA." "Could you spell that name?" they asked.³⁰ "Who is Deena?" wondered Carter Cornick. "What is her last name?"³¹

"Who do you think might have killed Letelier and Moffitt?" the FBI asked Landau.

"Pinochet."

"Again, please."

"Augusto Pinochet Ugarte, the president of Chile," explained Landau. "A-U-G-U-S-T-O. P-I-N-O-C-H-E-T."

"Slow down, please.... Would anyone else that you can think of want to or have reason to kill [Letelier]?"

"No."³²

IPS leaders, finally, ordered the agents to quit searching and leave.³³ It began its own investigation of the double murder.

The Chilean exiles at IPS reexperienced the terror of Pinochet's Chile. *Will there be another bombing? Maybe they'll target the institute this time.* Juan Gabriel Valdés, who would one day serve as Chile's ambassador to the United States and was then a young political science student and an associate at IPS, reported being followed by a Cuban three or four times in the months after the assassination, down Connecticut Avenue to IPS. He was also followed while in New York and again in Washington. Valdés also heard from a friend the rumor that he was next on DINA's list. He felt his phone was "definitely tapped." He heard beeps when he used it, and he was followed to places about which only those listening in would have known. Michael Moffitt also reported being followed twice, in New York and New Jersey.³⁴

>> Up in New Jersey, the Karpens, Ronni's parents, were largely spared from threats and surveillance but otherwise devastated. On the morning of the twenty-first, Hilda had been, in her words, "busy and excited," getting ready for Rosh Hashanah, when her daughter and her new husband would visit.³⁵ She was rushing to get to work at the family deli when Michael Moffitt called her from George Washington Hospital.

"It's not true!" she cried out. "She's my only daughter!"³⁶ Ronni's parents spent the day and night in lamentations. Their neighbor also went sleepless, he said, "because of the noise of those mourning next door."³⁷

Instead of celebrating the Jewish holiday with her daughter, Hilda and Murray buried her in King Solomon's cemetery in Clifton, New Jersey, on the eve of Rosh Hashanah. Four hundred attended the service, twenty-eight from IPS.[38]

At the funeral, reporters hounded the Karpens. Then they called them at their home and for months afterward sought them out whenever they went out. Ronni's death thus followed them, compounded by the ongoing investigation.

"There is nothing worse for a parent to suffer or endure than the loss of a child," said Murray. "Nothing."[39] Psychosomatic symptoms plagued the family. Hilda and one of Ronni's brothers developed duodenal ulcers. Murray took pain medication that "made him a different person," according to his wife: "Angry, short-tempered, constantly upset."[40] Murray suffered a grand mal epileptic seizure shortly after the bombing and almost choked to death on his own tongue. Ronni's older brother, Harry, tried to kill himself with a handful of sleeping pills and then was put under psychiatric care. Her other brother's college studies suffered.[41]

"A big piece of me died" with Ronni, recalled Hilda. Fifteen years later, she wrote, "the years have *not* made things easier. Time has not healed these wounds."

"We miss the grandchildren we will never have. We miss Ronni. I feel lost and alone without her."[42]

>> As soon as Michael Moffitt drove up to the Karpens' house in Passaic, the FBI said it needed to speak to him. Two days after the bombing, Moffitt could still smell the odor of burning flesh, which almost made him sick. To the agents, he recounted in detail the days before September 21, the ride to Sheridan Circle, and the explosion. When asked if anyone might want his wife or him dead, he said, "Everybody loved Ronni, but with me it might be different."[43]

Moffitt's trauma seemed to distract him from caring for himself. "For approximately five years following the bombing," he wrote in 1991, "my life was a living hell marked by total preoccupation with the bombing, sleeplessness, crying, alcohol abuse and a complete inability to remove it from my mind." He stayed with the Karpens for a while, sleeping in his wife's childhood bed. It felt "like living in a tomb." Until 1980, "I was a complex mass of anger, guilt and overwhelming sadness. I became basically non-functional." He remained on the IPS payroll, and "when I was introduced to dignitaries or financial supporters, I was always on display as the survivor of the murders — never a person in my own right."

"When I was not working on the investigation day or night, I started drinking heavily. Most nights I closed the bars down—drunk, striving to obliterate the present as well as the past. My house became a slum. I couldn't bring myself to clean up, mow the lawn or do anything. For months, all of Ronni's things remained around the house as if she was alive and I refused to allow anyone to take them away."

"I felt extremely guilty that I had survived. Guilty because I had not helped Ronni at the scene because I was trying to help Orlando. Guilty that I had survived and she hadn't particularly because I was responsible for her being in the car, guilty that I could not obtain justice for both of them."

"I had little interest in, or an inability to commit to, normal relationships with friends, family or others. Things that previously brought me great joy, such as social activities and athletics[,] became chores. I put on a significant amount of weight."[44]

While dressed in a green hospital gown on the afternoon of the bombing, still in shock, shuddering, his eyes red from tears, Moffitt had spoken crossly to national television reporters: "The United States government helped to overthrow the government of Allende and to put these dictators in power," he accused. "And they're responsible for killing my wife." He promised to enlist "people on Capitol Hill to cut off aid to the dictators in power." He spent several days giving more television interviews and writing an angry editorial for the *New Republic*, and ended the week at St. Matthew's Church alongside Isabel.[45]

After taking several weeks off, he came back to work at IPS. In 1977 he completed *The International Economic Order*, the pamphlet he and Letelier had begun that argued for a new architecture to the world economy to eliminate the inherent disadvantages of the developing world.[46] He also helped Isabel in sending out fund-raising letters, lobbying Congress, and pressuring FBI investigators. Throughout it all, he vowed revenge.

>> "I do not seek revenge. I seek only justice," was Isabel Letelier's own message. "Justice in the case of my husband and Ronni Moffitt will also mean justice for the majority of the Chilean people."[47]

Before September 21, 1976, Letelier had largely remained akin to an ambassador's wife. To be sure, she had taught Spanish and engaged in some appropriate activism as the founder of the Chile Committee for Human Rights, an educational nonprofit. But she was above all an artist. When Orlando died, her terracotta clay sculptures were on display at a cooperative gallery on Washington's P Street.⁴⁸ "After the coup," she said, "I stopped painting and turned to sculpture. I had seen death, I had seen mangled bodies, and I had developed a very tender feeling for the human body. We only have the skin that covers us, and bullets and knives enter so easily."⁴⁹

After September 21, Isabel's life changed drastically in three ways. First, she was now a single mother, with four young sons facing life choices.

"I had to do it myself, there was no point in feeling sorry for myself. I didn't want my kids to see it. The meals were on time, the clothes were clean, they kept going to school. I devoted all my efforts to making a normal life within the abnormality."⁵⁰

For Isabel personally, "My soul turned upside-down." "It was the loss of a companion of twenty years, with whom I shared so much. . . . I felt horribly alone."⁵¹ James Gordon, a psychiatrist who saw Isabel often in the following years, summarized the impact of the bombing on her: "Orlando was the center of Isabel's existence and with his assassination the center disappeared. Isabel's life was shattered."⁵²

When she buried her husband in Caracas, "never had I felt so abandoned." In Venezuela, when she inquired into returning to Chile, the Chilean Embassy stamped an "L" for "listed" in her passport, which barred her from her native country. "It was terrible," she recounted a decade later, tearing up.⁵³ "I had no visa to return to the U.S. I was totally isolated in Venezuela, totally helpless, with no job and no money. I truly feared that my children would go hungry. Finally, the U.S. Embassy in Venezuela paroled us into the U.S.A. for humanitarian reasons and I received a work permit."⁵⁴

"Orlando's family in their own grief, refused to reach out to either her or her children," wrote Gordon. "Her own family, except for her mother and one of her brothers, were too terrified of the reprisals from the Pinochet dictatorship to provide emotional or economic support."⁵⁵ One exception in Chile was Fabiola Letelier, Orlando's sister and a lawyer, who had worked to get him released from Dawson Island.⁵⁶

Back in Washington, said Isabel, "neighbors thought we were involved with terrorists if not terrorists ourselves. My children were isolated, angry, and unable to understand what had happened. For at least six years, very few [people] came to see us or visit us. Many times we felt shunned and alone."⁵⁷ Even at IPS, otherwise hardboiled activists were less than thrilled at being the targets of terrorists because of their association with Chilean exiles. Some were afraid to ride in a car with Letelier's widow. One was angry about IPS leaders having "signed us up for a death trip without asking."⁵⁸

Like the Karpens, some of Letelier's pain came out through her body. I "felt myself aging. . . . I could begin to feel myself growing weak and tired." She also put on weight, which depressed her. For years, she felt exhausted and forgetful.[59] Though she occasionally still displayed her art, she stopped producing it.[60]

As Letelier suggested, her boys were equally distraught. Saul Landau remembered seeing Pancho and one of his brothers on September 21. They looked like "glazed teenagers, no idea what had happened, so incredibly traumatized, between grief and incomprehension."[61] Many expected them to live up to their father's standards, something Isabel judged "Orlando would not have tolerated." Why be a painter and not a politician? some asked Francisco. The expectation that these young men would become martyrs for their father's cause only compounded their grief. It also "tore at the fabric of the relationship between them and Isabel," concluded Gordon.[62]

"I think that's a bunch of hogwash," countered Francisco years later. "We never even talked about it!"[63]

After his father's death, Cristián, the oldest at nineteen, "felt a deep sense of personal violation and fell into a prolonged depression."

Cristián had assumed he would follow in his father's political footsteps, but now that seemed impossible. He also had lost his faith in justice. He tried his hand at different jobs, with little success. He lived in Colorado, Washington, D.C., Copenhagen, Cuba, back to Washington, and New York. At twenty-three he headed to California and earned a master's degree in marine affairs. He eventually found success as an actor in B movies and as a fitness expert. He "absolutely" escaped the violence of Chile through the "bubble" of the movies. "I did my own sort of therapy" in California: martial arts, athleticism, modeling, and commercial after commercial.[64]

"Something is wrong, there are deep psychological issues I know I should be dealing with but don't know where to start," he wrote in 1991.[65]

José was seventeen and a freshman at the University of Maryland in September 1976. He worked part-time as Sears Roebuck & Co., and the murder of Letelier frightened his employers, who fired him. "To live in Washington D.C. in the late 70's and to have the name Letelier was for all practical purposes taboo; it was like having the plague." In 1979, he left Washington for the University of California, Berkeley, "where I felt the distance and the more liberal attitude of Northern California would permit me to function more normally." José found himself living on welfare, but he obtained a scholarship and, in 1984, a master's in arts with honors from Berkeley.[66]

Francisco, the third son, wrote of his own path: "Losing my father signified an immense change in my plans for the future and my expectations of institutions, justice, and education."

"The assassination was a powerful message to me. There really was no safety for individuals who spoke out and who had justice guide their acts."

"Adults would put their hands on my shoulder and tell me that I had a big responsibility," which "only served to accentuate my loss of direction."[67]

In summer 1977, Francisco and José went to the Eleventh World Festival of Youth and Studies in Cuba, and many there wanted them to come back for military training—they even offered training to Isabel. None of the Leteliers accepted—"I'm not really that into guns," said Francisco the artist.[68]

Francisco transformed his "burning rage" into "strength, into inspiration and action."[69] He first helped create a mural to his father in Washington's Rock Creek Park.[70] At eighteen he moved to Oakland and enrolled at the then-California College of Arts and Crafts. He met several artists, including Chile's René Castro. He earned a scholarship to Berkeley.

Like two of his brothers, he married a woman who had suffered similar hardship, in his case "great personal losses in her family because of political events."

Still, Francisco found it "hard to develop a sense of belonging to anything, anywhere, anyone."[71] He did join other artists as part of the Orlando Letelier Muralist Brigade. In the 1980s, he would trek down to Nicaragua to paint murals.[72]

The youngest, Juan Pablo, a high school senior in 1976–77, worked after school, he wrote, "to try to somehow fill up the hours of each day. I obviously felt a great distance with my peers due to the dramatic experience our family had lived.... My isolation was compounded by the hostility of many people toward myself and my family. Some of my friend's [sic] parents forced them to stay away from me out of fear that they too would become victims of terrorism. Others engaged in outrageous assaults on my father's character in efforts to protect or justify his killers."

He went to college in the Washington area to stay close to his mother. But, he recalled, his father's "absence made it extremely difficult to regain the family unity, which was so important to us in the past." At nineteen, he traveled to Mexico "in search of my latin [sic] roots." There, he studied economics as his father had. He lived off meager scholarships. He also took a grant to study in East Germany. He eventually returned to Chile "to seek a homeland, my father's roots and my identity with him."[73]

Between 1976 and 1991, Isabel Letelier and her four boys were together only once. As Francisco explained, "Orlando's murder deprived us [not only] of a father and husband but also of each other."[74]

"Death makes one very lonely," Isabel observed in late 1978.[75]

>> After caring for her family, Letelier's second great challenge was to continue her husband's work. Publicly, she did not let on that she needed the money. But privately, "we had to live with a small salary at a time when my sons needed support for their education. I could barely cope, really, with all of this, and with trying to raise my sons. We had debts. We had to sell our home. We were truly impoverished. The first years I could not buy clothes for myself or our sons. Both of my younger sons worked to earn money for our household."[76] Letelier and Moffitt both had life insurance through IPS, so their survivors received 1.5 times their salary.[77] Isabel soon moved out of the Ogden Street house and into a small brick colonial on 36th Street NW with a dogwood in front.[78] She could have gone back to something safe, such as sculpture or teaching, but neither paid enough. "You can't live off Spanish class with four sons," she explained in 2017.[79]

The bombing at Sheridan Circle threw her, theretofore a socially aware but not deeply political person, into the role of leader of Chilean exiles. Chileans now looked to this widow to carry on the consciousness-raising, human-rights-reporting, and sanctions-lobbying crusade of her husband.

Shortly after Orlando's death, IPS hired Isabel as the director of its Human Rights Project, director of the Third World Women's Project, and a member of the selection committee for the Letelier-Moffitt Human Rights Award, which would be given each year at a banquet around September 21. Her positions now required tireless speaking tours and countless hours of fund-raising. Letelier also joined many boards of nongovernmental organizations. She even wrote a report with Michael Moffitt in 1979.[80] Through her work, "she really influenced thousands of people, both men and women," assessed Francisco.[81]

One strategy she pursued was to identify as one of the perhaps half a million Chilean exiles scattered around fifty countries. She spoke of the grief, uncertainty, and hardship of her fellow expatriates. In 1978, as many as three-quarters of them were jobless, and exiles were "often physically or psychologically ill."[82] Letelier saw them as resilient, able to, for instance, recover from torture. But they needed help, especially in the United States, where the government left them to fend for themselves. In contrast, she said,

Canada offered "language programs, study programs, and jobs for people. In Holland and Sweden exiles are paid while they study. Cuba provides for the sick among exiles."[83]

She especially spoke to and for other Chilean women. In a speech to the U.N. Commission on Human Rights in December 1976, she argued that "the reason why I am here today, irrespective of my personal tragedy, is that as a Chilean woman I speak for the grief endured by thousands of women in my country and for their anger at the crimes committed by the DINA."[84] In June 1977, she wrote to President Carter on behalf of twenty-four women and two men on a hunger strike at the United Nations, for him to support an investigation of the 1,500 "disappeared" in Chile.[85] One of her IPS guests was the first ever to advocate against female genital mutilation. The Third World Women's Project was "the thing I've done that I liked the best," she assessed four decades later.[86]

As the months passed, Letelier traveled throughout the United States and Europe, from small college towns to bustling capitals. She directed a study updating and centralizing information on violations in Chile. She established a traveling Volkswagen van, called the Human Rights Mobile Education Project, to carry her message on panels and slides to churches and other communities around the United States. She established a speakers bureau.[87] She gave countless interviews to local reporters. She accepted posthumous awards on behalf of her husband.[88] All this she did while continuing to be the president of the Chile Committee for Human Rights.

》》 The third drastic change in Letelier's life was taking on the quest to bring her husband's murderers to justice.

In the months following the assassination, she spoke throughout the United States to focus attention on Pinochet's likely responsibility for the assassination. College and local newspapers covered her talks, as did local radio and television. Often with Michael Moffitt, she met with college presidents and church leaders.[89]

The ongoing IPS investigation seemed at first to reveal the lack of seriousness of the FBI investigation. While Saul Landau, Ralph Stavins, and other IPS associates uncovered evidence pointing to DINA, Eugene Propper and the FBI insisted on pursuing *all* leads. IPS criticized leaks at the attorney general's office and the FBI, the "harassment" of IPS, the smearing of liberal members of Congress, and theories about leftist assassins.[90] The FBI, meanwhile, judged IPS's own information to be invalid and declared that "under no circumstances" would it share intelligence.[91]

All these cul-de-sacs frustrated Isabel. Most maddening, however, were "the smear campaigns against Orlando and against myself. Someone wrote that Orlando was a KGB agent. Another that I had placed the bomb because Orlando had kept a mistress. A statement was made and published in the *Congressional Record* that I might be a Cuban agent. The press were constantly haranguing me, the FBI, reporters, on and on and on."[92] Even the Far Left got in on the blame game, pointing the finger at the CIA. Letelier considered this wrong both on the facts and as a strategy.[93]

Among the smears, none was so persistent as the accusation that Orlando was an agent for the communist Cuban government. It had emerged from anticommunist fire-breathers such as Senator Jesse Helms, Republican of North Carolina, and Representative Larry McDonald, Democrat from Georgia, who came back to the canard again and again.

Letelier-as-agent gained real traction beginning on December 20, 1976, two months after the assassination, when Jack Anderson and Les Whitten headlined their syndicated column "Letelier's 'Havana Connection.'" They had obtained from someone in the investigation—likely a Washington police officer—copies of the contents of Letelier's black Samsonite briefcase, in the Chevelle with him during the explosion. The briefcase contained Bayer aspirin, two Joan Baez records, a black sleeping mask, a booklet called *Promise of America*, a Dutch newspaper, an address book, and sundry paperwork and letters.[94]

Among these banal items, one document seemed damning: a letter to Letelier from Beatrice "Tati" Allende, daughter of the Chilean socialist president, written from Havana, where her husband was a Cuban official. She wrote that she would be sending Letelier a $5,000 payment "to support your work," followed by a monthly $1,000. Isabel admitted that Allende sent money but explained that it came from the Chilean Socialist Party in exile, not from the Cuban government. Anderson and Whitten remained suspicious.[95]

As if the leak of the documents were not enough, Letelier also learned that the Justice Department did not know exactly what had been in her husband's briefcase. She stormed into Gene Propper's office.

"Mr. Propper, I am astonished. . . . Is it possible that an inventory of the objects in the briefcase does not exist in the Justice Department?"

"You must understand, Mrs. Letelier, that many of the documents were in Spanish," said Propper lamely. "That's why the Police Department could not classify them. You know how the Police Department is. . . ."

"Well, I know that they're very inefficient."

"Mrs. Letelier, we can't have a conversation with this tone."

"And we haven't been able to get correct, responsible information. How can you know if a document is missing or if a document has been added later if there never was a list of the contents of the briefcase?"

"I assure you, Mrs. Letelier, that it is impossible that anything of the kind took place."

"Tell me, would it be possible for something like that to happen?"

"Who are you trying to implicate as the author of such an act?"

"Let's just say a ghost or something like that. I'm not yet accusing anyone in particular."

". . . In any case," Propper finally promised, "you may be very sure that you have all the contents of the briefcase."

"That's the same thing you told me some time ago. Nevertheless, several things have appeared since. Things which have been very efficiently distributed among right-wing journalists."

"I have nothing to do with that. It's impossible to control the press. We regret it deeply. We did everything we could."[96]

Also in response to the briefcase leak, Letelier founded the Action Committee on the Letelier-Moffitt Assassinations to counter the smearing of her husband in the media.[97] She made her own speeches calling for more transparency from both the U.S. and Chilean governments and labeling the briefcase controversy "a cover-up started by former CIA and FBI agents."[98] By early February of the following year, the FBI reported that the Havana money now carried "little significance in their investigation of Letelier's killing."[99]

Still, several journalists continued to paint Orlando Letelier as an "agent" of the Castro government, especially the many outlets associated with William F. Buckley and his *National Review*.[100] Rowland Evans and Robert Novak, for instance, denounced how some of Orlando's funds helped finance a trip to Mexico by liberal congressman Michael Harrington. They cited another briefcase letter, this one from Orlando back to Tati, that outlined his tactic of playing the human rights card with U.S. "liberals" so as to not associate them with his own socialism. To the columnists, this made for "a particularly embarrassing instance of idealistic liberal congressmen manipulated by the dashing, handsome Letelier."[101] Jeffrey Hart called Letelier "a Communist agent, a revolutionary leading a double life."[102]

"It is as if they want to prove that he deserved to die," said one Washington journalist who disapproved of the smear.[103] Former California governor Ronald Reagan was a notable voice in this endeavor, using his popular radio commentaries to spread the innuendo of anti-Castro journalist Virginia Prewett, for instance, that Marxists killed Letelier. "Alive he could be compromised; dead he could become a martyr. And the left didn't lose a minute in making him one," said Reagan. "I don't know the answer," he claimed disingenuously, "but it is a question worth asking."[104]

The day of the Evans-Novak "revelation," Isabel's attorney, Michael Tigar, opened the briefcase to the press to diffuse the rumors. The *Washington Post* observed that "it appears that the columns have followed the darkest possible interpretation of the scanty material."[105] Saul Landau explained the briefcase flap as a conspiracy "to distract attention from the suspected killers and to shield the repressive Chilean government." Tati sent the money because she was a party treasurer; she just happened to live in Cuba. The funds were not from the Cuban government but from Western European and U.S. labor unions and social democratic parties and religious groups.[106] Letelier wrote to the *Washington Star* to denounce that paper's own Jeremiah O'Leary and "other right-wing columnists," claiming they were being used for a "cover-up." Simply put, she concluded, there was no "mystery" in the briefcase.[107]

≫ "We're on the same side on this one," Gene Propper tried to reassure Letelier and her friends at IPS.[108] He and his team needed cooperation from the Letelier and Moffitt families, if only to keep them from complaining to reporters that the investigation was too slow or on the wrong track. "Saul," Carter Cornick similarly vowed to IPS's Landau, "I want to get the people who did this. I want all of them. And I can promise you that we'll go wherever we have to go to get them."[109]

A first meeting between Letelier and the FBI occurred on October 21, 1976, a month after the Sheridan Circle bombing. She was already annoyed that "according to Mr. Propper the idea of a passion crime has been dismissed. Yet he still persists in questioning me about it."[110] Attorney General Edward Levi informed her that he put "some 100" agents on the case and assured her, in her words, "that the investigation is still open, that more information is coming in daily from Caracas, and that they are very optimistic that perhaps in a month or so they will know what happened."[111] He also denied that Propper and his team "are ignorant of international relations" and reported "full cooperation" by the CIA, State Department, and the president. Letelier claimed to feel better, and she corrected erroneous reports that the FBI was not focusing on Chile. Isabel, Michael, and lawyer Tigar wanted to subpoena the CIA to force it to hand over its files on DINA and Cuban exiles.¹¹² In the hallway after the meeting, Tigar asked Propper, "Why not subpoena the CIA?" He responded: "If I issued a subpoena for records of the CIA that they didn't want to produce they'd say they didn't have them and then destroy them." *So much for "full cooperation,"* thought Tigar.¹¹³

On December 8, at a second meeting with Levi, Propper announced, "We've eliminated all leads except the political motive, the South American connection, the Chile-anti-Castro Cuban connection, and that's where the great bulk of the investigation is going." But he refrained from telling Letelier that he also had an eye on DINA, figuring IPS would leak it to the press and "any source we had down in Chile would dry up immediately."¹¹⁴

Levi's successor, Griffin Bell, at first denied Letelier a meeting, but then, advised as to the "political implications" of the case, he relented.¹¹⁵ At what was now, six months after the bombing, her third meeting with an attorney general, she, Moffitt, and others from IPS heard Bell's sympathies for their fallen comrades. Great, they responded, but what about a special prosecutor? Bell vowed in his southern drawl, "There won't be any special prosecutors while I'm attorney general."¹¹⁶

By August 1977, Letelier was growing impatient, especially after Carter met with Pinochet during the Panama Canal treaties signing. With Moffitt, she wrote the president and asked for a meeting "to discuss the assassinations and human rights questions raised by the murders."¹¹⁷ National security adviser Zbigniew Brzezinski recommended not meeting with them, "given the sensitivity of the evidence surrounding the assassination." He suggested instead that First Lady Rosalynn Carter see them "to convey our deepest sympathies."¹¹⁸ Brzezinski also saw "no reason to be defensive about seeing Pinochet given the context of the treaty ceremonies."¹¹⁹ He eventually wrote to Letelier offering a White House meeting with the president's counselor, Robert Lipshutz.¹²⁰ "Brzezinski didn't help at all," Letelier later recalled. "We could never get through to him. Never."¹²¹

By September, Letelier grew more trusting of Propper and the FBI, as Saul Landau wrote, "not because they are the authorities but because we grew to respect their honesty and integrity in this case." Largely, this conclusion stemmed from the Justice Department's admission that it now suspected DINA.¹²²

>> September 1977 signaled the approach of the first anniversary of the Sheridan Circle bombing. That month, Isabel Letelier participated in six events in Washington, in addition to more in Amherst, Boston, San Francisco, and Los Angeles.¹²³

To a crowd at DePaul University in Chicago, she described the last twelve months as "a terrible year in some ways, a wonderful year in others. Grief and pain, loneliness and anguish. But strength, determination and moments when I laughed and felt like a young activist, filled with the optimism that we usually associate with youth. It has been a year of bitterness, when I had to see Orlando and Ronni's murderer parade down the same street where Pinochet had his men detonated the bomb," she added, referring to the visit by Pinochet and Manuel Contreras to Washington.[124]

Letelier had spent much of the year appealing for contributions to what would be the Letelier-Moffitt Memorial Fund for Human Rights.[125] The assassinations, its call for donations explained, "symbolize the cruel and violent denial of human rights which is methodically on the increase in the world today."[126] She and Michael Moffitt helped raise $34,000, which went to fund their investigation of the assassinations, to organize memorial activities, and to support research in human rights violations.[127]

Isabel summarized her first year of life without Orlando: "I've had no time to be a sad widow. There has been too much to do."[128]

》》 The year 1978 started on a more hopeful note. "There was this convergence" between the families and IPS on one side and the Justice Department and the FBI on the other, said attorney Sam Buffone, who worked pro bono for the Letelier and Moffitt families for decades.[129] Michael Moffitt, the most abrasive among the family members, even praised Carter Cornick, the most abrasive among the investigators, as "a damn good cop."[130]

On March 1, 1978, Letelier finally got her meeting with Robert Lipshutz, counsel to President Carter. He candidly told her that "this case may not be resolved to everyone's total satisfaction." "The world is still waiting for a satisfactory conclusion of this case," she reminded him.[131] Her own recollection of the meeting was being told that the investigation would go the distance no matter the consequences. "We will not forget that promise," she responded.[132]

Of that, there would be no chance. Propper's letters rogatory had already landed in Chile.

11

Events Are Developing at Such a Rapid Pace

After the publication of the names "Juan Williams Rose" and "Alejandro Romeral Jara" in Chile produced no one, the U.S. embassy revealed to journalists, "We know the names are fictitious." It was tipping its hand to the Chileans that more was to come.[1] On March 2, 1978, the FBI leaked the photos of the two mystery men to *Washington Star* journalist Jeremiah O'Leary, whom Robert Steven of the State Department described as "very professional."[2] On March 3, the *Star* ran the story with the photos across its front page, including the threat that the U.S. government was ready to sever relations with Chile. That day, the photos were wired to newspapers around the world. Tips as to the men's identity began pouring in to the U.S. embassy and to newspapers.

The clock ticked away. On March 5, Chile's most influential newspaper identified "Juan Williams" as "Michael V. Townley, a North American electronic technician resident in Santiago from 1970."[3]

Eugene Propper learned of the breakthrough when Larry Barcella called him.

"Have you heard about Juan Williams?"

"What about him?"

"Then you haven't. You're too calm," said Barcella. "Are you sitting down?"

"Yeah, I'm sitting on a desk," said Propper. "What is it?"

"They identified Juan Williams down in Chile, Gene. The blond Chilean turns out to be an American named Michael Vernon Townley!"

"What? How do they know?"

"It was in *El Mercurio* yesterday down in Santiago," explained Barcella. "People are going crazy in Chile. ... A lot of people seem to know the guy.

He's a fuckin' American!"[4] The news that a U.S. citizen may be responsible for the death of Letelier and Moffitt "shocked U.S. officials" in Washington, reported O'Leary.[5]

Two days later, Chileans leaked the other man's name, and by March 9 the Department of State confirmed that "Alejandro Romeral" was "in all probability" Army Captain Armando Fernández Larios after an employee of the Organization of American States fingered him.[6] Even Fernández's sister Rose Marie in Centerville, Virginia, admitted that the photo looked just like her brother.[7]

After moving along at a snail's pace for a year and a half, the investigation suddenly overwhelmed the FBI. "In view of the fact that events in captioned matter are developing at such a rapid pace," the Washington office cabled to the director, "all offices conducting investigation in this matter are hereby requested to furnish summaries by teletype for the bureau, Washington Field, Newark, New York and Miami."[8]

A few days after receiving the letters rogatory, the Chilean ambassador in Washington, Jorge Cauas, flew back to Santiago and resigned, citing the accusations against his government as a cause.[9] Chilean newspapers, which chafed under the regime's censorship, suddenly found themselves free to broadcast all the details of this case since they piggybacked on a U.S. story. And *this* story sold newspapers! What's more, Chilean journalists used *el caso Letelier* to demand transparency from their government.[10] Questions arose everywhere in the press and diplomatic meeting rooms: How did Townley, the son of a wealthy executive, become a mechanic? How did he speak Spanish so well? Had he killed someone in Concepción? Whom did he know in the U.S. government? Was he CIA? "No way," said a former marine guard at the embassy. "If the CIA is hiring that kind of guy, this country is in real trouble!"[11] Who ordered him to kill Letelier? *Penthouse* magazine reported falsely that Chile paid Cuban exiles $1 million for the hit.[12] The most crucial question was, How did these two men obtain diplomatic passports to travel to the United States in 1976?

>> The press in Chile, however, also came to the defense of Pinochet. All mainstream newspapers saw in the letters rogatory an affront to national pride. None believed that a Chilean could be involved. Pablo Rodríguez, formerly of Fatherland and Freedom and now a columnist, smelled "a sordid CIA plot against Chile."

"This government has nothing to do with the Letelier crime," asserted Pinochet on March 10, breaking his silence on the case. He called the U.S.

request for the two men "a well-mounted campaign, like all campaigns mounted by the communists, to discredit the government. When the truth is known, it will be seen that in Chile there is innocence." He added, for good measure, that Fernández did not even look like the photo of "Romeral."[13] Throughout, Chilean officials claimed not to know Townley or where he was. No one seemed to know the location of the Williams and Romeral passports or who signed them. The practice was to burn returned passports every two years.[14]

But the truth did not exactly reveal Chilean innocence. Manuel Contreras no longer headed DINA, but Townley remained intensely loyal to him. When the scandal broke, the blue-eyed American received a call from Contreras.

"Everything will be fine, I think. My General Contreras wants to see me," Townley told his wife, Mariana Callejas, after hanging up. Contreras hadn't elaborated.

"I'm going with you."

"No. It's not a good idea. He wouldn't like it."

"I'm going anyway," insisted Mariana, headstrong as always. "I will not leave you alone with him."

It turned out that Townley would never have been alone with Contreras, who showed up in a three-car motorcade. Townley got into one car, Callejas in another, and Contreras was in the third. They drove to Nicos Pizza, where Townley walked up to Contreras, who sat in the back of his gray Peugeot, smiling softly. Callejas went into Nicos and there saw Fernández, in civilian clothes, so "very serious" that he would not look at her.[15] Instead he joined the two men in the car.

"I have arranged for you both to go down south, to the farm, where you will be safe from all this in case something should go wrong," the ex-DINA chief told his two worried subordinates.[16] Alternatively, Townley could flee Chile.[17]

"I won't leave Santiago," said Townley.[18] He had never disobeyed Contreras before, but he knew that Chile's south might prove a dungeon from which he would never emerge. "I told General Contreras that under no circumstances would I run away," Townley later recalled.[19] He also informed Contreras that he had secreted away files of his DINA crimes outside the country.[20]

Contreras let Townley and Callejas remain at their house in Santiago. He also arranged for a cover-up story: if forced to confess, Townley would say he had gone to Paraguay on an official DINA mission and returned to

Santiago; that he had never traveled to the United States; that Fernández was indeed to go to Washington, but merely to obtain a list of U.S. politicians sympathetic to Chile, and that his mission never took place. With Fernández, they agreed on the tale.[21] Contreras told the same lies to Pinochet and his cabinet, and even produced two other men as "Williams" and "Romeral."[22]

Sensing the flimsiness of Contreras's assurances, Townley and Callejas consulted a lawyer, Manuel Acuña.

After they had recounted recent events, Acuña looked at them in disbelief. "Do you have any idea of the seriousness of your predicament?"

"Yes," they said. "What can be done?"

The lawyer thought for a minute. "There's a real risk of death," he said, not exactly reassuring them. "If Michael dies, or disappears, the problem will vanish."

"But *I'll* talk," interjected Callejas.

"Sure, but your testimony is not very valid, you're not directly involved. What's more, you could disappear too. Since it will be difficult for Michael to hide in Chile, I suggest that you seek refuge in notoriety."

"What do you mean?"

"Go public, so that everyone knows you. The press is dying for news. Talk to them, talk a lot."

"But we can't tell the truth."

"That doesn't matter. Say anything. Get yourself noticed."[23]

Townley had to maintain the pretense that he was missing, so Callejas took naturally to dealing with the press, her talents as a storyteller serving her well at first. But she lied so often and outrageously that she lost all credibility with journalists. She first told the press that she was only a "close friend" of Townley and had not seen him in four years.[24] Later she admitted to being his wife and said he was hiding somewhere down south.[25] Two weeks later she said that her husband was with friends in Santiago but that he had "nothing to do" with killing Letelier. "He is not an assassin." After claiming she was tired of the media's lies, she lied that no Chilean was involved in the assassination.[26]

>> While Callejas fabricated, the U.S. government investigated. As soon as Townley's name was made public, agents at the Justice Department and the FBI frantically pieced together physical evidence against him, including bills indicating telephone calls he made from his sister's house in North Tarrytown, New York, and from a favorite Cuban Nationalist Movement bar to

that same house. Townley even called Guillermo Novo's direct number two days before the assassination. The FBI also found evidence of Townley purchasing espionage equipment in Florida and a receipt for paging devices in an apartment used by Alvin Ross.[27] The puzzle was coming together.

On March 18, the Chileans announced they would produce "Williams" and "Romeral" for questioning. Gene Propper and Carter Cornick landed in Santiago the following morning. Propper and his beard roused some suspicions among conservative Chilean officials—was he a hippie? a Jew?[28] The Americans met with their ambassador, George Landau, who explained that Townley's citizenship changed the U.S. strategy. "We'll tell them: 'Give him to us. He's ours,'" he told the visitors. That sounded good to Propper.[29] The Department of Justice also saw Townley as "the key who can link the Chileans presumably responsible for the commissioning of the murder of Letelier with the Cubans who allegedly carried it out."[30] In other words, they would only ask for Townley, but with his testimony they would take aim at all the coconspirators.

Unbeknownst to the Americans, Contreras was on the outs. On March 21, Pinochet personally grilled Contreras. When he found out that one of his most loyal subordinates had lied to him, he asked for his resignation.[31] The CIA assessed the move as calculated to take pressure off Pinochet, "but it could backfire. If Contreras is implicated, it will be difficult for Pinochet to escape guilt by association."[32] Once the most feared person in Chile, Contreras was supposedly "completely shocked" by his ouster.[33] Now out of the military, he also feared civil prosecution.[34]

The new head of the secret police, General Odlanier Mena, reported to Pinochet that Townley was probably just an "occasional informer" for DINA but that the tales told by Townley, Fernández, and Contreras were suspicious enough to merit investigation.[35] Many officers smelled the same rat.

At the same time, Chilean courts presented the two alternative "Williams" and "Romeral" to the Americans. The Chilean lawyer working for the U.S. government barely looked at the two imposters before telling the judge, "These are not the men we are looking for!"[36] "As far as I'm concerned," warned Propper, "the letters rogatory won't be complied with until you produce the men in the pictures."

Propper and Landau were outraged. They saw no trace of a manhunt and were certain that the Chileans were instead prevaricating while hiding Townley. Early on the morning of March 23, the ambassador demanded a meeting with Foreign Minister Patricio Carvajal. There, Landau abruptly dropped all the diplomatic politesse he had practiced over his career and threatened that, if Townley was not made to answer the U.S. government's questions, *all* U.S. relations with Chile would be endangered. This could mean a complete halt in trade, loans, investment, and diplomatic relations — a devastating blow to Chile. "Frankly, I don't believe your people are trying very hard," Landau blurted, landing the knockout punch. The Chileans threw in the towel.[37] Townley and Fernández would submit to judicial questioning.

It took six more days for Chile to produce Townley. On March 29 and 30, for 10.5 and 8 hours, respectively, the American-Chilean appeared for questioning by the head of army intelligence, General Héctor Orozco. He was driven to his testimony at the Ministry of Defense in a speeding Chevy Nova, bolted out before it screeched to a stop, and ran inside with two guards and his lawyer to avoid the over fifty journalists assembled.[38] The following day, a Chilean judge put to him the fifty-five questions sent by the District of Columbia's grand jury. Townley answered six before refusing to answer the rest on the grounds of self-incrimination. He denied any involvement in the Letelier-Moffitt assassination. Fernández did the same, except that he now added to his story having gone to Washington to visit his sister.[39]

The Americans knew Townley was lying about almost everything, so their goal became to question him back in the United States. They needed to get him out of Chile before he fled or was killed. On the evening of April 3, Cornick and Propper, joined now by FBI special agent Robert Scherrer from Buenos Aires, met with top Chilean intelligence officials and impressed upon them the "extreme urgency that the U.S. Government attached to the immediate expulsion of Michael Vernon Townley." The Chileans countered that Townley had an outstanding arrest warrant against him for involuntary manslaughter in Concepción, so they could probably deliver him only in about two weeks. The following day, Landau further pressed the acting foreign minister in what a colleague described with no little admiration as "some very firm table-pounding."[40]

"We wanted Townley and we wanted him the worst way," recalled Landau.[41]

Pinochet, meanwhile, still insisted on his government's innocence and that Contreras's resignation had "nothing to do" with Letelier. But he lifted the state of siege, released 400 prisoners convicted by military courts, and allowed key exiles to return.[42] On April 5, he added that his "conscience" was "clean." "We will do everything possible to get to the truth and see that those who are responsible are punished, whatever their position or nationality."[43] In truth, Townley's citizenship solved a problem for Pinochet. By turning over the American, he could claim to have collaborated with the United States while being vindicated that no Chilean was involved.

Townley heard rumors of his possible expulsion, which was a quicker process than deportation, but he judged the prospect unlikely. Besides, there was the warrant in Concepción, and the law provided twenty-four hours for an appeal before the Supreme Court.

Townley seemed to forget that the police state to which he pledged his loyalty operated outside the law when it suited it. On April 7, 1978, on the fifteenth floor of the Diego Portales building out of which Pinochet ruled, Pinochet's political team met, setting as its tasks avoiding expulsion and keeping Townley in Chile. Suddenly the French doors of the meeting room swung open and in walked Pinochet. The dictator rarely descended below his twenty-second floor. This meant something.

"Please continue, don't mind me," the strongman instructed his advisers while he paced behind their chairs. Then he interrupted: "We were doing so well, so well, ready to take off," no doubt referring to Chile's rapidly declining inflation. "And then this! This is a banana peel, *señores*!"

He seemed to ponder for a moment. "A banana peel!" he repeated. "If we step on it, the government will fall. *We* will fall!" As abruptly as he entered, he left the room. Pinochet's outburst seemed to change the momentum of the meeting. Talk of avoiding expulsion switched to handing Townley over. After all, a 1975 decree did allow the president to expel foreigners who violated residence requirements. On this Santiago would hang its legal case.[44]

The Americans in Washington soon came to an agreement with the Chileans: Chile would expel Townley if U.S. prosecutors promised to keep any information about DINA activities other than the Letelier-Moffitt assassination out of the press and from other governments. Propper also agreed to stay mum on the agreement itself.[45] The pact became known as the Montero-Silbert agreement.

Meanwhile, at her mother's house and with no idea where her husband was, Callejas received a call. It was Mena, the head of the secret police, calling her from her own home.

"*Señora*, please come to your house immediately."

As she sped her Fiat 125 home, Callejas wondered what has happened. *Had Michael died? Had he fled south?* She found Mena, a tall, distinguished man, standing next to her fireplace, surrounded by 100 or so security personnel. They had completely dismantled the second floor of her Lo Curro house that had served as a DINA office.

"I have bad news for you, *señora*," announced Mena. "Your husband is leaving."

"For Concepción?"

"No. For the United States. I'm sorry. There is no alternative. Your husband must be extradited. For the good of this country, because it is legal, because in truth the United States holds all the cards, . . . for *la patria*. It must be done."

"No, I will not allow it!" screamed Callejas. "You're making a grave error. I want to meet with General Pinochet."

"*Señora*, at this hour, that is not possible."

Callejas was driven to see Townley, who had already been taken into custody. She found him dejected, anxious, his face contorted in anguish. They said goodbye. Callejas was sure that her husband would soon die.[46]

At 9 A.M. on April 8, Scherrer was in his Santiago hotel room, about to brush his teeth (Propper had returned to Washington), when a man who refused to identify himself called.

"Get out to Pudahuel Airport right away," said the stranger. "Townley will be on the Ecuadoriana Airlines flight 052 scheduled to leave at nine forty-five. Don't worry about tickets and reservations. We'll take care of that. Please hurry, Townley's lawyer is maneuvering." Adding to the urgency was a rumor that two parachute regiments loyal to Contreras were to rescue Townley at the airport.

Scherrer called Landau, worried that Ecuadoriana Airlines might hold Townley in Ecuador, where it was scheduled for a layover. Landau brushed off his concerns: "We have to take the risk. It may be our only chance to get him."

A half-hour later, Scherrer and Cornick, leaving their luggage behind, were driven right onto the runway to the plane, where airport authorities had delayed the flight. A few minutes later, men with machine guns emerged from the airport, and a car approached and let out Townley, his hands cuffed at his waist. He walked up the steps, plopped himself in his seat, raised his handcuffed hands to his face, and wept. Across town, his lawyer was simultaneously presenting an appeal.

Cornick sat next to the prisoner. "Mike, you understand, don't you, that you are in deep trouble and you will be arrested as soon as we reach United States soil?"

"I didn't think you were taking me on a picnic with these handcuffs."[47]

In the wee hours of the next day, April 9, when the plane touched down in Baltimore, Cornick formally arrested Michael Townley.[48]

>> At this point, Propper did not even know what role Townley had played in the killing of Letelier and Moffitt or how the bomb had gotten under the Chevelle. He suspected the American was merely a courier between DINA and the Cubans. The evidence the Justice Department had on Townley was scant. They could prosecute him on passport fraud but little else. If he refused to talk, they might have no case.

Just as they were growing desperate, luck intervened.

On April 11, while Townley was held in Fort Meade, Maryland, an officer in Miami spotted a man who, underneath his shaggy brown wig, looked a lot like Guillermo Novo. Sitting next to him was a ringer for Alvin Ross. FBI agents soon were following the man who matched Novo's description riding in a gray Lincoln Continental registered to Ross. For three harrowing days, they followed, lost, and again found and followed Novo, Ross, and another man through Little Havana traffic, in restaurants, in bars, and in an apartment.

Finally, on April 14, the FBI was sure of the targets, had gathered enough agents, and had a signed arrest warrant. Agents pulled over the Lincoln and found in it not only Ross but a Derringer pistol, a .45-caliber automatic, two .38-caliber Smith & Wessons, a weighing scale, a large plastic bag full of cocaine, birth certificates for a large number of men, "and some wigs and other disguise materials." The cocaine—worth $30,000 on the street—was allegedly to finance an exodus to Mexico.[49]

In a nearby Holiday Inn, the FBI confronted Novo. When he saw the agents enter the lobby with local police, he "hurriedly got on the elevator" and, unbeknownst to Novo, so did an undercover special agent. Novo pressed the button for the eighth floor. "At the eight[h] floor," went the FBI report, "NOVO exited the elevator and started to walk to the right in the hallway, however, he immediately stopped as the hallway ended by the elevator." This was evidently not Novo's floor or even his hotel. "Novo then turned around and started walking in the opposite direction." The special agent then stopped him and asked him for identification, and Novo produced one bearing the name of Victor Trinquero. When prompted later for another ID, he gave Alvin Ross's. He eventually declared, once he was at the Miami FBI office, "My name is Guillermo Novo."[50] Novo was read his rights in Spanish and charged with violating his probation since he had fled authorities in June of the previous year. Ross was charged with conspiracy to make explosives and incendiary devices, making destructive devices, and storing high explosives.[51]

"I can't believe we got Novo today of all days, after all these months," said Cornick. "God must be an FBI agent."

Immediately hearing of this break in the case, Cornick and Scherrer informed Townley that they had Novo and Ross in custody. "Now it's every man for himself," Cornick told Townley. "The rats are leaving the ship."[52] Townley was "especially disturbed" hearing of Ross's cocaine possession, and Cornick and Scherrer had to explain "that the men were generally unprincipled individuals who dealt in unlawful activities to support themselves between their mercenary contracts."[53]

Townley knew he was cornered. "If they arrest the Cubans," he explained to Callejas, who flew to Fort Meade on April 12, "the Cubans could strike a deal. If I don't deal, I'll go to prison for entering the United States with false passports, at least twice, seven years per entry. They'd give me fourteen years."

"I see no other way but to make a deal," she told him.

Before he spilled his secrets, however, Townley insisted on speaking also with General Orozco, first, to guarantee his family's safety in Chile and, second, to be released from the DINA secrecy oath that had kept him so devoted to Contreras. "After all this," he told Callejas, "I owe him loyalty."

Take the deal, Orozco told the weary and isolated Townley, freeing him from his oath.[54]

On April 18, Townley signed an agreement with the U.S. attorney to give his full testimony. He pled guilty to one count of conspiracy to murder a foreign official. He would not have to discuss any DINA activities outside of the Letelier case. His sentence would be of no more than ten years in prison with the possibility of parole after three years and four months (a third of the maximum). He was also protected from extradition even though the United States and Chile had an extradition treaty—a first in U.S. history. Explaining a generation later the government's leniency, Carter Cornick recalled, "We had good circumstantial evidence" for a murder case against Townley. But "we did not have, in my opinion, a prosecutable case. So what we did was we made a deal with the *worst* possible guy. The government never does that. But without it, we had no case." At the FBI Academy in Quantico, Virginia, Townley paced and chain-smoked as he gave a detailed account of his homicide squad.[55]

On April 26, 1978, Michael Townley was formally charged in court with conspiracy—the first charge in the Letelier case. Dressed in a blue suit, dark striped shirt, and colorful tie, Townley showed no emotion. Propper asked for a $5 million bail, fearing that a DINA-like agency could pay a lesser sum and spirit Townley across the border.[56]

The testimony that Townley gave was invaluable. It confirmed all the suspicions of investigators and contradicted practically none of their other information. Townley even recreated the bomb for the FBI, placing it in an identical Chevelle to prove that he had indeed built the Letelier bomb. "It was an incredible moment," recalled Carter Cornick. "Townley turned white as paper and we were astonished. I could only say, 'My God, the damage is exactly the same on both cars!'"[57]

Over the summer, Townley wrote to Contreras and even to Pinochet, whom he had never met. His letters were largely analytical, pointing to where the government of Chile could have better strategized. Among Chile's missteps, he told Contreras, was the assassination of people outside Chile, which carried too many risks. Never did he express rancor against the two men who betrayed him and remained safe in Chile. He even pleaded for them to pay the Cubans the $25,000 they requested in early 1978 to flee the United States.[58]

In a more emotional, public statement made after his plea agreement, Townley told the Chilean nation as a whole that, after serving his sentence, he had every intention "to return to that country which I hold to be my true and authentic homeland." He reiterated his contention, made during his trial, that he considered both himself and Letelier to be soldiers in a war and thus fair game. "Intelligence and antisubversive wars are wars like any other war. They are wars in which people are killed and people die." Eliminating the leftist was nothing personal. "Mr. Letelier was an important soldier in the Marxist-Socialist ranks, a leader in a war which is using the capitalist society of the free world to attack and ruin our Chile, to cover up the causes and situations which prompted the Chilean armed forces to take action against their own principles in order to salvage and preserve the twisted social and economic wrecks left by the inept, unsuccessful and nefarious socialist experiment." His tone toward Contreras, however, was starting to harden. He disagreed with his expulsion and revealed that Contreras told him to lie and cover up his crime before Chile's investigators.[59]

》》 The expulsion and confession of Townley greatly moved along the Justice Department's case against the Cubans. In his statement, Townley had named ten coconspirators: Contreras, Pedro Espinoza, and Fernández in Chile, and seven Cuban Americans. Prosecutors discarded two of them and focused on the five who had provided material assistance to the conspiracy:

the Novo brothers, Virgilio Paz, Ross, and José Suárez.⁶⁰ On May 5, the FBI arrested Ignacio at his brother-in-law's "after a brief scuffle when he tried escape" through a basement window.⁶¹

Suárez and Paz—the two men who, most believed, had followed Letelier's Chevelle and detonated the bomb—were still on the lam. They were "believed to be hiding in one of the Spanish-speaking communities on the East Coast," and the FBI offered up to $20,000 for information leading to their arrest.⁶² The bureau, however, declined to put them on the Ten Most Wanted List because the added publicity would not help. "Rather than being ostracized for committing a crime abhorrent to the public, they are being embraced, protected, and sheltered by segments of the Cuban exile community."⁶³

As usual, the Cubans were uncooperative. Ross denied knowing anything about the cocaine found in his Lincoln Continental in Miami, and his prints were nowhere on the weapons. He claimed not to know Michael Townley.⁶⁴ And more threats attempted to halt the process. When Townley was arraigned at the U.S. district court in Hyattsville, Maryland, on April 10, an anonymous caller warned that the courthouse "would be bombed as Letelier's car." Five days later, Gene Propper himself got a call at his unlisted phone number. "You better watch out," said a male voice in unaccented English, "pay attention to the call made to the court house last week," then hung up. Propper reported the call to the FBI but refused to be protected by U.S. marshals.⁶⁵

On August 1, 1978, the U.S. government indicted the three Chileans and five Cubans in U.S. district court in Washington, D.C., a few blocks from the Capitol. There were ten counts. All but Ignacio Novo were charged with conspiracy to kill Letelier, with killing a foreign official, with killing Letelier and Moffitt (one count each) with a bomb, and with destroying the Chevelle Malibu Classic. Guillermo and Ignacio Novo were further charged with two counts each of lying to a grand jury, and Ignacio alone was charged with failing to report a felony—*misprision*, in legal parlance. Contreras was named as ordering the assassination; Townley, as a coconspirator but not a defendant.⁶⁶ Since Contreras's name came first in the indictment, the trial's name became *The United States of America v. Manuel Contreras el al.* But only those in custody—Alvin Ross and the Novos—would stand trial. These were the first charges ever filed in the United States against Cuban exile terrorists.⁶⁷

Michael Moffitt, for one, felt vindicated. The "United States Government has reached the conclusion that we have never strayed from. We said that, from day one, that the Pinochet Government was responsible," he declared. "We are pleased with the job that the Federal Bureau of Investigation has done so far. They operated in the face of domestic and foreign opposition and interference."[68] Even William F. Buckley, who had savaged Letelier over the contents of his briefcase, now had to admit that Chile had ordered the murder, though he still absolved Pinochet.[69]

As both sides prepared for a January 1979 trial, tensions mounted. A "substantial number" of witnesses for the prosecution feared "physical retaliation" and had to be placed under the protection of U.S. marshals. This included Townley and Callejas.[70] Five agencies cooperated with the prosecution team, which planned to call seventy witnesses. Orlando's sister Fabiola and her son came up from Santiago for the trial. "I have faith in North American justice," she said. On the side of the defense, little was made public, but Ignacio Novo said that the case would cost them collectively $100,000.[71]

On January 9, on the sixth floor of the court house, blanketed by snow, the trial began with unprecedented security, according to the FBI. Bomb-sniffing dogs prowled the halls of the courthouse a few blocks from the Capitol. Forty-four news organizations from around the world, including thirteen from Chile, were there, and they and all others first walked through a metal detector at the entrance of the building and then were searched and ID'd a second time before entering the courtroom. Riot police were on hand.[72] The courtroom itself offered only sixty seats, and some exchanged blows over the right to enter.[73]

The *New York Times* noted the schism in the audience. Supporters of Letelier "tend toward shaggy hair and rough loose clothes. They long to lead the poorer nations of South America away from the capitalism espoused by the Chilean junta headed by Gen. Augusto Pinochet." Friends of the Cubans, meanwhile, "seldom affect casual dress."[74]

Cuban Americans in the audience were unapologetic about the defendants. Paz's brother-in-law, Guido Guirado, said Letelier was *bien muerto y bien matado*, meaning that it was good that he was killed *and* that he was killed well. "Nobody will neutralize or stop us in our struggle against communism," he swore. "For now we are biding our time watching this trial," he added in a thinly veiled threat, "but if it doesn't go our way, then you will hear from us." He even set his sights on the FBI agents in the courtroom: "They threatened us and they will pay." Despite the healthy reward offered for Paz and Suárez's capture, he added, "never would any Cuban betray them. That's how we are. Nothing will make us talk."

"The government has nothing. They have shit," added Ross's daughter, Rosita. "They won't be able to prove anything because they rely on that degenerate, Townley. And he has no country, he has nothing and he would even sell out his mother."

Guirado claimed that in Union City, New Jersey, Cubans had called a general strike to protest the trial.[75] In actuality, they walked down Bergenline Avenue and demanded that shopkeepers close their doors for the day. "It was Capone-style," said one elderly man. "They put their stickers on my store window. I told them they had no right. They came back the next day and smashed my window.... Later, I sold my shop."[76]

Judge Barrington Parker, an African American Nixon appointee with an amputated leg, ambled up slowly on his crutches to his desk, adjusted his rimless glasses, and opened the proceedings in his slow, deliberate baritone.[77] He, like Propper, had received death threats before the trial, and Secret Service agents surrounded both of them, day and night, for its duration.[78] Unbowed, Parker denied a motion by the defense to move the trial out of Washington because of the intense publicity it had received.[79] What followed was the longest jury selection since Watergate. Over three and a half days, lawyers grilled 153 potential jurors, eliminating anyone who had any knowledge of Chile, Cuba, Letelier, Townley, or the Institute for Policy Studies. Finally, seven women and five men were chosen, all African Americans (70 percent of the District's population in 1980).[80]

His turn to testify, Michael Townley entered dressed in a dark blue pinstripe suit. While the judge, lawyers, and jury were out of the courtroom, the Cubans — both those on trial and those in the audience — lobbed insults and threats at him in Spanish while pretending to talk to each other: "Watch out, don't leave him alone!" "CIA traitor!" "CIA shithead!" "Faggot!" "Son of a whore!" "Cut out his tongue!" Townley, twenty feet away, glanced at one of the defendants but did not respond, and the U.S. marshals seated right behind the defendants, apparently unable to understand Spanish, did nothing.[81] The next day, Judge Parker rebuked the Cubans, and they apologized.

The prosecution, led by Propper, presented 26 witnesses and 123 exhibits over twenty days. Michael Moffitt testified, trying to contain his rage at the defendants. At rehearsal, Propper tried to calm him. "You know, Michael, Townley asked me to tell you that he's really sorry about Ronni. And I can tell you that I believe him. Whatever else you may think about him, Mike's a serious guy, and I really believe he feels that way, not about Orlando, but just about Ronni."

Moffitt's response: "You can tell Mike that if I ever have the chance I'll cut his heart out." On the stand, however, he kept his cool.

Isabel Letelier attended the trial. Before she testified, she summoned about fifteen journalists to show them the movie *Los Muertos No Callan* (The dead are not silent), in which she and Moy Tohá were interviewed by East German filmmakers on the ordeal of their martyred husbands.

On the trial's seventh day, Letelier took the stand. She wore a necklace with the black stone inscribed with the word "Isa" that her husband had carved for her at Dawson Island. Her testimony mostly went over his life as a leader of the exile resistance to Pinochet, establishing a motive for the defendants. "Her softly accented voice evoked suffering, determination, courage," observed her friend Saul Landau.[82] She perfectly did her job of extracting sympathy from the jury. Before the trial, while practicing, she had brought some of the investigators to tears.[83]

The prosecutor's case rested largely on Townley's testimony, which he had spent 200 hours rehearsing with him.[84] Over six days, he delivered a detailed, consistent, and largely composed testimony to what the *Washington Post* described as "a packed and rapt courtroom."[85] About his target he said, "He was a soldier and I was a soldier." "In his own way, within his own party, with his own actions, he was carrying on a battle against the Government of Chile," he explained. Asked whether he regretted killing him, Townley responded, "No sir. The person accompanying him, yes, very much so, sir."[86] Explaining further, he said, "I am not saying that I agreed with killing him, either. I received an order and I carried out the order to the best of my ability."[87] (Five months later Townley said he felt "a great sense of remorse for the death of Ronni Moffitt," and "if I could turn back the clock, I would voice my objections and find some excuse not to follow the orders. ... Violence is not the solution to a dispute.")[88] Other evidence included a stack of receipts demonstrating Townley's movements in the United States and Ricardo Canete's devastating conversations with Alvin Ross and Virgilio Paz.[89] Ross had even bragged about his crimes to a fellow prison inmate, who told the court that "Alvin Ross Díaz stands for everything I dislike in a human being."[90] Perhaps wisely, prosecutors chose not to call the unpredictable Callejas as a witness.[91]

The defense, meanwhile, presented eight witnesses over six days, but not the three defendants in custody. It chose the high-risk strategy of blaming the CIA for ordering Townley to kill Letelier, hoping that, as Ross said, "people everywhere would gladly accept the fact that the CIA would be held responsible."[92] A month into the trial, Ignacio Novo even laid out another conspiracy theory to a Dutch journalist: "This is a plot by certain sectors of the American Government ... to try to produce the fall of the Chilean Government and the elimination of the belligerent elements in the Cuban exile community. This by order, not by order, but by a petition of Fidel Castro, who has requested that."

Novo was "absolutely" sure that "we are going to be exonerated and found not guilty."[93]

Threats from the Cubans continued during the trial. One witness set to testify said his or her father received a call from Ignacio Novo, who did not bother to conceal his identity. Novo not so subtly told the father that he hoped his son or daughter's "health will continue to be good."[94] In August 1978, a letter mailed from Peru arrived for Townley. "You are a traitor," it read. "You have negotiated with the FBI to save your filthy hide. You will pay with your life. In no part of the world will you ever again live in peace. . . . Your wife and children are the most precious things you have. Don't allow the blood in their veins to stop running because of your treason." It was signed "Virgilio," likely referring to Paz.[95] Three days later, Propper took a call at his desk. "We're gonna blow off the legs of that fucking judge," said the voice at the other end, "and then we'll get his family, now or later. And then if we have time, we'll get you. But you're not a motherfucking black Communist lover."[96] During the trial, other Cuban Nationalist Movement (CNM) members bombed the Cuban Mission to the United Nations and Avery Fisher Hall in New York.[97]

The prosecution's case, too, almost went off the rails when Townley made a telephone call to a friend—taped apparently by a Contreras loyalist, and given to the defense—to whom he suggested he should have friends from around the world threaten Judge Parker so that he would remove himself from the case. Townley told the judge he was joking, and Parker refused to allow the tape to be played in court.[98]

On February 14, 1979, twenty-two U.S. marshals stood guard as the courtroom waited for a jury that had been deliberating for eight and a half hours. Guillermo Novo turned around to his friends, made a slashing gesture across his throat, and said in Spanish, "It's sure that they screwed us."[99] Soon after, the jury walked in, and the foreman read the unanimous verdict for Alvin Ross and Guillermo and Ignacio Novo: guilty on all counts.[100] The Cubans stared blankly as their relatives sobbed and shouted at Judge Parker, "Nigger! Black son of a bitch!"[101] As they left the courtroom, Guillermo Novo and Ross raised their fist and shouted *"¡Viva Cuba libre!"*[102]

On March 23 came the sentencing. Now the Novo brothers did make statements, both denying any part in the Letelier assassination. "I have done no evil" is how Guillermo put it, while admitting that he did violate his parole to travel to Chile, where he met with Townley. Both brothers saw the trial as scapegoating the CNM, which Guillermo described as "an honorable organization, whose main goal is the liberation of Cuba from the foreign Communist oppressor, the defense of our culture and traditions, and indeed, the defense of our western Christian civilization." Reading his twenty-three-page statement, Guillermo segued into the conspiracy theory about a U.S.-Castro deal when Judge Parker cut him off: "You don't have the right to get on the soap box and give a political speech."[103]

U.S. Attorney Earl Silbert made his own impassioned plea—for a severe sentence. The verdict, he argued, should have nothing to do with the defendants' ideology but with crimes of "savagery" that "undermine the very fabric of society." The defendants had a chance to provide evidence, like Michael Townley, but they chose instead to lie to a grand jury. Judge Parker's sentence, he said, "is important to the widow of Mr. Letelier. It is important to the husband of Ronni Moffitt." Parker seemed to agree: "In the nearly ten years of service as a trial judge of this court, I have not presided over a crime as monstrous and coldblooded as the two murders committed on the morning of September 21st of 1976." He added that being naturalized American citizens did not affect the defendants' sentencing, but he did scold them because "you brought in, and imported and brought with you a brand of terrorism, fanaticism, and hatred which has no place in this country." He sentenced Guillermo Novo and Alvin Ross to life in prison, while Ignacio received eight years—the maximum sentence for each. There was screaming in the courtroom as Parker read the sentences, but he brushed it off: "They will be all right. They are just emotional."[104]

>> But emotion would translate to action. Two days after the sentencing, at 8:46 P.M., a bag checked in for a flight at Trans World Airlines Terminal in Kennedy Airport in New York exploded while on its way to the plane. The damage was largely contained to the metal cart in which it blew up, but four baggage handlers suffered light injuries. The dynamite in the bag went off too early; it was meant to destroy the plane because TWA was flying charters to Cuba. That same day, two more bombs went off in Union City and West New York, New Jersey. One shattered the windows of an enterprise shipping medicine and goods to Cuba; the other, at the New Jersey Cuban Program, which worked with refugees. Omega 7, an organization that sometimes overlapped with CNM, claimed responsibility for all three terrorist acts.[105] The FBI sought Virgilio Paz and José Suárez in connection with the bombs in New Jersey.[106]

Since the Letelier-Moffitt assassination two and a half years earlier,

Cuban exiles had become even more aggressive. A diplomatic gambit called "The Dialogue" begun in September 1978 between a moderate Cuban American "Committee of 75" and the Castro government had further divided the community by freeing 3,000 political prisoners and allowing 4,000 Cuban Americans to visit Cuba. Some Castro haters fretted that the betrayal of the revolution would be forgotten. One reverend, his office bombed, said rapprochement was "an economic threat to those people who were charging $700 to get packages into Cuba via Canada" since normalization with Cuba would sharply lower such costs. Those who opposed terrorism, said another community member, declined to complain because they were not citizens.[107]

The bombings persisted. In late October, shortly before 10 P.M., a bomb exploded just outside the Cuban Mission to the United Nations in Manhattan. The flash was seen for a block in all directions, the sound heard two or three blocks away.[108] A month later, Eulalio José Negrín, a member of the Committee of 75, was killed by a fusillade of automatic weapons as he climbed into his car in Union City. His twelve-year-old son, sitting in the car, was not hurt. A Hispanic caller claiming to be from Omega 7 declared afterward, "We will continue with these executions until we have eliminated all of the traitors living in this country." Negrín was the second Committee of 75 member slain in 1979.[109] Many more received death threats.[110] In early December, another bomb exploded outside the Cuban Mission, and then another blew a gaping hole through the Soviet Mission on East 67th Street. Another still hit the Soviet airline Aeroflot.[111]

While, in the mid-1970s, many complained that the FBI ignored Cuban exile terrorism, by 1980 the FBI regarded Omega 7 as "the most dangerous terrorist organization in the United States" and placed "the highest priority" on dismantling it. As of March 1980, however, it had made no arrests.[112] A group of law students working with the New Jersey Civil Liberties Union and the New Jersey Council of Churches reported that, despite more than 100 bombings or attempted bombings in the last two years, they had seen "no special effort by the Department of Justice and Federal Bureau of Investigation to coordinate federal, state and local police agencies around the country to investigate and prosecute these groups. There have been no recent congressional or statewide legislative investigations of Cuban exile terrorist activities."[113]

12

Prisoners, Survivors, and Judgment Creditors

Shortly after Michael Townley confessed in April 1978, he, his wife Mariana Callejas, and their children were placed under the U.S. Federal Witness Protection Program. Townley's father, mother, sisters, and brothers were also offered protection.[1] For about a year Callejas and their children went back and forth from Townley's undisclosed location on the American East Coast to her home in Santiago. When with her husband, she and the children hated the isolation and grew homesick for Chile.

Townley was officially given his reduced prison term in May 1979. Awaiting his sentence, he worried about how to pay for the lawyers, the house, and the long-distance phone calls. He and Callejas sold their refrigerator, stereo, and a few pieces of furniture, which netted them only $1,500. It turns out they did not own the Lo Curro house, or any other property anywhere, and Townley had nothing to his name save for some clothes and a few hundred dollars.[2] Witness protection did pay his daily expenses in the United States, and the Chilean government helped with bills—belatedly and reluctantly. Townley stewed over what he now considered a betrayal by Manuel Contreras and Pinochet, two leaders to whom he had been ruinously loyal.[3] His wife's continuing loose talk to the media—"the real guilty one is President Pinochet. I feel for him the same respect as for an African dictator"—made Townley anxious that the regime would retaliate against her or the children, eject them from their house, or find out where he was. He bemoaned his inability to "control her," but wrote resignedly, "she is the owner of her thoughts and I do not have the right to try to censure her."[4]

After sentencing, a probation officer interviewed Townley and family members to assess his psychological state for a first parole hearing. His mother found it "hard, impossible to accept the fact" of her boy being involved in an assassination. Vernon Townley, Michael's stern father, faced no such obstacle. "It would not have happened to a more deserving fellow," he said frostily of Orlando Letelier's murder, though he added that his son was "stupid" to have joined the plot. Townley himself told the probation officer that he had stopped drinking, smoking, and using drugs. "He has not felt the need of psychiatric or psychological counseling and feels that in that regard he is an ordinary person suffering from no delusions, etc. He did indicate that he thought he had a 'slightly undeveloped inferiority complex.'" He "now believes that political action should be nonviolent and take place in the public arena." But the officer doubted Townley's remorse, saying he usually fabricated "some type of rationalization to mitigate his culpability":

> For example, . . . he spoke about his being "bothered" about the death of Mrs. Moffitt and his feelings after he saw the photographs of what the bomb had done to her body. But at the same time, he inferred that Mrs. Moffitt's relationship with Mr. Letelier went beyond that of working colleagues, and therefore Mrs. Moffitt was leaning close to Orlando Letelier when the bomb went off. When he told us that and the fact that if she were sitting up straight that she would not have been killed, he gave the undersigned the distinct impression that Mr. Townley was, in part, blaming Mrs. Moffitt for her own death.

She concluded that "Michael Townley still does not fully appreciate the criminal, personal, and moral laws he so harshly violated."[5]

Townley served his sentence at the Federal Correctional Institution, Englewood, a low-security prison near Denver, under a false name and phony crime.[6] He described to a friend his fate as "worse than that of a normal prisoner. I cannot have contact with the outside in a normal way. . . . I have to live a story 24hrs. a day, 365 days a year and the first mistake in that may be my last. . . . The pressure is strong!"[7] Townley eventually earned his high school degree in prison and began to read law in the legal office and advise fellow convicts, among whom he became "popular and appreciated," according to Callejas. He taught Spanish to the bikers and English to the Mexicans.[8]

When Townley went to prison, Callejas settled back in Chile, to live in lonesome, insecure poverty in her mansion in Lo Curro. There, they both feared for her life, and Townley implored her to carry a pistol.[9] Every morning, she recalled, the children had breakfast while she warmed the motor of her Fiat 125. As she put the key in the ignition she would think, *Well, this could be the last moment of my life.* Another car bomb could easily take her, the

Chilean regime simply blaming it on "international communism."[10] Despite Callejas publishing a work of fiction, the writing community politely dismissed her. Regime loyalists called her a traitor, while opponents feared she still worked for the secret police. Assuming she was under surveillance, she and her few remaining friends never met. "No matter," she said defiantly to the Chilean press. "I enjoy my loneliness. I have my kids in Lo Curro, where I live, among the trees and rabbits. . . . As long as I have books to read and paper to write on, I don't despair."[11]

To an American journalist, she confided that "I'm just hanging on to the little blue pills of valium and trying to keep sane until the end." About the future of Chile, she was an optimist. "There will never be a DINA in Chile again," she claimed. "Michael was only a screw inside a gigantic machinery. Now the screw is missing and the machine is grinding to a halt."[12]

After three years, Townley went up for probation again. In meetings with lawyers, he griped about the secrecy and bureaucracy of his protection. "He spoke of himself as a victim . . . of what had happened in Chile," wrote one lawyer. "He described himself as 'un herido ambulante,' 'the walking wounded.'" Townley now criticized the entire Chilean regime for concentrating all power into one person, Pinochet.[13] Despite his good behavior, the parole board must have sensed his lack of remorse—it denied him parole. In April 1983 he finally earned parole. But before he left prison, he was re-arrested for extradition to Argentina for the 1974 murder of Chilean General Carlos Prats. However, a judge rejected Argentina's request, and on July 25, Michael Townley was a free man—though one who had to live the rest of his life clandestinely. He was forty years old.[14]

Townley met with Callejas one last time. They spent several days together in Philadelphia and on the beach, walking hand in hand, "to see, I suppose, if we could make it work again after everything," she recalled. "We both knew it was not to be."[15]

>> While Townley went to prison, Isabel Letelier saw Chile for the first time since 1974. In summer 1978 the junta decreed a selective amnesty, letting a few hundred Chilean exiles return. These included prominent politicians—and Letelier.[16] The practical reason for her short trip was to file for the restoration of her husband's nationality. This would serve two purposes: to provide her and her children with survivor's benefits and to make possible the conviction of her husband's killers, since Chilean law stated that murderers of a non-Chilean abroad could not be tried in the country.

When she deplaned on November 24, exactly four years after she left, what she described as "a huge throng of clamoring reporters and photographers" surrounded her.[17]

"Why have you come back?"

"For deeply moral motives," she responded. "I have a duty to the memory of my husband. I have a duty also to my children, to whom he taught to love their country, and a duty to my in-laws, who taught my husband to love Chile more than life itself."

"Why did you participate in anti-Chilean protests in the United States?"

"Nothing that I do is against Chile," she said calmly.[18]

"Do you plan to marry Michael Moffitt?"

Isabel paused. She had to get used to such conspiracy-minded questions from a right-wing press still in thrall to Pinochet. "You folks are living in a fantasy world," was her reply.[19]

Two days after landing, she held a press conference, where she called the stripping of her husband's nationality "an affront to International Law and the basic rights of natural law." She denied seeking revenge and put up with more sidetracking questions—about Orlando's briefcase, about his infidelity, about CIA involvement in the assassination.[20] She added that this was an opportunity for the cabinet ministers who signed the decree "to ease their consciences" by revoking it.[21]

A relative who attended a family reunion for Letelier on November 28 observed she "was a dervish of activity" and "looked exhausted."[22] The FBI said she "reported being constantly followed by approximately four or five unmarked vehicles, which were occupied by men from the Chilean intelligence service.... They had made their surveillance obvious but they, at no time, had harassed her or hindered her movements."[23] Ambassador George Landau judged that "Mrs. Letelier has handled this delicate visit with considerable adroitness. In public statements she refuses to be drawn into polemics. She apparently has touched base with a number of sectors." "So far," he concluded, "she has given the G[overnment] O[f] C[hile] no ammunition to be used against her."[24]

On December 1, Isabel met with the subsecretary of the Ministry of Justice, who refused to answer her questions.[25] She also filed her claim against her husband's loss of nationality at the Supreme Court of Chile.[26] That evening, she attended a folk music concert where the audience cheered her rapturously.

Upon her return, Letelier summarized for her lawyer "the excitement, fear, tension, and happiness of my brief visit to Chile," which she found "extremely rewarding. The press coverage was impressive in spite of the government's efforts. People came and embraced me in the streets, and in church, and everywhere I went. I received hundreds of phone calls and letters. In a way, it was too great an homage to receive when you are alive."[27] Though she scored no legal victories, she created a favorable public atmosphere for the Letelier cause.[28]

Letelier came back stateside about one month before the beginning of the trial of Alvin Ross and Ignacio and Guillermo Novo. Jumping back into the details of the assassination was an ordeal for her and Michael Moffitt.

"I was consumed in preparing for it," Moffitt recalled of the trial, during which his father died. "I believe the murders . . . broke his heart and killed him. On his deathbed, when he needed me most, I was not there." His father's ulcerative colitis, a condition that developed after Ronni's death, destroyed his digestive system. While the conviction of the Cubans "raised our hopes about justice, my personal problems continued. My heavy drinking continued and while I had sexual relations with a number of women, they were totally devoid of emotion and more often than not, promiscuous in nature. I had no regular friends, was estranged from my family and felt totally alone."[29]

By about 1981, Moffitt's involvement in the case "began to wane." He moved to New York and embarked upon a career as a financial consultant. For years, he dealt with his survivor's guilt in therapy. He earned an advance on a book and published it in 1983. "As a result, my mental health and professional life improved, and I was able to resume a more normal life."[30]

For Isabel Letelier and the rest of Institute for Policy Studies (IPS), the guilty verdict against the Cubans had its drawbacks. They feared retaliation. IPS head Robert Borosage extracted a promise from the Washington mayor's office for round-the-clock police surveillance of IPS offices. He also recommended that staff not work after 9 P.M. for a few weeks. "If you are here, turn on several office lights to give the appearance of a crowded office." For the time being, IPS was going to be a less welcoming place. "We must be more assertive about asking strangers who they are, who they wish to see, and escorting them there."[31]

More personally, Letelier found herself "slandered, despised, ostracized, impoverished and finally, as a family, separated."[32] In 1980 she first went to a psychiatrist. He diagnosed her as suffering from survivor's guilt and posttraumatic stress disorder. She lived with "recurrent and intrusive recollections of the event, recurrent dreams, hyper-alertness and anxiety, sleep disturbance, guilt about surviving when another has not, trouble concentrating as well as chronic anxiety and depression." In his professional opinion, Isabel's PTSD would continue "for the remainder of her life."[33]

In public, she had to refight old battles with right-wing propagandists such as Reed Irvine of Accuracy in Media, rebutting his "nonsense" about her husband being a Cuban agent. To the charge that he was not a liberal, she responded, "Orlando never pretended he was a liberal. He had been a member of the Chilean Socialist party since 1959, and he was proud of this fact."[34] When Peter Kornbluh, then a young staffer at IPS, obtained permission from the Washington mayor's office to erect a modest plaque in memory of Orlando Letelier and Ronni Moffitt in Sheridan Circle, Irvine and others were at it again, opposing "a monument to a Communist agent."[35] Privately, Letelier wrote to a friend that these personal attacks were becoming "intolerable." "At times, I feel discouraged."[36]

》 Nevertheless, Letelier forged ahead with her many activities, which included almost constant travel—and lawsuits. Letelier and Moffitt sought any justice they could, and they felt that the criminal indictments against the Cubans, even were they to result in sentences, would not begin to remedy sufficiently the wrong done by Chile. Lawyer Michael Tigar even toyed with the idea of suing the CIA to the tune of $1,000,000 per death for failing to prevent the assassination, but he apparently abandoned the idea.[37]

More realistically, one week after the issuance of criminal indictments by the U.S. government against the Chileans and Cubans in August 1978, Tigar, on behalf of Letelier, her four sons, and Michael Moffitt, filed a civil suit in U.S. District Court for the District of Columbia against the Chilean government, Contreras, Pedro Espinoza, Armando Fernández, Michael Townley, Alvin Ross, and Guillermo Novo.

Tigar, fifty-three at the time, grew up in California with a unionist father at Lockheed. At twelve years old, when Tigar informed him that he wanted to be a lawyer, his father handed him a book on Clarence Darrow. "That is the kind of lawyer you should be," he told the boy. "Darrow was for the people." With a likely photographic memory, Tigar made first in his law class at the University of California, Berkeley three years in a row and edited its law review. He was active in the free speech movement. As a result, a Supreme Court clerkship offer under Justice William Brennan was withdrawn after Brennan received criticism of Tigar's activism. Tigar ended up at the Washington law firm of Williams & Connolly, and he represented well-known leftists such as Abbie Hoffman, Angela Davis, Cesar Chavez's son Fernando, and H. Rap Brown. During the Chicago Seven trial, where his client was David Dellinger, he was briefly jailed for contempt of court.[38]

The civil suit Tigar filed in 1978 sought unspecified monetary damages for the "wrongful deaths" of Letelier and Moffitt.[39] "The government of President Augusto Pinochet has taken the people we loved from us and have caused all of us immeasurable personal grief," said the relatives. "We hold Gen. Pinochet and his government directly responsible. The government of Chile has invaded the streets of Washington to assassinate someone under the protection of the U.S. government and has murdered a U.S. citizen."[40]

Officially, the civil and criminal cases were unrelated. But the litigants hoped that this civil trial would allow them to make discovery motions and subpoena documents that might help the criminal case. The Italian government in the Bernardo Leighton attempt or the Argentine government in the Prats murder might also use such unsealed documents. "Without a doubt," explained Letelier to a reporter, "the direct responsibility of Pinochet will be made plain."[41]

When the criminal case ended in February 1979, "all of a sudden," recalled Sam Buffone, Tigar's partner, "the civil case became much more important. This was now the vehicle to place responsibility where it belonged, on the highest level of the Chilean government."[42] Buffone complemented Tigar well in that he specialized in white-collar criminal defense and federal sentencing.[43]

It was the first wrongful death case ever brought against a foreign nation in the United States.[44] It also went beyond the suit against the individual Cubans and Chileans by accusing the Pinochet government directly. However, the unprecedented nature of the case also presented its greatest obstacle: the Foreign Sovereign Immunities Act (FSIA) recognized that national governments were the ultimate arbiters of laws, and therefore that one could not sue a foreign government. Such was the principle of "sovereign immunity."

Buffone and Tigar thought they spotted a loophole, however. Then known as Title 28, section 1605(a)(5), of the U.S. Code, the 1976 version of FSIA, effective in January 1977, excluded from sovereign immunity "tortious" matters, or situations of extreme negligence. Weren't two murders by car bomb in Washington the perfect example of tortious actions? asked the lawyers. Their case made several claims: that the defendants conspired to deprive Letelier and Moffitt of equal protection under the law; that their use of explosives was negligent and reckless; that they committed intentional, willful, and malicious assault and battery causing death; that they violated the "law of nations" by torturing, unlawfully confining, and assassinating Letelier and others; and that they caused the death of an internationally protected person.[45]

The ball was in Chile's court. Santiago had sixty days to respond after the documents were translated and served that same week. It scrambled to hire U.S. defense lawyers and pay them the $250,000 retainer they demanded. Contreras allegedly offered up his house as collateral.[46] Meanwhile, the firm of Tigar & Buffone froze Contreras's assets at Riggs National Bank on Pennsylvania Avenue in Washington, D.C.[47]

The defense lawyers apparently advised the government of Chile not to respond to the court's documents, and none of the defendants appeared in court. But Santiago did send diplomatic notes to the State Department arguing that sovereign immunity protected it and that, besides, Chile was innocent.

The Ronald Reagan State Department forwarded the documents to Chile but otherwise stayed away from this civil action. Buffone's letters to Secretary of State George Shultz went unanswered. In the only meeting that Letelier and Moffitt obtained, they were ushered into a tiny room used for making photocopies, where a junior officer in charge of the Southern Cone listened to their pleas. "Pure insult," Buffone called it.[48]

The Chilean strategy of stonewalling failed. On March 11, 1980, U.S. District Judge Joyce Green let the suit proceed without the defendants being present. She ruled that a foreign government was "not immune from lawsuits that allege responsibility for negligence or for internationally wrongful acts."[49] She rejected Chile's argument that Congress, in drafting FSIA, only intended to hold accountable foreign governments for private acts, such as auto accidents, while political assassinations were public deeds by a government. "Whatever policy options may exist for a foreign country," she wrote, "it has no 'discretion' to perpetrate conduct designed to result in the assassination of an individual, . . . action that is clearly contrary to the precepts of humanity as recognized in both national and international law."[50]

"We haven't had this kind of development in the case in a very, very long time," rejoiced Michael Moffitt on Channel 9 news that day.[51]

On June 20 the trial began. The firm of Tigar & Buffone worked pro bono, but IPS shouldered the other legal costs both in the United States and in Chile, and Letelier sharpened her fund-raising skills.[52] Lawyers Tigar and Buffone presented hundreds of exhibits and witnesses from the criminal trial. Unlike the trial of the Cubans, they linked Contreras to Pinochet. The families calculated what Orlando and Ronni would have earned over the years and thus requested between $900,000 and $1,500,000 for Isabel and the children and between $405,000 and $916,000 for Michael. To this would be added reparations for suffering and punitive sanctions.[53] Judge Green pulled out a blackboard, did her own math, and agreed.[54] She praised the commitment, compassion, and skill of the Tigar & Buffone team.[55]

On November 4, Judge Green ordered the defendants to pay $4.95 million in damages to the two families. To $510,000 in compensatory damages, she had added $2 million in punitive damages and more than $2.4 million in compensation under wrongful death statutes, in addition to $110,000 for the lawyers (which they donated to the Letelier-Moffitt Memorial Fund for Human Rights).[56] At an IPS press conference the following day, Tigar explained that $2.95 million of the judgment involved all the defendants, including the Republic of Chile, and that the rest must be sought from Contreras and the other individuals named in the suit. "The most important significance of this decision," explained an IPS memo, "is that it, for the first time, names the Republic of Chile as a responsible party to the assassination of Orlando Letelier and the murder of Ronni Karpen Moffitt. It is a moral victory." It was also the first time that a U.S. court provided a civil remedy to an act of international terrorism.[57]

"Even though nothing can bring them back," said Michael Moffitt of the decision, "it feels good that one can achieve some measure of justice in this case."[58] Since Chile owed them millions, Letelier, her sons, and Moffitt were now officially "judgment creditors."

Tigar noted that the opponents of international terrorism could now count on the courts. "Terrorism is not a partisan issue," added Tigar. "The full cooperation of President-Elect Reagan's administration is expected in the carrying out of this judgment." Reagan had said in his campaign that "there is no room worldwide for terrorism. There will be no negotiation with terrorists of any kind."

》 "It will be a long and difficult effort to obtain the assets of the Chilean government," predicted IPS. Indeed, Chile was served notice within a month but did not respond. And if Santiago did not yield to pressure from diplomats, members of Congress, and other governments, what could one do?

File another lawsuit. The government of Chile had assets in the United States. Among these were bank accounts, but Santiago was "moving massive amounts of money to Canada."[59] Luckily for Tigar and Buffone, LAN-Chile, the republic's state-owned airline, also had planes at airports throughout the United States. At Kennedy International Airport was one such plane, a Boeing 707 freighter. The lawyers hit upon the idea of filing in a New York court to empower U.S. marshals to seize—*attach* was the legal term—this property in order to pay the $2.95 million in compensatory damages ordered by Judge Green. "We intend to leave the Chileans no place to hide," said Tigar.[60]

The ability to attach LAN-Chile's assets to the civil judgment rested on whether Michael Townley had used its planes in the Letelier conspiracy and had done so with the collusion of its employees. In his testimony, Townley had asserted that he carried packages aboard LAN-Chile planes and that the airline knew about it but not that some were explosives. The airline did know he worked for DINA.[61] One journalist accused Townley of traveling in the pilot's cabin and not registering as a passenger.[62]

Investigations by the FBI, Justice Department, a grand jury, and the House Government Activities and Transportation Subcommittee confirmed that Townley's testimony was essentially accurate. And they found more: LAN-Chile pilots, about 90 percent of whom knew Townley, abused their informal exemption from strict customs searches. They not only allowed Townley to smuggle small packages but also brought them onboard themselves, including the Fanon-Courier paging device that served as a detonator in the Letelier car bomb. LAN-Chile employees also bumped up Townley, Fernández, and Liliana Walker to first class for free, allowed Townley to bring on overweight luggage, helped him rent a car, loaned him money for a ticket when he ran out, and carried explosives to the Cubans after the assassination to replenish their supplies. It was even rumored that pilots had handed over the controls of a plane to Townley while over U.S. airspace. Meetings to plot the murder were allegedly held in the LAN-Chile executive lounge and office at Kennedy Airport. DINA, it was revealed, had ordered the pilots to help.[63] In December 1978, a senior LAN-Chile employee also withdrew from Contreras's U.S. bank account $25,000, which he never paid to the Cubans.[64]

Many of these claims became public in the spring of 1980, as Isabel and Michael's lawyers filed their suit. LAN-Chile denied all wrongdoing.[65] By May, the U.S. government banned LAN-Chile from flying to Los Angeles while the investigation was ongoing.[66] A Chilean magazine speculated that, if the airline's flights to Miami and New York City—38 percent of its operations—were also cut off, the loss would be devastating.[67]

In July, the House investigation came to its own conclusions. It found that no evidence contradicted Townley's claim that LAN-Chile employees were unaware that they carried DINA explosives. Nevertheless, "it is plain that they did afford special treatment to packages transported for DINA agents, and that this behavior was widespread." The most dangerous substance carried on LAN-Chile planes, they found, was lead trinitroresorcinate, a highly volatile explosive. Subcommittee chairman John Burton also tore into Federal Aviation Administration (FAA) official Richard Lally for his outfit's "complete failure to comply with Order 1650.3 governing investigations into the foreign air carrier security program":

> *Burton*: Have you filed a report on a 1650.3 form?
> *Lally*: No, sir, we did not.
> *Burton*: So you violated your own directives.
> *Lally*: We may have been technically in administrative violation of our own directives, but that is a judgment.
> *Burton*: Is there something in your directives that gives you the discretion to make a judgment whether or not to follow them?
> *Lally*: No, sir.[68]

Lally and the FAA finally did conduct an investigation, writing to the CIA and interviewing LAN-Chile employees. Unsurprisingly, it produced no incriminating information.[69] Because LAN-Chile pilots and staff had not known about explosives on board, and because few of the other allegations could be proved, it had violated no regulations on security or hazardous materials. Sure, LAN-Chile had been too chummy with Townley. But these were "minor violations," not to mention five years old.[70] The FAA recommended the case be closed.[71] The State Department, parroting the FAA's rationale, refused to revoke LAN's permit to fly in the United States on the grounds that LAN did not *knowingly* participate in the assassination.[72]

Still, LAN's officials grew nervous and began to lease aircraft from other airlines so that its property could not be seized.[73] Then came the one-two punch. On March 18, 1983, the case now three years old, the actual trial against LAN took place, and Judge Charles Brieant ordered the airline's assets frozen, its planes grounded. (However, the operations office at Kennedy Airport claimed to be unaware of the order, and it allowed a LAN plane to take off.) Buffone and his firm had convinced the judge that LAN-Chile not only was involved in the plot but also was wholly owned and controlled by the Republic of Chile. Judge Brieant also ordered the Chilean government to appear in court to explain why Michael Moffitt—probably because of his economic expertise—should not be appointed receiver to run LAN's U.S. operations until the $2.95 million, now augmented by $800,000 in interest, was paid.[74] In the days that followed, another federal judge, Morris Lasker, ordered LAN put into receivership unless the airline posted a bond of up to

$4 million.⁷⁵ The U.S. district court did appoint Moffitt as the receiver, and LAN-Chile did deposit the bond but also appealed the order.⁷⁶ LAN's Boeing 707 continued to land at Kennedy Airport.

At this point, the case against LAN had overshadowed the civil case against the government of Chile, so Letelier clarified the issue for the press. "There is only one trial here, not two as some believe," she said. "Our fight is not with LAN, but against the Republic of Chile, against its present government. It fulfills a promise that we, the families, made to the corpses of our loved ones: that we will not quit until justice is done."⁷⁷ One of her lawyers added that the case "demonstrates to repressive regimes throughout the world that if refugees are pursued and harmed here, American courts provide a forum in which to prove the harm and force the regime to pay."

Until November 1984, prospects seemed bright for the judgment creditors. A lawyer from Buffone's office wrote in April that he "expected [to see] the bonding company writing a check to the plaintiffs in the amount of about $5 million in ten to twelve months."⁷⁸

Then misfortune befell the case. A court of appeals for the Second Circuit reversed the decision of the district court. It interpreted FSIA as intended to compensate for commercial losses, not political assassinations. FSIA therefore ensured a "right without a remedy." The court further found that the district court had "improperly ignored defendant LAN's separate juridical status from the Republic of Chile."⁷⁹

Letelier, Moffitt, and their lawyers were crestfallen. The only recourse left to them was the Supreme Court, and the first step was to come up with $4,000–6,000 just to produce a "petition by certiorari"—a request to send documents from a lower court to the Supreme Court.⁸⁰ They did so, but in mid-1985 the Supreme Court declined to review the case. "Plaintiffs are now without a remedy," Letelier's lawyer concluded.⁸¹

Francisco recalled that his mother never expected to win this civil case. She was surprised to almost win, and not when she lost.⁸²

In 1988, the House Judiciary Committee unanimously endorsed H.R. 3763 to amend FSIA to allow for damages to be recovered by victims of terrorist attacks. "Should any foreign state ever again choose to perpetrate an act of terrorism against Americans," its sponsor told the Congress, "the bill ensures that Americans will have a remedy." Unfortunately for the Letelier and Moffitt families, H.R. 3763 died in the Senate.⁸³

》》 Two months before Judge Green ordered massive damages paid to Letelier and Moffitt, on September 15, 1980, devastating news came in. A federal appeals court overturned the convictions of Alvin Ross and the Novo brothers. Two key prosecution witnesses against Ross and Guillermo Novo, Sherman Kaminsky and Antonio Polytarides, had been inmates in the same cell block. Their testimony that the Cuban Americans confessed to the assassination was not particularly crucial, and the prosecution had done nothing to induce these confessions. But on June 16, three months after the Cubans' sentencing, the Supreme Court ruled the testimony of jailhouse informants inadmissible. The appeals court did offer the opinion that "Guillermo and Ross, based on the evidence at the trial, were guilty," and it suggested they be retried. It also ruled that Ignacio Novo was unfairly tried along with the other Cubans and should have instead been given a separate trial for merely knowing of the assassination plot, a crime less severe than murder.[84]

"Full justice still seems distant in the Orlando Letelier case," the *New York Times* editorialized.[85] "Tremendously disappointed" is how assistant U.S. attorney Larry Barcella described his response to the decision. It turned out that Judge Barrington Parker, who first tried the Cubans, had hesitated both to allow the inmates' statements and to try Ignacio with the others. But he had gone ahead anyway.[86] The U.S. Attorney's Office first tried to get an appeals court to review the decision, but it refused, so a retrial was set. Guillermo Novo and Alvin Ross were out on a $200,000 bond each, paid by a group of six Cuban expatriates. Among them were a bank president and owners of a meat store, a meat plant, and a clothing store in northern New Jersey, who formed the "Committee for the Bail of Novo and Ross" and collected the $400,000 in three swift weeks. Most who contributed took out mortgages on their homes, and the banker of the group provided the loans.[87] The Cuban exile financial network remained alive and well.

With Eugene Propper now retired from the U.S. Attorney's Office, Larry Barcella headed the prosecution team for the retrial of the Cubans. It began in early May 1981, with Michael Townley and Isabel Letelier giving essentially the same testimony as in 1979 and Judge Parker again presiding.[88] Once more, the prosecution's case rested on Townley's "polite and emotionless" testimony, which he gave wearing a conservative blue suit, his hands folded before him.[89] This time, however, the defense was able to play the tape of Townley "joking" about threatening Judge Parker, thereby savaging his credibility. "If you don't swallow Townley, you don't swallow the case," said a defense attorney to the jury.[90] Defense lawyers also now claimed not that the CIA killed Letelier but that Townley and DINA alone did it, without the help of Cubans, who were "scapegoats."[91] "The beauty of a retrial is that you're not stuck with your original defense," said one of the Cubans' attorneys, all but admitting to fabricating the previous the-CIA-did-it theory.[92] When asked if this defense contradicted the previous one, he responded, "You don't have to be consistent. You just have to win."[93]

On May 30, after deliberating seventeen hours, the jury of eight women and four men acquitted Guillermo and Ross of all murder and conspiracy charges. The jury also cleared Ignacio of aiding and abetting the conspiracy. Jurors only found Guillermo guilty of making false statements to a grand jury.[94] It was a stunning reversal of fortune for the Cubans.

After the foreman read the verdict, Cubans in the audience clasped hands and sobbed in joyful disbelief. The defendants embraced their lawyers. Ross said he would "put my life together, start working and try to overthrow Castro." "Justice has been done," exclaimed Guillermo Novo. Walking out, he saw Saul Landau of IPS staring at him in dismay. Novo glared back "murderously," Landau recalled, hissed, and told Ignacio loudly enough in Spanish so that Landau could hear, "Now we can finish off the rest of these communist pigs."

Landau stuck out his tongue, and—"thbpbpthpt!"—blew him a raspberry.

Guillermo's eyes narrowed and he took a few steps toward Landau. Immediately, FBI Special Agent Robert Scherrer stepped between them and flashed Novo his holstered gun. Novo backed off.

"That was stupid," Scherrer told Landau, shaking his head. "That man is a murderer." Landau learned later that year that Novo put a hit out on him. He lived the rest of his life watching his back and avoiding Union City, New Jersey.[95]

In late June, Judge Parker did order Guillermo Novo to prison for four and a half years for perjury.[96] Novo and Ross also signed affidavits in late 1981 to the effect that neither had ever accumulated any real estate, stocks, or savings of any kind. Only through fund-raising had they been able to pay their lawyers and their bail money.[97] Contributions from friends, relatives, businessmen, and sympathizers, two banquets in New Jersey, and a telethon in Miami kept them out of prison.[98]

Parker also reduced Ignacio's sentence to time served, and he was freed in October—but not before prison officials confused him for his brother and freed Guillermo instead! Guillermo went to his family's home in Jersey City. Two days later he was back in prison.[99]

>> By the early 1980s, Isabel Letelier's quest for justice on U.S. territory was seemingly at an end. She and Michael Moffitt, with the help of count-

less allies in the State Department, Justice Department, and law offices, had investigated the case, identified all the guilty parties, had Michael Townley expelled to the United States, sent him and three Cubans to prison, and initially won damages from the Republic of Chile. These were significant victories against terrorists and violators of human rights—more than anyone had thought possible—and they had already begun to change the way the U.S. government dealt with international terrorism. Through it all, Isabel had remained hopeful but realistic, passionate but even-keeled, fierce but kindhearted.

Yet the defeats were perhaps more significant. Townley only served a short sentence. Chile and its airline admitted to nothing and paid no reparations. Only three Cubans went to prison, and only briefly, while Virgilio Paz and José Suárez remained at large. Letelier's response to the acquittal of the Cubans was telling of her focus. "I think justice has different ways of showing itself."[100] To her friend Joan Baez she explained, "If [Novo and Ross] were found 'not guilty' it's only because the jury was convinced by the strong evidence against the Chilean government."[101]

Most galling of all, Contreras, Espinoza, and Fernández remained free men, and they did so because the man responsible for it all, General Augusto Pinochet, was still in full control down in Chile.

PART THREE

Prosecution

»

13

Cover-Up

On August 1, 1978, the day that Manuel Contreras was indicted in Washington, D.C., along with fellow Chileans Pedro Espinoza and Armando Fernández and the five Cubans, the Chilean government, citing treaty obligations, announced the preventive detention of the three Chileans following a formal request for extradition from the U.S. government.

The unhappy task of arresting Contreras fell to Minister of Justice Mónica Madariaga. She showed up, accompanied by a general, at the former DINA chief's tony residence on Príncipe de Gales in La Reina, Santiago.

"Will you go to jail while Chile considers the extradition order?" she asked him.

"No, I will not," he said through a half-open door. Machine gun in hand, Contreras threatened to shoot anyone who got near. For an entire day, he refused to surrender. Madariaga persisted, Contreras called his lawyer, and the following day at dawn he finally conceded. "If I go anywhere, it will be to the [Santiago] Military Hospital."[1] In the months that followed, the former chief of the secret police sent two death threats to Foreign Minister Hernán Cubillos, who signed the original arrest warrant.[2]

Isabel Letelier and her allies in the U.S. government soon learned that they could expect such resistance not only from Contreras but also from most in the Chilean government. Chilean intransigence became the dominant theme of the Letelier saga between February 1978 and October 1979. The Pinochet government was not operating under a different truth; it was merely concealing it. Said a source close to the U.S. investigation, "They know what the real story is and they know that we know."[3]

≫ The day after the letters rogatory hit the front pages of U.S. newspapers, on February 23, 1978, five months before the arrest of Contreras, U.S. Ambassador George Landau braced for a judicial battle — "probably the most arduous one in the legal history of Chile," assessed one writer.[4] No one in the U.S. government harbored any illusion that Chile would seriously try Contreras, Espinoza, and Fernández. Therefore, the legal path to justice was to extradite the three men.

The first step along that path? Recruit legal help. Landau reported on a local Santiago lawyer that Washington might consider, Alfredo Etcheberry, whom another U.S. ambassador would call "a fascinating man, sort of diminutive in size but huge in brain power and with a very big heart."[5] Etcheberry had earned his law degree from Columbia University in 1954. "An excellent jurist and a well-known opponent of the regime," Landau called him, but warned, "he will be regarded here in many quarters as lacking objectivity and prejudiced against the regime."[6]

Etcheberry assessed the legal landscape facing his American clients. A 1900 bilateral treaty (ratified in 1902) did compel Chile to extradite those charged with crimes in the United States, but there were two huge loopholes: not "if the offense . . . be of a political character" and not if the individual were a Chilean citizen.[7] The Bustamente Code that emerged from a 1928 Havana conference further held that American republics could not extradite one another's citizens. The United States had not signed it, but Chile had signed and ratified it.[8] In 1933, a third pact (ratified in 1935) promised that Chile would try its citizens if it chose not to extradite them.

For Chile, expelling or extraditing a foreigner such as Michael Townley was one thing; a native, quite another. Why would Pinochet subject himself to such humiliation? He had already gotten flak from the Right for giving up Townley. The *New York Times* speculated in May that Pinochet would probably order the army to try the three Chileans if only to "prevent extradition until trial action here is completed."[9] Finally, it was impossible to ask for extradition until a U.S. grand jury indicted the Chileans, which was not likely until late summer 1978.

》》 Unlike in the United States, in Chile judges are also in charge of investigating crimes. So on March 1, 1978, the Chilean Supreme Court entrusted to Judge Marcos Libedinsky the investigation of what would become known as the "passports case," the only instance of illegal activity *in Chile* that Chilean officials considered worthy of prosecution.

Simultaneously, the cover-up within the Chilean government deepened. It had begun when Fernández had heard of the killing of Letelier and had gone to DINA headquarters. There, Espinoza dismissed his concern. "Don't worry. It is very probably that the Letelier attempt was done by the opposition to discredit the Government because next week the foreign minister will be speaking at the U.N. That is what you have to say." That last sentence made Fernández doubt the sincerity of his former chief of operations, and the face Espinoza made confirmed that this was indeed a cover story.[10] Fernández never discussed Letelier with Townley, but from that day on, he later said, "I knew I was involved in the assassination."[11]

In spring 1978, when the press reported Fernández's trip to Paraguay, Contreras instructed him to deny going to the United States. When the lie became untenable, Contreras modified the cover story: "You were there a few days and came back. Don't worry. I will take care of all. There is no problem." What about the false passports story? asked Fernández. Contreras told him to say he and Townley got them from a now-dead foreign ministry official whom Fernández had never met. As the heat rose on Fernández, he again went to see Contreras, this time at his beach house, where Contreras changed back to his original lie:

"Forget the trip to the U.S. You never travelled there."

"How can I deny?"

"Deny it."

They finally agreed to call it a trip related to CODELCO, the state-owned copper agency. But, added Contreras, "You should never say that you ever saw or went to see Letelier, or Pinochet would throw me out of the Army."

In mid-April, after General Héctor Orozco, the chief of intelligence, came back from the United States with Townley's truthful declaration, which contradicted Fernández's, he was furious. Orozco put Fernández in an office, said "you are incommunicado," and left him there. Four hours passed. Later that afternoon, Orozco called.

"The hour of truth has arrived," announced the general. "You're going to the U.S. I have spoken to the U.S. Justice Department and to Townley. Townley has confessed the whole thing." Orozco said he and the Justice Department had agreed that no officers would be extradited but that Contreras would spend ten years in Chilean prison, Espinoza five, and Fernández one.[12]

Fernández insisted on the CODELCO story, but Orozco cut him off: "Don't lie here." He showed him declarations by Townley and Espinoza, who had also confessed. Orozco then confronted Contreras with these three declarations. With Fernández waiting outside Orozco's office, Contreras spent half an hour with the general. According to Orozco, Contreras admitted he gave the order to Espinoza to hire Townley.

"Who ordered *you* to order Espinoza?" said Orozco.

"I received an order," was Contreras's terse reply.

"From whom?"

"Ask the Chief." This could only be a reference to Pinochet.

"You can't declare this," concluded Orozco, aware of the political ramifications of implicating Pinochet. At this point, Fernández recalled a "commotion" from inside the office, including "people running."

"Orozco," assessed the CIA, "was obviously given orders by Pinochet to accept Contreras's cover story."[13] Whatever happened behind those doors, Orozco then reversed himself and "became a major architect of the cover-up," according to a U.S. ambassador.[14] He instructed Fernández and Espinoza to make false declarations before the Chilean Supreme Court. The general gave each back their truthful testimony for them to tear up.[15]

Fernández "felt like shooting Contreras" for manipulating him so. The former DINA chief twice ordered his subordinate to retain his lawyer, but Fernández refused, preferring to choose his own. They argued, and they never saw each other again.[16]

Seeing this discord in the ranks, members of the junta began to doubt Contreras's innocence. Pinochet could see it in their faces. He called Contreras to testify before the cabinet.

"Colonel," said Pinochet, "I want you to answer three questions: One, did DINA have anything to do with Letelier's assassination? Two, did *anyone* from our government? And three, who do you think did it?"

"To the first two questions, I have to answer *negative*, my general. With respect to the third, I believe the CIA did it."

Pinochet turned to his cabinet. "You see? That's the truth. You are excused."[17]

Such was Contreras's response when he would be questioned about Letelier for the rest of his life: the CIA did it, and Townley was its agent. The story fed into the prejudices of many on the left *and* right while it conveniently absolved all the Chileans. Contreras's lawyer spread the story and expanded upon it by suggesting that the Cubans—and even Ambassador Landau—were also CIA agents.[18] In truth, in April Contreras admitted to a close confidant that he had authorized the killing on direct orders from Pinochet and that he had told Orozco.[19]

If all else failed, Contreras crafted an insurance policy. He claimed to have shipped twelve to fourteen boxes of incriminating DINA documents out of Punta Arenas to an unknown European destination aboard the West German freighter *Badenstein* on April 20.[20] Those documents, he made it known, placed responsibility for the assassination squarely on Pinochet, and they would come to light were anything to happen to him.[21] It was also said that Contreras had poured gasoline over several other papers and burned them; his successors found what they considered to be too many "silences" in DINA's records.²² Many denied these stories, and Contreras may have fabricated them to disconcert anyone gunning for him.

≫ On May 22, Assistant U.S. Attorney Gene Propper flew back to Santiago to wade in these legal and political waters. It was his third trip to Chile, now accompanied by Larry Barcella, who kept a photo of Contreras on a door in front of his desk and thought about the crime "just 15 to 20 times a day," he said.²³ The Americans moved around town, engaged in secret meetings, and refused to respond to journalists who shouted, "Prosecutor Propper, Prosecutor Propper!" "As in a Peter Sellers movie," recounted the *Washington Post*, "photographers hanging out of Fiat windows chased an embassy station wagon at high speeds through a market district, scattering chickens as they went, trying to take pictures of Barcella and Propper." "Who's Afraid of Propper?" asked *Qué Pasa* magazine, and every news outlet seemed intent on answering, "Not us." "National public opinion" is getting annoyed, declared *La Tercera*. How could these *gringo* investigators move around so freely? Would this be allowed in other countries? Papers speculated about Propper's "James Bond-equipped" briefcase, the specially built car they said was flown in for his use, and even his romantic life while in Santiago.²⁴

The CIA identified a "growing anti-American campaign" in Chile. In early May, members of an AFL-CIO delegation invited by Chilean union leaders were jailed when they tried to hold an unauthorized rally.²⁵ One rally that did occur, and was reported on favorably, involved the burning of a U.S. flag.²⁶ In a switch from Allende's days, anti-U.S. sentiment this time came from the Right. A columnist for *La Tercera* denounced "North American imperialism" and its "assault on the nation's dignity." Washington was merely disguising its imperial aggression as a concern for human rights, he added.²⁷ Pablo Rodríguez, formerly of Fatherland and Freedom, saw the AFL-CIO visit, the rhetoric of Senator Ted Kennedy, editorials in the *New York Times*, and the work of Chileans on human rights as a vast conspiracy to "overthrow the Government of the Armed Forces."²⁸ In the week after Propper landed, Chilean headlines included "Yankee Insolence," "FBI Go Home," and "Chile Says NO to U.S. Arrogance." Many angry letters to *El Mercurio* were from Chileans tied to Pinochet—a sure sign of coordination.²⁹

Not surprisingly, Chileans declined to cooperate with the U.S. investigation when they realized it would lead to a request for extradition. Specifically, they refused to let Americans interview Fernández or to take sworn testimony from the Paraguayans who were believed to have given passports to Townley and Fernández.[30] On June 21, Deputy Secretary of State Warren Christopher received a report that the Chilean foreign minister, Hernán Cubillos, would not even speak with him.[31]

The following day, Pinochet hosted a diplomatic dinner in the full-dress uniform of a Chilean general, and that evening he had a twenty-minute private talk with U.S. Ambassador George Landau. "Pinochet, who normally drinks very little, had two scotch and sodas," reported the ambassador. "His face grew redder and redder as he talked to me."[32]

"You are causing me a great deal of trouble," Pinochet began, looking intently at the ambassador.

"I'm sorry to say that we do not believe we have received the cooperation your government promised us in this matter," Landau answered.

Pinochet felt betrayed by the United States, he said. He mentioned an editorial in the *Washington Post* calling for his resignation and assumed U.S. government officials had planted it. "That kind of thing will not happen here," Pinochet vowed. "Tomorrow I shall close *La Segunda* as punishment for publishing an interview with a fool who took the side of *The Washington Post*."

The dictator's temper rose. "You and your government can meddle in Chilean affairs and bring back political parties," he ranted. "Maybe you can. And if you do, you will cause another bloody revolution. People will die.... But I am warning you that I will not allow it."

Pinochet pointed to the Chinese ambassador across the room. "You see that man over there?" he asked. "Do you see him? Well, I can go to him. Believe me, Chile can turn to China. We are not married to the United States. I could even turn to the Soviet Union. They would help. They would do anything to hurt you."

"Excuse me, Mr. President," said Landau. "I want to make sure I understand you. Do you really mean that last statement? Do you really mean that you could become an ally of the Soviet Union?"

"Absolutely!" said Pinochet.[33]

Recalled Landau with understatement, "My relations with Pinochet were very cool afterwards."[34]

>> Partly to confer with Landau but mostly as a public signal of displeasure toward Santiago, the State Department recalled the ambassador on the very day of his confrontation with Pinochet. "The Chilean authorities have not been forthcoming on important requests for information in the Letelier-

Moffitt murder case pending by the Justice Department for some time," said a spokesperson in damning diplomatic language.[35] Once in Washington, Landau and U.S. diplomats discussed the pressure they could put on Pinochet to cooperate. Although Congress had cut off aid to the Chilean regime in 1976, there remained $20–30 million in the military supply pipeline. The State Department suspended a shipment of bomb parts and put the Defense Department on notice that more suspensions might come.[36] Suspending the bomb parts was an easy decision since California longshoremen, in support of the investigation, refused to load them onto a ship. Deputy Secretary Christopher also insisted on mentioning Chile's continuing human rights problem, thus connecting it with the Letelier investigation.[37]

In late June, Chile conceded the interview with Fernández and the Paraguayan testimony, and so Landau returned to Santiago. "Mutual cooperation has been reestablished," the secretary of state declared.[38] In a late July deposition to the FBI, Paraguay's chief of intelligence swore not only that Contreras asked for passports for "Williams" and "Romeral" and that Paraguay issued them but also that Paraguay canceled them after the men were refused U.S. visas. The Chileans had then obtained visas from the U.S. consulate a month later.[39]

By August 2, after his machine-gun-in-hand surrender, Contreras, along with Espinoza and Fernández, was under watch on the sixth floor of the Santiago Military Hospital, a detention site far cushier than a jailhouse. It appears that Contreras moved freely within the hospital. According to the FBI, he enjoyed "a fairly spacious room in the hospital, equipped with a sofa, desk and special telephone."[40] Contreras apparently wrote some memoirs and read spy novels. Fernández also could leave his room, sitting in on medical operations and learning dialysis. But three guards watched him day and night.

In his own, likely more Spartan room, Fernández grew uncomfortable with the cover-up. He didn't like the lies and felt abandoned, at bay. He let it be known that he pondered a trip to the United States to resolve the matter. He was immediately called in to the Ministry of Defense, where he met with none other than Pinochet.

"I'm told that you want to go to the United States," began Pinochet.

"That's a lie."

"I know it is the truth."

"The truth is, not that I want to go to the United States, but that I *am going* to the United States." Fernández was especially upset at being confined for what he considered other people's crimes.

"Don't worry," the dictator told him. "Be a good soldier, tough it out, and this problem will have a happy end." Fernández twice attempted to resign his commission in the Chilean Army, and twice Pinochet personally refused to accept it but without returning the army captain to military duty, likely so that Fernández could benefit from professional immunity. Fernández therefore remained in limbo, unwilling to defect and sully the reputation of his fellow soldiers.[41] The cover-up was working.

In late August, Contreras phoned the CIA station chief in Santiago for a meeting, but it was declined. His lawyer, Sergio Miranda Carrington, and other representatives communicated with CIA and State Department lawyers that the former DINA chief may be "forced" to reveal ugly secrets about the U.S. government if Washington tried to extradite him.[42] Warren Christopher's response: "The U.S.G[overnment] will not, repeat NOT, be subject to blackmail."[43]

Miranda, Contreras's lawyer, was a self-professed Germanophile, to say the least. During World War II, he recalled, "I identified more with the cause of the Germans than with those of Asiatic communism or North American capitalism."[44] In his early twenties, he engaged in conservative politics and earned a scholarship to the University of Munich, where it was said that he offered to defend Nazi war criminals at the Nuremberg trials after the war.[45]

A trip to Greece convinced him of the superiority of its ancient culture. He learned Greek in 1952, read Greek classics every night, and wrote two unpublished manuscripts—in Greek—about Homer and Sparta. He defended Pinochet's military coup as a return to ancient values. "For me the word *dictatorship* is highly honorable. It comes from Ancient Greece. Greek dictators governed with the people in the interest of the nation and dispensed with oligarchs and economists."[46]

So what do you say? Miranda asked the State Department about the blackmail that Contreras threatened.

"Fuck him, that's what I say," said Francis McNeil of the American Republics Bureau at the State Department. "Let him say anything he wants, but we're going after him," he told Gene Propper.

Propper smiled. "That's great, Frank," he said. "Would you put it in writing?"

"Not quite in that language."[47]

And "Fuck Pinochet," McNeil added for good measure. "We would not submit to blackmail," he told the Defense Department. The CIA felt the same.[48]

On September 1, the United States informed Chile that it would ask for extraditions. Pinochet felt forced to ask for Contreras's resignation.[49] By

November, loyalists to the former DINA chief began to organize Committees for Assistance to the Defense of Manuel Contreras.⁵⁰ It was rumored for a while that Contreras had committed suicide; another time, that he would be assassinated.⁵¹

However, any hopes inside Chile that the Pinochet regime would fall or even fully abandon Contreras were soon dashed. El Mamo was a fighter. Throughout his career, the Chilean had never let subordinates take the fall for his decisions, and they repaid Contreras now with protection. Former DINA officers called on friends throughout the bureaucracy to support their former leader. And most in the military rejected the very notion of civilians investigating them or giving them orders. Some were ready to rise up in revolt, it was rumored. To prevent his own extradition, on April 7, as the Chilean government was deciding to expel Townley, Contreras had led a convoy of a dozen vehicles filled with his most loyal supporters, armed to the teeth and driving to the homes of officials to drum up support. If necessary, he thought, he would head south and ensconce himself inside a fortress.⁵²

》》 Isabel Letelier and Michael Moffitt followed this saga closely and wondered if justice would come to their loved ones' killers. Moffitt, for one, was skeptical. "I don't think there is anyone who seriously believes that General Pinochet will voluntarily give up people who could trace the murder of Mr. Letelier and my wife directly to his doorstep," he told the press. "Sources very close to the investigation tell me the chances are probably less than 10 percent that we'll get an extradition."⁵³

Letelier was more optimistic, thinking that the case might even free Chile as a whole. "General Pinochet's days are numbered," a State Department official told her. "Ironically, your husband's murder has become the instrument which all of Pinochet's enemies have begun to use to rid themselves of the bloody tyrant." She heard similar appraisals from friends in Chile.⁵⁴

In September 1978, Letelier prepared a speech aimed at U.S. audiences that revealed her ability to place her husband's case within a larger struggle. "What will happen if Pinochet refuses extradition?" she asked. "To some, this might mean that the international terrorist network operated by several military governments in Latin America with the help of anti-Cuban terrorists will feel free to commit other crimes." In contrast, "to bring to trial members of the DINA will mean to place on trial this entire, inter-governmental apparatus. . . . The international community is standing up for the most basic human right, the right to life free from the dread assassin's bullet or bomb."

"The time for shock and tears is past," she declared. "We have learned too much in these two years to believe that this tragedy was a singular event, or that the men who planted the bomb were aberrations from a more benign, authoritarian norm."

"You have begun to correct those defects in your democracy which played a part in the training of these terrorists," she congratulated her American listeners. "For this, the whole world is glad."[55]

>> In the fall, now faced with a formal extradition request from Washington, the Chilean government publicly swore that it was fully cooperating and asked the press to keep its coverage of what it considered a purely legal matter respectful and subdued.[56] The press obliged. One national television report devoted about forty-five seconds to the news, followed by a three-minute commentary against the indictment.[57] The government-owned *El Cronista* accused the U.S. Department of State of harboring political objectives. Pinochet promised, "The Government will not fall on account of the Letelier case."[58]

Meanwhile, the case now fell into the hands of a different judge, Israel Bórquez, president of the Chilean Supreme Court. The seventy-three-year-old jurist had never challenged Chile's military rulers, even though they had set aside the constitution he swore to uphold. The CIA explained that the Supreme Court was "neither dominated by the Pinochet regime, nor totally independent of it." It "has been subject to [the] regime's pressures in the past," the agency noted. "The court will also be moved by nationalist sentiments, by its own pride in its legal reputation, and by its desire to reach a decision that will stand international scrutiny."[59] However, Pinochet had just appointed Bórquez in May precisely because he figured Bórquez was predisposed against extradition. In August, Pinochet met secretly with the judge to urge him not to extradite, saying the blow to the army's reputation would be fatal. According to the CIA, Bórquez said he would do "everything possible to see that the Court complied with his request."[60]

The court's legal options were essentially three: to find that there was insufficient evidence to warrant an indictment, to determine that the crime was political and therefore also deny the extradition request, or to find the evidence strong enough and either extradite the defendants or try them in Chile.

The U.S. government deluged the Chileans with 700 pages of supporting evidence, photographs, and film, all contained in a twenty-five-pound box "elaborately bound with metal rivets and diplomatic ribbons to prevent tampering and photocopying," wrote journalist John Dinges. Landau delivered the evidence to Cubillos on September 20, along with the formal extradition request.[61]

A few days later, Bórquez made an unusual decision. Invoking a criminal proceedings rule called a "summary," he barred not only the press from his hearings but also all the lawyers. This meant that Alfredo Etcheberry, working for the U.S. government, would be prevented from cross-examining the accused or any witness and would have no chance to clarify the evidence.[62] Etcheberry filed an appeal, but the Supreme Court unanimously rejected it. Propper was enraged. He and U.S. diplomats considered rescinding the extradition request and just exerting diplomatic pressure.[63] Submitting the request had trapped them. They had officially placed their trust in Chile's courts and were now bound to accept their decisions.

Other shenanigans took place in the fall. In October, it came to light that persons close to Contreras at the Santiago Military Hospital handled copies of the secret U.S. evidence within a day or two of Landau delivering them to Cubillos. The Supreme Court denied any involvement: "It couldn't be, they didn't get it here."[64] Landau suspected the documents were copied at the Foreign Ministry after they left Cubillos's office.[65] It was revealed later that Contreras told Fernández that he himself had a copy.[66]

On October 17 and 18—a full month after the extradition request—Fernández gave his testimony to Bórquez. He denied all knowledge of a Letelier mission and said he went to the United States with Townley to meet with the CIA's Vernon Walters. The questions, on the whole, were soft:

Why would DINA send you, of such low rank, to meet with Walters?

"Walters was only to give me some information about members of Congress," answered Fernández.

Why would DINA send Townley to meet Walters if Townley had only technical expertise?

"I figured it was because Townley spoke English."

At the close of the two days of questioning, Bórquez walked out of his chambers and was surrounded by reporters. He was "visibly tired and definitely irritable," as his answers demonstrated:

"What did you ask Fernández?"

"Dumb question. All you newsmen ask are stupidities."

"Is Espinoza next?"

"Check with God."

"But judge, the press needs to inform—"

"What do I care?"[67]

The following day, Pedro Espinoza wove exactly the same yarn as Fernández, and so did Contreras the following week.[68] Contreras, ensconced in the Santiago Military Hospital, had been complaining of various ailments and arrived at the court with an ambulance trailing him. Around twenty women greeted him.[69] Unlike Espinoza, who used a decoy to elude the press, Contreras freely answered all the reporters' questions:

"Did you play a role in the Letelier investigation?"

"I no more participated in the Letelier assassination than in the murders of the Kennedy brothers and of Martin Luther King."

"What about the 'disappeared'?"

"I am more interested in the 'appeared,' those who continue plotting. It is they who make accusations. The Marxists will never forgive our victory over them on September 11, 1973."

"Did DINA ever do any 'dirty work'?"

"No, never. Whatever work is done for the good of the fatherland is clean." He specifically denied that DINA ever operated in a foreign country.[70]

On November 22, a powerful bomb shook the home of Judge Bórquez. He was not hurt, and he announced publicly that he would not be intimidated. While many may have suspected leftist guerrillas, General Odlanier Mena said the bomb was probably the work of former DINA loyalists.[71]

>> As 1979 rolled around, Bórquez continued pouring over the evidence, and more came in from U.S. investigators and Etcheberry. On January 5, the Supreme Court upheld a decision not to set bail for Contreras and Espinoza. El Mamo then attended his twenty-two-year-old daughter Mariela's wedding to an army lieutenant. There he hobnobbed with the hundreds who attended, including many generals. Espinoza used his own freedom to visit military friends. Fernández, known as "quite a ladies' man," visited discotheques.[72] When the trial of the Cubans began in Washington on January 9, many speculated that Bórquez was holding off on ruling until after that faraway trial was concluded.[73] When the Cubans were found guilty, Propper also connected the two cases, saying the Washington verdict "should make it easier for us" to win extradition in Chile.[74] But few in Chile made the link or even paid much attention to the Washington trial, dismissing it as a judgment on Townley and the Cubans, not on Chile.[75]

From February to May 1979, as Bórquez deliberated, legal experts weighed in and Landau feared that "under the Chilean legal system our case was not as strong as we believed."[76] Nobody could identify a precedent where the head or former head of any secret police was extradited.[77] Chilean jurisprudence complicated what was already a muddled treaty situation.

First, conspiracy to commit a crime was not in itself a crime in Chile. Second, while the Chilean Supreme Court was considered independent, it had never deliberated on a case of security under Pinochet. Finally and most important, Chilean jurists were not in the habit of considering plea-bargained testimony of the kind Townley had given to be admissible in court because defendants were expected to lie.

The "Willoughby gambit" briefly gave hope to the Americans. On March 26, Federico Willoughby, a former Pinochet private secretary and press spokesperson for whom Fernández had worked as a bodyguard, invited Alfredo Etcheberry to lunch. He told him that the army was most concerned about the extradition of Fernández—one of theirs, who was low ranking, had already served nine months, was just following orders, and ignored the purpose of his mission. If this captain were extradited, army officers feared, any one of them could be next. A week later, Willoughby proposed a deal: give up proceedings against Fernández, and we will hand over the two bigger fish, Contreras and Espinoza.[78] In May, Willoughby even traveled to Washington and met with Townley, Barcella, Propper, the FBI's Carter Cornick and Robert Scherrer, and others in the Embassy Row Hotel and the U.S. Courthouse.[79] U.S. authorities rejected the deal because Fernández was not willing to admit that he *did* know he was helping to kill Letelier. This marked a major misstep by the United States, because while Fernández suspected that his surveillance of Letelier made the exile some kind of target, he did not figure out that he was part of an assassination plot until September 21, 1976. While the Willoughby gambit failed, it suggested that Fernández could be "flipped"—a precedent that would come in handy one day.

Finally, at 9 A.M. on May 14, all the lawyers in the case received Bórquez's forty-five-page decision, dated the previous day. The judge accepted the U.S. evidence as valid yet found it unconvincing for the purposes of an extradition. He also, however, found enough contradictions in the statement of the three Chilean officers that he ordered a military court to begin its own investigation that might lead to an indictment. "Not to concede extradition does not equal innocence," he specified.[80] Because of this last ruling, wrote Landau, "the Borquez decision is better than we had anticipated."[81]

Still, it was not good. Contreras's satisfaction with the verdict was evidence of that. "Chilean justice is professional," he beamed. "Truly, it has earned and deserves our trust."[82] Etcheberry, feeling "disappointed, but not discouraged" by the "unsatisfactory" decision, appealed to a five-judge panel of the Supreme Court, whose decision would be final.[83]

In Washington, meanwhile, the State Department declared it was "gravely disappointed by the decision" and recalled Landau again.[84] It defended its decision to trust Bórquez as "the only viable and legally acceptable method in which to proceed."[85] It was also politically realistic, since the Chilean press was largely united behind Bórquez's decision. (*Hoy*, the Christian Democratic paper, was the lone dissenter, and the Chilean government shut it down for two months.)[86]

Bórquez did not enhance his reputation, however. Two weeks after his decision, he declared that "Americans are very good actors and famous for believing in the gullibility of others.... Imagine, to constitute a grand jury of the court of the District of Columbia, they choose, including Judge Barrington Parker who presided, only little brown people from Washington — perhaps in order that they might be able to hide their embarrassed blushes."[87] This bigoted swipe at the all-black jury in the Washington case enraged many stateside, Isabel Letelier among them. "His racial slurs only make too clear the general disrespect and contempt for human beings which characterize the Pinochet regime," she declared about Bórquez. "Racism and Fascism go hand in hand."[88]

With arguments now fully before the Chilean Supreme Court and his job done, Gene Propper resigned from the Justice Department and joined the Washington law firm of Lane and Edson. "The Letelier case has been a most significant part of my life for the past three years," he wrote to Letelier. "Many persons in the United States Government devoted a great deal of time and personal effort to the solution of the monstrous crime that took place on September 21. We did so because it was our job and because of the heinous nature of the crime. During that time I have come to know and like you and other people in the Institute [for Policy Studies]. While we did not always agree, I think we developed a relationship based on trust, respect and understanding."[89]

>> The appeals hearing in Santiago began on July 11, 1979. This time around, it was open to the public. Thirty-five foreign and twenty-four Chilean correspondents reported from the Supreme Court, and one radio network broadcast the trial in its entirety.[90] Before the five somber justices, Etcheberry did his best to rehabilitate Townley's credibility and to argue that plea-bargained testimonies were valuable. "There is nothing immoral in this. In the United States, the practice of obtaining evidence that makes it possible to prosecute the big fish in exchange for leniency is considered to serve the public interest." "Let the voice of reason be heard," he pleaded in his sonorous voice. As he left the courthouse, a crowd of 300 cheered him.[91]

Behind the scenes, the draft of the Court's decision was shown to Pinochet, who, the CIA found out, "insisted that it be toughened to exclude any possibility that the extradition case could be revived. The language was changed to comply with Pinochet's order."[92] On October 1, the panel handed down its decision upholding Bórquez's ruling. Its 132-page decision said that U.S. evidence created a suspicion but not "a well-founded presumption" of the defendants' involvement in the assassination. In fact, the panel made things worse for the prosecution in that it reversed Bórquez's instruction to open an investigation. The only door it left open — a significant one, it would turn out — was that the eighteen-month-old passport fraud case, which had gone nowhere, was to be expanded to include the assassination if new evidence came to light. Its case number was 192-78.[93]

"I am not happy," said Etcheberry to the press.[94] Neither was Larry Barcella, who confided to a Chilean newspaper that Americans felt "absolutely disillusioned." "A jury in the United States found guilty other people implicated in this case with the same evidence," and the level of evidence necessary for an extradition is generally lower than for an indictment, he explained.[95] Both the *New York Times* and *Washington Post* saw in the trial a travesty of justice. Pinochet claimed he would have obeyed any ruling by the courts, but, he added, "Chile doesn't accept pressure from anyone."[96]

Foreign Minister Cubillos felt comforted by former secretary of state Henry Kissinger when the two had breakfast two days after the denial of extradition. Flirting with treason, Kissinger told Cubillos that the Supreme Court's decision was correct, insulted top Carter officials, and told the Chilean to treat this White House with "brutality." "This is the only language they understand."[97] Later that day, even the current secretary of state, Cyrus Vance, contradicted subordinates by promising Cubillos, "I'll try to lower the pressure.... This is a manageable issue."[98]

>> Given the ruling, Bórquez ordered Contreras, Espinoza, and Fernández freed from the Santiago Military Hospital after 450 days in holding. Now in retirement, Contreras went back to his ranch house in a posh neighborhood of Santiago. Foreseeing the dissolution of DINA, he had arranged for himself and his top commanders to be cared for in houses "gifted" by the Chilean government.[99]

14

The Ghost Who Haunts Our Chile Policy

After the failure of the extradition request against Manuel Contreras, Pedro Espinoza, and Armando Fernández in the fall of 1979, Pinochet loyalists may have believed that their ordeal was at an end. But *el caso Letelier* remained front and center in U.S.-Chilean diplomatic relations. For a decade starting in the late 1970s, Chile lost the United States as a reliable patron, and the Letelier-Moffitt assassination was the leading cause. The case largely ran parallel to larger efforts by Presidents Carter and eventually Reagan to liberalize the politics of Chile. "The Pinochet government was sort of hoping that this issue would go away, and it couldn't go away," recalled a U.S. deputy chief of mission at the embassy in Santiago. "It was too important."[1]

>> As soon as Michael Townley's photo appeared in Chilean newspapers, it seemed more than just a coincidence that the Pinochet government took its foot off the necks of the Chilean opposition. The break in the Letelier case was "an obvious catalyst" for this liberalization, assessed the *Washington Post*, even though Pinochet attributed his newfound moderation to having saved the Chilean economy.[2] Letelier developments also compelled ordinary Chileans to discuss politics in public. In May, Santiago announced it would allow the U.N. Commission on Human Rights to visit Chile later in the year.

Still, personal liberties could not be taken for granted. A "state of emergency" still remained, the secret police still detained many in the torture center of Villa Grimaldi without due process, and union elections, strikes, collective bargaining, and political parties all remained banned. On May Day, the government broke up the first labor demonstrations since the coup—

though the violence was minimal. Pinochet also rode out a hunger strike meant to get him to admit to the disappearance of over 600 leftists.

"Things are vastly improved," summarized one diplomat, "but the bottom line is that there's nothing to prevent the government from going back. There hasn't been an institutional leap. Most of the generals haven't seen the light."[3]

One had glimpsed it, however. General Gustavo Leigh Guzmán, the commander of the air force and a member of the junta, now called for a rapid return to civilian rule. Similar grumblings came from the navy and business circles. Business leaders had never liked the Far Right's fascistic view of a government managing the economy.[4] Leigh went further. The CIA assessed that Leigh was trying to "portray Pinochet as a loser" and get him to step down, saying he had "lost control of [the] situation in Chile" mostly because of his handling of the Letelier case. While countless civilians now admitted that the regime had tortured dissidents, many in the military were dismayed at how Pinochet handed over Townley.[5] One junta member called the scandals swirling around Pinochet the "Chilean Watergate." The CIA wondered whether the Letelier case "will ultimately bring down the Pinochet regime."[6]

In late July 1978, in the so-called air force massacre, Pinochet fired Leigh after the general criticized him to a foreign correspondent.[7] Eight generals who were passed over as his successor resigned, and eleven more quit in solidarity. In all, nineteen of twenty-one air force generals resigned en masse.[8] Was this, as one diplomat said, a sign that "the rule of the military junta is nearly over"?

More likely, Pinochet was purging his regime. One memo to U.S. National Security Adviser Zbigniew Brzezinski assessed that "Leigh had hoped to hang on until the Letelier case indictments came out, calculating that this would shift the balance of forces in his favor. The imminence of the Letelier case indictments, however, apparently motivated Pinochet to press for Leigh's ouster."[9] The CIA agreed, tying the Leigh ouster to the Letelier murder. "Because it is widely believed that Contreras would not have acted without president Pinochet's consent, the president expects a rough time ahead and has been working to consolidate his political position." Pinochet was going to "tough it out, relying on his military and popular support as well as on his belief that he himself cannot be indicted in the Letelier murder."[10]

Chile was also straining its relations with Washington because of two border disputes. Against Argentina, Chile tussled over sovereignty over Picton, Nueva, and Lennox Islands at the mouth of the Beagle Channel, the southern tip of South America. Queen Elizabeth II of England arbitrated and granted the islands to Chile, but Argentina, claiming them since 1904 and fearing its navigational rights threatened, rejected the solution. Both countries mobilized troops to the frigid waters but accepted a successful papal mediation. To Bolivia, meanwhile, Pinochet had proposed swapping land that would restore the access to the sea that Bolivia had lost a century earlier, while granting new territory to Chile. But the scheme ran afoul of a Chile-Peru treaty, and the Bolivian government broke ties over the dispute. Throughout, the State Department provided no diplomatic support to Chile.

A few weeks before Judge Israel Bórquez's decision not to extradite Contreras and the two others, Pinochet again showed his annoyance at U.S. pressure. "Power will be handed over when the time is ripe — but I won't be rushed into this," he warned. "You won't believe me, but I'm as democratic as you Americans are. I trust the people all right; but they're not ready."[11] After the denial by the courts, Pinochet rejected political normalization in his state of the union message and even accused the Carter administration of being soft on "Soviet imperialism" in Latin America. He lamented a "vacuum created by the country that should be the leader of the free world."[12]

▶▶ Forces in Washington, meanwhile, tussled over whether to punish Chile even before Santiago's courts rendered a verdict on extradition. On August 2, 1978, in what the *Washington Post* called a "confusing sequence of events," Rep. Tom Harkin of Iowa, an ally of the international human rights community, called for cutting off all arms shipments to Chile until the three Chileans were extradited. Harkin was responding to the indictment in Washington of the three Chileans plus the five Cubans the day before and to the discovery by longshoremen in the Port of Oakland that the United States had yet to ship $24,817,827 in military equipment remaining in the pipeline despite an earlier cutoff. "This equipment includes revolvers and ammunition, hand grenades and equipment that can be used to further directly repress the people of Chile," Representative Pete Stark of California argued, adding that such equipment "could be further used by Chilean agents to come into this country and murder residents of this country, as suggested by the indictments brought yesterday."[13] The amendment passed by voice vote.

Immediately, however, the Justice Department mobilized its congressional liaisons to tell members of the House that such action was premature. The Chileans would see this not only as interference in their internal affairs but also as a ploy to bring down the Pinochet regime. It would backfire. Late in the same afternoon, Republicans overturned the amendment, 243 to 166.[14]

The U.S. business community was also in no rush to pressure Pinochet on Letelier—or on any other human rights issue. During the extradition trial, the Anaconda Copper Mining Company penned contracts to invest an additional $1.5 billion in Chile, Chase Manhattan Bank prepared to open its first branch there, and Goodyear, Exxon, St. Joe Minerals, Superior Oil, and Falconbridge all expanded their investments or planned to. "I don't think we spent five minutes talking about human rights when the board made the decision to invest in Chile," said one Goodyear manager. While a Citibank manager claimed that "we don't mix business and politics," it was instead clear that companies such as Anaconda and Dow Chemical were returning to Chile precisely because of Pinochet's repression of unions and political dissent. As Ralph Cox, president of Anaconda, admitted, "We have come back to Chile not only because of the mining prospects, but because this Government has created a climate of confidence for investment." U.S. banks had also provided about $2 billion in credit to Chileans.[15]

Among politicians and human rights advocates, however, Robert Steven, the Chile Desk Officer in Foggy Bottom, "could not emphasize enough how much Letelier now dominated everything. If I went to a meeting of any sort in the Department and tried to argue for any consideration on another Chile issue, I was shot down." Ambassador George Landau was never recalled to Washington for any other issue.[16]

After the May 1979 denial of extradition, Senators Ted Kennedy and Frank Church beseeched President Carter to suspend all assistance to the Pinochet regime, recall all military personnel from Chile, and, in a broader measure, deny bilateral and multilateral aid to countries harboring terrorists.[17] House liberals such as Harkin, who sent a petition to Carter for harsher measures, also felt they had held their fire long enough and were now ready to cut off all aid to Chile. "We must take strong action against this act of terrorism," the representative wrote to the *New York Times*, "and in so doing, steady the standard of human rights and human dignity that trembles with each such act."[18] The most damaging sanction, which Isabel Letelier and Michael Moffitt advocated, would have been for private U.S. banks to stop lending to Chile, cutting off billions. Nongovernmental organizations blitzed Capitol Hill and Foggy Bottom with demands for pressure on Chile.[19] The State Department demurred, saying that it had to see through its commitment to the Chilean courts and let the appeals process go forward.[20]

The definitive October 1979 denial of extradition by the Chilean Supreme Court signaled that the time for a decision had come. "I do not wish to break relations," Carter wrote in the margin of a memo from his deputy secretary of state.[21] The president also never seriously considered Letelier and Moffitt's request to ban private loans. So what was left for the State Department to do?

First, it issued a strongly worded statement that took the unusual step of calling the three defendants "terrorists."[22] Second, it recalled Ambassador Landau for the third time over the Letelier case. Finally, the State Department mulled over nineteen sanctions to punish Chile, and the turf battles in Washington began. The Defense Department did not want to lose its attachés and military mission in Santiago. The Latin Americanists at Foggy Bottom argued that Washington should avoid the word *terrorist* lest it lose all influence on Santiago. The National Security Council agreed. The only State Department office arguing for tough sanctions were the human rights folks under Assistant Secretary of State Patricia Derian and her deputy Mark Schneider. They wanted the U.S. government to establish "the satisfactory resolution of the Letelier case and human rights and a return to democracy as our primary interests."[23]

In late November 1979, Carter followed the advice of Secretary of State Cyrus Vance and National Security Advisor Zbigniew Brzezinski and chose only five sanctions: reducing the U.S. mission in Chile, terminating by the following January the $6.6 million in military sales left in the pipeline of already approved sales, phasing down and perhaps eliminating the Military Group, which was doing liaison work with the Chilean military; suspending Export-Import Bank financing in Chile; and ending guarantees by the Overseas Private Investment Corporation.[24]

Harkin called the measures "despicably weak." Only eight of the eighty staffers at the embassy would leave, as would only two out of the four "Mil-Group" members. The delay of the military sales termination meant Chile would receive most of its $6.6 million in weapons. Finally, there had been no Export-Import Bank financing in five years or any Overseas Private Investment Corporation loan since 1970.[25] Senator Kennedy agreed that the sanctions fell "far short of a tough and vigorous action against terrorism." "The President must show that the United States can be a leader in the fight against terrorism," he said, having already announced that he would make a run for the Democratic presidential nomination against Carter in 1980.[26]

Foreign Minister Hernán Cubillos crowed, with reason, that Chile would easily endure such sanctions.[27] Ambassador Landau portrayed Cubillos as "not particularly bothered" by the "small pinpricks" but concerned that Washington might not support Santiago in case of a war with Argentina. Landau himself called the sanctions merely "symbolic."[28] Many observed that the failure of the Letelier extradition actually strengthened Pinochet's rule because of Carter's failure to follow through on his threats. Demonstrating his newfound political capital, Pinochet purged his cabinet again.

"All right, we bluffed," summarized a high-ranking U.S. official. "They called our bluff, and we lost."[29]

More painful for Chile, however, was a 1980 Carter decision separate from the sanctions. He excluded the proud naval power from participating in the annual Unitas 21 naval exercises to be held that fall with Argentina, Brazil, Peru, and other Latin American nations. It was the first denial of an ally in such an exercise for political reasons in twenty-one years. After the news made the front pages in Chile, Cubillos showed up at Landau's residence in Santiago "visibly exercised." The foreign minister said Argentina or Peru would see the snub as "an open invitation to play rough with Chile" in Beagle Channel negotiations and called the cancellation of Unitas "the last straw."[30] "As a reprisal," recalled Landau, "Pinochet gave orders that no cabinet officers, no general officers would come to our Fourth of July reception at the residence. So that was the type of relations that we had. Not very good."[31] The United Nations also voted 93 to 6 with 28 abstentions to condemn Chile for violations of human rights, and the U.S. secretary of the treasury denied loans to Chile based solely on human rights failures, explaining that he would have voted yes were it not for the Letelier case.[32]

The Chileans "were just hoping and praying that Reagan would win the November presidential election," Landau recalled.[33] The Republican Party kept warm relations with the Pinochet regime. Reagan himself, in his radio commentaries, had called Letelier an "unregistered foreign agent" with links to "terrorist groups," and he accused defenders of Letelier of waging a "hard-line human rights campaign."[34]

Once Reagan was elected U.S. president, the Chilean elite rejoiced. He was initially friendly to a regime his administration saw as a partner in global anticommunism.[35] Shortly after his inauguration, he rescinded Carter's already watered-down sanctions, including the Unitas ban. In July 1981, the administration began backing multilateral bank loans to Chile, and Reagan's U.N. ambassador, Jeane Kirkpatrick, voted against a special human rights rapporteur to investigate its abuses.[36] The following month, Kirkpatrick made her own visit to Chile, carrying the message that Washington wished to normalize relations. She called the Chilean government's relationship to the Letelier case "indirect, remote" and, given the failed extradition request, considered the case "closed."[37]

In 1981, the Reagan administration, helped by archconservative Senator Jesse Helms of North Carolina, also repealed the 1976 Kennedy-Harkin amendment that had prohibited U.S. military aid, sales, or training to Chile. However, the repeal also required that Reagan "certify" that Chile had made significant progress in complying with international human rights, was not aiding or abetting international terrorism, and had taken steps to bring to justice the killers of Letelier and Moffitt.[38]

Certification was the fulcrum compelling Reagan's continued pressure on Pinochet. Because of this legislative necessity, the Reagan State Department found itself under the gun to either extract concessions from the Chileans or stand accused of ignoring its own pledges on human rights and terrorism.[39]

>> Pinochet did hold his plebiscite in September 1980, with Chileans checking "Sí" or "No" on a new constitution for Chile—the "Sí" option was adorned with a star. In the previous year, the Catholic Church estimated, about 3,000 Chileans were arrested for political reasons, and half were beaten or tortured. Ted Kennedy called the vote a "perversion of democracy."[40] Still, Pinochet won two to one and declared that the Carter administration should now "leave us alone."[41] His timetable now called for another plebiscite in early 1989 on a presidential candidate to be chosen by the junta. Assuming that candidate was Pinochet—everyone did—he would serve until 1997. Loyalists began to call this process "protected democracy," a way for the military to exclude from the political system Marxists and anyone else who betrayed the "Chilean spirit."[42]

By 1981–82, however, the Chilean economic boom of the late 1970s went bust. The gross national product tanked by 14 percent, and unemployment skyrocketed to 30 percent. Reagan's high-interest monetary policy stabilized inflation but also made it impossible for much of Latin America to dig itself out of massive debt, and Chile had the highest debt per capita of any country in the world. Many firms went bankrupt, including large conglomerates.[43] The crisis emboldened the opposition, political arrests and tortures ticked back up, and 300,000 exiles remained unable to return. In May 1983, the copper miners' union organized Days of National Protest against an increasingly isolated Pinochet, who soon looked around South America to see new democracies in Argentina, Brazil, Peru, Bolivia, and Uruguay. Democrats also overthrew Pinochet-like tyrants in Haiti and the Philippines.

>> Both the Left and the Right in the United States overestimated the primacy of human rights in the Letelier case. One national security staffer ex-

plained that, in the Carter administration, "our actions resulting from the Letelier case are not, in the first instance, a human rights matter. They represent an expression of our national sovereign interests.... (This explains, for instance, why we are harder on Chile than on Argentina which has a worse human rights record.)"[44] This concern with sovereignty rather than human rights continued under Reagan, who declared that "acts of state-sponsored terrorism against the U.S. will meet swift and sure punishment."[45] Secretary of State Alexander Haig agreed that Santiago had "not helped its case" in the Letelier matter.[46] This despite the fact that, as Ambassador James Theberge wrote to the secretary of state in March 1982, "in my judgment and that of my senior staff, the Letelier case offers no chance of success."[47]

There were other pressures beyond the injury to U.S. sovereignty. Congress required some progress, which led columnist Mary McGrory to call Letelier "the ghost who haunts our Chile policy." "Letelier, from the grave," she explained, "can do what no witness of steady human rights deterioration in Santiago can accomplish—and that is stop certification in its tracks."[48] U.S. public opinion was further moved by the publication of popular books about the assassination and the critical success of the movie "Missing," about the disappearance of a U.S. citizen during the Chilean coup.

By 1983, the Reagan honeymoon with Pinochet had run its course. Santiago proved loath to collaborate on human rights, even more so on Letelier. As Larry Barcella of the Justice Department said of the Chileans, "They haven't done spit. In fact, they've been dilatory and obstructionist."[49] Even had Pinochet handed power over to the democratic opposition, the U.S. government still needed progress on the Letelier case to have military-to-military relations. Given these pressures, officials led by Elliott Abrams, assistant secretary of state for human rights and humanitarian affairs, began to argue that "democracy promotion" had to be universal to be credible. "You can't go around saying you're for freedom but we don't care about South Korea, we don't care about South Africa, and bashing only the Soviets and Cubans," explained Abrams.[50] Abrams himself had evolved since the earlier 1980s, when, upon hearing mention of Letelier, had asked, "Wasn't he some kind of a communist?"[51] He now found a kindred spirit in Haig's more moderate successor, George Shultz. When White House Chief of Staff Don Regan suggested softening up Pinochet with a state visit—an honor reserved only for America's closest allies—Shultz shut him down: "No way. This man has blood all over his hands. He has done monstrous things."[52]

"We are not trying to overthrow Pinochet," Shultz told Reagan in late 1985, "but there is increasing evidence that he is becoming an obstacle to the gradual evolution in Chilean politics that would favor our interest in a peaceful transition to a civilian elected government."53

On July 2, 1986, Rodrigo Rojas, a nineteen-year-old high school dropout who had lived in Washington, D.C., since the age of ten and was a legal U.S. resident, went to Chile "to find himself," as his mother said. As Rojas walked with a Chilean woman down the streets of a slum during a general strike, three or four men in military uniforms, black grease on their faces, jumped them from the back of a truck, beat them, poured gasoline on them, and set them afire. Then they wrapped them in blankets, drove them to another neighborhood, and dumped them in a ditch. Rojas died several days later from burns over 65 percent of his body.

Isabel Letelier mourned a young man she knew well. "Rodrigo was a very special kid. He had a desperate need to talk, discuss. He would come into the door when I was busy and sort of provoke me with something until I ended up talking to him."54

Complaining of "glacial progress" in investigating such crimes, the U.S. government increased pressure on Chile, this time from both the White House and Congress.55 Calls for economic sanctions and votes against Chilean loans at multilateral banks multiplied. The Letelier and Moffitt families joined Ted Kennedy for one of his statements, and the *New York Times* praised Reagan's "sensible policy."56 Yet there always remained significant opposition in the Defense Department, the State Department, and even Congress. Kennedy's 1987 Democracy in Chile Act, for instance, was to impose additional sanctions on Chile but was never enacted. In Santiago, meanwhile, the aggressive Ambassador Harry Barnes, often pitted against his own administration, pressed Pinochet as of his arrival in late 1985. As a result, recalled wife Betsey Barnes, "Pinochet hated my husband, and I was never sure what he and his DINA might be prepared to do about him—this man whose mission, they had decided, was to 'destroy Pinochet.' I carried with me the memory of Orlando Letelier."57

》》 The lack of firm direction against Pinochet's terrorism was not merely due to clashing U.S. interests or partisan politics. By the 1980s, the U.S. government had never developed a coherent policy against international terrorism, especially if aimed at targets inside the United States. The Office of Strategic Services and its successor, the CIA, had both limited themselves to preventing terrorism abroad, and the Kremlin's interest in international assassinations had faded after 1961. The Department of Justice, meanwhile, stayed away from crimes committed abroad. In the John Kennedy and

Lyndon Johnson administrations, *terrorist* largely meant an insurgent or guerrilla, not someone who targeted U.S. citizens.

Facing a rash of hijackings—some of which included U.S. citizens, U.S. airlines, or U.S. territory—the Richard Nixon administration gave birth to the first executive branch institutions to respond permanently to international terrorism. Still, through the 1960s and 1970s, agencies tended to keep terrorist issues away from the president, especially when the event took place outside U.S. borders.

They also collaborated poorly. As historian Tim Naftali explained about the Letelier assassination, "Working group discussions in the wake of that attack, the first successful political assassination in the capital since 1865, betrayed an unwillingness of both the State Department and the CIA to share with the working group or the FBI what it knew about Operation Condor."

Still, the Letelier case helped spur presidential action. On September 16, 1977, almost a year after the bomb in Sheridan Circle, Carter signed Presidential Security Memorandum 30, which gave the National Security Council an active role in counterterrorism—a novel term at the time—while the State Department remained the lead agency. The National Security Council also now had an Executive Committee on Combating Terrorism.[58]

>> By mid-1987, the Reagan administration had almost completely settled on a policy of openly criticizing Pinochet's human rights violations and encouraging a free and fair public consultation, now a referendum scheduled for late 1988. It decided not to back a $250 million loan for Chile at the World Bank, and U.S. government aid funds now expressly went to support human rights in the country. It also presented five diplomatic notes to Pinochet asking to resolve the Letelier-Moffitt case, and the Chileans gave negative responses to all five.[59]

A major push in this direction—though a secret one at the time—was the CIA's May 1, 1987, report titled "Pinochet's Role in the Letelier Assassination and Subsequent Coverup," released only in 2016. In it, the agency reviewed its files on Letelier and concluded it possessed "convincing evidence that President Pinochet personally ordered his intelligence chief to carry out the murder" and "stonewall[ed]" on the case to hide his involvement and, ultimately, to protect his hold on the presidency." The agency added that Pinochet had been less than forthcoming about Contreras and strong-armed the Supreme Court in the extradition case. Large paragraphs remained excised and may have laid out more specific evidence. But, regardless, this was a remarkable finding—that Pinochet ordered the hit on Letelier.⁶⁰ Though just about everyone involved had already reached the same conclusion, from Isabel to the FBI and members of Congress, never had they claimed to have evidence.

The CIA report was so explosive that Secretary Shultz explained it to President Reagan, who showed little interest in Chilean affairs while in the White House. "We are heading into an extremely difficult 12–18 month period with Chile," the secretary wrote on October 6. "President Augusto Pinochet is determined to succeed himself as President by whatever means will ensure success." Like others, he reiterated his disgust at Chile's injury to U.S. sovereignty, "a blatant example of a chief of state's direct involvement in an act of state terrorism, one that is particularly disturbing both because it occurred in our capital and since his government is generally considered to be friendly."⁶¹ The memo encapsulated one of the great meanings of the Letelier assassination: it evoked U.S. policy makers' fear of losing control over the Cold War.

In a surprise nail-biter, Chilean voters recaptured the reins of their nation's future. The "No" won the referendum in October 1988. In December 1989, elections went off peacefully. A democratic government headed by a civilian, Patricio Aylwin, replaced the Pinochet dictatorship on March 11, 1990, along with a new congress.

After the 1989 vote, U.S. vice president Dan Quayle was to have a conversation with the departing Pinochet. The statement he made first congratulated him on the elections but followed with an admonition about the remaining bone of contention in U.S.-Chilean relations: "I urge you to support our efforts to seek justice for those responsible for the assassination of Orlando Letelier and Ronni Moffitt, an act of international terrorism committed on the streets of the capital of the United States."

"The United States insists on the resolution of this case. We will not normalize relations until this is done."⁶²

15

No More Lies Are to Be Told

Months before the Letelier car bomb, Armando Fernández, then an army lieutenant, was summoned to his father's study. Alfredo, a seventy-year-old retired colonel in the Chilean Air Force, "was a very serious man," recalled his son. "A very, very serious man." The son walked to his father cheerily, out of uniform and sporting long hair, and sat down sideways on a chair.

"What do you want?" he asked the elder Fernández.

"No, put the chair in front of me, because what I am going to say to you, I want to look into your eyes when I do."

"All right." Armando adjusted the chair. "So what do you want?"

Colonel Fernández asked his son for his badge from DINA, the secret police. He looked at it, unimpressed, and laid it down between them.

"Armando, please leave DINA! Go back to the army. You were born to be a soldier, not an intelligence agent. You are a good soldier. Please leave!"

The son refused.

The father pressed on. "Look Armando, I know you. And I know your loyalty for your superiors. And one day, you are going to end up in jail. None of your superiors are going to protect you. And the only man who can protect you will be me, but I will probably be dead. You must go. Tomorrow."

Fernández paid him no mind. He was young and wanted to play James Bond games. *My father doesn't know anything*, he told himself.[1]

Alfredo died in 1977, and when Michael Townley's declarations came the following year, the younger Fernández lied about his missions to the United States and Paraguay, as Pedro Espinoza, Manuel Contreras, and Augusto Pinochet himself told him to.

For years, Fernández continued to draw his military salary and receive promotions but was relieved of his duties. From 1980 to 1982 he worked in a cement factory in Viña del Mar. He returned to Santiago to manage a store in San Miguel that sold jogging clothes and swimsuits. All of it bored him.

By the mid-1980s, his friends and former colleagues wondered why he was still on leave after five years. He would complain about his superiors and sometimes be told that he should "cool it." "I ran into Pinochet twice in restaurants after that. He shook hands, said hello, asked about my mother, and asked why I was wearing a beard and a mustache."[2]

Fernández lived what he described as a "bohemian" life and became a regular at the shadowy Oliver bar, where drinks were among the most expensive in Santiago.[3] Its decor recalled the Roaring Twenties, with images of flappers and limousines on the walls, black and gold matchboxes, green and white tablecloths, and large dark windows that shielded its patrons from the stares of the outside world. It all screamed "tacky gangster." Sometimes Fernández would go with friends and, rakish as ever, would spend evenings propositioning female patrons. Mostly, however, he drank alone, taciturn, listening to a lone black man playing a saxophone. Other patrons knew him as a *duro*, a tough guy. They largely left him alone.

One night, the bearded Fernández came in wearing a Montgomery duffle coat and began to drink alone. Soon after, other officers dressed as civilians, some former academy classmates of Fernández's, came in. After a few drinks, one walked up to him and berated him for betraying the Chilean Army's most cherished values. "How could you have lowered yourself to being a terrorist?"

Irate, Fernández pulled out a pistol from his coat pocket. The officers rushed him and knocked it to the floor, along with him. Fernández, seeing he was outnumbered, slowly dragged himself across Oliver's dirty carpet to his weapon, got up, put it back in his pocket, pulled his hoodie over his head, and walked out without saying a word.[4]

>> Equally in miserable, early-1980s limbo was the Letelier legal case in Chile. After October 1979, when the Supreme Court had definitively ruled against the extradition of the three Chileans, it had left Isabel Letelier and her allies but a glimmer of hope. They might expand the scope of the "passports case" of fraud to include the Letelier-Moffitt assassination—but only if the prosecution could uncover new evidence. Orlando's parents and sisters asked to be considered part of the lawsuit. On December 30, 1980, that dim hope became dimmer as a Santiago military judge dismissed all charges against the three men, ruling a "definitive stay" over what became also known as case 192-78.

Another year passed, and most gave up hope, but not Fabiola Letelier. Her nephew Francisco called Orlando's sister "brilliant. She's the brains in the family. She is an old-school lawyer and has a savant ability to remember names and dates."[5] Fabiola carried herself erect, with piercing eyes and a long, narrow face. A lawyer and "definitely a communist," as an acquaintance called her with a smile, by now Fabiola had years of experience fighting the Pinochet regime.[6]

Like Isabel, she had married and had four children. But then she also obtained a law degree from the University of Chile. "I had to spend nine months doing nothing but studying," she recalled, "and of course my husband was opposed to it. My husband is one of those exemplary Latin Americans, very *machista*, who thinks that women ought to simply stay home and raise the children. He had nothing to do with our children's upbringing; that was one reason why we broke up."

In her early thirties, she moved to the United States for eight years. On one hand, the southern struggle for civil rights impressed her with its summons to justice. But on the other hand, the 1965 U.S. military intervention in the Dominican Republic "moved me deeply" toward opposing U.S. power. She began inching further left. As a cultural attaché with the Chilean delegation to the Organization of American States, she felt surrounded by "servants of imperialism."

When Allende took power, Fabiola returned home and worked in diplomacy. After the Pinochet coup, "I was arrested and held in the basement of the Interior Ministry. I was very anxious because I was Orlando's sister. I was afraid for his life because I thought he had been in La Moneda [Presidential Palace] with Allende."[7] Before the coup, she was a Christian Democrat, a moderate. "The coup, and the events after the coup, sent her extremely to the left," recalled her nephew.[8] Her son Fernando toyed with joining the revolutionary Left, and she had to get him out of the country. Her advocacy for political prisoners began with her brother.

Two months after the coup, she got to talk to Pinochet but could never get to Dawson Island to visit her brother. When she did see him as a prisoner, in the basement of the War College, he said, "Fabiola, as long as I live, as long as I can breathe, I will fight against this dictatorship, for this is the most irrational, most horrible system you could ever imagine." The words pained her but also inspired her to work for the disappeared. As of 1974, she handled exile cases for the Pro-Peace Committee. When it was forced to disband, she worked with the Catholic Church, heading the Vicariate of Solidarity's projects to free political prisoners and investigate cases of disappearance from 1978 on. She always threw herself into her work; "I would say I have sacrificed much personally." From 1982 on, she moved to a lay human rights advocacy organization. From there she took time off to appeal the "definitive stay" ruling in the Letelier case.[9]

Her partner in this was Jaime Castillo, a prominent Christian Democrat and lawyer, a former minister of justice and Allende opponent, and a human rights activist like Fabiola. Within two days after Reagan appointee Jeane Kirkpatrick said she wanted to normalize relations with Chile in late 1981, plainclothes agents stormed into the sixty-seven-year-old Castillo's home, beat him, dragged him into a car, and dumped him along with three others on the Argentine border. Kirkpatrick apparently acknowledged that Castillo's work on the Letelier case was one of the reasons for his exile.[10] Castillo landed in the United States, and Isabel was incensed. When the government "resorts to something so blunt as expelling the lawyer in a case against the Government," she said, "the last traces of law in Chile are gone."[11]

In response to the appeal, on January 14, 1982, the Chilean Supreme Court reversed the military judge's ruling, finding that that court's investigation "does not clearly establish the innocence of the accused and for that reason the definitive dismissal cannot proceed."[12] That reversal changed the status of the case from "definitive stay" to "temporary stay." Many in Chile saw this as a declaration of the guilt of the three Chileans. It was not. Nor did this judgment reopen case 192-78, and the Supreme Court itself would not pursue any investigation.[13]

But its decision meant that the case *could* be reactivated. Fabiola and Castillo could gather and present evidence—*new* evidence—for a motion to reopen the case. Unfortunately, they had to present it to the military district attorney first, and then Santiago's military court, both disinclined to help. Even if they did, the evidence would also need to be presented at the Supreme Court.

For years, nothing that Fabiola or Castillo found or filed with the military court convinced it to reopen the investigation. On September 11, 1985, Fabiola was even detained along with thirty people for attempting to hold memorial ceremonies for President Allende.[14] The passports-homicide case remained what one U.S. ambassador called "technically open but practically inactive."[15]

Contreras, meanwhile, filed his own motions and had time on his side as the statute of limitations on passport fraud inched closer. In 1985, a military court granted the former DINA chief's request to dismiss entirely the suspended investigation into the passports. The Letelier family appealed the ruling, which was still pending in early 1987.

▶▶ By the mid-1980s, now-Major Armando Fernández's conscience seriously gnawed at him. His father's admonition to live an honorable life finally sunk in. "I must clear my name," he vowed. "I must clear the name of my father."[16] He also wanted to show other Chilean soldiers "that they do not need to blindly follow orders and that superiors should not abuse the loyalty of young subordinates."[17]

Fernández expressed his doubts to his sister in New York. She flew down to Chile and encouraged him to leave the country. But to defect was no snap. All military officers were prohibited from leaving the country without permission—probably among the reasons Pinochet kept him on the payroll. His brother had once been stopped at the airport when security agents mistook him for Armando. And if anyone in the Chilean government found out what he was thinking, he would surely end up in prison for the rest of his life—or dead. Was it worth it?

In 1986, Fernández finally decided it was time to be, as he said, "a man."[18] Early that year, Chilean lawyer Alfredo Etcheberry sent an urgent message to the Justice Department's Larry Barcella, saying he had heard through Federico Willoughby, who had attempted to mediate a surrender of Fernández in 1979, that Fernández may defect.[19] A Chilean also approached George Jones, the chargé d'affaires at the U.S. embassy in Santiago, "out of the blue," to discuss a prospective unnamed defector. After several conversations, it became obvious that the man meant Fernández, who "was very much afraid of talking directly to anyone in the Embassy and for that matter so were we," recalled Jones. "At this point we had no way of knowing if this were a set-up or what it was." Getting out of Chile was one problem. Once in the United States, recalled Jones, "we are going to have to tell him that he is going to be subject to prosecution in the United States for his role in the assassination. If you tell him this is he still going to come? No way."[20]

By April, Fernández had agreed, through his U.S. attorney Axel Kleiboemer, to his sister's recommendation that he meet with Department of Justice officials. He also let it be known he wanted "a permanent home in the U.S.," reported a U.S. official to Elliott Abrams, Reagan's head diplomat for human rights, adding wryly, "He no doubt prefers that this not be San Quentin." The Justice Department considered a plea bargain for parole, but it hesitated to provide witness protection to a foreigner who had abetted a terrorist act on U.S. soil.[21] At the embassy in Santiago, only the ambassador, the CIA station chief, and Jones knew of a possible meeting. The Americans were concerned "if somehow word got out, that Fernandez Larios would disappear into a military cell and never be seen again until you heard the noise of the firing squad."[22]

The first face-to-face between Fernández and U.S. officials took place on November 7, 1986. Without telling her why, Jones asked to borrow an embassy secretary's apartment, which Pinochet was likely not bugging. He got his driver and bodyguard to drive him home in the middle of the day.

"That's all for today. Nothing else on the schedule."

"Are you sure you don't want us to stick around?"

"No!"

They left. Jones grabbed a bottle of scotch, "which I always found to be helpful in breaking the ice in a Latin environment and put it into a paper sack and went out and caught a taxi, the only time I ever caught a taxi in Chile in front of my own house, and went to the apartment—the nearest thing to playing cloak and dagger that I ever got involved in." Etcheberry was also there. Fernández, without telling his hosts, also invited Willoughby. "The ice did get broken," recalled Jones. "Fernandez was stiff and somewhat nervous at [the] beginning but relaxed as [the] meeting progressed and responded readily and apparently straightforwardly to questions," reported Ambassador Harry Barnes.[23]

These early meetings were about establishing trust and discussing the security and logistics of further meetings, not grilling Fernández. Fernández was afraid the U.S. government would just arrest him and transport him stateside. U.S. diplomats feared a ploy by Santiago to embarrass Washington and definitively close case 192-78. Both sides arranged meetings by communicating sometimes through spy signals, including a rolled up magazine. Fernández's lawyer implored him to tell the whole truth and nothing but the truth, adding that one of the U.S. investigators "hates you. . . . He wants to put you in jail for the rest of your life. If he catches you lying, that's where you'll be. So tell the truth. Anything you say will be tested by various means including polygraph."

"I asked for a meeting," Fernández assured them. "No more lies are to be told."

In mid-January 1987, while still in Santiago, Fernández told his story. On the murder of Letelier, not much was new. Yes, he followed him and reported on his movements. No, he did not know the true identity of Liliana Walker, the woman who played his wife, and no, he did not know Letelier was to be assassinated, though the thought crossed his mind. (This time, the Americans believed him, though polygraphs later showed "consistent signs of deception in Fernandez's disclaimers.")[24]

More novel was the narrative of his fourteen months under guard at the Santiago Military Hospital during the extradition investigation. For the first time, American officials heard all the details about Pinochet's orchestration of the cover-up: General Héctor Orozco's extraction of truthful testimonies from all three Chileans and his turnabout move to bury them, Pinochet's own hospital visit to Fernández to keep him quiet, and Espinoza and Contreras's own roles in the cover-up. The story about Pinochet giving Contreras the order to kill Letelier was secondhand, Espinoza having relayed it to Fernández. It therefore contained "no irrefutable smoking gun that would tie Pinochet to ordering the crime itself," wrote the State Department.[25] After a ten-hour interrogation of Fernández by a team from the State and Justice Departments and the FBI, the story hung together. "We are unanimous in finding Fernandez credible," concluded Ambassador Barnes.[26]

The State Department patted itself on the back for its counterterrorist determination. "We do not forget," diplomats wrote in one report.[27]

U.S. officials in Santiago also talked about where they and Fernández could meet to further strategize. Chile? So many places were tapped. One time Kleiboemer rode in a car with embassy officials at 2 A.M. because "we had run out of safehouses," wrote Barnes.[28] Argentina? Too many Chileans there. Brazil, meanwhile, seemed a safe alternative. Fernández could fly to Rio de Janeiro without a passport, and the CIA found out that his name was not on Chile's no-fly list.[29] His cover story? He was going to the Marvelous City to meet a lover. The embassy agreed to either have "a pretty girl" meet him at the airport or at least have him return to Chile "with pictures of himself on a beach with a girl."[30]

Fernández told his actual girlfriend that he was going on vacation to the south of Chile. The night before leaving, to avoid raising suspicion, he went one last time to the Oliver bar with his friends and told them, "All right, let's have drinks."[31] On January 22, he filled out an embarkation form at Santiago's Pudahuel Airport for a commercial Varig Airlines flight, showed his national ID card, and went through the police checkpoint. "It took all my courage," he later related in his broken English, which a judge forced him to speak since he had lived in Washington as a child. "I say 'hello.' They say 'hello.' And I walk. I walk to the airplane. I sit and I say *rápido, rápido, rápido.* And the plane takes off, and I was very glad."[32]

While Fernández was in the air headed to Rio, Jones broke the news to the rest of the senior embassy staff in "the most dramatic single meeting that I ever had in the Foreign Service." The ambassador and Jones then told the Chilean minister of the interior, and "we had another stunned audience."[33]

In Rio, Fernández, now afraid he might be extradited, was subjected to a polygraph (that he had offered to take) and "additional intensive debriefing" over four days.[34] Notably, while hooked up to the lie detector, Fernández swore that he had participated in no other crimes, not even during the 1973 coup.[35]

Kleiboemer negotiated for Fernández to plead guilty to one count of acting as an accessory after the fact to the murder of an internationally protected person. In exchange, the U.S. government dropped long-standing murder charges and promised not to hand over Fernández, who considered himself "a marked man" in Chile. Fernández was flown from Rio to New York using a safe passage letter from the U.S. embassy rather than a passport or visa. From there, on January 31, he landed at Andrews Air Force Base near Washington, D.C., on the FBI director's own jet, where heavily armed agents in flak jackets escorted him off the plane and confined him in a windowless room slightly larger than a closet. *Have I done the right thing?* Fernández wondered.[36]

On February 4, the U.S. attorney for the District of Columbia made the deal public along with most of Fernández's story. That same day, Fernández confessed to the same Judge Barrington Parker who had tried Townley and the Cubans. "I have come to clear my name," he declared in a firm, clear voice.[37] Parker, however, refused to abide by the government's promise of a maximum seven years in prison; he set it at ten years. *This is a dream. I must wake up*, thought Fernández as he stood in front of Parker. "But it was not a dream. I was there," he told a reporter. "I take a chance to go to jail 10 years. [But I] don't care! Ten years, 20 years, a life! . . . Is more important that my name is not going to be in a case of murder."

His final thought was for Alfredo Fernández. "I think my father is going to be — now is — very happy."[38]

The same could not be said for Fernández's longtime girlfriend in Chile. She was shocked to hear he was not going to marry her as he had promised a half year earlier. Another disappointed Chilean was the husband of one of Fernández's conquests, who had threatened him with a gun and was hunting him.[39]

Meanwhile in Washington, Secretary of State George Shultz congratulated the team that had brought Fernández to U.S. justice, especially FBI Special Agent Stanley Pimentel and U.S. Assistant Attorney David Geneson, "both of whom undertook personal risk in meeting with Fernández in Chile." Typical of the Reagan administration, Shultz held this out as a victory against terrorism, not for human rights.

Fernández asked his lawyer to convey privately his remorse to Isabel Letelier.⁴⁰ In the courtroom, she took the stand. "I look around myself, and I don't see the murderer of my husband in this room. He is Augusto Pinochet and he is in Chile. I have no reason not to forgive somebody who asks me for a pardon, so I forgive him."⁴¹ "I would have loved to forgive more people," she recalled decades later, but, apart from Michael Townley, Fernández was the only coconspirator to do penance.⁴²

On May 6, before a packed, hushed courtroom that included Fernández's sister and Isabel, Judge Parker walked slowly to his bench, put on his tiny reading glasses, and handed down the sentence: from twenty-seven to eighty-four months after granting credit for the fourteen months during which Fernández was confined at the military hospital in Chile. The Chilean would be eligible for parole in ten months. Fernández accepted the sentence "as an honorable man."⁴³ "Yesterday I had only a past," he added. "Today, I have a future."⁴⁴ He was thirty-seven.

Fernández did not enjoy his time in prison, where he had to share a tiny cell and to clean latrines for much of the day. But on September 10, 1987, barely four months into his stay, Judge Parker changed Fernández's sentence to the already served twenty-one months in U.S. prisons and Chilean hospitals. Fernández claimed he refused to enter the Witness Protection Program.⁴⁵

"When they sentenced him, I knew his sentence was short," was Isabel Letelier's reaction. "But I didn't think it would be *that* short."⁴⁶

>> Letelier felt vindicated by the first conviction of a Chilean military man in U.S. courts. "Ten years ago the Pinochet administration killed my husband," she told reporters, "and now a young officer has proved that that was true."⁴⁷ To the Chilean press she expressed skepticism that Santiago would in fact collaborate, since it had not done so in the cases of Rodrigo Rojas and others. She hoped Fernández's testimony changed something, "but if it's only to cause a stir, two days of news and it's over, that would be a shame."⁴⁸

The same day Fernández testified in Washington, Ambassador Barnes asked the Chilean government to hand over Contreras and Espinoza immediately for trial in the United States. Chile would answer no, in due course, though it did soon after pass along Fernández's testimony to the military court. Chileans speaking to the press were circumspect. The minister of interior, for instance, limited himself to saying that the Fernández defection had "various and diverse implications," without naming one.⁴⁹ All insisted that Chile would collaborate and that the legal and political facets of the case were discrete. Only Pinochet expressed a strong opinion of Fernández in public: "In my view he is a deserter."[50]

Privately, the Chilean ambassador in Washington, Hernán Felipe Errázuriz, wrote to the Ministry of Foreign Relations that "we were surprised" by Fernández's testimony and that "the American strategy is unpredictable." He gathered that several U.S. entities were coordinating to isolate Chile. Liberal activists attacked Chile on human rights grounds, unions called for boycotts, Congress pushed through resolutions, and pressures even came from the Commerce, Treasury, and Labor Departments. Meanwhile the Iran-Contra scandal kept President Reagan "immobile" against Congress and the State Department. Errázuriz predicted a "conflict between Chilean legalism and American pragmatism" and warned against treating the Letelier case as a purely legal one because it was inherently political. The attitude he suggested? "Cordial firmness."[51]

The CIA made a mirror assessment of Chile's internal politics after the Fernández revelations "provoked an uproar in Chile, shocked the armed forces, and stunned Pinochet." The dictator cut short a vacation to return to Santiago for a nighttime meeting with his ministers and Ambassador Errázuriz. The army wanted to charge Fernández with desertion. Senior officers also wanted Espinoza and Contreras turned over to Washington. "Pinochet, however, has given no indication that he will be guided by this view."[52]

In spring 1987, Ambassador Barnes spoke privately with members of the Chilean Supreme Court, and the State Department and the surviving family members began to coordinate their next steps. Isabel Letelier could not make the meeting, but Michael Moffitt and Ronni's father Murray Karpen were there. They "expressed a great deal of skepticism, but were willing to give us the benefit of the doubt," wrote the State Department. All agreed that Washington should drop its request for extradition because Pinochet would again shift the burden to the courts, who would take another year and a half to almost certainly again reject the petition. Washington should instead insist that Chile expel Contreras and Espinoza under Article 24 of the Chilean Constitution. Once in the United States, the two Chileans could be judged, serve their sentence, and return to Chile if they wished.[53]

On May 11, 1987, the U.S. government formally asked Chile to "arrest and expel" Contreras and Espinoza. While mulling over the request, Pinochet reeled from a divine intervention: Pope John Paul II, while calling for more democracy in Chile, also asked the dictator not to close the Letelier case. Top Chileans described Pinochet during these days as often in a fury, slamming doors, walking out of meetings, and blaming the CIA for orchestrating protests in Chile and plotting to kill him—in cahoots with Soviet agents, no less.[54]

Pedro Espinoza presented an additional problem. He had been assigned as administrative counselor in the Chilean embassy in South Africa. From December 1985 to May 1987, Chilean diplomats sheltered him in Pretoria. Soon after U.S. officials learned he was not on Chilean soil, armed guards reportedly escorted him back to Chile to prevent his capture by U.S. authorities.[55]

On May 22, a military court of appeals, prompted by the Leteliers, reversed a lower court's closing of the passports-murder case. But it only returned the case to "suspended" or temporary status. This meant new evidence was still a precondition for an investigation to be opened. In June, Chile formally rejected expulsion through a diplomatic note.[56]

U.S. diplomats in Santiago were disappointed but not surprised. On July 7, they briefed lawyers Fabiola and Castillo and Orlando and Isabel's son Juan Pablo. The next step would be to request that the Chilean executive formally petition for the reopening of case 192-78. To smooth out this process, U.S. diplomats asked the Leteliers to delay their own response. "The family was clearly taken by surprise, and immediately expressed misgivings," wrote Jones of the embassy. "Let's get all the details that the Chilean government has, for instance on Liliana Walker," suggested Juan Pablo.[57] In August, the Letelier family, this time backed by a U.S. diplomatic note, petitioned the lower military court to reopen case 192-78, but in October the court refused, claiming that the Fernández evidence lacked any "probative value." The same day, the Leteliers filed another appeal.

Why not ask for the extradition of Orozco or someone else? Fabiola had asked at the same July meeting. General Orozco had sought out the truth from all three Chileans, heard it, and then, under orders from Pinochet, actively suppressed it. In January 1988, the U.S. government presented Orozco with more than 200 questions. In April, the Chilean Supreme Court refused to require the general to answer all but twelve, and the answers he did give proved evasive or false. "In the legal field," a sympathetic Chilean lawyer estimated, "the United States doesn't seem to have any other major moves left here."[58]

On and on it went. In January 1989, another letter rogatory requested answers to 113 questions from seven Chilean officials and diplomats, and the Supreme Court accepted all the questions. There was brief hope when, in response to those questions, a former Chilean ambassador to Washington, José Miguel Barros, divulged a conversation he had had in 1978 with a retired air force brigadier general, Enrique Montero Marx, who had investigated the killing of Letelier.

"This genius of intelligence mounted an operation to assassinate Letelier," General Montero had said.

"To whom are you referring?" asked Barros.

"The former chief of the DINA, Manuel Contreras."[59]

Save for his memory and his notes taken in 1978, however, Barros had no proof. Asked on television if what he told the judge were true, the surprised Barros retorted, "Of course!"[60] In March, however, a military judge decided that Barros's testimony did not warrant reopening the case, and the Leteliers appealed again to the Supreme Court.[61]

"I have not had a single success in any Court," said Fabiola dejectedly in June 1989.[62]

All these proceedings were complicated by Chile's justice system, in which military courts handled some civilian matters, some cases had both military and civilian judges, and some passed from military trials to civilian appeals courts. Also not helping was that many who played official roles in the case, such as ambassadors and military judges, themselves had been in top posts during the killing of Letelier.[63]

》》 While the Letelier case languished in Chile's courts, in the early 1990s it benefited from two breakthrough arrests in the United States.

José Dionisio Suárez, one of the two Cuban Americans on the lam, was now fifty-one with peppered hair and beard and gray-tinted glasses. He had divorced his first wife in 1979, and in 1981 in Puerto Rico, he married a twenty-one-year-old Mexican called Elizabeth Góngora. In 1990, they had been living in St. Petersburg, Florida, for six years, including three years in Elizabeth's small ranch house, now with a fifteen-month-old son, Juan.[64] Sources in the New Jersey Cuban American community apparently informed the FBI of his location. Neighbors knew him by a version of his real name, "José Suárez." He was a painter who worked little, suffered from chronic migraines, and rarely left the house.

The arrest was ludicrously easy. The local FBI bureau knew of his location for two weeks. Agents called him at twenty minutes past midnight on April 12, 1990, told him how and when to turn himself in, and he complied without resistance. Such a surrender was anticlimactic for a man who had spent eleven and a half months in jail rather than testify to a grand jury and who was also wanted in connection with bombings in New York and New Jersey and for a murder in Puerto Rico. His wife believed that "José is basically a scapegoat. He had no role in the bombing whatsoever. He tells me he was in New Jersey selling cars at the time."[65] Góngora also thought that her husband had been cleared of all charges along with other Cubans and that for that reason they lived out in the open. He had not.[66]

In Santiago, Fabiola Letelier and Castillo were confident that the new evidence from the arrest of Suárez would force the opening of the passports-murder case.[67] "The case is not closed," summarized Isabel.[68] In a lengthier interview, she described Suárez as no mere bystander but "the brains of the Cuban National Movement, a dangerous international terrorist group. Of all those characters, he is the shrewdest." Now, in 1990, she was more hopeful than ever since 1978. "Once more we see the flowering of justice, that dodgy lady who comes and goes in this Letelier case, while the dead are not dodgy but rather persistent."[69]

A week after the arrest, Suárez, dressed in a blue prison jumpsuit, appeared in front of a U.S. magistrate in District of Columbia Federal Court for a five-minute bail hearing. The ten crimes he was charged with could carry a life sentence. Suárez pleaded not guilty. He was ordered held without bond.[70]

Suárez needed a good lawyer, and the Cuban exile community once again provided. Góngora held a news conference to declare her husband's innocence and to announce the formation of a nonprofit corporation to pay his legal fees.[71] Days later, the Fund for the Defense of Dionisio Suárez had already raised thousands of dollars.[72] On May 4, four Spanish-language stations in Miami, with Guillermo Novo soliciting on air, held a twelve-hour radiothon for Suárez that raised $30,000, three times what they had raised against cancer and heart disease.[73] Three U.S. towns handed Suárez their key to the city.[74]

When the trial began in September 1990, fourteen years after the crime, Suárez changed his plea to guilty. In exchange, prosecutors agreed to drop five counts, to press for a sentence of no more than twelve years, and not to charge Góngora for hiding him. Protecting her was "his primary concern all along," said his lawyer.[75] In late November, U.S. District Judge Aubrey Robinson handed down the maximum sentence of twelve years.

>> Five months after the sentencing of Suárez, on April 19, 1991, the American television program *America's Most Wanted* aired a typical sensationalist episode in which it identified criminals at large, described their gruesome crimes, and entreated viewers to call into the program's 1-800 number with leads. The show was not only a hit with audiences but also remarkably

effective at nabbing criminals, serving as an all-points bulletin to millions of households. By that date, *America's Most Wanted* had already helped in the arrest of 147 suspects.⁷⁶ It would contribute to more than 400 arrests in its eight-year run before the Fox television network would cancel it in 1996, to the dismay of law enforcement officials.⁷⁷

Months before the episode aired, Sam Buffone, the attorney for Isabel Letelier, received a call from the show's producers asking for information for a segment on Virgilio Paz. *Oh no, this is the last thing I want to be associated with*, thought Buffone. Since the FBI had failed to find Paz while his mug shot hung on the walls of police stations for fourteen years, Buffone figured *America's Most Wanted* was a waste of time. "Everyone laughed at me for talking to them."⁷⁸ Francisco Letelier also dismissed the producers: *Whatever. You're just exploiting this thing.*⁷⁹

During those years, the FBI had gotten tips that Paz was in the Caribbean or South America.⁸⁰ In fact, he had settled in South Florida in 1980 and, since 1985, had owned Greenheart Landscape Maintenance in Boynton Beach, a middle-class suburb south of West Palm Beach. In 1991, he was thirty-nine and living under the name "Francisco Luis" or "Frank Baez," with a wife and two children. One neighbor had confronted him several times over his loud stereo or television, twice calling the police. Once, after officers left, Paz banged on her door with four or five male friends behind him. When she answered, he shouted, "Don't you ever call the police on me again!" "I was shaking I was so upset," she recalled. A fellow landscaper thought Paz generally friendly but with a strange habit of changing his name. Besides "Frank Baez," he had used two others, including "Ronaldo McDonaldo." "And I'm not kidding," said the man.⁸¹

Before *America's Most Wanted* aired on a Friday night, a former Cuban Nationalist Movement friend rang up Paz to warn him. "Why don't you get the fuck out of there?" Paz moved his family to a nearby safe house, where they watched the program together.⁸² As it ended, it showed different photos of Paz shaved, with a beard, and with glasses. "If you see this man," said the host, "alert the authorities to his whereabouts. He is one of America's most wanted criminals." In the following days, Paz not only refused to hide but also went out in public to minimize the chances of assassination. The FBI received fifty-two calls about men who looked like Paz.⁸³ At least one identified him correctly. The FBI took a few days to authenticate the tip, and on Tuesday, April 23, at 7:30 A.M., just as Paz was leaving for work, FBI cars surrounded his truck and a helicopter chuffed overhead. An agent walked up to the truck, opened its door, and pressed a gun into Paz's left ear. The Cuban slowly reached around to unbuckle his seatbelt. "He didn't seem really surprised," said Miami office Special Agent William Gavin. "He said he was glad he didn't have to live as a fugitive any longer. Of course, he could have done something about that a long time ago."[84]

Like Suárez, Paz was held without bond, pleaded not guilty at first, and changed to guilty for the trial that began in July in federal district court. In exchange, the prosecution recommended a maximum of twelve years.[85] For his sentencing on September 12, Paz was impeccably dressed in gray flannel pants and a blue sports coat. He pleaded for clemency from Judge Robinson, who had, ten months earlier, sent his friend Suárez to prison. Paz's lawyer argued that his client had been a "pawn in a much bigger game" and that surely the crime's importance had diminished in the thirteen years he was on the lam. "I can't give him credit for being a fugitive," Robinson retorted.[86] She also gave him twelve years.

>> In Santiago, Juan Pablo Letelier called the arrests of the two Cubans "very good news" and predicted that they would accelerate the legal struggle in Chile. He added that the press was incorrectly reporting that the "last fugitive" from the Letelier murder had been caught. "The main fugitive remains free," he said, "General Manuel Contreras."[87]

Michael Moffitt also saw the Cubans' trials in perspective: "This has been a 15-round fight," he said in an interview. "We are in round 13 or 14, and for the first time I think we are winning."[88]

16

Fight until the End

"For years after the coup, and after Orlando's death, I was impatient, very impatient," Isabel Letelier told a British journalist in 1981. "I wanted the world to know what Fascism was. I wanted the world to act, the world to change. Now I have become patient." Around the same time, the chumminess of the early Reagan government toward Pinochet had sparked a wave of repression in Chile, partly accounting for Letelier's cooled ardor. "Human rights is apparently not in vogue," said one forlorn liberal member of Congress, and the Chilean government declared Letelier persona non grata, barring her from returning. "But I am not depressed," she specified.[1] "I am convinced that there is no useless pain."[2]

Her sons were all adults now, and Letelier remained active in the 1980s. At the Institute for Policy Studies (IPS), she ran the Human Rights Project, which concentrated on investigating violations of rights in the Americas. In 1980 it found a "consistent pattern of gross violations of human rights" by the United States, Chile, and Guatemala.[3] She held receptions and fund-raisers not just for Chile but also for Haiti, Puerto Rico, and Paraguay. She worked on behalf of the indigenous Mapuche, raised awareness about women in the developing world, and toured with tapestries depicting scenes from the Pinochet dictatorship. "She is a haven for the oppressed," said her friend Saul Landau. "She cares about all sorts of people no one is interested in." She spoke from Rio and Lima to Helsinki and Paris, with frequent stops on Capitol Hill. Picketers called her a communist.[4] At the premiere of the 1982 movie *Missing*, she spoke to Sissy Spacek, who portrayed the wife of Charles Horman, an American disappeared during the 1973 coup. "At the very same time you were searching in the film for your husband," Letelier told Spacek, "I was looking in real life for *my* husband."[5]

In many ways, Letelier said, she was "haunted" by Orlando's murder. A large poster of him hung in her office. Five years after the car bomb in

Sheridan Circle, she was still shocked by its audacity, especially when driving through Sheridan Circle. "Can you imagine, plotting an assassination in Washington, D.C., on Embassy Row? And [the Cubans] knew... that there were two Americans [in Orlando's car], and they couldn't have cared less. Why did they do it there? And why in Washington?"[6]

Letelier's sons continued along their various life paths. Francisco had become an accomplished artist. José Ignacio got married and had a son called Orlando. Cristián struggled in Hollywood. Juan Pablo, the youngest, was increasingly involved in politics. At twenty, while paying his own way to earn a bachelor's in economics and international politics at Washington's Georgetown University, Juan Pablo meditated on being his father's son. "For some people, that's a burden.... For me, it's not a mystical inspiration. But ... I know what should be done."[7] His next stop was graduate school in Mexico, "not only for the perspectives my studies will give me," he wrote to a friend, "but also because it will serve as a 'bridge' to Chile."[8] Once in his parents' land, he would become "a functional member in the construction of a new democratic society there." He had not been since late 1974. In the meantime, he abided by his mother's words the day his father died: "Remember not to hate anyone."[9]

In 1983, Juan Pablo returned to Chile, traveling light and not sure he would stay. As he and others walked out of a public building after celebrating an anniversary of the Chilean Socialist Party, a squad of armed security officials carried them away. His mother, back in Washington, faced a potentially worse nightmare than when the regime killed Orlando—joining thousands of other Chilean mothers worrying about disappeared sons. "I do not know where my son [is or where] the prisoners are being detained," she wrote in anguish. "Nor can I find out what—if any—charges have been leveled at him and the others."

Letelier suggested that the failed criminal and civil trials in the United States emboldened Pinochet. "Is this cause and effect?" She wondered. "I don't know. I am a widow and a mother of four fatherless sons, one of whom returned to Chile to struggle for a return to democracy and is now in an unknown prison."[10] Luckily, Juan Pablo was released soon after.

Isabel and Juan Pablo were in it for the long run. "There is a large group of people who will fight until the end," she said. "We will keep working toward justice, toward peace until the very last breath," she said, pausing, "on this earth."

Then she smiled. "I'm 49. I'm just beginning."[11]

By mid-1983, she was fifty-one and had been away from Chile for almost ten years save for a brief stay in 1978. On that trip, her efforts to restore her husband's nationality had met with failure. In June 1983, the Chilean government announced that 128 leading political exiles—the "jet set," as a Chilean paper called them contemptuously—could return to Chile without conditions.[12] Letelier was elated when she saw her name among the 128. She understood her status as akin to "winning the lottery without buying a ticket. We don't know the rules of the game. But I do know that my return is not a 'favor' from the government but rather the result of ten years of struggle."

She returned to Chile for ten days in July and was struck by the lingering 8 P.M. curfew. "It's hard to fathom how, for ten years, eleven million people can be treated like minors!" she marveled to a Chilean journalist.[13] To a friend, she wrote that her short trip was "very exciting and moving. It was difficult for me to take in all of the changes in such a short period of time, but little by little I will become reacquainted with my country." Resettling in Chile, however, seemed out of the question because she had no way to earn a living there while, in Washington, her IPS job paid the bills with meaningful work. She was in Santiago for the Third National Day of Protest. "It was amazing to see the resounding and overwhelming protests of the majority of the Chilean people," she wrote a friend. "Such protest would have been impossible only a year ago."[14] She made additional short trips in the coming years, for instance, when Orlando's father died in 1984.

As the Pinochet regime came under increasing fire in the late 1980s, the Letelier family's work against it intensified. Isabel concentrated her IPS work on the Southern Cone of Latin America. She paid special attention to women and indigenous rights, cultural rights, the role of the Catholic Church, and U.S. policy. She organized public conferences, seminars, and forums and put out publications that included her *Human Rights Updates*.[15]

Juan Pablo moved back permanently to Chile the same month that his mother returned. He lived for a while with his brother Pancho. "It 'freaks' me a little to head south from Mexico," he wrote, "but in a good way."[16] He was arrested again, during the Fourth National Day of Protest, but only for a few hours. "He is a great source of information for us," wrote Isabel, "and keeps us up to date on all the latest developments."[17] Juan Pablo also helped his aunt Fabiola with the Letelier case, as did Jaime Castillo, who also returned from exile in 1983.[18]

For perhaps the first time, in 1987 at only twenty-six, Juan Pablo spoke to the media, to say that Armando Fernández's testimony exposed Chile's court system as a sham.[19] Thoughtful, charismatic, and schooled in economics and politics, the Leteliers' youngest son was slowly replacing his mother as the spokesperson of the family. He wore his dark hair long and straight, usually with a beard on his thin, ascetic face, and spoke Spanish with a trace of an American accent.[20]

Juan Pablo had a tough time adjusting to life in Chile. He ventured there out of a desire for "self-definition," he said, but "everyone expected things from me, friend and foe alike." He was lonely and saw several psychologists. "Doors were constantly closed in Chile for different reasons. For those who did not share my father's ideas I was an outcast. I became active in the movement for a return to democracy in Chile and was jailed on many occasions, my house was repeatedly ransacked, many of my personal belongings were stolen, including my car on one occasion." For his first four years in Chile, he lived first in the apartment of an uncle who was a priest, then alone in a "marginal" Santiago neighborhood.[21] Eventually, he grew active in the "No" campaign that led to Pinochet's defeat in the plebiscite. In 1989, while socialists generally did not poll well, Juan Pablo, just twenty-eight, won the most votes in a nine-person race for deputy from a rural district south of Santiago. He now represented the Socialist Party in the Chilean legislature.[22]

After about 1983, Isabel Letelier was in a live-in relationship with Miguel Sayago, a Chilean photographer in Washington. In the late 1980s or early 1990s, she stopped working at IPS, took a sabbatical year to Chile, and then retired permanently with Sayago to Santiago, where she volunteered for various causes.[23]

There, she was known as Isabel Morel, not Letelier.[24]

>> When President Patricio Aylwin and the new Congress took power on March 11, 1990, they formed an eight-person commission headed by politician Raúl Rettig to investigate the human rights violations of the Pinochet era. The Rettig Report that came out a year later had its flaws. It was prohibited from naming perpetrators, and a 1978 amnesty law protected those perpetrators from Chile's courts. But the 2,000-page tome stood as a rousing indictment of the regime's illegitimacy—Pinochet's "ironclad" control over DINA, the impunity offered by the courts, and a general state of "internal war."

The Rettig Report also declared that Orlando Letelier and Ronni Moffitt were "victims of an act of terrorism committed by agents of the Chilean state, specifically DINA."[25] It was the first admission by the Chilean government of its responsibility for the assassination.[26]

In a response to the report, President Aylwin suggested that victims would be awarded cash reparations and maybe more. That was music to the ears of the U.S. government, which was still trying to get Chile to take "appropriate steps" to resolve the Letelier-Moffitt case before the Pentagon could sell military equipment to Chile. Since the 1970s, because of the assassination, Chile had instead purchased arms from South Africa, Israel, and Great Britain. It had also begun manufacturing its own.[27]

The idea of reparations from the Chilean government arose as soon as it became clear that the civil suit that ultimately concentrated on Chile's national airline, LAN-Chile, was exhausted. In 1986, Isabel Letelier, Michael Moffitt, and Ronni Moffitt's father, Murray Karpen, began meeting with State Department lawyers to ask if the U.S. government could help. "There is no doubt that feelings continue to run high" among these survivors, reported the State Department. "Mrs. Letelier wants us to twist Chile's arm for democratization, but seems to have the strongest appreciation of the limitations on our ability to do so." Ronni's father was "still clearly deeply upset over the death of his daughter" and demanded the toughest sanctions. "If Libya had done this you know very well we would not have permitted them to continue to operate in our economy the way Chile does," he told U.S. diplomats.[28]

Moffitt, involved again in legalities after years of absence, was still intent on punishing Chile. He had hated testifying in trials in the early 1980s, when "I had to sit in a courtroom and tell it all before hundreds of strangers. The defendants used to smirk and joke. I wanted to kill them." He continued to suffer from the trauma. "I still jump when an automobile backfires or when a car that is driving too fast screeches to a halt to avoid hitting a child, dog or cat.... I fear for the lives of my second wife and my children—that they may some day be ripped away from me the way Ronni was.... Each time I plan an automobile trip with my family, I am plagued by images of the bombing and obsessively check the car and watch for danger on the road.... To this day I cannot watch violence or bloodshed on television or in movies and if I do not turn my head, I become physically ill."[29]

Lawyer Sam Buffone demanded, among other things, that Washington publicly embrace the court judgment against Chile, now up to $5 million with inflation. The shaming power of the Letelier survivors over the U.S. government had not completely abated, admitted the State Department's lawyers. "At this time when pressure on Chile is growing, it would clearly not be opportune to have Buffone and his clients publicly stating that we are protecting the Chilean government and, despite their (genuine) patience over the years, are now stonewalling when presented with a simple request that we associate ourselves with a valid court judgment."[30]

By mid-1987, Assistant Secretary Elliott Abrams presented a first diplomatic note to the Chilean government that requested compensation for the families. He suggested the money could be granted ex gratia, a common concept in international law that meant Chile would not admit guilt or responsibility. Reparations would also not be explicitly tied to Manuel Contreras and Pedro Espinoza.[31] Chile did not agree to Abrams's proposal, but the idea was out there, percolating.

In April 1988, using a rare legal procedure called "espousal" by which a government takes on the claims of individuals, the Reagan administration sent another diplomatic note, this one requesting the Letelier-Moffitt compensation in the name of the U.S. government. On October 12, one week after Pinochet's loss in the plebiscite, it demanded $12 million. The sum added the costs incurred by the U.S. government in investigating the killings to the $5 million legal judgment rendered in 1980 in federal district court.[32]

Not surprisingly, the Pinochet government rejected the request, saying it "had no role in the crimes." Shortly after, Contreras again tried to blackmail the U.S. government. He claimed to have reached an "understanding" with four "gringo" officials to protect him and Pinochet in exchange for Contreras's own silence about President George H. W. Bush, who helmed the CIA when it worked with Contreras. Embassy officials feared a possible "Contreras-initiated terrorist act." But in Washington, Deputy Assistant Secretary Michael Kozak was not cowed: "I would be mighty surprised if any U.S.G[overnment] person made any such deal with this piece of dog shit."[33]

The timing of Washington's espousal responded not only to the Chilean plebiscite but also to a bill out of the House of Representatives and now in the Senate amending the Foreign Sovereign Immunities Act to allow victims of terrorism to seize foreign assets. "It is unconscionable to permit a foreign government to avoid responsibility for acts of terrorism while it benefits from U.S. commerce through its assets in this country," declared Howard Berman, Democrat of California, the bill's sponsor. The State Department, along with conservative Republicans, wanted to kill the bill out of fear that other countries, for instance, Libya, would retaliate against U.S. property if bombed or attacked. State lawyer Abe Sofaer called Buffone and "offered a truce": if the families and their allies in Congress would drop the amendment, Washington would publicly espouse their cause.[34]

In 1990, the new, civilian government desperately wanted the resumption of U.S. aid to Chile, so it was open to compensating the families. In January, Letelier and Moffitt told Senator Ted Kennedy's staff that they wanted three things from Chile: a trial for Contreras and Espinoza, an admission of responsibility by Chile for the car bomb, and monetary compensation. On the last point, "the families would be happy with $3 million," but the State Department held out for a higher figure.

Talks took place over all three demands but focused for now on the more easily obtainable one: reparations.[35] In May 1990, the Aylwin government agreed to compensation in principle, and as a quid pro quo, the State Department promised tariff preferences and aid programs to Chile.[36] To find the magic number that would satisfy Chile, the families, and the State Department, both countries on June 11 signed an agreement to use the Treaty for the Settlement of Disputes That May Occur between the United States and Chile, penned by Secretary of State William Jennings Bryan in 1914. It called for setting up a commission to determine the amount of compensation. Commissioners included an American and a Chilean, accompanied by jurists from Great Britain, Venezuela, and Uruguay—the Bryan Commission, it would be called.[37]

Letelier got wind of accusations from Chile that she was being bought off at the price of dropping demands for justice against Contreras and Espinoza. She called Sam Buffone.

"I don't want us to be seen as people pushing for compensation," she told him. "If we have to sacrifice something, it has to be the civil part." She was ready to give up millions of dollars in compensation for the mere chance to try the two Chileans.

This is not a choice we should have to make, thought Buffone. He got assurances from Santiago and Washington that, despite the ex gratia nature of the payment, Chile would not concede its liability for murder.[38] He also released a statement: "We are not being bought off," it said. "The more critical and important question, the more difficult question for Chile, is, what will be done to bring the responsible parties to justice? Will they be extradited to the U.S. or tried in Chile?"[39] Juan Pablo also tied the Letelier matter to a larger struggle for justice. "If this case goes nowhere, nothing can be expected in other cases of human rights violations."[40]

The Letelier team's "relentless quest for justice" impressed U.S. diplomats.[41] Congress also took advantage of the Chilean Congress signing off on the Bryan Commission, as well as a private letter of assurance from Aylwin to Bush, to certify Chile in December 1990. "The Letelier case has cast a shadow over U.S.-Chile relations since 1976," assessed a U.S. official. "Now that the years of military dictatorship have ended and Chile has returned to its democratic traditions, it is in our mutual interest to put this troublesome legacy of the past behind us."[42] It would also preclude an embarrassment during President Bush's upcoming state visit to Santiago.

Throughout 1991, the Chilean Congress dawdled on the compensation issue, afraid the Leteliers and Moffitts would come back for more or that others would piggyback on the case. Finally, in January 1992, the Bryan Commission ordered Chile to pay $2,611,892. It was just short of the $2.9 million the families had requested. They calculated the financial loss that each death subtracted from the potential income of the families and added moral damages and medical costs. Letelier and her four sons collected $1.2 million in financial support, plus $160,000 in moral damage and $16,400 in medical costs for her and $80,000 for each child. Moffitt collected less because he had remarried. Still, he netted $233,000 in loss of financial support plus $250,000 in moral damages and $12,000 in direct costs. The Karpens received $300,000 in moral damages plus $20,000 in medical costs. The remaining $100,492 went for court and other costs.[43]

"A shining victory for the rule of law," Ted Kennedy called the award. "Never again can a dictator expect to commit international acts of terror with impunity."[44] In May, Chile accepted the ruling. Recalled U.S. Ambassador to Chile Charles Gillespie, "I don't think that the families were overjoyed by the amount of the money involved in the settlement. However, like everybody else, they were probably relieved that the matter had been brought to a close."[45]

The Leteliers used some of the money to help Orlando's mother in Chile. Juan Pablo used his to pay some debts from his congressional campaign and his U.S. college tuition. Still, "nothing can heal the pain of the assassination of my father," he reminded the press in Chile. "What matters to us is justice, that the guilty ones be judged in Chilean courts and there be no mantle of impunity."[46] Fabiola actually saw the reparations as "negative," seeing—not inaccurately—the prime motivation of both governments as restoring normal diplomatic relations, not achieving justice. "I'm not saying that financial reparations are not legitimate, but the essential response to a crime should be a criminal sanction."[47]

After so many twists and turns, the saga of the civil trial over the Letelier assassination was at an end. It had set several legal precedents. A legal analyst concluded that, "from resurrecting a 76-year-old treaty, to lobbying Congress and the State Department, to pressuring foreign governments to seize Chilean assets, the [Letelier] campaign against terrorism broke new ground in international law."[48]

>> The Letelier family's experiences around the return of democracy spoke to the uncertainty that would mark Chile's 1990s. José Ignacio Letelier moved back to the country in 1989, just as the Aylwin government was about to take over. He found the once great Letelier clan "basically disbanded" and himself frustrated at not being able to, like other favorite sons, benefit from "the connections passed on by their fathers who are senators, cabinet members or the president of Chile." Neither he nor his wife, both professionals with advanced U.S. degrees, could find jobs. Many Chileans assumed that the Leteliers were wealthy, but José had to depend on his little brother, Juan Pablo, to survive at first. "The order of the day is 'reconciliation,'" he noted of Chilean politics. Many saw the Letelier case as instead reopening old wounds.[49]

For now, the Leteliers experienced significant closure. In addition to receiving compensation, in May 1990 Isabel finally obtained the return of Orlando's Chilean nationality.[50] In late 1992, she used some of her award to repatriate his body from Venezuela to Chile. The family had long vowed that they would not bury their patriarch in his native country until he was made a Chilean again, and in a democratic Chile. Now they could follow through on that promise.

The remains landed on November 1 at the Santiago airport, where a decree was read restoring Letelier's nationality. Two days later, the lower house of the Congress honored him. On November 4, the Venezuelan delegation in Santiago attended a ceremony at which dignitaries received the remains. A funeral mass followed at the Iglesia de la Recoleta Dominicana, and then a burial in the Central Cemetery, attended by President Aylwin, three of Orlando's sons, and thousands of others.[51] On Orlando's black marble headstone were the defiant words from his Madison Square Garden rally eleven days before his death:

> I was born a Chilean,
> I am a Chilean,
> And I will die a Chilean.[52]

17

I'm Not Going to Any Jail

In 1991, as the Rettig Report cataloged the atrocities of the recently defeated Pinochet regime, Manuel Contreras defied the reality it described. He admitted that DINA interrogated prisoners, but he considered them prisoners of war. There was no torture by his outfit, he assured a journalist. He met the publication of the report with derision, calling its conclusions "a half truth," its commissioners biased, and the very investigation a mockery of a process that belonged only in the courts — courts that had served Contreras and Pedro Espinoza so well.[1]

Of his own role as the former head of DINA, Contreras expressed no remorse. "I have nothing for which to ask forgiveness. . . . My conscience is clear."

Contreras felt untouchable. As he bragged to journalists, "Today still there are DINA people located in top positions in the government," and they pledged to protect him in order to preserve themselves.[2] His self-assuredness and the timidity of the Rettig Report both reflected the larger deal that the military had struck with the civilian-led Patricio Aylwin government: Pinochet, the guaranteed commander in chief of the Chilean Army until 1997, pledged to stay out of political affairs in return for Aylwin leaving the military alone and forgoing any prosecution of human rights violators. The military also received eight seats in the Senate, effective veto power over foreign policy, and 10 percent of copper export proceeds.[3] While Aylwin received the Rettig Report in a solemn ceremony, the military and judiciary both dismissed it.[4]

"What happened to my *papá*," recalled Manuel Contreras's son of the early 1990s, "was that his judgment grew cloudy, he could not grasp what was happening to the country at the time. I told him to watch himself, that his power could not last forever, that he should be ready for what came after the military government. But he wouldn't listen. My father has always been stubborn, taken with his own ideas. He was always right, always had to have the last word. My father had so much power that he lost all sense of reality."

Since 1978, when he had lost his DINA post, El Mamo had begun drinking to excess while listening to recordings by Argentine crooner Leo Marini. He and Maruja, their marriage essentially over, slept in separate bedrooms. Manuel watched television alone until he fell asleep, secure in the notion that his nightstand harbored his revolver, machine gun, and two grenades.

After his forced retirement, Contreras founded the first private security company in Chile, Alfa Omega, controlled several other companies, and owned stock in a bank and an armored vehicle company. In 1985, the removal of a section of his stomach to fight colon cancer slowed him down considerably. He would eventually need a colostomy bag. Contreras notably made public his long-standing affair with his secretary, Nélida Gutiérrez, who, unlike his wife, satisfied his culinary and perhaps other tastes as well. In 1987, he left the house he still shared with Maruja. Nélida insisted they be married — "because you have to respect the laws of Earth," she said.[5] In 1989, he was asked if he had any regrets. Only one, he said: not having been harsher against "the Marxists."[6]

At one dinner with business associates and former military colleagues, El Mamo, a few drinks in him, reminisced about the 1975 funeral of Spain's dictator Francisco Franco, which Contreras had attended with Pinochet. Thousands of Falangist Blueshirts, he recalled, had raised their arms in salute of their departed leader while intoning their anthem, "Cara al Sol" (Facing the Sun).

The recollection brought Contreras to tears. "That's the kind of mystique we need in Chile!"

Seizing the moment, one of the faithful suggested, "Take the government, my general, we'll back you!"

"Yes, my general! You know that many would be on your side!" another chimed in.[7]

For now, Contreras demurred on both marrying Nélida and reentering government. Instead, he went to live, mostly alone, in the south of Chile, a dozen miles from the nearest town of Fresia. His ranch, El Viejo Roble (The Old Oak), was down dirt roads so narrow that roadside vegetation whipped car windows. An ex-DINA man commanded the army division that protected Viejo Roble. Through a business called Tegualda, Contreras ran a wood and woodchips processing plant and exported timber and pellets produced on his nearly 2,000 acres. In a winter-white ranch house made of larch, he still read military history books in his small study, which was decorated with a poster of Jesus, a photo of the Pope, several portraits of his grandchildren, and an imposing picture of a topless, buxom brunette. He rode horses every morning and owned six German shepherds and a hundred cows—among them one named "Fabiola." Locals occasionally reported seeing him gambling at the nearby lake resort. He never flew anymore; when he had business in Santiago, he preferred to drive the fourteen hours. Surrounded by trees, cattle, and the snow-capped Andes, the old man was decidedly no longer at the center of Chilean life.[8]

>> With the economy humming along at an average 6.3 percent growth rate from 1990 to 1993, many essentially shared Contreras's complacence.[9] In 1990, fully 41 percent of Chileans described 1973 more as a civil war than as a military coup against democracy, and the previous year only 17 percent considered themselves direct or indirect victims of human rights violations by DINA and others in the regime.[10] From 1989 to 1994, the proportion of Chileans who considered human rights a priority fell from 28 percent to 7 percent.[11] The country was in a mood to, if not forgive, at least forget.

Pinochet helped set the mood with his not-so-subtle threats to bring back the dictatorship. Before Aylwin even took power, he asserted, "No one is going to touch my people. They day they do, the rule of law will come to an end."[12] In 1992, 40 percent of Chileans polled said they feared a military coup.[13] On May 31, 1993, while Aylwin was in Europe, Pinochet and twenty generals, wearing combat uniforms, observed approvingly while soldiers with painted faces rappelled from helicopters in an exercise supposedly simulating an assault on a radio station while "Ride of the Valkyries" blared from the San Bernardo military base. Pinochet also called soldiers to their barracks and deployed elite black berets outside the armed forces building in downtown Santiago while army generals met inside.[14] The display of force compelled the Aylwin government to hold secret talks to allay the army's concerns about the investigation of its human rights violations, its corruption, and its independence from the president. There was also evidence that the military conducted electronic spying on civilian politicians. Such intimidation was meant to quash investigations into the financial improprieties of Pinochet's son and daughter—the infamous "Pinocheques" case.[15] Chile's right-wing political party, the Independent Democratic Union, reinforced the loss of memory by arguing that a hierarchy existed within human rights, the less important of these being subject to violation in pursuit of the "common good."[16]

In such a fraught political and legal atmosphere, the Letelier case stood out as an exception, but also not. On one hand, caving to U.S. pressure, Pinochet had explicitly exempted the crime from the Amnesty Law of 1978 that absolved his henchmen of atrocities committed up to that year. For that reason, the Rettig Report had publicly placed the blame for the Letelier assassination on "agents of the Chilean government, namely DINA agents," something it dared not do in other cases when it had the information.[17] The case's exceptional status, it then seemed, precluded a Letelier verdict, if one ever came, from setting a legal precedent in the prosecution of Pinochet era human rights violators.

On the other hand, the case was not only legal but also political. Its very prosecution might awaken the memories and stiffen the spines of more timid Chileans, who might alter the politics of forgetting and make the Letelier case mean something to all Chileans. For instance, the reparations paid to the surviving Leteliers and Karpens and to Michael Moffitt mirrored compensations awarded to over 4,500 relatives of human rights victims by the end of 1992. In addition, the Letelier crime was not alone in being subject to prosecution because the Amnesty Law did not forbid justice in the case of around 500 opponents of the regime killed after 1978.[18] While Aylwin accepted the Amnesty Law's principle that violators would not be prosecuted, he noted that nothing prevented the crimes from being investigated. Applying what became known as the Aylwin doctrine, he ordered the judiciary to investigate and the armed forces to collaborate.[19] In an even greater seeking of loopholes, a judge later argued that pre-1978 disappearances could be prosecuted because, being unsolved, they should be considered ongoing crimes.

>> In early 1980, the Chilean lawyer working for the U.S. government speculated that the only break in the Letelier case would emerge if Liliana Walker were to come out of the cold.[20] Walker was arguably the most mysterious person in the Letelier saga. "Walker"—a pseudonym for Mónica Lagos, a hostess and later sex worker on the DINA payroll—had been hired by Pedro Espinoza to act as Armando Fernández's wife on his surveillance mission to Washington in the summer of 1976. By all accounts, she had played no substantive role in the conspiracy. She had met Michael Townley and Orlando Letelier briefly, but she largely spent her days in Washington separately from Fernández, shopping and sightseeing.

Nearly everyone dismissed her as a person of little importance. "There are two types of women. You might go out a couple of times with a woman like this, but you would never take her to a restaurant," Fernández said of Walker. "She came from a lower social life. Her fingernails were uncared for." He believed, erroneously, that Espinoza ignored who she was and, more accurately, that she was not a DINA employee.[21]

For years after the assassination, U.S. and Chilean investigators struggled to identify "Liliana Walker." The earliest documented guess as to her past came in May 1978 by Robert Scherrer, the FBI's man in Argentina, who identified her as "a high class call girl" but whose name no Chilean seemed to know.[22] The FBI in Washington speculated that she might be "a highly trained DINA agent."[23] In the absence of any photo of her, an artist made a *portrait parlé*, but Townley said it looked nothing like her. By August, her name became public and the press in Santiago reported that no one by the name of Walker in Santiago knew of her.[24] Neither did anyone by that name have a Chilean passport.

Immediately, countless Chileans, military and civilian, took a stab at who she might be. A secretary for the military? The wife of a DINA operative? The daughter of a Nazi sympathizer? A West German-Chilean captain in the Chilean intelligence service? A woman in a Carmelite convent in Caracas?[25] One prospective informant asked the U.S. embassy for $200,000 in exchange for his supposed exclusive on Liliana Walker.[26] Some thought she did not exist; others, that she was a man dressed as a woman.[27] Others still speculated that she was Mariana Callejas, Townley's wife. "No, I am not her," Callejas disabused the press, "despite the fact that, based on her physical description, I wouldn't mind."[28] One magazine cataloged nearly fifty potential identities.[29] It seemed inconceivable to U.S. officials that DINA would have hired her without knowing her real name—Espinoza, long her handler, no doubt did, but other Chilean officials seemed sincerely baffled. Still, the Americans were wary of asking the Chileans about any possible leads lest the Pinochet government "disappear" them.[30]

In 1988, as Chileans began to see the light at the end of the dictatorship's long, dark tunnel, a fisherman named Marco Linares contacted the U.S. embassy saying that he, unlike those who had come before, knew the true identity of "Liliana Walker." By now, embassy staff had received perhaps dozens of such boasts. Still, in mid-June, Linares met with the political officer in a Santiago restaurant and handed him a letter from "Mónica." The letter's author claimed to have once been Espinoza's lover but to have had no contact with him or with Manuel Contreras since 1980. The embassy staff found Linares "unconvincing" because he looked suspiciously relaxed and professional and asked for money in return for his information. Still, the story seemed similar to one they heard from a former radical youth leader, who had revealed Walker's real name — Mónica Lagos.[31]

Meanwhile, the Letelier family tried to keep its legal case alive using the mere possibility of the surfacing of Liliana Walker. In February 1989, it asked the Second Military Court of Santiago not only to reopen the passports case but also to investigate the whereabouts of Walker. Two months later, a judge ruled against the family, which failed to have him removed on the grounds that he had worked for DINA during the Letelier assassination.[32]

On April 17, 1990, Chileans awoke to a dramatic front-page headline in that morning's *La Época* newspaper: "I am Liliana Walker," it declared in large font, accompanied by a 1976 passport photo. It turned out that Marco Linares got it right. Walker's real name was Luisa Mónica Lagos Aguirre, but she went by "Mónica." The letter she had written in 1988 was authentic. "I wish to lift this weight off my conscience," she had written in a longer version of her story since the Letelier assassination.

She was in Miami on September 21, 1976, when she heard about Sheridan Circle. "I have to admit that I felt a brief but intense sense of guilt. It was terrible to see Orlando Letelier's destroyed car. It was terrible to know I had been involved in such a thing."[33] She immediately returned to Chile, where she met Espinoza at the airport and handed him back Liliana Walker's passport. She continued seeing him — and traveling for DINA, to Venezuela, Peru, back to the United States — but sensed that their relationship was "always more intense" and beyond what she considered "appropriate."[34] He advised her to break up with her leftist boyfriend and reassured her that she was safe from any Letelier-related prosecution. In 1978, when the FBI came sniffing around Santiago, Lagos panicked and demanded a meeting with Contreras. He and Espinoza gave her some cash and said to go live with her parents. Intelligence services, she recalled, "completely forgot about me."

She got engaged to a man, but when she told him of her participation in the Letelier assassination, he left. In Los Angeles at the time, she returned to Chile in May 1979, devastated. "I was in a deplorable physical and mental state. I felt persecuted, I believed that they could kill me anywhere, that DINA was everywhere." She went to see Contreras, who again assured her, "Don't worry. You're fine, just fine."[35]

Later that month, when Chilean courts rejected the extradition of Contreras, Espinoza, and Fernández, Fernández got in touch with Lagos, telling her of his own abandonment by DINA. Three months later, Espinoza asked to see her. "My first instinct was to tell him to go to hell," she recalled, "but I knew what that beast was capable of if it were wounded." They agreed to keep in touch, which he did occasionally from his post in South Africa. When he stopped calling, Lagos went looking for *him*. "He was my *only* security blanket," she recalled.

The 1980s were not kind to Mónica Lagos. She lived with her parents and found herself as destitute as she had been before DINA. She was no longer welcome in the high-end brothels, so "I joined the sordid world of low-level prostitution, where it was necessary to consume alcohol, drugs, and do all sorts of insane stuff." She became an alcoholic and a drug addict. In about 1982, she had a daughter, Paula. For months in 1985, she lived in a "vegetative state" under psychiatric care, taking up to twenty pills at a time.[36] She finally reached her sister Diana, who, with their mother, rescued her from the psychiatric hospital. One psychiatrist diagnosed Lagos with "acute schizophrenia," her father reported. Friends described her as suffering from a "persecution complex."[37] "She always said 'they' were after her," recalled one, "and sometimes she'd start to cry because she thought they were about to kill her." Lagos would return to psychiatric hospitals or would leave Chile just to feel safer.

Upon returning from one trip abroad, she climbed aboard a Chilean bus and ran into a DINA agent. She had changed her appearance completely, yet he recognized her. "Liliana!" he said, using her DINA alias, and she got off immediately, terrified. She had her number deleted from the Santiago phonebook.

At home, she followed radical diets to lose weight and dyed her natural blonde hair dark.[38] She smoked marijuana, her parents admitted in shame.[39] She spent most days in a single room watching television, spoke only with family members, and rarely went out or interacted with neighbors.

When Fernández defected in 1987, she recalled, "I thought of doing the same, but there were too many obstacles." Chief among these was fear of Chile's secret police. She also had no money for a lawyer.

By 1990, at thirty-seven, she was no longer addicted to drugs or alcohol, she wrote, "but I suffer from intense episodes, which often seriously alter my personality."[40] Since 1980, she had several times attempted suicide. She slit her wrists. She tried to poison herself. She fantasized of testifying in a Washington courtroom and staying in the United States.[41]

The mystery behind Liliana Walker proved too tempting for a Chilean press fascinated by the Letelier case and enjoying increasing press freedom.

On April 8, a source approached a reporting team from *La Época* with a tip about Walker's identity—including an address in the district of Providencia, in Santiago.[42]

At 2 P.M. on Sunday, April 15, one of the newspaper's cars crept cautiously to the corner of Amapolas and Montenegro Streets. Middle-class families ate lunch in their homes. The tree-lined streets were quiet and deserted. The car approached the address on Amapolas, flanked by several other two-story townhomes. Manuel Salazar, the national editor of *La Época*, got out and approached the gate. It was locked. Salazar looked through the windows, half covered by curtains. A tan Doberman-boxer named Ruby came to the window, barking at the reporter. Salazar rang the bell on the gate and waited. Finally, a young man opened a second story window:

"Yes, what is it?"

"*Buenas tardes*. Is Mónica Lagos here?"

"Who are you?"

"I need to talk to her. It's important."

"One moment." The young man came down and opened the door. "What's this about?"

"Listen, it's something important that I have to discuss with her."

"Well, tell me what it's about."

"It concerns a trip she took to the United States. . . . Please tell her—"

"Who are you?"

Salazar pulled out a business card, while Ruby continued barking.

"Wait here," said the man, and went back in the house. A few seconds later he came out. "She's not here."

Doubtful, Salazar insisted. "Please tell her that it's very important that I speak with her. It's vital."

"She is not home. I'm alone with my grandmother."

"Can I speak with your grandmother?"

The young man hesitated, and then seemed resolved. "Please don't insist. Mónica is not here."

"Can I wait for her?"

"I don't know how long she'll be. She's coming back tomorrow."

"But—" began Salazar, seizing on the contradiction in the boy's last two sentences.

"She'll be back tomorrow, ok?" said the boy, now visibly annoyed. He walked back to the house.

Lagos has to be in that house, though Salazar. *Why else would the young man have entered and returned so quickly?* He and a colleague spent that afternoon and evening staking out the house. The next morning, April 16, curious neighbors walked up to the *Época* vehicle, inquiring into its business. Salazar was reluctant to say too much, lest they call the police. Shortly after 9 A.M., an old woman emerged from the Lagos house with a tote bag.

"That's got to be her mother!" exclaimed Salazar and jumped out of the car. "*Buenos días, señora*. Are you Mónica Lagos's mother?"

"Yes, *señor*."

Salazar asked her to let him speak to Lagos and revealed he was a journalist. Tears fell from the old woman's blue eyes. "Why don't we go into the house?" she said.

Before they crossed the threshold into the house, a voice came from inside. "Who is it, *Mamá*? What does he want?" The old woman tried to explain, but the voice grew anxious. "No, no. Go away! Please go away. *Mamá*, shut the door!" Salazar insisted, and finally the voice from inside the house said, "Ok, I'll come out, but let's speak outside." And out came a thin woman, her blonde hair in a bun, wearing a blue denim jumpsuit and thick mascara.

"What do you want? Who are you? Can I see your credentials?"

"We believe you are Liliana Walker, the woman who accompanied Captain Armando Fernández Larios to the United States, in the days leading to the assassination of Orlando Letelier."

"You're wrong. I—"

Salazar cut her off with more details from her life, all accurate.

"Please, lower your voice!" she said. "The neighbors!" They went inside, but still she was reluctant. Salazar offered to bring in someone she trusted, and she gave him a lawyer's name.

With him present, she revealed the story that appeared in the following day's paper.[43] She also handed *La Época*'s reporters a note: "I have been afraid, very afraid for a long time. But no more. The truth needs to be told, and I am ready to help . . . to go to court if I'm asked. I was always ready, but no one ever asked."

"I also want to ask forgiveness from the Letelier family. What I did, I did without knowing it would end in such a horrific assassination."[44]

When the story broke, all of Chile realized that Liliana Walker "was a woman, not the ghost many imagined," as Fernández said.[45]

The evening after she gave the interview, Mónica left her house with her parents in a Datsun 150-Y, surrounded by a SWAT-like police team. Ruby stayed behind. With friends, Mónica left a forty-page diary, which she considered life insurance in case something happened to her. Within days, she received threatening phone calls. So did *La Época*. Police placed her and her family under round-the-clock protection by ten heavily armed men, but the government did not at first investigate, interrogate her, or charge her with anything.⁴⁶ Four days into her escape, the press snapped a photo of her with dark glasses, refusing to answer questions.

Mónica Lagos's coming out coincided with the ascension of Patricio Aylwin to power barely a month earlier. It also came a mere five days after the announcement of the arrest of José Suárez in Florida. A tide seemed to be turning.

》 As usual, Isabel Letelier cut to the heart of the matter. The true meaning of the Mónica Lagos confession was not its sensationalism. "The importance of this woman," she reminded the press, "is that she confirms Armando Fernández Larios's story." That story "was treated in Chile as a bunch of lies told by a traitor to the army." Now, all of Chile knew "that this woman says she came to Washington with him."⁴⁷

Meanwhile, Fabiola Letelier prepared a petition for the Supreme Court to reopen the passports-homicide case. She did not try to contact Lagos, but Lagos did say she had documents that proved her story. (It turned out that she thought U.S. authorities could track down receipts from the purchases she had made in Washington fourteen years earlier.)⁴⁸

On April 24, the Chilean Supreme Court responded to Fabiola's petition by ordering the reopening of case 192-78 and vowing to appoint a new investigative judge. Its main reason? The reappearance of Mónica Lagos.

"It's about time," said Letelier from Washington. She called the new investigation "extraordinarily positive, not only for the Letelier case but also for all other cases of human rights violations."⁴⁹ "Let's hope history won't repeat itself," said the more skeptical Fabiola, "where the case is reopened, two or three motions filed, and then shut down again." In the past, she explained, a dozen documents had gone missing with no explanation from the court. Now, a proper judge should investigate everything Lagos claimed, and "Contreras must be made to testify."⁵⁰

The next day, the Supreme Court handed to case to Raúl Rozas, a military prosecutor, who questioned Lagos for four hours. She looked stressed, wrote one journalist, but she allegedly confirmed that DINA hired her for the trip to Washington and that, in her two meetings with Contreras, she understood that her superiors worked for him. After the testimony, she was sent to a detention center, allowed to talk to no one but her guard, and spent her days walking around her cell.⁵¹

This confinement of a witness charged with no crimes concerned Fabiola, as did the battery of psychological tests she was given. Was the military trying to make her look mentally incompetent? The early May arrest without charges of journalist Manuel Salazar was also worrisome, but he was freed the next day.[52]

At the end of the month, the Ministry of Foreign Relations suddenly declared it was done reviewing 3,000 passports from 1974 to 1979 and was closing the passports case, which Fabiola interpreted as a tactic to obfuscate the real mission of Liliana Walker.[53] More serious still, Rozas did exactly what Fabiola feared and announced that, after questioning Lagos, he was releasing her and would take no further action on the case.[54] Fabiola filed a complaint, and she and Juan Pablo called for a special investigative judge or *ministro en visita* on the grounds that, Orlando's nationality having been restored retroactively, he was now considered a citizen when killed, which made his case solvable in Chilean courts.[55] On June 5, the Supreme Court rejected the request. By late summer 1990, Fabiola and Juan Pablo had filed a total of seventy-two motions before Chilean tribunals, without advancing the case one step. "This presages a kind of non-justice," she worried.[56]

》 The absence of justice persisted for another year. But in February 1991, Minister of Justice Francisco Cumplido ushered through a series of judicial reforms, among these the transfer of most cases from military to civil courts. The "Cumplido Laws," however, kept crimes committed by military personnel within military courts. Aylwin was also careful not to pressure the military too much because the Right dominated the Senate and the Supreme Court refused to reinterpret the Amnesty Law. Pinochet also denied Aylwin's request to force the retirement of Pedro Espinoza.[57]

In March, the Supreme Court tried to delay the case by claiming it could not accept jurisdiction because the military court had pending an appeal from a lower military court to close the case. In April, that military court upheld the lower court's decision, its three military judges outvoting the two civilians. Military prosecutors jumped on the chance to ask the Supreme Court to close case 192-78 permanently.[58] At the same time, however, just as news of Virgilio Paz's arrest in Florida reached Chile, the military court modified the stay on the Letelier case from "definitive" to "temporary," two of the military judges voting to study the case further.

As usual, U.S. pressure on diplomats to nudge Chile began with the human rights community and its allies in Congress. The House of Representatives expressed its concern to President George H. W. Bush. Harry Barnes, now the former ambassador, joined the International League for Human

Rights in Chile to meet with Aylwin and the Leteliers. "Fifteen years after the crime," wrote the league's Scott Greathead, "its resolution is the single most important issue in bilateral relations between the two nations."[59] U.S. officials, as a result, told Chilean counterparts that no free trade agreement was possible as long as the Letelier-Moffitt case remained unresolved. The U.S. government also promised the Letelier and Moffitt survivors that, if Chile did not prosecute, Washington would again request extradition, humiliating Aylwin.[60]

In March, President Aylwin and his foreign ministry formally petitioned the Supreme Court to appoint a special prosecuting justice — a *ministro instructor* — to review the Letelier case, based on a Cumplido law that allowed the civil review of a military crime if that crime affected Chile's foreign relations. Few on the Letelier side were hopeful because Pinochet had stacked the seventeen-justice Court in his favor before his departure.

To make matters worse, the clock was ticking. The fifteen-year statute of limitations on homicide in Chile was to expire on September 21, 1991, in just a few months, so indictments had to be filed before then or justice would never come to Letelier and Moffitt's killers.

Suddenly, events turned in the Letelier family's favor. In early July, the Supreme Court rejected the closing of the case. On July 15, on a 9 to 7 vote with one judge not voting, the Court acceded to Aylwin's request to appoint a *ministro instructor*. The jurist they chose was one of their own, Adolfo Bañados, the newest justice and the only one not appointed by Pinochet. One of his daughters described Bañados as "timid, introverted, and affectionate."[61] He shied away from interviews. He wrote poetry and painted. In his early seventies, he remained in great shape by hiking the Andes. His peers knew him as a conservative but also a sharp, energetic intellectual and a fiercely independent, by-the-book investigator.

His decisions proved a roller coaster for the Letelier family. He had voted to reject Aylwin's request and stated that reopening the investigation would require "an extraordinary circumstance, a finding that new facts exist."[62] He quickly announced he would reopen the case but stated he would do so *de oficio*, meaning on his own initiative and not in response to petitions. Then again, he requested all the Cuban Americans' testimony from U.S. courts.[63] Fearing this was all going too sluggishly, Letelier lawyer Jaime Castillo announced he would submit a complaint accusing Contreras and Espinoza of the murder, to force Bañados to review files and rule. One week later, on August 1, Bañados officially reopened what was still commonly known as the passports case. Three weeks later, he barred Contreras, Espinoza, and Lagos from leaving the country.

Contreras sensed the shifting winds. "I will always collaborate with justice," he had previously claimed, but now he called for a writ of prohibition against Bañados on the basis that the jurist was unconstitutionally going after past crimes. He was unsuccessful.[64]

On September 20, 1991, the day before the statute of limitations was to expire, Bañados quietly issued indictments against Contreras and Espinoza, charging them with murder and the malicious use of false passports. That was enough to keep the statute from expiring. Two days later, the two were arrested. The indictments became public. Contreras was back as a detainee in the military hospital, as he had been for over a year during the failed extradition process a dozen years earlier.[65]

"This is the most important development since 1978, the first step towards real justice," exuded Fabiola Letelier.[66] Through Bañados, whom Isabel recalled as being "so careful" in his interrogation of her, she met Juan Bustos, who became her principal attorney and who did most of the legal work while Fabiola became the family's spokesperson. "I had spoken a lot for many years" by that time, Isabel later recalled.[67]

The investigation proceeded largely in secret, the press reporting the names of those questioned by Judge Bañados but none of their testimony. Throughout, both sides barraged Bañados with petitions to either facilitate or delay the investigation on every technicality imaginable.

Contreras faced his first ever unfriendly interrogator. His son, who visited him in prison three times a week, claimed that his father was a victim of "cruelty" and "political persecution." He accused "extreme Marxists" of forging documents.[68] When Contreras *père* read the transcript of his twenty-minute interview, he claimed it did not correspond to what he said. The next day, he ratified it.[69]

For others, the process was cathartic. "I thought I would feel rage, wrath," said Juan Pablo, who witnessed El Mamo's testimony. "Instead I felt contempt."[70] Like his mother, Juan Pablo saw the greater significance of the case: "Justice is being done, or at least beginning to be done, not only in the Letelier case but also in hundreds or thousands of other cases." Fabiola attributed the breakthrough to the transfer of the case to civilian courts. The hard-headed lawyer also let the public glimpse a rare show of emotion: "Personally, I am very happy, because at many points throughout these years, I grew discouraged. I felt we were beating our heads against a brick wall."[71]

The questioning over, Bañados, in pretrial hearings starting in November, argued the government's side before five of his colleagues, who were to decide whether to formally charge Contreras and Espinoza with murder and to clear the way for a criminal trial. This stage was critical. If the Supreme Court accepted the evidence presented by Bañados, a conviction down the road was all but assured. According to one human rights activist, "This is the test case to see if there is real justice in Chile." Few were reassured to learn that Contreras, from his suite in the military hospital, talked to Pinochet by phone almost every day.[72] Hundreds of families with relatives who disappeared under Pinochet looked intently at these proceedings with the hopes that they would set a precedent—or at least act as symbolic retribution. It would be the first sign that human rights violations in Chile were not cocooned in what Fabiola decried as "total impunity. And in that context, the Letelier case is a symbol."[73] She and other lawyers from both sides also presented their case to the Supreme Court.

On November 18, the Court announced it had reached a decision. Defense lawyers were sure they had convinced the judges not only that Bañados had no jurisdiction but also that the passport fraud charges were time barred. Isabel, Juan Pablo, and Fabiola waited outside the courtroom surrounded by other family members and the families of disappeared or executed Chileans.

Suddenly, the court spokesperson emerged. In a trembling voice, he read the decision: "The resolution of the 20th of September is . . . CONFIRMED."

At these words, "a huge applause filled the courthouse," wrote lawyer Jaime Castillo, "which even included the guards inside the building."[74] The Court's vote had been close, 3 to 2, to uphold the indictments and support the investigation by Bañados. Contreras and Espinoza remained under arrest, and the investigation could proceed. The Letelier family was thrilled. President Aylwin called it "major news."[75]

Asked if he was satisfied, Bañados, who had worked without pause since September, replied, "Actually, I'm tired. There is no need to inject personal feelings in this."[76]

On November 27, government officials came to the military hospital to take Contreras's mug shot and fingerprints. Rather than submit to this routine procedure, the former head of the secret police locked himself in his hospital room bathroom for two hours. The officials waited and waited and eventually gave up.[77] "He was taking a shower," explained his lawyer the next day, when again the officials showed up and waited a half hour outside his door while he refused to be booked by mere civilians. By threatening to strike down all his other motions if he persisted with this childish reticence, Bañados eventually forced Contreras to show up at the registrar's office.[78]

Contreras and Espinoza were soon out of prison on $2,700 bail each, but it was now they who complained of anonymous threats, along with their lawyers.[79] The next fourteen months told a story of back-to-back delaying tactics by the Contreras-Espinoza lawyers. They even gained approval from the Supreme Court to request President Bush to answer four questions from his time as CIA director. In June 1992, Bush—as well as Venezuela's Carlos Andrés Pérez—testified via letters rogatory.[80] Secrecy shrouded the entire process.

>> The public phase of the trial—the presentation of the evidence—began on February 17, 1993. For it, Bañados chose the Fourth Chamber of the Supreme Court, one of the smallest in the building, and moved around furniture so as to keep the seats to sixteen: four for prosecution lawyers, three for defense lawyers, four for the press, and the remaining five for the Letelier family and other lawyers. Twenty media organizations asked for a seat but received only one for radio, one for dailies, one for television, and one for the foreign press. Only pen and paper could be used; no recordings of any kind were allowed.[81] Over forty witnesses were to testify, six days a week.

Contreras remained contumacious when facing civilian justice. Citing continuing death threats, his lawyer claimed his client could not testify in the Fourth Chamber but only in military barracks. "At no time have we seen any hostile attitude from anyone," Fabiola Letelier retorted, obviously running out of patience.[82] Frustrating to Contreras's lawyers was that Espinoza, in contrast, demanded no such protection. Bañados ordered Contreras to testify in the courtroom. Still, Contreras showed up in Santiago only after he was personally served a subpoena at his remote ranch in southern Chile and after Bañados promised to double or even triple security at the courthouse.

Contreras's petition contradicted his words. Asked by a reporter about the threats, he boasted, "I have received threats by phone and I pay them no mind. I've had twenty assassination attempts against me. Don't think I'll be bothered by a mere threat." Contreras also repeated to the press the lie that DINA only collected intelligence and never disappeared anyone.

"Did you give the order to kill Orlando Letelier?"

"Are you serious? What a stupid question." The CIA killed Letelier with the connivance of Venezuela's secret police, he explained. "I ask forgiveness for nothing."[83]

In his own testimony, Espinoza essentially turned on Contreras, stating that Contreras gave all the orders while he, Espinoza, merely did administrative and analysis work. He denied knowing of Michael Townley's mission to Washington.[84]

In another interview, Contreras upped the number of attempts against him to twenty-one, repeated his accusation against the CIA, claimed there were no disappeared under Pinochet, and, when asked his main virtue, he answered, "honesty."

For good measure he added, "I will not spend a day in any prison."[85]

》》 After the questioning ended and Chileans anxiously waited several months for a verdict, a strange case caught the public's attention, one that only thickened the cloud of terror lingering from the Pinochet regime.

Eugenio Berríos was a biochemical engineer for DINA who stood accused of helping develop sarin gas in spray cans in Michael Townley's Santiago home. In late 1991, Judge Bañados issued a detention order for Berríos, calling him to testify against Contreras and Espinoza. But the chemist disappeared. In May 1992, he was secretly moved to Uruguay. In November of that year, in the resort town of Parque del Plata some thirty miles outside Montevideo, he broke a window from inside a white bungalow, climbed out, and ran to a neighbor, whom he told he was being held prisoner and was about to be murdered.

He told this story again at the local police station, but only after an army captain had already stopped by for help in recapturing a deranged "Chilean prisoner."[86] When Berríos entered the station, he said he had "been abducted by the Uruguayan and my country's armies," adding that Pinochet had ordered him killed. Half an hour later, the district police chief arrived with uniformed army troops and carried away Berríos, who supposedly recanted his story. That night, he was escorted to Brazil.[87]

In mid-1993, while the Supreme Court considered the Contreras-Espinoza indictments, the story again hit the front pages when Berríos allegedly sent a handwritten letter to the Uruguayan consul in Milan, Italy. "Don't look for me," it said. "It is impossible to find me."[88] According to some reports that year, Berríos was dead. It was rumored that his body had been found without a head or limbs in the Plata River near Montevideo. Another rumor said he was in the custody of the Mossad, the Israeli secret police—or of the CIA.[89]

To Fabiola Letelier, the disappearance of Berríos told her she was on to something. "Berrios knows things about Pinochet and Contreras that would be so damaging, it was better to get him out of the country," she said.⁹⁰ The Berríos case also suggested that Operation Condor was alive and well or at least resurging. "It tends to prove that the coordination [between South American countries] is still operating," Fabiola explained.⁹¹ It elevated tensions in Chile and Uruguay between the civilians and military, the former accusing the latter of continuing its illegal, ideological war.

In 1995, the chemist was discovered dead on a beach in Uruguay, two gunshots in the back of his neck. Twenty years later, fourteen defendants were found guilty and sent to prison.⁹²

》》 The media attention showered on the increasingly intricate Letelier case seemed to help shift Chilean public opinion. While in fall 1991, 55 percent believed that Contreras ordered Letelier's assassination, two years later, as everyone awaited the ruling, that number had increased to 71 percent.⁹³ Meanwhile, the Left in Congress was able to defeat a proposed law that would have transferred pending cases of human rights violations involving 200 military officials in secretive civil court hearings. Perhaps emboldened by the Letelier case, a group of judges increasingly refused to transfer cases to military tribunals, called high-ranking officers to testify, and revived dormant cases. Like many others, Fabiola Letelier saw her work as central to this quest for justice. "The Letelier case is going to be the first case in which a prison sentence is handed out and I think, considering the magnitude of abuses and the years that have passed, that it is immoral [that it took so long]."⁹⁴

On November 12, 1993, Judge Bañados announced that he had issued a verdict and a sentence, yet he refused to make them public until the accused had been notified. As a lawyer in the case, Fabiola was privy to the ruling. She walked out of the judge's chambers into the hallway of the court building. Surrounded by reporters, she told them: "Guilty." Contreras was sentenced to seven years; Espinoza, six. Bañados had wanted fifteen and twelve years, respectively, but reduced the sentences given the time that had passed. He absolved the defendants of the passport fraud charges since the crime had occurred before September 21, 1976, and so the statute of limitations had expired.⁹⁵

"Today is a day of great hope for all Chileans," Fabiola told the press. She acknowledged that the sentences were light but emphasized that justice had been done. The murder convictions of Manuel Contreras and Pedro Espinoza were the first instance of military officers being brought to justice for human rights violations during the Pinochet years.⁹⁶

Five days later, Contreras arrived at the courthouse in a car that screeched to a halt. Wearing dark glasses and a well-cut suit, he was whisked inside by bodyguards while cameras clicked away and a handful of protesters shouted, "Sonofabitch murderer!"[97] When he reemerged, he repeated his position: "I'm not going to any jail, because justice is going to prevail."[98]

He and Espinoza both appealed to the Supreme Court. They remained free on bail.

18

The Fear Is Over

By 1995, a full year after Judge Adolfo Bañados's sentencing of Manuel Contreras and Pedro Espinoza, the Supreme Court of Chile was ready to hear their appeal and issue a final verdict on a crime that was almost twenty years old. In the previous year, it had reviewed seventeen tomes of documents totaling 8,500 pages, with twenty additional tomes of annexes.[1] On the first day of the trial, the court reporter tallied the paperwork so far: 2,090 proceedings undertaken, 349 testimonies given, 903 documents filed, 305 official letters, 27 expert reports, 23 inspections, 22 letters between judges, 461 presentations by lawyers, and about 2,000 court statutes and dispositions.[2]

The Fourth Chamber of the Court was initially to handle the case. Its five judges—two Pinochet appointees, two Aylwin appointees, and a final judge appointed by Aylwin's successor, President Eduardo Frei—were a political mixed bag, their collective record on human rights cases being neither the worst nor the best. All were white men between sixty-one and seventy-nine years of age.[3]

》》 Each side in the case jockeyed to increase its leverage on the court. Contreras's and Espinoza's lawyers wanted the hearing of five appeals to the 1993 ruling to begin as scheduled on January 3. Being Chile's summer, with many away on vacation, the timing would minimize the public's attention to the case, which would benefit the defendants. Defense lawyers also thought the present composition of the court was favorable to their clients, since any new appointees would be Frei's and therefore bound to be more devoted to the rule of law than were Pinochet's.[4] Isabel Letelier and her four sons, however, successfully filed for a suspension of the appeals, an overt delaying tactic that moved back the Court's proceedings to late January, to enhance what Fabiola Letelier termed "transparency" and "publicity." After years of filing for stays, it was now Contreras's lawyer who called Fabiola's maneuvering "truly grotesque."[5]

Public opinion became salient in this final phase of the case because, for the first time in Chilean history, court proceedings would be televised and broadcast live to the entire nation. The Supreme Court signed an agreement with five Santiago-based channels, all of which would share a single camera feed from the courtroom.[6] Chile scholar Peter Kornbluh called the 1995 case "the O. J. Simpson trial of Chile," referring to the infamous California double-murder case whose televised proceedings captivated U.S. audiences that same year.[7] Some Chileans were overjoyed that the truth of the Letelier assassination would finally be diffused to all Chileans. Others bemoaned that "Chilean justice is inching closer to what has become of North American justice."[8]

Requests for space within the courtroom were so numerous that the Court changed the venue to the larger Second Chamber while keeping the same judges. On the first day of the trial, January 25, 106 people filled its seats. Apart from the judges and their staff, these included thirty-six journalists, including ten from abroad; eleven lawyers; five leaders of political parties; the vice president of the Senate; a half-dozen military leaders, seated behind the defense; leaders of the Communist Party; the daughters of Carlos Prats, another Contreras victim; the human rights attaché at the U.S. embassy; representatives of human rights organizations and of families of the disappeared; and Isabel and Juan Pablo Letelier.[9] Inside the courtroom, the audience remained calm. Outside the courthouse, dozens of relatives of the disappeared protested and handed out flyers, and police closed off traffic on Compañia Street.

》》 The defense presented no new arguments or evidence but merely again denied that DINA had tortured anyone or even operated abroad, and it cast doubt on the credibility of Michael Townley. Contreras's lawyers asked for a verdict of not guilty, or at least a sentence that would not require time in prison. They even had the temerity to complain that the trial had become "politicized."[10]

Letelier's lawyer, Juan Bustos, countered by asking for life in prison, arguing that a sentence of six or seven years would be more commensurate with the crime of aggravated theft, not double homicide. "This trial marks the history of Chile and a symbol of a history we do not wish to see repeated," he told the court. He compared the arrogance of the defendants to that of Macbeth, who believed in his omnipotence on the basis that Birnam Wood could not move up Dunsinane Hill—until it did and the reckoning came. "This trial has shown us clearly that Manuel Contreras and Pedro Espinoza enjoyed a similar omnipotence and imagined that their crimes would never be punished and that time would dilute their prosecution."

"But the time has come for destiny to be fulfilled," he concluded. "The hour has arrived in which justice will be done and the punishment called for by law given to the criminals."[11]

Other parties followed these opening statements by presenting evidence. The national police argued against any form of house arrest for Contreras based on a "psychosocial" report that concluded that the former head of a secret police that had killed thousands possessed "no awareness of his crimes and no desire to change." Any therapy would likely be wasted "on a subject that possesses a merely instrumental adaptation to norms, so that he internalizes none of them when they clash with his interests or expectations." Espinoza, his own report said, also denied his crimes "as a defense mechanism." He "exhibits a diminished self-criticism, distrusts others, and presents as aggressive and rigid."[12]

>> After the Supreme Court retired to deliberate on the case, Chile agonized. The choices the Court was facing were essentially three: option one, confirm the lower court ruling because no new evidence surfaced; option two, find the defendants guilty with lower but firm prison terms; or option three, issue a guilty verdict but lower the sentence to five years or less of "conditional liberty," largely justified on the passage of time.

As the public mood and the evidence seemed to turn against the defendants, and as the judges pledged to rule strictly based on the facts, fewer and fewer believed that the Letelier case threatened democracy in Chile, say, with the return of the dictatorship. Still, many worried that a guilty verdict might prompt riots or the use of force by Contreras's still powerful loyalists. After all, he *had* vowed never to go to prison. And some human rights groups promised to riot if option three was chosen. Minister of Justice Soledad Alvear found herself having to lecture and threaten Chileans about the rule of law. "The citizens in our country obey the final ruling of the courts; therefore, I urge all citizens to do so, and if not, there are legal mechanisms contemplated in our legislation to force compliance with the Tribunals of Justice."[13] Even the Socialist Party, of which Juan Pablo was a member and that handed out stickers with Orlando's face and the words "Chile Needs Justice" on them, felt the need to reassure the military that its campaign targeted Contreras, not all of Chile's armed forces.[14] There were reports of politicians from the ruling Concertación political alliance threatening the Court with political reprisals if Contreras and Espinoza did not serve time. The Court postponed its verdict until the tense climate eased.[15]

Pinochet ratcheted up the tension. In late April, a three-hour meeting of army generals ended with heads of units told to return to their garrisons and be on alert against any "unpleasant surprises." Asked what this meant, Pinochet teased reporters: "You figure it out." Unofficially, the mobilization was a rebuke to "Chile Needs Justice," which, despite its assurances, spread fear among the military. "Yes, there is preoccupation. . . . We are all one institution," one general said about the military. "A man does not leave that institution, even upon retirement."[16] One right-wing politician vowed the army would defend itself if attacked.

To an extent, the fear on the right was warranted because Contreras would indeed be the first domino to fall. As the Left's Sergio Bitar explained, "We had to build a narrative, saying, The institutions are one thing, the criminals another — separating persons from institutions. We know that that was not true, but we needed some logic to push our policies!"[17]

The continuing defense of Contreras in public seemed to shift public opinion. An April poll found that the proportion of Chileans who thought Contreras guilty had declined back to 55 percent from the 71 percent of 1993.[18]

As rumors circulated that the five judges of the Supreme Court had reached a unanimous decision, the generals met again on May 22 to now pledge to accept the verdict.[19] Three days later, a bomb scare took place at the Supreme Court. Many, including the Archbishop of Santiago, felt the need to reassure the public.[20]

To nervous giggles from journalists, President Frei joked, "I think the house is in perfect order. No problem at all. . . . Why? Is there a problem?" When they insisted on a serious answer, the president obliged:

"The country is mature and I think we will accept this decision as any mature democracy would."

"What about the military?"

"I believe that all the country's institutions will accept it."[21]

Contreras's son, Manolito, said he might die alongside his father rather than let him be arrested.[22] Fabiola called his statement "a provocation and a call to violence."[23] It certainly seemed to stir the community around Viejo Roble, Contreras's southern ranch. In the days prior to the verdict, seventeen trucks driven by farmers showed up at the compound's gate in solidarity with Contreras. Nearby, the army dispatched 80–150 Special Forces soldiers commanded by two generals, along with two helicopters and at least three armored cars.[24] The mission was apparently to prevent the "gratuitous humiliation" of Contreras. At the head of it was Brigadier General Eugenio Videla, who headed to Contreras's farm for a negotiation.

"General," Videla told Contreras, "on the instructions of the minister and my General Pinochet, I have come to propose to you that you go either to Easter Island or Chaitén." The choice was bleak: either thousands of miles off the coast of Chile or in a tiny township even farther south.

"I will not flee like a guilty man, and I will not go to prison," replied Contreras.[25]

》》 On the day that the Supreme Court announced its verdict, back in Santiago, the courthouse was also under extra security. Police installed a double containment barrier around the palace and several nearby military buildings. Busloads of Special Forces troops arrived to patrol in and around the courthouse.[26]

Starting at noon on May 30, more than 200 people gathered on the second floor of the Palace of the Tribunals. Most were lawyers or human rights workers, joined by dozens of reporters, including some from Spain, Argentina, Finland, and elsewhere. They waited. Then they waited some more. "The air was thick with anxiety," observed one Chilean reporter.[27] Several times came the announcement that the court was about to announce, but each time another announcement informed those assembled that the court's photocopier had burned out and so the announcement would be delayed.

Finally, at 6:15 P.M., Carlos Meneses, the secretary of the Supreme Court, walked up to the forest of live radio and television microphones. Cameras flashed furiously, blinding Meneses. When he began to speak, a deep hush fell over the crowd. "The Fourth Chamber of the Supreme Court has handed down its ruling in this appeal and has confirmed the decision reached by Judge Bañados." Meneses added that the Court unanimously upheld the sentences of seven and six years for the defendants—it had chosen option one. At Meneses's words, a deafening cheer erupted from the crowd. Two decades of waiting were over. People hugged and, tears streaming down their faces, sang the national anthem.[28]

Outside the courthouse, where thousands had gathered, masked demonstrators, venting their pent-up anger at police and the military, threw rocks and Molotov cocktails and injured twelve police officers. These in turn fired tear gas and arrested forty-four. Two hours later, President Frei sat behind his desk in La Moneda Palace. With the Chilean flag by his side, he gave a nationally televised address to ask Chileans to "receive this decision with tranquility and a serene spirit."[29]

Fabiola, the other lawyers, Isabel, Juan Pablo, and brother José Letelier—now an architect for the Ministry of Regional Planning—all were simultaneously given the verdict in an adjoining room. They embraced and let the joy and relief wash over them. Isabel, dressed all in black, held her two sons' hands, and they walked out to face the media. For the family, Juan Pablo acted as spokesperson. "The Supreme Court has shown the courage to administer justice," he said. "This is a struggle not only for our family, but for all Chileans."[30] José reiterated that, "if the armed forces feel aggrieved, it is their problem; there was no intention to harm. . . . We have shared a lot of happiness today because this is one of the few deeds that has gone to judgment."[31] His mother thanked God for all those who had stood by her side since September 21, 1976. Squeezing their arms, she noted her sons' strength throughout the ordeal. Decades later, she recalled that day as "beautiful. People were so happy. Everybody was so happy. I embraced one thousand people."[32]

Fabiola was, uncharacteristically, the more emotional Letelier on this occasion. "At this instant I feel a profound sense of joy, because I believe that, for the first time in Chile, we have achieved a just sentence," she told reporters in a faltering voice.[33] Several others rejoiced at the ability of Chile's new democratic institutions to pass such a major test. "This day is happier than the day that democracy returned to Chile," said the president of the Association for the Disappeared and Detained.

The U.S. embassy in Santiago had stayed advisedly quiet during the trial, not willing to taint it. But on the evening of the 30th, it issued its congratulations to the Chilean government: "We are gratified that justice has prevailed."[34] From the United States, Michael Moffitt called the decision satisfying, though not ideal. Sam Buffone and Gene Propper both judged the sentences unusually short; in the United States, Propper calculated, the defendants would have each received twenty years to life in prison.[35]

Conservatives who lamented the decision saw it as an attack on all uniformed personnel. The armed forces themselves kept an eerie silence, emitting no statement. Pinochet's daughter, Lucía, said the army was "wounded, upset, saddened. [My father] considers that the Army saved this country, fixed it up and handed it back, gently and voluntarily—without bloodshed—to the civilians, to the politicians and even his worst enemies from the past. But the enemy fails to appreciate these moral values, and, instead of weighing things, it persecutes one of the Army's generals and an active-duty brigadier."[36]

Moderate Chileans, meanwhile, celebrated the integrity of the democratic system, evident in the independence of the courts and the separation of powers. Many also seemed eager to move on, to bury with the Letelier verdict any suggestion that the Pinochet government as a whole, the armed forces, or the former dictator himself were also guilty. *La Tercera*'s editorial on the verdict was titled "Healing Old Wounds" and expressed relief that the Supreme Court had explicitly denied the participation of "the highest authorities of the government" in the crime.[37]

Espinoza penned a public statement in which he reiterated his innocence and his honor to have served "the glorious Army of Chile, victor and never vanquished" yet also announced his willingness to obey the verdict.[38]

On the day of the verdict, while crowds in the courthouse celebrated, Contreras's lawyer, Sergio Miranda, approached the press, the contracted muscles of his face unable to mask his discomfort. "I don't know what the general's reaction will be," he told the press, "but I don't think it will be applause."[39]

>> Contreras let his reaction be known in a television interview from Viejo Roble the evening of the ruling. It did not begin well, the general calling Chile's elected civilian rulers "Marxist scum . . . who act mercilessly to destroy the armed forces."[40]

Did you expect this ruling?
"With this type of judge, yes."
But you always said you believed in Chilean justice and not in North American justice. Do you maintain this?
"No, now I don't believe in Chilean justice, not in those who just emitted this ruling."
So who killed Letelier, the CIA?
"Absolutely it was the CIA."
Will you flee?
A general "never runs from a battle," he asserted. Because he was not a coward, neither would he ever contemplate suicide.
Will you go to jail?
"I am not going to any prison," he reiterated, "while there is no true justice." He claimed his right to yet another trial.[41]

The defiance of Contreras even to the venerated Supreme Court now openly grated nerves among the establishment. One minister called his declarations "an act of arrogance." The right-wing party Renovación Nacional judged his "tone" to be "simply unacceptable," and the Christian Democrats agreed.⁴² When the minister of the interior threatened the use of force to bring Contreras in, the general responded, "He can say what he wants. My comrades in arms support me absolutely." Asked who these comrades were, he answered, "a whole army."

"I will do everything that is necessary from a legal standpoint," he said, before adding, " — or any other." ⁴³

Contreras had been ordered to begin serving his sentence within forty-eight hours. "At the moment they come for me, I will decide what is necessary," the general said. "I am a winner and do not want to lose." ⁴⁴

The Chilean Army itself kept the country on edge. On June 1, two days after the verdict, twenty-seven generals met behind closed doors.

When one exited, he was asked, "General, is the institution upset?"

"What do you think?" was his response.

"Were you analyzing the ruling?" another was asked.

"Of course. We're not analyzing soccer matches!"

Hours later, Pinochet and his top staff met with Minister of Defense Edmundo Pérez Yoma. When Pérez Yoma emerged, reporters pointed their cameras at him.

"The Army will obey the ruling," he declared, to great relief.

Was that it? The military would not assist Contreras in resisting the Court's order? Editorial cartoonists seemed to think so. One drew a military man explaining to a seated Contreras, "You did not understand, general. 'The Army *complies with* the ruling,' not '*attacks* the ruling,'" playing on the similarity between the words *acata* and *ataca*. Another portrayed a hand in military uniform cutting the umbilical cord of a baby bearing Contreras's face.⁴⁵

However, the deadline passed for Contreras to surrender. Three days later, Pinochet was interviewed on television only to declare, "I believe Contreras. I have always believed Contreras." ⁴⁶ Pinochet added that his position was a personal, sentimental one and that the Court must be obeyed. And there was apparently no contact between the two men after the ruling. But the disagreement of the commander in chief of the army with the Supreme Court left many wondering if the military would be emboldened to resist the enforcement of the ruling.

》 Rumors, fears, and delays frustrated the Leteliers. Juan Pablo, raised a Catholic, said he was "ready to forgive, if those who hurt me repent and ask for forgiveness." "Most important is that the fear is over." He judged Contreras to be dishonoring the uniform by failing to accept the ruling.[47]

Although the Leteliers vowed that they were not out to persecute the armed forces as a whole, others admitted the broader implications of the case. One sociologist said that, although the case was legally against only two people, the trial pitted civilians against the military regime, especially its terrorism.[48] Human rights groups in Chile, while not as powerful as those in neighboring Argentina and facing a more popular military, still felt reenergized by the Letelier case to press lawmakers for legislation to void the 1978 Amnesty Law.[49] Some who cheered the verdict had carried placards reading, "Today Contreras, Tomorrow Pinochet."[50] The *Washington Post* wrote that Contreras "represents the decline of a once feared species: the authoritarian Latin American general." In several other South American countries, it noted, the "once coddled" abusers of human rights were now in the crosshairs of public opinion and legal prosecutors.[51]

>> For now, the target was Contreras. A week after the ruling, the Supreme Court acceded to one of the general's requests. Counting the 472 days that Contreras and Espinoza had served in the Santiago Military Hospital in the 1970s and in 1991, it shortened their sentences to six and five years, respectively. Friends of Contreras around Viejo Roble also petitioned President Frei to pardon the general, but that went nowhere, as did Contreras's other appeals in early June. Again, Contreras claimed that his poor health precluded him from serving time in any prison other than his beloved military hospital. Fabiola Letelier called his bluff. "All of Chile has seen the former general Contreras in press conferences, with a defiant, arrogant attitude, discrediting the Judiciary authorities, discrediting everyone, while coherent in his fanaticism. He himself has said that he is fine."[52] "No Chilean believes the story that Contreras is ill," agreed Juan Pablo.[53]

Sunday, June 11, 1995, witnessed one of the oddest events of the Letelier saga. At 3 A.M., Contreras, still holed up behind his fences in Viejo Roble and all his legal appeals exhausted, received a call from an intelligence captain named Helmut Schulback.

"Headed your way is the military operation of the year," he warned Contreras. Schulback explained that a line of buses carrying ninety policemen was on its way to Viejo Roble.

I see, thought Contreras. *They're coming for me.*[54] (Judge Bañados denied the existence of a warrant.)[55]

Claiming he wanted to avoid a confrontation in front of his girlfriend,

Nélida Gutiérrez, and his daughters, Contreras decided to leave his ranch. Right before he did, a major power outage knocked out all cell phone reception in nearby Fresia. Contreras's son, seemingly reading this as a police tactic, grabbed a machine gun and fired as many as a hundred rounds — until his sisters took his weapon from him. "I hoped to see someone in front of me, to riddle him with bullets, because he came into my house," said Manolito.[56] His father, meanwhile, drove thirty-six miles to a nearby military base called Sangra, where the army commander sheltered Contreras. In the evening, with no arrest coming, he returned to Viejo Roble.

Two days later — one magazine called it "Black Tuesday" — proved even stranger. It began at 10 P.M. the previous evening, when Carlitos, a twenty-something worker on the Contreras ranch, walked out the front door with a surprise for the nearly 100 freezing journalists camped out there: an entire slaughtered lamb, to be roasted on a spit. As the reporters dined on this barbecue, in Santiago the defense minister assured leaders of the government coalition that "everything was under control" in the transfer of Contreras to Santiago. A few hours later, at 1:20 A.M., two of Contreras's best friends left in a car with a man masked in an army green balaclava sitting in the back.[57] At 2:25, three military Jeeps, with twelve black berets in them, entered Contreras's compound. At 3:30 A.M., one of the Jeeps left through one of the property's secret exits, carrying the general and driven by his son-in-law. Five minutes later, the two other Jeeps exited through the main entrance, escorting a red Subaru in which sat Contreras's girlfriend and daughters. Reporters waiting outside the gates, unaware of the decoy operation, followed the convoy. For some reason, the three Jeeps met up on the way to the nearby town of Osorno and, once there, engaged reporters' cars in a chase around town and then split up again to lose them.

The cat-and-mouse game continued to the Osorno airport. There, at 9 A.M., a Citation 2 nine-person aircraft owned by the army took off carrying a VIP who looked a lot like Contreras, headed to Los Carrillos airport in Santiago. Unbeknown to reporters, minutes before the Citation 2 took off, an Army Hughes 500 combat helicopter — this one carrying the real Contreras — had left the same airport headed for the Naval Hospital of Talcahuano, near the southern city of Concepción.

The entire operation — which involved three planes, three helicopters, and three decoys, according to one count — was a ruse coordinated by several branches of the armed forces, without the knowledge of either the police guards around Viejo Roble or the civilian government. For hours, the government and Judge Bañados had no idea where Contreras was. The police who came to "arrest" him hours later, however, did likely know, because they brought only one vehicle.[58] Once he was ensconced in Talcahuano, base officials prevented the police from serving Contreras with an arrest warrant.[59]

Pinochet later explained the motivation for the June 13 operation. "We had to get General Contreras out and avoid a humiliation. We had to prevent this circus. That's why we acted so. We cannot have a general of the Republic vexed!" Discussing the case more broadly, he banged his fist on the table and shouted, "This was an unfair trial! They fabricated a court ad hoc, similar to the court in Nuremberg!"[60] Pinochet also admitted that the operation was meant to delay Contreras's transfer to prison.[61] One political scientist later assessed this as a key moment when most Chileans wondered if the military truly subordinated itself to civilian authorities.[62]

"Black Tuesday" set the nation on edge more than anything that year. On the same day, President Frei had to reassure the public that the constitution would be respected. After Pinochet's explosive comments, the president suspended a planned trip to Brazil. A Supreme Court judge threatened "contempt" against those who opposed complying with its ruling. On June 14, a loud boom exploded in Santiago, and only later did the air force announce that an F-5 fighter breaking the sound barrier had caused it. Military helicopters also hovered over the capital. One journalist called this series of events "the most serious situation created since the beginning of the transition [to democracy]."[63]

"Before General Pinochet spoke, we felt the crisis was a manageable one," said a human rights activist. "But this has now become the most serious challenge the democratic government of Chile has faced from the military." "This incident won't help our image at all," bemoaned a senior industrial executive with an eye to negotiating Chile's entry into the North American Free Trade Agreement.[64]

Chile's media was completely engrossed in the drama, devoting to it hours of coverage and several pages daily. One journalist called it "our Gulf War," the first war covered nonstop by global media. "In the last thirty days, and especially since early June, the country has thought of nothing else but the Letelier case and the reactions of the condemned military men."[65]

Obviously emboldened by Contreras's example, Pedro Espinoza began to declare that not only was he, like the general, not feeling well but also that, well or not, he would serve his sentence only at an army communications command center. It was the only place, he said, "adequate for a military man, one which gathers the conditions of honorability, security, and tranquility."[66] Nothing doing, responded Pinochet. On June 20, the military stripped Espinoza of his rank, and Chilean police thereafter arrested him without incident. Immediately, the Chilean stock market rallied. "This is one step more but this case will only end when they are both in jail," commented Juan Pablo.[67]

All that remained was the "fat cat," as one Chilean political leader called Contreras. At the naval hospital, military doctors worked to find a condition that would justify his stay there. Still refusing to surrender, the sixty-six-year-old had an already diagnosed colon cancer and possible bone cancer. He was also diabetic and hypoglycemic, had a large hernia that needed surgery, and suffered from cardiac arrhythmia and arterial hypertension, reported a slew of doctors who sometimes contradicted one another.[68] The Supreme Court ordered new medical evaluations, which again delayed his arrest. On June 27, he was transferred to a new hospital for testing.

The tests were over on July 6. Contreras's colon cancer had not metastasized, doctors found, and a move from one detention center to another would not worsen his hypertension or hypoglycemia. The hernia surgery was necessary but could be delayed. Doctors declared the general safe for transportation to prison. But because of the surgery he needed, Contreras again appealed to postpone the move, and an appeals court in Concepción agreed to review it.[69] More appeals followed throughout July. He was operated on late in the month and then returned to Talcahuano.

The ludicrousness of the Contreras delays took its toll on Chilean public opinion, 80 percent of which now believed him responsible for Letelier's murder, with 8 percent considering him innocent and the rest undecided. Still, 41 percent still doubted he would go to prison, and 38 percent felt democracy in Chile was endangered.[70] It did not help that, in mid-July, conservative senators introduced legislation to end legal investigations into the murders of more than 900 political prisoners still unaccounted for. They failed.[71] Against them were other legislators who proposed giving the president the power to order military officers into retirement and to strip the military of its ability to appoint some senators. On July 24, Pinochet ended a meeting with the defense minister by saying, "Minister, you know we don't want to stage another coup d'état. So don't force us to do so."[72]

>> Adding another level of dispute to the Chilean winter of 1995 was the controversy over where Espinoza and Contreras might serve their sentences. In the early 1990s the idea of building a special prison for military personnel arose. In 1993 the defense minister dismissed the idea. But by early 1995 there

were 1,100 lawsuits against military personnel; in January, the news came that the special prison would be built.[73]

The location chosen was Punta Peuco, twenty-five miles north of Santiago, named after a Chilean bird of prey, a raptor that enjoys warm, fresh meat.[74] It seemed apt.

Many on the left called the project at best a waste of money, at worst a five-star luxury that barely registered as punishment and made a mockery of the judiciary. The Right, meanwhile, feared its friends in the military would be insufficiently protected. Yes, it would cost a lot, answered the government, but it would not be run by the military but, rather, by the same force that ran all prisons. Special prisons existed in many countries, including for the military, and military prisoners, if not isolated, might be the target of common prisoners.[75] The important principle was that the military allowed two of its own to be confined outside a military installation. As the Contreras-Espinoza verdict drew closer, the government stepped up construction of Punta Peuco. It opened five days ahead of Espinoza's move-in on June 19.

Punta Peuco's realities largely justified suspicions of the Left. The facility cost $2.7 million to build. Its staff of sixty-one could handle 100 prisoners, but for months Espinoza was the only one. Managing Espinoza's stay cost almost $21,000 a month, compared to less than $800 for a common inmate.[76] Inside, Espinoza's suite was like a hotel's. It contained not only a separate closet and bathroom with a shower but also a new bed, a nightstand, a desk, a separate living room to receive guests, and another room with a couch and a television.[77] He enjoyed three visitation days per week, walks around the courtyard, reading materials, and a special low-salt diet.[78] "It may sound odd, but it's a rather pleasant place. It's nice to be inside," said a politician who visited Espinoza. "The windows were made in a way that you don't see any bars."[79]

The military was still dissatisfied. On a Saturday in late July, a thousand military officers and their families drove down for a solidarity "picnic" outside the prison, during which they waved flags and sang the national anthem.[80] Within weeks, Pinochet struck a deal with the government whereby army officers would be deputized as prison guards—breaking the promise of a Punta Peuco not run by the military.[81]

>> For months, Contreras further delayed his transfer to Punta Peuco by recovering from hernia surgery. On October 10, the Supreme Court ruled

that Contreras had to leave the hospital by October 23. Nine days later, it rejected his final appeal. Finally, on October 20, 1995, Manuel "El Mamo" Contreras left the naval hospital and turned himself in to Punta Peuco. In another operation involving a helicopter and then a convoy, at 1:40 A.M. on October 21—nineteen years and a month after the car bomb in Sheridan Circle—he stepped silently out of the white van that carried him to the prison. Dressed in a blue jacket and red tie, "he looked sad," said witnesses. Still without saying a word, he let the prison doctor look him over, and then guards walked him to his suite, accompanied by uniformed generals.[82]

"With this, a chapter is closed," President Eduardo Frei said that day. "The law has been fortified, justice has shown its dominion, and Chile has won."[83] When the Chilean magazine *Ercilla* published its yearly retrospective, it dubbed the Contreras trial the "event of the year."[84]

"We are content, very content," said Juan Pablo in his family's name. "It has been several years."[85] Added Fabiola, "Now, I believe, Orlando Letelier can truly rest in peace."[86]

EPILOGUE

Intellectual Authors, 1996–2018

Rather than six years as sentenced, Manuel Contreras would spend all his remaining twenty years in some kind of detention.

To be sure, his tenure in Punta Peuco was more of a sinecure than a sentence. At first, Espinoza and he did not get along, the brigadier considering Contreras a traitor for a reason he never specified. Once the prison filled with other inmates, Contreras reminded them that they owed their comforts to him—even though he had provided information that allowed their prosecution. The army, afraid that the two men would spill sensitive information about it, installed five officers and sixty-six subofficers on the inside of the prison, walled off from the civilian guards on the outside. As a consequence, said a fellow prisoner, "El Mamo's parties and the birthdays of Espinoza were veritable carnivals."[1] Contreras spent his days reading and writing his memoirs. He played pool and watched TV. He enjoyed a private doctor and even a chef.

Meanwhile, 35,000 Chileans testified about political crimes under the Pinochet regime. The prosecution of Contreras over the killing of Orlando Letelier motivated not only Chileans to pursue other cases but also investigators in other countries. In 1995, lawyers for Spanish diplomat Carmelo Soria, also killed in 1976, accused Contreras and Espinoza of obstructing their investigation, and they used Michael Townley as a witness. The same year, Italians convicted Contreras in absentia to twenty years for the 1975 murder attempt on Bernardo Leighton and his wife in Rome. Partly through documents that came to light in the 1995 Letelier case, they identified a shooter—Pier Luigi Concutelli—and confirmed that Townley arranged the hit through an order from Contreras.[2]

Contreras did publish memoirs, which largely reflected a "fog of war" defense for his crimes. He painted Chile as in a state of chaos prior to 1973, one that justified his extreme methods, and alleged that Salvador Allende's government initiated the cycle of violence. Most observers expressed grave doubts about his evidence.[3]

In 2001, after six years in Punta Peuco, he was placed under house arrest in one of his daughters' homes. In 2003, a judge indicted Contreras for orchestrating the 1974 bombing assassination of Carlos Prats and his wife in Buenos Aires, and later that year, in a historic ruling that defied the 1978 Amnesty Law, the courts sentenced him to twelve years for the 1975 DINA disappearance of a leftist militant, Miguel Angel Sandoval.[4] To that would be added a life sentence for the Prats murder. By this point, Chilean jurists argued that crimes against humanity—*lesa humanidad*—superseded the Amnesty Law and that therefore *any* crime that met the standard, not just disappearances, could be prosecuted.[5] The Amnesty Law itself, however, remained on the books.[6]

Not until 2005 did the police serve Contreras another arrest warrant. As one could have predicted by now, Contreras did not show up for his 8 A.M. order to surrender. This time, neither Pinochet nor the army would protect him with helicopters and decoys. Instead, he remained defiant from inside his daughter's house. A judge immediately declared him in contempt. At 11 A.M., nine police cars and twenty-five officers surrounded the Contreras property.

"I'm not going anywhere. If you want me, you'll have to kill me first!" Contreras vowed to the lead officer from his office.

"We don't want it to come to that, *señor*," said the officers.

"Then tell the judge I'm not going."

"I'm not a messenger."

"Then I don't accept *your* message either!"

Then Contreras rushed to his desk and opened a small drawer to pull out a weapon—which, being under house arrest, he never should have had. A scuffle ensued, during which El Mamo tried to wrest a pistol from one of the officers. Police had no choice but to wrestle the seventy-six-year-old to the ground to handcuff him.[7] "I'm a general! Traitors!" Contreras yelled. As police brought him before a judge, protesters spit and threw fruit and eggs at him.[8]

The avalanche of sentences that soon buried Contreras made him obsessed with his legal standing and his legacy. He concluded that no one knew the law better than he. He even came to blows with his best lawyer.[9] By 2007, courts had added several rulings—and 129 years—to El Mamo's fate.[10] An additional fifteen-year sentence in 2008 marked the hundredth conviction stemming from human rights abuses during the Pinochet era.[11] By 2011, he was serving twenty-eight sentences from the Supreme Court totaling over 300 years, including two life sentences. He remained involved in sixty-nine other cases.[12]

His new prison, Penal Cordillera in Santiago, was another five-star affair for condemned former military officers that surpassed even the comforts of Punta Peuco. In his own cabana, El Mamo enjoyed heating, long visits, satellite television, a well-stocked bar, and an Internet connection. Penal Cordillera also featured lush gardens, a pool, and tennis courts. Four years into that sentence, another psychiatric evaluation found the now eighty-year-old with an undiminished memory, perspicacious, even affable.

In 2013, Contreras appeared on CNN Chile to deny he was in a prison at all.

"So what do you call this?" asked the incredulous journalist, looking around.

"A military enclosure."[13] He added that the prison guards were there to "hold his cane."[14]

In September of that year—the fortieth anniversary of the coup—the Chilean government, largely to punish Contreras for his untoward comments, shut down Cordillera. In a video for all to see, Espinoza and Contreras filed out and climbed into a van that would carry them . . . back to Punta Peuco. Contreras walked into a cell that now reeked of humidity and emulsified oil. In 2014, journalist Juan Cristóbal Peña visited him there. "Rather than the ruthless dictator he had been," related Peña, "I saw in front of me a helpless grandfather, with cloudy eyes, who had on his wall a collage of photos of his grandchildren. Contreras was old and sick, but very lucid."[15] He was no longer the star inmate he had once been. When he asked a former DINA man to help him with an electric problem, the man refused, saying, "To you, I don't want to talk."

In 2010, after just divorcing his wife, he married his longtime lover Nélida, but he divorced her, too, a few years later. "It was time," said son Manolito. "My *papá* grew bored of Nélida."

"For the first time in his life," confided the son in 2015, "my father is starting to be afraid. I see it in his eyes, in how he moves. He sees that he's dying and is afraid. He's afraid of death, of pain, of the unknown."[16]

Around 10:30 P.M. on August 7, 2015, Juan Manuel Guillermo Contreras Sepúlveda, after being hospitalized for nearly a year with kidney problems, died in the Santiago Military Hospital. At eighty-six, he was serving fifty-eight sentences totaling 526 years, with fifty-six cases pending.[17]

Outside the hospital, dozens of protesters celebrated the passing of the man responsible for over half the murders, disappearances, and torture under Pinochet. He never admitted to any of the atrocities. They chanted "Murderer!," waved Chilean flags, and toasted with champagne in paper cups. "I'm really happy," said one, "but it's a conflicting emotion because this murderer died of illness but he should have suffered much more, just like many comrades suffered."[18] "Happy trip to hell, murdering son of a bitch!" one sign read.[19] Some on the right discreetly offered their condolences to his family, and a few tweeted them.[20]

>> Though as usual less dramatic, Espinoza's story followed Contreras's closely. He was tried and often convicted of several other kidnappings/disappearances, including the Prats case and several as a member of the "Caravan of Death." He spent years in Punta Peuco and in Cordillera. A Paris court also sentenced him in absentia to life in prison for the murder of four French citizens. In 2015, he received seven years for killing Charles Horman and Frank Teruggi, two U.S. citizens rounded up in the postcoup crackdown and depicted in the movie *Missing*.[21]

>> After serving a reduced sentence of seven months in a U.S. prison for doing surveillance on Orlando Letelier, Armando Fernández spent the following decade living a middle-class existence in a condominium in Kendall, a Miami suburb. Living in the United States under special immigration status, he set up an import-export business called Fervic Corp. and supposedly repaired cars on the side. He lived quietly, never disturbing neighbors with more than a *buenos días* or *buenas tardes*.

In March 1999, a process server showed up to Fernández's condo at dawn. He was being sued in U.S. federal court in Miami. In 1973, the papers alleged, as part of the Caravan of Death, he had helped torture Winston Cabello, a young leftist economist. Bound in the back of an army truck, Cabello was stabbed several times and thrown into a mass grave with twelve others. Now four members of Cabello's family, helped by the Center for Justice and Accountability, sought compensatory and punitive damages in a civil case. "For 25 years my family has waited for justice to prevail," explained Zita Cabello-Barrueto, Cabello's sister. Fernández maintained his innocence.

In July of that same year, the Chilean Supreme Court ruled that the 1978 Amnesty Law no longer applied to cases of disappeared people. A Chilean judge, Juan Guzmán, took the opportunity to indict thirty military officers, including, in September 1999, charging Armando Fernández with nineteen counts of kidnapping—none related to Cabello. The following month, the Chilean Supreme Court approved Guzmán's request to extradite Fernández from the United States to Chile. The approval established yet another Letelier-related legal precedent: the United States had asked for his extradition in the 1980s (and been refused), marking, as far as anyone could tell, the first time one suspect was subject to back and forth extradition requests between two countries.[22]

The turn of the millennium thus had Fernández facing a civil trial in the United States and a potential criminal trial in Chile. In the latter case, the deal he struck with Washington in 1987—to prevent his extradition to Chile—worked. U.S. criminal law also did not allow prosecution for either extrajudicial killings abroad or torture abroad before 1994.

However, the Miami civil trial went ahead, the first one in the United States for a violation of human rights committed in Chile.[23] In the courtroom, Fernández, fifty-three—heavier, balder, and with reading glasses—explained he was "just a young lieutenant" in 1973 and denied knowing of any crime committed by the Caravan of Death. He did admit to being in Copiapó on the day the crime took place and hearing of the order to haul thirteen prisoners onto a truck.[24]

As the jury deliberated, it took a break to ask the prosecution team how much they evaluated the damages owed for Cabello's death. The elated lawyers, now confident in their victory, responded, "There is no number, use common sense." On October 15, 2003, the jury found Fernández liable for crimes against humanity, extrajudicial killing, torture, and cruel, inhumane, and degrading treatment of Cabello. It imposed $4 million in damages. That night, the Cabello family danced the cueca in a Miami restaurant.[25] In 2005, a court of appeals upheld the verdict.[26]

By 2018, every year the Chilean government ritually asked Washington for the extradition of Fernández, who lived under an assumed name, on yet another murder. Every year, the U.S. government refused.[27]

》》 Michael Townley's other crimes while in the employ of DINA dogged him for decades. In 1983, an Argentine judge sought Townley's extradition for the 1974 murder of Carlos Prats and his wife, and the Justice Department, claiming a plea agreement loophole, cooperated in presenting the case to the Federal District Court in Washington, D.C.[28] A federal magistrate, however, turned down the request just months after Townley was paroled.[29] In

Epilogue

1986, Stockholm police inquired into Townley's apparent testimony in 1979 that Chile gave him orders to kill Olof Palme, the Swedish prime minister and Orlando Letelier collaborator gunned down in early 1976.[30] The case remains unresolved. In 1995, Townley testified in Rome in the Leighton case and testified again in the 2000s and 2010s. In 2018, he remained under witness protection.

Mariana Callejas de Townley, struggling to make a living as a writer in Chile, was denied an immigration visa for the United States in 1988 and even to join her husband in the Witness Protection Program.[31] "I feel that my future, as a writer, has ended in Chile for political reasons," she wrote at the time. "But while I was in the U.S. I explored in the field of literature and I feel that I do have a future as a writer in the U.S., where there is freedom to write about any subject."[32] In 1989 she flew to Nevada and obtained a divorce from Townley. She also joined the "No" referendum protests against Pinochet. In her 1995 memoirs, she expressed pride at never changing her name or hiding what she had done for DINA.[33] In 2008, a Chilean judge sentenced Callejas to two ten-year prison terms for the Prats murder; according to both Contreras and Michael Townley, it was Callejas who first pressed the button, unsuccessfully, to detonate that bomb.[34] An appeals court confirmed the ruling in 2009, but in 2010 the Supreme Court lowered her sentence to five years. In 2015, she and fourteen other DINA agents were indicted for the Soria murder, the court finding that Soria was tortured and killed in her Lo Curro home. But Callejas never served a day in prison. In August 2016, at eighty-four, plagued by dementia, she died in a care home in Santiago.

》》 The Cuban Americans who helped Townley kill Letelier and Moffitt thrived in their U.S. enclave communities. A diminishing but still powerful slice of Florida's Cubans continued to offer shelter to terrorists, despite counterterrorism laws passed in the 1990s. Guillermo and Ignacio Novo and their Letelier-Moffitt collaborators never worked together again, but they were now funded by the Cuban American National Foundation and Miami businessman Jorge Mas Canosa, whom Guillermo served as bodyguard. In 1995, U.S. government documents revealed, Guillermo shipped explosives to Cuba while ostensibly running a furniture store in Miami.[35] Even some in the federal government implicitly tolerated illegal activities. "I welcome the opportunity of having anyone assassinate Castro," said Representative Ileana Ros-Lehtinen, Republican of Florida, before she served as chair of the House Foreign Affairs Committee from 2011 to 2013. She had also lobbied for the release of José Dionisio Suárez and Virgilio Paz.[36]

Paz served seven years in prison, and Suárez was released on probation in 1997 after eight years, but both remained in custody of the Immigration and Naturalization Service because of a 1996 law that subjected noncitizens convicted of violent crimes to automatic deportation. The Cuban American National Foundation came to Paz's rescue, arguing that deportation to Cuba would subject him to torture in Castro's prisons, thus violating the U.N. Convention against Torture. Florida Governor Jeb Bush also lobbied his brother, President George W. Bush, to release Paz and Suárez, who was in an identical predicament. In 2001, the Supreme Court that elevated Bush to the presidency ruled that the Immigration and Naturalization Service could not hold such detainees indefinitely, and Paz and Suárez walked out in August of that year.[37]

Paz called the Letelier-Moffitt car bomb "a grave human error," all but admitting his guilt. "At the time I was 23–24 years old. I was a young man full of ideas. Unfortunately, I saw myself involved in that." He expressed regret for Ronni Moffitt's death and claimed that, if he could speak to Isabel Letelier, "I'd tell her that her husband was a soldier for his cause."[38] Clarifying that his client was not admitting guilt, Paz's lawyer added, "He's sorry in a humanitarian way. The same way we're sorry for Mother Teresa and Mahatma Gandhi." On Facebook in 2015, Paz confirmed that "giving up or losing our youth, families, and bringing suffering to our loved ones" were all "worth it."[39] In interviews in the 2000s and 2010s, most of the Cuban Americans involved in the Letelier hit confirmed their involvement while disputing mere details.[40]

"This is a fantastic day because I'm going to embrace my wife and children," said the sixty-two-year-old Suárez upon his release.[41] He vowed to write a book, but either he never did or it was not published.[42] Instead, he started a house painting company in Miami and displayed his own oil and acrylic paintings in 2007.[43] As of 2016, both Paz and Suárez still lived in Florida. Alvin Ross, whose conviction was overturned in the early 1980s, lived quietly in Union City, New Jersey.

In Panama in 2000, Guillermo Novo, in his mid-sixties, was arrested, along with convicted terrorist Luis Posada Carriles and two others in a plot to assassinate Fidel Castro using thirty-three pounds of explosives with their fingerprints on them. Guillermo's brother Ignacio died in 2004 while Guillermo was in prison—"one of the most difficult moments of my life."[44] That year, the four Panama plotters were found guilty but then immediately pardoned by the outgoing Panamanian president, Mireya Moscoso.[45] George W. Bush administration officials denied any collusion in the pardon, but many suspected that Cuban American politicians such as Ros-Lehtinen played a part, and the White House declined to condemn the actions of the men.[46] In May 2004, when Bush gave a speech in Miami, Paz and Suárez were there, offering hearty applause.[47]

》》 Carter Cornick of the FBI retired in 1988 and by 1990 had founded Counter Terrorism Consultants, Inc., with Robert Scherrer, Gene Propper, and Larry Barcella.[48] He gave occasional interviews on the Letelier case.

Scherrer retired from the FBI in 1988 with multiple sclerosis, and Isabel Letelier and the Institute for Policy Studies celebrated him with a Letelier-Moffitt Special Recognition Award.[49] In his acceptance speech, he hinted that other federal agencies had advance knowledge of the Letelier bombing: "I'm sorry the FBI did not do anything, but no one told us. . . . They could have. . . . They should have. . . . It was just pure incompetence."[50]

Larry Barcella joined a law firm. He died in 2010 from bladder cancer.[51]

》》 Augusto Pinochet turned eighty right after Contreras entered Punta Peuco. Soon after, he had a pacemaker and used a hearing aid. Suffering from shortness of breath, limping, he stepped down as army commander in chief on March 11, 1998. But he created for himself the title of senator for life, over the objections of 60 percent of Chileans and a lawsuit from President Eduardo Frei's party because the title granted him full immunity from criminal prosecution. "Thank you! Thank you, my country! I have been your soldier, and that makes me happy," he said with a hoarse voice as thousands protested, throwing rocks at police who fired back with tear gas and a water cannon.[52]

The former dictator's semiretirement would not be as peaceful as he imagined. On October 16, 1998, Pinochet rested in a private room at the London Clinic, undergoing treatment. Just before 11 P.M., Sergeant David Jones of Scotland Yard arrived with a small group to arrest him. A Chilean Army captain in charge of Pinochet's guards stood in his way.

"You have to leave at once," Jones warned.

"I cannot leave my general," said the captain. "I'm a Chilean military officer, and I only take orders from my superiors."

"You can either leave nicely, or you can leave by force," said Jones. When one of the guards reached into his pocket, the British police tensed up, since none of them was armed. But the guard merely pulled out a cell phone, and the guards were led outside the building.[53]

The arrest of Pinochet, issued by Spanish judge Baltasar Garzón, shocked all Chile observers around the world. "When I read it," said Murray Karpen, Ronni's father, "I said, 'There is a God.'"[54] Francisco Letelier, like his mother, saw the bigger picture. "There are some who, like me, are not so concerned about whether Pinochet goes to jail—he is, after all, 82 years old. It is more important that we as a world society recognize that a man like Pinochet is someone who should be submitted to justice and investigation. It is more important that the world know the truth."[55]

In November 1998, Great Britain's highest court rejected Pinochet's claim of immunity, allowing the Spanish extradition request to go forward.[56] Many, including members of Congress, the Institute for Policy Studies, and the Justice Department's Larry Barcella, publicly urged the State and Justice Departments to make all its relevant documents available to Garzón and to request extradition and indict Pinochet himself for the Letelier-Moffitt assassination.[57]

A major declassification project began, some of which reinforced the claim that Pinochet was the intellectual author of the Letelier assassination. Over the years, almost everyone involved in the case assessed that Pinochet was not only aware of the plot but also ordered it, and that Contreras was the key to proving it. "Pinochet unaware of all of this? That's inconceivable," said Cornick. "He knew. He had to know, but short of a confession or Contreras's testimony, we can't indict him." "I have no doubt," agreed Cornick's colleague, Robert Scherrer. "The problem is we can't prove it—unless Contreras implicates him."[58]

Contreras, in an effort to lower his sentence, did file an affidavit in February 1998. He stated that "only [Pinochet] as supreme authority of DINA had the power to order the missions that were executed.... Always in my capacity as delegate of the President, I carried out strictly what was ordered."[59] Contreras's son said his father felt "abandoned by his peers and by all the businessmen who grew rich thanks to the military regime and who now pretend not to know him."[60] When asked directly for a response, Pinochet seemed relaxed. "It is very difficult to answer this question because there are many things I ordered him to do, but which things? I had to exercise power. But I could never say that I was actually running DINA."[61]

In December, Garzón indicted Pinochet "for the crimes of genocide, terrorism and torture," naming more than 2,500 victims, including Letelier and Moffitt. Pinochet would spend sixteen more months in Great Britain while his lawyers argued that he was too senile to stand trial.[62] Fabiola Letelier had witnessed that pretense before with Contreras, and again did not buy it. "One day he is walking in his garden in England, the next he is depressed in a wheelchair."[63]

But it worked. In March 2000, the House of Lords ruled that Pinochet "would not at present be mentally capable of meaningful participation in a trial."[64] Home Secretary Jack Straw released him. Days later, he was back in Chile.

Days after *that*, the U.S. Justice Department reopened a grand jury investigation aimed at indicting Pinochet. Officials told Isabel Letelier they were "vigorously" pursuing the case. The possibility of getting Chile to extradite Pinochet was remote, all admitted, so the goal was different. "You've got to send a message with [terrorist] investigations, no matter how far back they go," said an FBI counterterrorism official.[65] Justice officials did obtain permission from Santiago to interview forty-two witnesses there.[66] Declassifications also revealed that Pinochet asked Paraguay for the phony passports for Michael Townley and Fernández.[67] Letelier thanked Attorney General Janet Reno for the probe, which suggested the existence of an order from Pinochet to Espinoza to murder her husband, but no document ever surfaced. The incoming Bush administration failed to follow up.[68]

Emboldened during the absence of Pinochet, Chilean judges launched a spate of investigations. A year after the old man's arrest, twenty-five other officers were charged with murder, torture, and kidnapping, including Armando Fernández.[69]

The government of Ricardo Lagos created a second truth commission, and the resulting Valech Report of 2003–4 was more comprehensive in its findings than the Rettig Report had been. In late 2004, victims won a monthly pension of $220 from the Chilean government. Under the first Michelle Bachelet administration that followed, the executive gave support for judicial prosecutions.[70] By then, too, Judge Guzmán and others had brought charges against 160 officers in 365 cases.[71] By the 2010s, wrote one scholar, "Chile had compiled one of the most active and complete records of judicial accountability anywhere on the continent, and perhaps in the world."[72]

As serious was the scandal unleashed by a 2004 U.S. Senate investigation into terrorist funding. Motivated by the attacks of September 11, 2001, it uncovered secret holdings of $8–16 million in bank accounts held by Pinochet in Washington, D.C.'s Riggs Bank. Prompted by the revelation, a Chilean legal agency discovered a series of secret accounts held by Pinochet, family members, and collaborators. Such evidence of self-interest was a blow to those of Pinochet's followers who always considered him ruthless but selflessly patriotic.[73] It was the Riggs scandal that turned Chilean public opinion against the former dictator.[74] Since he had no declared income other than his $40,000 yearly salary, many drew the obvious conclusion that he had either pilfered the treasury or taken bribes.[75]

Again, in late 2004, Contreras indirectly implicated Pinochet in the Letelier assassination by saying, "General Pinochet needs to assume his responsibility." As always, many believed he was about to unveil the infamous cache of documents allegedly secreted abroad that would incriminate his former boss, but Contreras never did.

In 2000, Chilean courts stripped Pinochet of his senator's immunity and then indicted him on over 177 counts of torture, murder, and other crimes. Thus began years of court appearances. Before a judge at the Military Club in Lo Curro in November 2005, the two men entered into a shouting match:

> *Pinochet*: You were the leader of DINA, general, that should be clear once and for all!
> *Contreras*: Yes, general, but *you* were the one who gave all the orders—that, too, should be clear!

For two hours and twenty minutes, the two went at each other in this way, desperate to shed responsibility for acts they had so proudly touted for decades. Contreras later told the court, "*El Presidente* knew exactly what DINA and its director did or did not do."[76]

The confrontation demonstrated, first, that Pinochet's claims of senility back in London were a lie and, second, that Contreras did not have documents that implicated Pinochet in any crime. In May 2005, Contreras only produced a thirty-two-page detailed spreadsheet of the kidnappings, killings, and grave sites of 580 people disappeared under Pinochet. He added, "The president of Chile personally arranged and directed the actions" of those who killed Orlando Letelier. He presented no evidence, but with that statement, he finally made a direct connection between Pinochet and the Letelier-Moffitt murders.[77]

The following year, Contreras implicated Pinochet and his son in a cocaine manufacturing and smuggling scheme overseen by Eugenio Berríos.[78] But none of it would end up sending Pinochet to prison, and it did not help that Contreras was a known liar whose accusations were imprecise and questioned by investigators. On December 10, 2006, Pinochet died in the

Santiago Military Hospital before any verdict came down. He was ninety-one. Asked what he felt when his former boss died, Contreras responded, "Nothing."[79]

Isabel Letelier did feel something. "I was not happy. I was appalled that he had died without being sentenced. . . . I hope that [he] will be remembered [for what he was]: a coward, criminal, and thief."[80] A U.S. colleague of hers added that, although he never went to prison, Pinochet "certainly died in disgrace, [and] having Contreras point the finger at him contributed to that."[81]

On his deathbed, Pinochet issued a statement that included the phrase, "I take political responsibility for everything that was done."[82] But he never admitted guilt or apologized for any of his crimes, including the worst state-sponsored assassination in U.S. history. Chilean courts refused to pursue the case against him, and the Bush administration dropped Pinochet from its long-dormant investigation.[83] "It is very easy to say you were the intellectual author of a crime," Pinochet once beamed, referring to the Letelier assassination. "But to prove it? That's not easy."[84]

>> Saul Landau, a close friend of both Leteliers who wrote about the case for decades, died in September 2013, two days prior to the Chilean coup's fortieth anniversary. Lawyer Sam Buffone, who worked pro bono for the Leteliers for years, died in April 2015.

The Karpens remained largely out of the limelight but continued to mourn their daughter and sister. In 2002, father Murray, now retired, wrote to the *Washington Post* to express his displeasure with U.S. hesitation in indicting Pinochet.[85] Brother Michael Karpen did something similar.[86] Murray died in 2009. In June 2012, an appeals court in Chile ordered the government to open a separate investigation into the assassination of Ronni Moffitt. The case remained open in 2018.[87]

Michael Moffitt lived a quiet life in the world of finance, specializing in socially responsible investment. He stayed away from the Letelier case in the 1990s.[88]

Of the two Letelier boys who settled in the United States, Francisco remained the most politically vocal, penning opinion pieces or open letters.[89] He developed as an artist and muralist before settling in Venice, California, in 1997. Much of his art revolved around the themes of human rights and social justice. At the time, he lived on the same property as his brother Cristián.[90] In 2016, to coincide with the fortieth anniversary of Sheridan Circle,

Francisco directed a mural at the sculpture garden of American University in Washington, D.C., where his father had taught. It depicted not only Letelier and Moffitt but also other activists whom they inspired. "This project celebrates the way that tragedy was turned into a legacy of activism, of landmark cases in global justice, of continuing to build a world in which justice and international cooperation are real and felt."[91]

In Chile, José moved to remote Easter Island, employed in public works until at least 2017. That same year, Fabiola, in her late eighties, continued to work on human rights cases, including those of exiles who filed class action suits for reparations.[92] Juan Pablo was several times reelected as a deputy. President Bill Clinton, on a visit to Chile in 1998, stopped to shake hands with him before an address to Congress.[93] In May 2003, Juan Pablo was accused of bribery in relation to a truck repair shop and investigated by a judge friendly to his political rivals. But the court cleared him, the judge himself was investigated, and Isabel and even Chileans across the aisle swore that the accusations were spurious. In 2005, he won a senatorial seat and became a fixture in Chilean national politics, writing significant labor and environmental legislation.[94]

All the brothers except José gathered in Washington in February 2018 to unveil a statue of their father in front of the Chilean ambassador's residence, near where he was killed more than forty-one years earlier. "We are all older than he was when he died," observed Francisco, adding that his father's martyrdom sent one clear message: "The world can be better."[95]

Isabel Letelier continued to live in Santiago, retired but making art with her own kiln and buying and selling real estate. She no longer lived with Miguel Sayago, but the two remained good friends. In her eighties, she had an accident that damaged her cerebella and she lost vision in one eye. Despite some vertigo, in 2017 she remained lucid and an avid reader.

>> The historical legacy of the Letelier affair is challenging to reckon with, intersecting as it does with many salient themes of the last century. It no doubt stands as one of the most consequential assassinations of the Cold War. Certainly, it provided hope that ordinary people—survivors of terror, mourning family members, investigators, lawyers, diplomats, and their allies in nongovernmental organizations—could obtain justice against tyrants and terrorists even when their own governments were less than forthcoming. FBI and Department of Justice agents and mid-level diplomats grew frustrated by the unwillingness of successive White House occupants to confront Pino-

chet, an ally in the Cold War. Pledging to do their jobs, these bureaucrats allied with activists and especially with Isabel Letelier, who wielded significant shaming power.

The most concrete impact of the Letelier case, however, was on the prosecution of human rights violators in Latin America. "What the U.S. did in investigating this case has had *enormous, enormous* impact in Latin America," journalist John Dinges said in 2016. "The beginning of the uncovering of all these human rights crimes—of Operation Condor, of the internal workings of the security services, all of that began with the FBI investigation. It was the first penetration of the interior workings of these intelligence forces."[96]

In Chile, the Letelier quest for justice brought about the dissolution of DINA and eventually defanged the Amnesty Law. It forced the Reagan government and Congress to "certify" Pinochet's human rights progress, putting decisive diplomatic and financial pressure on his regime. The cause célèbre defied the judicial system and won, inspiring others to pursue their own cases and prompting many confessions.[97] As scholar Cath Collins suggested, even its weaknesses revealed strengths: its being an exception to the Amnesty Law exposed the arbitrariness of that decree, and its exposure of the civilian deference to the military stiffened the spine of Chile's democrats.[98] Contreras and Espinoza were the first of Pinochet's military officers to go to prison and among the first Cold War violators of human rights in Latin America or anywhere to do so. The case sparked a movement that has adjudicated more than 1,000 cases of human rights violations in Chile alone.

For all the legal precedents set by the case, its impact was also political and psychological. As Ambassador Juan Gabriel Valdés explained, the case "produced an idea that human rights were... an area of international politics ... and that you had to take that into consideration, it was not a matter to be taken lightly." Cold Warriors could no longer dismiss talk of human rights as Soviet propaganda. "The military had to say, 'We respect human rights.'" The case also changed the Chilean Left's perception of the United States, at least under President Carter. Now Washington could be perceived as a "foe" of Pinochet.[99]

In the United States, Isabel Letelier saw the most important consequence of the case being the annual Letelier-Moffitt Human Rights Award, an occasion to educate many about the world's foremost champions of human rights.[100] Son Francisco agreed, adding that the prize gave all who won it wind in their sails and built a community of like-minded people.[101]

The U.S. side of the story also demonstrated the transnational power of human rights. The civil case against Chile represented the first wrongful death case ever brought in the United States against a foreign nation, and it culminated in a successful restitution. In 2017, the Center for Justice and Accountability estimated that more than a thousand human rights abusers had moved to the United States. In June 2016, a jury in an Orlando, Florida, trial found a former Chilean Army lieutenant liable for his role in the torture and extrajudicial killing of folk singer Víctor Jara. Since 1980, human rights attorneys used the Alien Tort Statute of 1789, among other laws, to pursue accountability. The Center for Constitutional Rights first argued that the statute, originally intended to apply to cases such as piracy, assaults on diplomats, and debts to foreign countries, could also relate to cases of assaults against common principles of international human rights law such as torture. In 1984, one U.S. court found that, "for purposes of civil liability, the torturer has become—like the pirate and slave trader before him—*hostis humanis generis*, an enemy of all mankind."[102]

In terms of terrorism, the Letelier affair razed the U.S. intelligence community's wall separating domestic from international events. "The FBI had no clue about how to investigate terrorism before this case. They hadn't really done it," recalled Eugene Propper of his Letelier investigation. For that matter, neither did any other agency in Washington, including the CIA. Carter Cornick agreed: "This was the first case of international terrorism, state-sponsored terrorism in Washington. I was involved in a specialty that did not exist in the mid-'70s. Terrorism was a Category 3 priority in the FBI. . . . It was the first time we were dealing with a foreign government as a suspect."[103] Counterterrorism was truly in its infancy. Cornick's bomb squad, for instance, had just been formed in 1976. And the Letelier assassination was the last major FBI case not to be computerized.[104]

"They told us from the beginning that this case could not be solved because of all the international political implications it carried," continued Cornick. "There were too many firsts. But we established, through this case, the policy of the U.S. government with respect to terrorism. I believed that the effort set a precedent for similar cases."[105] Coming as it did amid a wave of international terrorist acts committed in the United States, whether from Palestinian hijackers or Cuban American bombers, the Letelier case blurred the lines between domestic and international terrorism. The 1970s were also a decade in which secret police such as Iran's SAVAK, South Korea's KCIA, and DINA committed "direct assaults upon exiled citizens" in the United States. This went well beyond the practice of most countries, which just had "agents in the U.S. for intelligence purposes." Iran and South Korean even admitted that they spied on their own citizens in the United States.[106] The Letelier case and others caused the U.S. government to shatter its illusions of splendid isolation from terrorism and to force its security agencies to work together.

Blending human rights and counterterrorism advances, the case produced additional legal firsts: the first deal against extradition when the United States had an extradition treaty with another country, the first charges ever filed in the American legal system against Cuban American terrorists, the first conviction of a Chilean military man in U.S. courts, and the first live telecast of Chilean court proceedings. In civil courts, the case became the first filed under the Foreign Sovereign Immunities Act that dealt with terrorism and led to improvements in the civil prosecution of state sponsored terrorism in U.S. courts. It marked the first time that a U.S. court provided a civil remedy to an act of international terrorism. In 1996, it led to a law that stripped immunity from a foreign state when damages were sought against specific terrorist acts, including "extrajudicial killing."[107]

As Sergio Bitar concluded decades later, the Letelier case initially showed that you could commit assassinations under a veil of silence "but in the end it will explode," meaning that truth would emerge and international institutions would keep national criminals accountable.[108]

>> "The Letelier assassination in retrospect was one of the more stupid things done by any government," said U.S. diplomat Robert Steven.[109] That certainly is true. Pinochet, Contreras, and Townley did not understand the implications of car bombing a former ambassador and a U.S. citizen in the heart of Washington, D.C. It took decades, but their monstrous deed backfired, contributing in no small part to ending their ideological dream, their government, and, in the last two cases, their personal freedom — all these the results of the actions of simple investigators and activists moved by the fighting spirit of a lone widow.

ACKNOWLEDGMENTS

Many colleagues, archivists, and others are to be thanked for helping tell the full story of the Letelier search for justice. First come Isabel Letelier and two of her sons, who agreed to be interviewed on a topic that was no doubt painful to recall even after forty years. All those who agreed to be interviewed by me, whose names appear in the bibliography, were gracious with their time.

The archival hunt for documents was more arduous than I imagined, and I thank many for mapping it out for me. At the National Security Archive in Washington, D.C., Peter Kornbluh was an early, essential source on all things Letelier, and Mary Curry patiently helped secure the needed boxes. Thanks to Paul Adler for telling me about Institute for Policy Studies records at the Wisconsin Historical Society, where Paul Hedges, Simone Munson, Lisa Saywell, and Amy Sloper were consummate professionals. Fiona Dove at the Transnational Institute in Amsterdam was welcoming, and that city's International Institute of Social History contained a few precious nuggets (again, thanks to Paul Adler for putting me on that scent). Kathryn Bondy of the State Department eased my access to the new releases of documents in 2015 and 2016. In Santiago, Chile, Miriam Del Carmen Guzman Morales, Emilia Beniscelli Troncoso, and Oscar Alvarez Santos went above and beyond in unearthing the personal records and photos of the Letelier family.

Many at the University of Oklahoma were crucial in helping me with research, including Department of International and Area Studies Chair Mitchell Smith, his assistant Rhonda Hill, librarian Karen Rupp-Serrano, and especially research assistants Chelsea Burris and Lilli Kiehl (now Lebeau). The department also provided a sabbatical in 2015 to speed up the research.

Evan McCormick was a lifesaver with a handful of illuminating documents from the Chilean Foreign Ministry. Colleagues and friends helped me think through ideas and process my findings. Thanks to Mary Dudziak, Claudio Fuentes, Greg Grandin, Julie Greene, Meredith Hindley, Elizabeth Cobbs Hoffman, Margaret Power, Jeremi Suri, Vanessa Walker, and, at my new academic home of Temple University, Bryant Simon.

At UNC Press, I thank Chuck Grench for believing in this book, Greg

Weeks and an anonymous reviewer for their perceptive yet encouraging readings, and the amazing production staff. As with many of my books, Heather Dubnick did a masterful job with the index.

Finally, my love goes out to my kids, Luc and Nico, for being patient while Papa was away on work trips, and to Cindy, for talking me through my anxiety over this book.

I dedicate this work to my mentor, Michael H. Hunt, who passed away in April 2018. I feel his influence throughout my projects and will miss him dearly.

NOTES

ABBREVIATIONS

AA	Archivo de la Administración, Santiago
ADST	Association for Diplomatic Studies and Training
CIA	Central Intelligence Agency
Cubillos	Papers of Hernán Cubillos Sallato
CV	curriculum vitae
DNSA	Digital National Security Archive Collection, Chile and the United States: U.S. Policy toward Democracy, Dictatorship, and Human Rights, 1970–1990, National Security Archive, Washington, D.C.
DOS 2015	Department of State, Additional Release: Chile Declassification Project, 2015
DOS 2016	Department of State, Additional Release: Chile Declassification Project, 2016
FBI	Federal Bureau of Investigation
FOIA	Freedom of Information Act
Hoover	Hoover Institution Archives, Stanford, California
IISH	International Institute of Social History, Amsterdam
IPS	Institute for Policy Studies Records
LC	Letelier Collection
LP	George W. Landau Papers
NSA	National Security Archive, Washington, D.C.
NYT	*New York Times*
OL	Fondo Orlando Letelier
TI	Records of the Transnational Institute
TNI	Transnational Institute, Amsterdam
WHS	Wisconsin Historical Society, Madison, Wisconsin

INTRODUCTION

1. Orlando Letelier, quoted in Elizabeth Subercaseaux, "Isabel, te tengo una sorpresa," *Caras* (Santiago), [May?] 1990, 6. All translations are mine.
2. Martin Walker, "The Fight for Bread and Roses," *Guardian*, March 3, 1981.
3. Isabel Letelier, interview by the author.
4. Michael Moffitt, quoted in Alexander Cockburn and James Ridgeway, "Why Chile's Secret Police Killed Orlando Letelier," *Village Voice*, October 4, 1976, 11.
5. FBI Newark field office, memo to director, September 23, 1976, Letelier (FOIA) documents produced by the FBI, vol. 1, box 1, LC, NSA.

6. Michael Moffitt affidavit, July 16, 1991, DOS 2015.

7. Michael Moffitt, quoted in Eugenio Gutiérrez, "Michael Moffitt: 'No olvidaré ese horror,'" *Caras* (Santiago), [May?] 1990, 8.

8. Dinges and Landau, *Assassination*, 209.

9. Branch and Propper, *Labyrinth*, 18.

10. Moffitt affidavit.

11. Officer Walter Johnson, quoted in Dinges and Landau, *Assassination*, 209.

12. Branch and Propper, *Labyrinth*, 18.

13. District of Columbia Department of Human Resources, certificate of death, September 24, 1976, IPS, WHS.

14. Freed and Landis, *Death in Washington*, 10.

15. Moffitt affidavit.

16. Dinges and Landau, *Assassination*, 211–212.

17. Quoted in Subercaseaux, "Isabel," 6.

18. Dinges and Landau, *Assassination*, 212.

19. Isabel Letelier, interview by J. Teunissen and A. Steenhuis, February 2, 1977, audio recording 1534A/303, IPS, WHS.

20. Quoted in Subercaseaux, "Isabel," 6.

21. Isabel Letelier, interview by the author.

22. Quoted in Varas and Orrego, *El caso Letelier*, 19.

23. Quotations mixed together from Isabel Letelier, interview by the author; Subercaseaux, "Isabel," 6; and Dinges and Landau, *Assassination*, 212, 213.

24. Isabel Letelier, interview by the author.

25. Isabel Letelier affidavit, August 2, 1991, DOS 2015.

26. Quoted in Rodríguez, *El asesinato*, 22.

27. Isabel Letelier, interview by the author.

28. Moffitt affidavit.

29. Quoted in Raquel Correa, "'Ahora estoy en paz,'" *El Mercurio*, June 4, 1995, D2.

30. Francisco Letelier interview.

31. Cristián Letelier interview.

32. Isabel Letelier, interview by the author.

33. Quoted in Correa, "'Ahora.'"

34. Kornbluh, *Pinochet File*, 341.

CHAPTER 1

1. Dinges and Landau, *Assassination*, 28.

2. Del Solar, *Orlando Letelier*, 2.

3. Isabel Letelier affidavit, August 2, 1991, DOS 2015.

4. Isabel Letelier, interview by J. Teunissen and A. Steenhuis, February 2, 1977, audio recording 1534A/303, IPS, WHS.

5. Francisco Letelier interview.

6. Isabel Letelier interview, IPS, WHS.

7. Cristián Letelier interview.

8. Isabel Letelier interview, IPS, WHS.

9. Cristián Letelier interview.

10. Francisco Letelier interview.

11. Isabel Letelier interview, IPS, WHS.
12. Isabel Letelier, interview by the author.
13. Francisco Letelier interview.
14. Isabel Letelier interview, IPS, WHS.
15. Del Solar, *Orlando Letelier*, 1, 2.
16. Francisco Letelier interview.
17. Del Solar, *Orlando Letelier*, 5.
18. Isabel Letelier, interview by the author.
19. Quoted in Del Solar, *Orlando Letelier*, 8.
20. Dinges and Landau, *Assassination*, 30.
21. Isabel Letelier interview, IPS, WHS.
22. Del Solar, *Orlando Letelier*, 9.
23. Isabel Letelier, interview by the author.
24. "Tiempos turbulentos," *La Nación* (Buenos Aires), special report, 1995, 15.
25. Isabel Letelier interview, IPS, WHS.
26. Isabel Letelier, interview by the author.
27. Isabel Letelier affidavit.
28. Francisco Letelier interview.
29. Isabel Letelier interview, IPS, WHS.
30. Quoted in Luis Ulibarri, "Orlando Letelier: Al servicio de la vida misma," *Revista Paloma* (Chile), September 3, 1973, reproduced in *The Clinic*, September 11, 2013, www.theclinic.cl/2013/09/11/orlando-letelier-al-servicio-de-la-vida-misma.
31. Isabel Letelier, interview by the author.
32. Isabel Letelier interview, IPS, WHS; Isabel Letelier CV up to 1986, folder 34, box 46, IPS, WHS.
33. Ulibarri, "Orlando Letelier."
34. Isabel Letelier CV.
35. Isabel Letelier interview, IPS, WHS.
36. Isabel Letelier, interview by the author.
37. Isabel Letelier interview, IPS, WHS.
38. Javier Urrutia, quoted in Del Solar, *Orlando Letelier*, 14.
39. CIA, biographic sketch of Orlando Letelier, c. January 1971, DNSA.
40. Del Solar, *Orlando Letelier*, 14, 34.
41. CIA sketch.
42. "Orlando Letelier" [editorial], *Washington Post*, September 22, 1976, A16.
43. Isabel Letelier interview, IPS, WHS.
44. Isabel Letelier affidavit.
45. Cristián Letelier interview.
46. Quotations from Raquel Correa, "'Ahora estoy en paz,'" *El Mercurio*, June 4, 1995, D2; and "Tiempos turbulentos," 20.
47. Isabel Letelier, quoted in James Gordon, psychiatric evaluation of Isabel Morel Letelier, August 2, 1991, DOS 2015.
48. Gordon evaluation; see also Isabel Letelier affidavit.
49. Isabel Letelier interview, IPS, WHS.
50. Isabel Letelier CV.
51. Dinges and Landau, *Assassination*, 37.
52. Del Solar, *Orlando Letelier*, 35; see also 33–37.

53. Quoted in Correa, "'Ahora,'" D2.
54. Dinges and Landau, *Assassination*, 27.
55. Quoted in Elizabeth Subercaseaux, "Isabel, te tengo una sorpresa," *Caras* (Santiago), [May?] 1990, 6.
56. Juan Pablo Letelier affidavit, August 2, 1991, DOS 2015.
57. Isabel Letelier, interview by the author.
58. Gordon evaluation.
59. Orlando Letelier, quoted in CIA sketch.
60. Cristián Letelier interview; Tom Hayden, "An Exiled Son of Santiago," *Nation*, April 4, 2005, www.thenation.com/article/exiled-son-santiago/.
61. Harmer, *Allende's Chile*, 78, 176.
62. CIA sketch.
63. Ambassador Orlando Letelier, report on presentation of Orlando Letelier's credentials to President Nixon, March 2, 1971, and National Security Council memorandum of conversation, Washington, D.C., March 23, 1971, both in DNSA; Harmer, *Allende's Chile*, 121.
64. Ambassador John Hugh Crimmins interview, ADST.
65. Dinges, *Condor Years*, 176.
66. Tad Szulc, "U.S. Seeks to Keep Cubans Isolated," *NYT*, December 20, 1970, 23.
67. Benjamin Welles, "'We Don't Have Any Friends Anyway': Loans," *NYT*, August 15, 1971, E6.
68. Harmer, *Allende's Chile*, 181.
69. Dinges and Landau, *Assassination*, 50.
70. FBI Washington, D.C., field office to director, November 3, 1976, Letelier (FOIA) documents produced by the FBI, vol. 5, box 1, LC, NSA; Michael C. Jensen, "Chilean Break-Ins Puzzle Watergate Investigators," *NYT*, May 29, 1973, 17.
71. Ambassador Juan Gabriel Valdés interview; transcript of interview, New York, February 7, 1975, folder CIA, box Series A-C, Carpetas temáticas, OL, AA.
72. Del Solar, *Orlando Letelier*, 26.
73. Letelier, quoted in Ulibarri, "Orlando Letelier," 7.
74. Hayden, "Exiled Son."
75. Del Solar, *Orlando Letelier*, 40.

CHAPTER 2

1. Childress, *Pinochet's Chile*, 30.
2. FBI interview of Eduardo Frei, December 20, 1976, Letelier (FOIA) documents produced by the FBI, vol. 20, box 2, LC, NSA.
3. For more on fascism in Latin America, see Briones, *Ideología*, 78; dos Santos, *Socialismo o Fascismo*, 23; and Viñas, *Qué es el fascismo*, 13. For more on Nazis in Chile, see Mount, *Chile and the Nazis*.
4. Viñas, *Qué es el fascismo*, 13.
5. "Nazi Party in Chile Revived; Top Leader Stresses Anti-Semitism," Jewish Telegraphic Agency, September 12, 1963, www.jta.org/1963/09/12/archive/nazi-party-in-chile-revived-top-leader-stresses-anti-semitism.
6. Etchepare and Stewart, "Nazism in Chile," 579.
7. Raúl Morales Alvarez, quoted in Salazar, *Contreras*, 19.

8. Etchepare and Stewart, "Nazism in Chile," 585, 589.
9. Talbot, *Devil's Chessboard*, 106.
10. Franz Pfeiffer Richter, quoted in "Nazi Party in Chile Revived."
11. "Partido Nacional Socialista Obrero de Chile," *Wikipedia*, es.wikipedia.org/wiki/Partido_Nacional_Socialista_Obrero_de_Chile (accessed November 27, 2018); Etchepare and Stewart, "Nazism in Chile," 594.
12. Eva Vergara, "Victims of Chile Colony Hope German Documents Bring Justice," Associated Press, April 28, 2016, bigstory.ap.org/urn:publicid:ap.org:59dd7a22c8594c079a e5160d64e0daca.
13. *Report of the Chilean National Commission* (Rettig Report), 639–42; Sebastian Rotella, "Siege May Force Colony to Yield Its Secrets," *Los Angeles Times*, June 25, 1997, articles.latimes.com/1997-06-25/news/mn-6655_1_secret-police/2.
14. Etchepare and Stewart, "Nazism in Chile," 579.
15. Salazar, *Contreras*, 20.
16. Contreras's mother in law, quoted in Peña and Tobar, "Manuel Contreras," 17–18; "Juan Cristóbal Peña desentraña vida de 'El Mamo' marcada por su infancia, Pinochet, Dios y la DINA," *El Mostrador* (Santiago), August 8, 2015, www.elmostrador.cl/noticias/pais/2015/08/08/juan-cristobal-pena-desentrana-vida-de-el-mamo-marcada-por-su-infancia-pinochet-dios-y-la-dina/.
17. "El retador incorregible," *Qué Pasa*, June 3, 1995, 24.
18. Peña and Tobar, "Manuel Contreras," 24.
19. Vial, *Pinochet*, 233–34.
20. Pilar Molina Armas, "¡Ay de los vencidos!," *El Mercurio*, June 4, 1995, D8.
21. Peña and Tobar, "Manuel Contreras," 22.
22. Quoted in "La hora de Contreras," *Qué Pasa*, February 27, 1993, 11.
23. Bitar interview.
24. Quoted in Peña and Tobar, "Manuel Contreras," 26.
25. Salazar, *Contreras*, 27.
26. Molina, "¡Ay de los vencidos!" D8; "Aficionado a novelas de acción," *La Tercera* (Santiago), June 1, 1995, 11.
27. Quoted in Dinges, *Condor Years*, 27.
28. Quoted in F. P., "El militar, el hombre," *Ercilla*, May 26, 1995, 29.
29. Vial, *Pinochet*, 234.
30. Quoted in Tina Rosenberg, "Force Is Forever," *New York Times Sunday Magazine*, September 24, 1995, 44–45.
31. Alenjandro Barros Amengal, quoted in Salazar, *Contreras*, 23.
32. Molina, "¡Ay de los vencidos!," D8.
33. F. P., "El militar."
34. Quoted in "Perfil sicológico del general Contreras," *La Tercera* (Santiago), June 2, 1995, 9.
35. Quoted in "Juan Cristóbal Peña desentraña."

CHAPTER 3

1. Kornbluh, *Pinochet File*, 341.
2. Malcolm Coad, "General Whom the Roman Gods Protect," *Guardian*, January 29, 1990.

3. Transcript of television program, "World in Action—the DINA," WNET New York, January 19, 1977, Letelier (FOIA) documents produced by the FBI, vol. 22, box 2, LC, NSA.
4. Dinges and Landau, *Assassination*, 59.
5. Saul Landau, introduction for TNI/IPS booklet, undated, box 249, TI, IISH.
6. Isabel Letelier, interview by the author.
7. Joshua Partlow, "Behind the Sunglasses," *Washington Post*, October 19, 2008, BW02.
8. Francisco Letelier, "Victims of Pinochet Are Still Hoping for Justice," *Irish Times*, December 23, 2004, 14.
9. Cristián Letelier interview.
10. Coad, "General."
11. Childress, *Pinochet's Chile*, 22–24, 28.
12. Transcript of grades of Isabel Morel, Colegio Argentino del Sagrado Corazón, Santiago, November 25, 1940, folder no. 1, box Objetos personales Isabel M., OL, AA.
13. Childress, *Pinochet's Chile*, 28.
14. O'Shaughnessy, *Politics of Torture*, 9-12, quotations on 64.
15. Pinochet, quoted in Malcolm Coad, "Obituary: General Augusto Pinochet," *Guardian*, December 11, 2006, 30; Childress, *Pinochet's Chile*, 28–29.
16. Monte Reel and J. Y. Smith, "A Chilean Dictator's Dark Legacy," *Washington Post*, December 11, 2006, A01.
17. Coad, "General."
18. Quoted in Laurie Goering, "The Sins of the Father; Son of Chile's Secret Police Chief Releasing August Book," *Hamilton Spectator*, May 15, 1993, A11.
19. Pilar Molina Armas, "¡Ay de los vencidos!," *El Mercurio*, June 4, 1995, D8.
20. "Manuel Contreras, Head of Chile's Spy Agency under Pinochet, Dies Aged 86," *Guardian*, August 8, 2015.
21. Oyarzún, *Augusto Pinochet*, 241; Contreras, *La verdad histórica*, 11.
22. Steve J. Stern, forward to Collins, Hite, and Joignant, *Politics of Memory*, xi.
23. Childress, *Pinochet's Chile*, 65.
24. Dinges, *Condor Years*, 44–45.
25. Salazar, *Contreras*, 24.
26. Goering, "Sins of the Father," A11.
27. Peña and Tobar, "Manuel Contreras," 32.
28. Vial, *Pinochet*, 254.
29. Dinges and Landau, *Assassination*, 133–34.
30. Dinges, *Condor Years*, 65; Dinges and Landau, *Assassination*, 132.
31. Pascale Bonnefoy, "Manuel Contreras, Chilean Spy Chief under Pinochet, Dies at 86," *NYT*, August 9, 2015, 21.
32. John Dinges, "Chile's Murder, Inc.," *Inquiry*, January 8–22, 1979, 21.
33. Salazar, *Contreras*, 55, 126.
34. Peña and Tobar, "Manuel Contreras," 32.
35. Sebastian Rotella, "Siege May Force Colony to Yield Its Secrets," *Los Angeles Times*, June 25, 1997, articles.latimes.com/1997-06-25/news/mn-6655_1_secret-police/2.
36. Goering, "Sins of the Father," A11; "Juan Cristóbal Peña desentraña vida de 'El Mamo' marcada por su infancia, Pinochet, Dios y la DINA," *El Mostrador* (Santiago), August 8, 2015, www.elmostrador.cl/noticias/pais/2015/08/08/juan-cristobal-pena-desentrana-vida-de-el-mamo-marcada-por-su-infancia-pinochet-dios-y-la-dina/.
37. Salazar, *Contreras*, 123.

38. Douglas Grant Mine, "The Assassin Next Door," *Miami New Times*, November 18, 1999, www.miaminewtimes.com/news/the-assassin-next-door-6357449; Barnes memo to secretary of state, Santiago, March 12, 1987, DNSA.

39. Mine, "Assassin Next Door."

40. McSherry, *Predatory States*, 154.

41. Shultz memo to American consul in Rio De Janeiro, Washington, D.C., January 22, 1987, DOS 2015; McSherry, *Predatory States*, 154.

42. Quoted in Jorge Escalante, "Missing: Espinoza, González y el misterioso gringo Davis," *El Mostrador* (Santiago), February 3, 2015, www.elmostrador.cl/noticias/pais/2015/02/03/missing-espinoza-gonzalez-y-el-misterioso-gringo-davis/.

43. "La ficha de Espinoza," *Qué Pasa*, June 3, 1995, 26.

44. Dinges and Landau, *Assassination*, 62, 63.

45. Isabel Letelier, interview by the author.

46. Dinges and Landau, *Assassination*, 63; Isabel Letelier, interview by the author.

47. Saul Landau, "Two Deaths in the Morning," *Mother Jones*, December 1976, 19.

48. Orlando Letelier, quoted in Tad Szulc, "A Very Quiet Horror," *Playboy*, February 1977, 114.

49. Orlando Letelier, quoted in Landau, "Two Deaths," 20; Isabel Letelier testimony, May 13, 1981, folder Isabel Crim. Case Testimony, box 18, LC, NSA.

50. Juan Pablo Letelier, "English Project: Autobiography," [1976?], folder 1, box 45, IPS, WHS.

51. Dinges and Landau, *Assassination*, 69.

52. Letelier, "English Project."

53. Francisco Letelier, "Now the World Will Know the Truth," *Los Angeles Times*, October 21, 1998, articles.latimes.com/1998/oct/21/local/me-34692.

54. "Entrevista con Isabel Letelier," *Areíto*, vol. III, nos. 2–3, [late 1976?], 12, folder Publicaciones, box Temas varios subfondos Isabel M., OL, AA.

55. Paraphrased from Letelier, "English Project."

56. Orlando to Isabel, September 12, 1973, folder Letelier, Orlando (recibido de parte de OL), box Correspondencia entre Isabel y Orlando, Subfondo Isabel Morel de Letelier, OL, AA.

57. Isabel Letelier, interview by the author.

58. Dinges and Landau, *Assassination*, 74–75.

59. "U.S. Tried to Hide Truth in Death of Envoy, Widow Says," *Grand Rapids Press*, February 10, 1978, 1.

60. Isabel Letelier testimony.

61. Letelier, "English Project."

62. James Gordon, psychiatric evaluation of Isabel Morel Letelier, August 2, 1991, DOS 2015.

63. Isabel Letelier, quoted in Martin Walker, "The Fight for Bread and Roses," *Guardian*, March 3, 1981.

64. Isabel Letelier, quoted in "U.S. Tried to Hide," 1.

65. Juan Pablo Letelier, quoted in Raquel Correa, "'Ahora estoy en paz,'" *El Mercurio*, June 4, 1995, D2.

66. Letelier, "English Project."

67. Francisco Letelier, quoted in Tom Hayden, "An Exiled Son of Santiago," *Nation*, April 4, 2005, www.thenation.com/article/exiled-son-santiago/.

68. Isabel Letelier testimony. A Washington, D.C., newspaper discussed his whereabouts fifteen days after the coup, so Isabel must have known by then: Jeremiah O'Leary, "Chile Coup Divides Families," *Washington Star-News*, September 26, 1973.

69. Marvine Howe, "Top Allende Men Reported on Isle: Writer Says They Are Held in 'Concentration Camp,'" *NYT*, February 27, 1974, 7.

70. Orlando Letelier, quoted in Szulc, "Horror," 182.

71. Quoted in Freed and Landis, *Death in Washington*, 116.

72. Orlando Letelier, quoted in Szulc, "Horror," 182.

73. Dinges and Landau, *Assassination*, 77.

74. Isabel Letelier, interview by the author. A note from his doctor sent to the Chilean government is Kanof letter, Washington, D.C., November 21, 1973, folder Estado de salud, box Series D-E, Carpetas temáticas, OL, AA.

75. An example is Orlando to Isabel, Dawson Island, November 18, 1973, folder Letelier, Orlando (recibido de parte de OL), box Correspondencia entre Isabel y Orlando, Subfondo Isabel Morel de Letelier, unnumbered, OL, AA.

76. Bitar interview; Orlando to Cristián, José Ignacio, Francisco, and Juan Pablo, Dawson Island, December 22, 1973, folder Letelier, Cristián, box 5, Correspondencia entre Orlando Letelier y terceros, OL, AA.

77. Bitar, *Dawson*, 82.

78. Landau, "Two Deaths," 20.

79. Isabel Letelier, interview by the author.

80. Orlando Letelier, quoted in Szulc, "Horror," 184.

81. Isabel Letelier testimony.

82. Dinges and Landau, *Assassination*, 78.

83. FBI Washington, D.C., field office to director, November 3, 1976, Letelier (FOIA) documents produced by the FBI, vol. 5, box 1, LC, NSA.

84. Orlando to Isabel, Puerto Arenas, January 24, 1974, folder Letelier, Orlando (recibido de parte de OL), box Correspondencia entre Isabel y Orlando, Subfondo Isabel Morel de Letelier, OL, AA.

85. Isabel Letelier, quoted in Elizabeth Subercaseaux, "Isabel, te tengo una sorpresa," *Caras* (Santiago), [May?] 1990, 6.

86. Correa, "'Ahora,'" D2.

87. Isabel to Orlando, Santiago, December 11, 1973, folder Enviados a Orlando, box Correspondencia entre Isabel y Orlando, Subfondo Isabel Morel de Letelier, unnumbered, OL, AA.

88. Orlando Letelier, quoted in Szulc, "Horror," 184.

89. Orlando to Isabel, Dawson Island, October 27, 1973, folder Letelier, Orlando (recibido de parte de OL), box Correspondencia entre Isabel y Orlando, Subfondo Isabel Morel de Letelier; Isabel to Maruja (Orlando's sister), Santiago, December 4, 1973, folder Maruja, box Corresp. entre Isabel Morel y terceros; Isabel et al. letter to Junta de Gobierno, Santiago, December 13, 1973, folder De esposas de detenidos a Junta militar, box Temas varios subfondos Isabel M.; Fabiola letter to Orlando, Santiago, December 20, 1973, folder Letelier del Solar, Fabiola, box 5, Correspondencia entre Orlando Letelier y terceros; Frances Heacock Smith, open letter, Washington, D.C., August 19, 1974, folder National Committee to Defend Letelier, box 1 Organizaciones, Carpetas temáticas, all in OL, AA.

90. Isabel Letelier testimony.

91. Isabel to Orlando, Santiago, November 11, 1973, folder Enviados a Orlando, box Correspondencia entre Isabel y Orlando, Subfondo Isabel Morel de Letelier, OL, AA.

92. Holton to Abourezk, Washington, D.C., May 23, 1974, Letelier (FOIA) document produced by the Department of State, February 6, 1980, vol. 1, box 8, LC, NSA.

93. Steven interview.

94. U.S. Ambassador to Chile David Popper to secretary of state, August 2, 1974, DNSA.

95. Dinges and Landau, *Assassination*, 80, 81.

96. Orlando Letelier, quoted in Szulc, "Horror," 186.

97. Juan Pablo Letelier, quoted in Correa, "'Ahora,'" D2.

98. Letelier, "Now the World."

99. Manuel Trucco, quoted in Cornick to Propper, October 8, 1976, Letelier (FOIA) documents produced by the FBI, vol. 11, box 2, LC, NSA.

100. Lewis H. Dinguid, "Chilean Ex-Leaders May Be Freed," *Washington Post*, August 16, 1974, A20.

101. CIA memo, September 13, 1974, and CIA to director, September 16, 1976, both in DNSA.

102. Eugenio Gutierrez, "Diego Arria: 'El general Pinochet me dijo que Letelier era muy peligroso,'" *La Época*, May 7, 1987, 9.

103. Landau, paraphrasing Pinochet, in Saul Landau and Isabel Letelier, Meaning of the Letelier-Moffitt assassination, September 22, 1992, audio recording, 1531A/393, IPS, WHS.

104. Arria, quoted in Gutierrez, "Diego Arria," 9.

105. Pinochet, quoted in Del Solar, *Orlando Letelier*, 58.

106. "Nada sabía de mi libertad: Letelier," *La Segunda* (Santiago), September 11, 1974.

107. Szulc, "Horror," 186; Patricio Carvajal Prado, safe passage, Santiago, September 10, 1974, folder Visas, box Series S-V, Carpetas temáticas, OL, AA.

108. Michael Moffitt, quoted in Kenneth Bredemeier, "Court Told Letelier Spoke of 'Enemies,'" *Washington Post*, January 17, 1979, A5.

109. Bitar, *Dawson*, 204–5.

110. Dinges and Landau, *Assassination*, 84.

CHAPTER 4

1. Dinges and Landau, *Assassination*, 158–60.

2. Dinges, *Condor Years*, 132, 130; Callejas, *Siembra vientos*, 105.

3. Kornbluh, *Pinochet File*.

4. Manuel Contreras, quoted in Dinges, *Condor Years*, 12.

5. McSherry, "Tracking the Origins of a State Terror Network." Many authors believe that Contreras wrote to Pinochet asking for $600,000 to "neutralize" opponents abroad. But Andrew and Mitrokhin, in *World Was Going Our Way*, 87–88, expose this "letter" as a KGB forgery.

6. Dinges, *Condor Years*, 133.

7. Weld, "Spanish Civil War."

8. Quoted in Dinges, *Condor Years*, 120.

9. George Landner Jr., "FBI Bugging of Chilean Offices Told," *Washington Post*, November 12, 1976, A1.

10. Dinges, *Condor Years*, 5, 13, 123.

11. Contreras to Corte Suprema Chile, December 23, 1997, folder Contreras: Apelación

de Sentencia, box 28, LC, NSA; Laurie Goering, "The Sins of the Father; Son of Chile's Secret Police Chief Releasing August Book," *Hamilton Spectator*, May 15, 1993, A11.

12. Christopher Marquis, "C.I.A. Says Chilean General in '76 Bombing Was Informer," *NYT*, September 19, 2000, A6; Kornbluh, *Pinochet File*, 216.

13. Kornbluh, *Pinochet File*, 216.

14. Dinges, *Condor Years*, 103.

15. Ryan interview, ADST.

16. Kissinger (drafted by Philip Habib) to embassies in Buenos Aires, Santiago, La Paz, Brasilia, and Asunción, August 16, 1976 (sent August 23), folder George W. Landau the Letelier Case (Chile) (1 of 2), 1976–2006, box 3, LPJ Hoover.

17. Quoted in "Kissinger Blocked Demarche on International Assassinations to Condor States," States News Service, April 10, 2010.

18. Dinges and Landau, *Assassination*, 92.

19. Townley testimony, p. 1584, criminal case no. 78-367, January 18, 1979, Washington, D.C., box 25, LC, NSA.

20. Michael Townley, quoted in Branch and Propper, *Labyrinth*, 506.

21. Larry Jackson, "Chile: On Exporting Political Murder" [letter to the editor], *NYT*, May 7, 1978, E22.

22. Quoted in John Dinges and Kenneth Bredemeier, "The Assassin," *Washington Post*, January 22, 1979, A1.

23. Rosalind Andrews [probation officer], postsentence report on Michael Townley, May 29, 1979, DNSA.

24. Freed and Landis, *Death in Washington*, 27.

25. Dinges and Bredemeier, "Assassin," A1.

26. "Townley Profile," undated, folder 59, box 38, IPS, WHS.

27. "Appearance by Townley before Attorney General Hector Orozco and Chief Clerk Jaime Vergara," box 11, LC, NSA.

28. Callejas, *Siembra vientos*, 151, 152.

29. Mariana Callejas, quoted in Cecilia Domeyko, "La última version de Mariana Callejas," *Hoy*, March 7–13, 1979, 8.

30. Enrique Lafourcade, quoted in Jack Chang, "Downstairs from Her Glittering Chilean Salon, There Was a Torture Chamber," McClatchydc.com, August 3, 2008, www.mcclatchydc.com/news/nation-world/world/article24494053.html.

31. Callejas, *Siembra vientos*, 18, 29.

32. Branch and Propper, *Labyrinth*, 484.

33. Domeyko, "La última version," 8; Dinges and Landau, *Assassination*, 95.

34. Branch and Propper, *Labyrinth*, 485.

35. Callejas, *Siembra vientos*, 127.

36. Branch and Propper, *Labyrinth*, 485–87.

37. Jeremiah O'Leary, "Townley's Wife Knew of Plot to Kill Letelier," *Washington Star*, June 11, 1978, A1.

38. Mariana Callejas, quoted in Dinges and Landau, *Assassination*, 95.

39. Branch and Propper, *Labyrinth*, 488, 489.

40. Dinges and Bredemeier, "Assassin," A1.

41. Mariana Callejas, quoted in Domeyko, "La última version," 8.

42. Callejas, *Siembra vientos*, 65.

43. Quoted in Branch and Propper, *Labyrinth*, 493.
44. Testimony of Mariana Callejas to federal grand jury, Washington, D.C., June 6, 1978, Letelier/Moffitt exhibit file no. 1, box 12, LC, NSA.
45. "Townley Profile."
46. Michael Townley, "'Distortion' on Chile" [letter to editor], *Guardian*, April 13, 1980.
47. Branch and Propper, *Labyrinth*, 496.
48. BBC, "Inside Story: Assassin: The Pursuit of Michael Townley," 1992, LP, Hoover.
49. Quoted in Callejas, *Siembra vientos*, 30.
50. Dinges and Landau, *Assassination*, 103; David Burnham, "C.I.A. Had Contact with American in Letelier Case," *NYT*, January 11, 1979, A10.
51. CIA source, quoted in "Periscope," *Newsweek*, March 20, 1978.
52. John Tipton, quoted in Dinges and Landau, *Assassination*, 109.
53. Quotations from Landau to secretary of state, Santiago, March 8, 1978, DNSA.
54. Transcript of proceedings, *United States of America v. Guillermo Novo Sampol, Alvin Ross Díaz and Ignacio Novo Sampol*, criminal case no. 78-367, January 18, 1979, Washington, D.C., box 25, LC, NSA, 1585.
55. Jaime Eyzguirre, quoted in Pollack, *New Right*, 32; Díaz, *Patria y Libertad*, 100–101, 16; Weld, "Spanish Civil War."
56. Pablo Rodríguez, quoted in Pollack, *New Right*, 38; Díaz, *Patria y Libertad*, 101.
57. Patricia Verdugo, "Pablo Rodríguez, 'el jefe,'" *Hoy*, April 4–10, 1979, 21–22; Freed and Landis, *Death in Washington*, 55; Salazar, *Roberto Thieme*, 75.
58. Salazar, *Roberto Thieme*, 21, 23, 114, 118.
59. Hernán Millas, "Qué se hizo Patria y Libertad," *Hoy*, April 4–10, 1979, 20–21; Salazar, *Roberto Thieme*, 80; Fuentes, *Memorias secretas*, 80–81, 104.
60. Dinges and Landau, *Assassination*, 103.
61. Unidad Popular, quoted in Millas, "Qué se hizo," 20.
62. Dinges and Landau, *Assassination*, 41.
63. Fuentes, *Memorias secretas*, 338.
64. Dinges and Landau, *Assassination*, 109; Díaz, *Patria y Libertad*, 31, 36.
65. Pablo Rodríguez, quoted in Díaz, *Patria y Libertad*, 41, see also 65.
66. John Dinges, "Figure Sought in Letelier Case Called U.S. Citizen," *Washington Post*, March 6, 1977, A1.
67. Salvador Allende, quoted in Millas, "Qué se hizo," 21.
68. Callejas, *Siembra vientos*, 37.
69. Michael Townley, quoted in Dinges and Landau, *Assassination*, 106.
70. Mariana Callejas, quoted in Fuentes, *Memorias secretas*, 146–47.
71. Branch and Propper, *Labyrinth*, 494, 496.
72. Roberto Thieme, quoted in Fuentes, *Memorias secretas*, 154; see also 147, 153.
73. Quoted in Fuentes, *Memorias secretas*, 153; Branch and Propper, *Labyrinth*, 496.
74. Callejas, *Siembra vientos*, 46.
75. Quoted in Fuentes, *Memorias secretas*, 163; BBC, "Inside Story."
76. Quotations from Fuentes, *Memorias secretas*, 166–68, 154.
77. Kornbluh, *Pinochet File*, 168; Dinges and Landau, *Assassination*, 113; Landau to secretary of state.
78. Callejas, *Siembra vientos*, 52; Dinges and Landau, *Assassination*, 115; Branch and Propper, *Labyrinth*, 499–500.

79. Callejas, *Siembra vientos*, 56.
80. Branch and Propper, *Labyrinth*, 501.
81. Dinges, "Figure Sought."
82. Jeremiah O'Leary, "Assassin's Wife to Go to Chile," *Washington Star*, February 22, 1979.
83. Callejas, *Siembra vientos*, 16.
84. Freed and Landis, *Death in Washington*, 99.
85. Dinges and Landau, *Assassination*, 103–4.
86. Townley to lawyer, April 4, 1973, quoted in Fuentes, *Memorias secretas*, 246.
87. Branch and Propper, *Labyrinth*, 501.
88. Andrews postsentence report; Dinges, *Condor Years*, 75–76; Dinges and Landau, *Assassination*, 130.
89. Mariana Callejas, quoted in Dinges and Landau, *Assassination*, 130.
90. Varas and Orrego, *El caso Letelier*, 38.
91. O'Leary, "Townley's Wife," A1.
92. "Secuestro de un diplomático," *La Nación* (Buenos Aires), special report, 1995, 12.
93. Mariana Callejas, quoted in Chang, "Downstairs."
94. Pia Barros, quoted in Chang, "Downstairs."
95. Quoted in "Secuestro," 13.
96. Cockerell to Propper, London, June 14, 1978, unmarked vol., box 8, LC, NSA; see also Callejas to federal grand jury.
97. Callejas, *Siembra vientos*, 122.
98. Cockerell to Propper.
99. Callejas, *Siembra vientos*, 122, 123.
100. "La muerte emprende viaje," *La Nación* (Buenos Aires), special report, 1995, 18.
101. Callejas, *Siembra vientos*, 123.
102. Dinges and Landau, *Assassination*, 141.
103. Kenneth Bredemeier, "Agent Details Letelier's Death," *Washington Post*, January 19, 1979, A1; McSherry, *Predatory States*, 141.
104. John Dinges, "Chile's Global Hit Men," *Nation*, June 2, 1979, 1.
105. Carter Cornick, quoted in Karen De Young et al., "'This Was Not an Accident. This Was a Bomb,'" *Washington Post*, September 20, 2016, www.washingtonpost.com/sf/national/2016/09/20/this-was-not-an-accident-this-was-a-bomb/?utm_term=.57984422ebde.
106. Callejas, *Siembra vientos*, 12.

CHAPTER 5

1. Cmiel, "Emergence of Human Rights," 1233.
2. Keys, *Reclaiming American Virtue*. See also Renouard, *Human Rights*, 6–7. For an admirably transnational and detailed look at the larger human rights movement, see Kelly, *Sovereign Emergencies*.
3. Schoultz, *Human Rights*, 75.
4. Cmiel, "Emergence of Human Rights," 1246.
5. Sikkink, *Mixed Signals*, 57–58.
6. Cmiel, "Emergence of Human Rights," 1235.
7. Patrick Symmes, "The Man Who Would Not Disappear," *Washington City Paper*,

September 22, 1995, www.washingtoncitypaper.com/news/article/13006608/the-man-who-would-not-disappear.

8. Delia Vergara, "Kennedy habla de Chile," *Hoy*, November 22–26, 1978, 12.
9. Lobbyist and Kissinger, quoted in Schoultz, *Human Rights*, 93, 111.
10. Cmiel, "Emergence of Human Rights," 1234.
11. Renouard, *Human Rights*, 88.
12. Schoultz, *Human Rights*, x, 19–20, 90.
13. Volk, "Politics of Memory," 18–22.
14. Schoultz, *Human Rights*, 84.
15. Kathleen Teltsch, "Torture in Chile Said to Continue," *NYT*, September 11, 1974, 15.
16. Schoultz, *Human Rights*, 129–30.
17. William D. Rogers, quoted in Kornbluh, *Pinochet File*, 227.
18. Schoultz, *Human Rights*, 198; Kornbluh, *Pinochet File*, 223.
19. Vergara, "Kennedy habla," 12.
20. John Davis Lodge, quoted in Schoultz, *Human Rights*, 57; see also 52–57.
21. Kornbluh, *Pinochet File*, 224–25.
22. Orlando Letelier, *Groene Amsterdammer* (Amsterdam) interview, March 3, 1976, translated and quoted in FBI Washington, D.C., field office to director, November 3, 1976, Letelier (FOIA) documents produced by the FBI, vol. 5, box 1, LC, NSA.
23. Donna Packer, quoted in Beverly Fisher, memorial for Ronni Moffitt, September 26, 1976, folder 12, box 96, IPS, WHS.
24. Hilda Karpen affidavit, July 25, 1991, DOS 2015.
25. FBI Newark field office to director, October 21, 1976, Letelier (FOIA) documents produced by the FBI, vol. 3, box 1, LC, NSA.
26. Michael Karpen, "Ronni Karpen Moffitt—Supergirl," U.S. Senate, 99th Cong., 2nd sess., *Congressional Record* 132, no. 144 (October 17, 1986): S17140–41.
27. Beverly Fisher, "Tribute to Ronni Karpen Moffitt for Dupont Circle Rally," Washington, D.C., September 22, 1976, folder 12, box 96, IPS, WHS.
28. Baltimore office to FBI director, November 30 and October 27, 1976, both in Letelier (FOIA) documents produced by the FBI, vol. 3, box 1, LC, NSA.
29. Karpen, "Ronni Karpen Moffitt."
30. Fisher memorial; Alexandria office to FBI director, October 28, 1976, Letelier (FOIA) documents produced by the FBI, vol. 3, box 1, LC, NSA.
31. Fisher memorial; Branch and Propper, *Labyrinth*, 86.
32. Richard Prince, "Second Victim of Blast Was 'Warm, Vital and Active,'" *Washington Post*, September 22, 1976, A9.
33. Hilda Karpen affidavit.
34. Flyer for "The Letelier Seminars," August 1979, box 178, TI, IISH.
35. Joshua Muravchik, "The Think Tank of the Left," *NYT*, April 26, 1981, SM19.
36. Fisher, "Tribute"; Fisher memorial.
37. Dinges and Landau, *Assassination*, 208.
38. Michael Moffitt affidavit, July 16, 1991, DOS 2015.
39. FBI Albany office report, October 5, 1976, Letelier (FOIA) documents produced by the FBI, vol. 3, box 1, LC, NSA.
40. Moffitt affidavit.
41. Michael Moffitt statement, September 22, 1976, box 277, TI, IISH.
42. Michael Moffitt draft essay, May 20, 1976, box 277, TI, IISH.

43. Laurie Ann Kaye, paraphrased in FBI Washington, D.C., field office to director, September 28, 1976, Letelier (FOIA) documents produced by the FBI, vol. 1, box 1, LC, NSA.

44. Anonymous, quoted in Cornick to Propper, October 8, 1976, Letelier (FOIA) documents produced by the FBI, vol. 11, box 2, LC, NSA.

45. Moffitt affidavit.

46. Michael Moffitt, address at St. Mark's Cathedral, Washington, D.C., December 26, 1976, reproduced in *Monthly Review*, December 1, 1976, reproduced in www.tni.org/es/node/13701.

47. Moffitt affidavit.

48. Moffitt statement.

49. Letelier had had discussions about teaching at the University of California, Berkeley and the State University of New York–Buffalo. Barnet to Letelier, October 11, 1974, folder 12, box 13, IPS, WHS; Patricio Carvajal Prado, safe passage, Santiago, September 10, 1974, folder Visas, box Series S-V, Carpetas temáticas, and Letelier to Alegría, Caracas, October 22, 1974, folder Alegría, Fernando, box 1, Correspondencia entre Orlando Letelier y terceros, both in OL, AA.

50. Juan Pablo Letelier, quoted in Raquel Correa, "'Ahora estoy en paz,'" *El Mercurio*, June 4, 1995, D2.

51. Quoted in Dinges and Landau, *Assassination*, 8.

52. Raskin and Barnet to TNI Planning Board, Washington, D.C., November [4?], 1974, folder Barnet, Richard S., box 2, Correspondencia entre Orlando Letelier y terceros, OL, AA.

53. Moffitt affidavit.

54. Orlando Letelier, "The Chicago Boys in Chile: Economic 'Freedom's' Awful Toll," *Nation*, August 28, 1976, 137–42. See also Letelier, *Chile*.

55. Isabel Letelier speech, Chicago, September 10, 1977, folder 37, box 52, IPS, WHS.

56. Tom Wicker, "Propping Up Chile," *NYT*, May 23, 1976, E17.

57. Isabel Letelier affidavit, August 2, 1991, DOS 2015.

58. Saul Landau and Ralph Stavins, "The Meaning of the Letelier Assassination," December 1976, Letelier (FOIA) documents produced by the FBI, Bulky Serial—Part 2, box 7, LC, NSA.

59. George McGovern, quoted in David Burnham, "McGovern Testifies about Meetings with Letelier," *NYT*, January 17, 1979, A7; Freed and Landis, *Death in Washington*, 12; Rodríguez, *El asesinato*, 37.

60. "El intenso exilio de Letelier," *La Nación* (Buenos Aires), special report, 1995, 29.

61. Saul Landau, "Two Deaths in the Morning," *Mother Jones*, December 1976, 21.

62. Joe Eldridge, quoted in Jack Anderson and Les Whitten, "Two Chilean Exiles' Lives in Danger," *Washington Post*, October 7, 1976, E25.

63. Bitar interview.

64. Valdés interview.

65. Cavallo, Salazar, and Sepúlveda, *La historia oculta*, 133.

66. Isabel Letelier, quoted in "Intenso exilio," 28.

67. Dinges and Landau, *Assassination*, 86.

68. Branch and Propper, *Labyrinth*, 86; Washington, D.C., field office to FBI director, September 26, 1976, Letelier (FOIA) documents produced by the FBI, vol. 1, box 1, LC, NSA; "Intenso exilio," 27; Gallagher to Deegan, and Washington, D.C., field office to FBI

director, September 30, 1976, both in Letelier (FOIA) documents produced by the FBI, vol. 1, box 1, LC, NSA. Accounts differ as to whether Pérez-Soto was the aunt or the niece of Arria's wife.

69. Orlando Letelier, quoted in FBI Washington, D.C., field office to director, December 9, 1976, Letelier (FOIA) documents produced by the FBI, vol. 14, box 2, LC, NSA.

70. Quoted in Dinges and Landau, *Assassination*, 86.

71. Branch and Propper, *Labyrinth*, 85.

72. Isabel Letelier, quoted in "Intenso exilio," 28.

73. Washington, D.C., field office to FBI director, December 9, 1976.

74. Michael Moffitt, quoted in Washington, D.C., field office to FBI director, September 30, 1976.

75. Francisco Letelier interview.

76. Washington, D.C., field office to FBI director, October 2, 1976, Letelier (FOIA) documents produced by the FBI, vol. 1, box 1, LC, NSA.

77. Orlando Letelier, quoted in Dinges and Landau, *Assassination*, 90.

78. However, Beverly Ann Leigner claimed to have been Orlando's mistress for over sixteen years, up to his assassination, and that Isabel knew about it: FBI San Francisco field office to director, November 20, 1976, Letelier (FOIA) documents produced by the FBI, vol. 7, box 1, LC, NSA. Isabel Letelier, quoted in Dinges and Landau, *Assassination*, 90. See also Washington, D.C., field office to FBI director, September 26, 1976; "Intenso exilio," 27, 29; and Cornick to Propper.

79. Orlando Letelier, quoted in Washington, D.C., field office to FBI director, December 9, 1976.

80. Orlando Letelier, quoted in Landau, "Two Deaths," 21.

81. Juan Pablo Letelier affidavit, August 2, 1991, DOS 2015.

CHAPTER 6

1. Ché Guevara, quoted in Saul Landau, "Guillermo Novo and Me," *Counterpunch*, September 19, 2003, www.counterpunch.org/2003/09/19/guillermo-novo-and-me/; Antonio de la Cova, email communication with author, December 13, 2018.

2. FBI Miami special agent in charge, memo to director, February 3, 1977, Letelier (FOIA) documents produced by the FBI, vol. 21, box 2, LC, NSA.

3. Frank O'Connor and Stanley Ross, quoted in Peter Kihss, "Three Castro Foes Arrested in Firing of Bazooka at U.N.," *NYT*, December 23, 1964, 8.

4. Ignacio Novo, quoted in Barnardo de la Maza, "Cubanos en el exilio hablan para *Qué Pasa*," *Qué Pasa*, March 20, 1978, 13.

5. Philip Walsh, quoted in Kihss, "Three Castro Foes," 8.

6. FBI Miami special agent in charge to director.

7. Timothy Robinson, "Arrest of Missing Parolee Is Ordered," *Washington Post*, June 7, 1977, C3.

8. Didion, *Vintage*, 34.

9. Manuel Hevia Frasquieri, "Guillermo Novo Sampol: ¡Yo no soy un terrorista!," *La Jiribilla*, April 12–22, 2005, www.latinamericanstudies.org/belligerence/bill.htm.

10. FBI Miami field office to director, July 5, 1979, Letelier (FOIA) documents produced by the FBI, vol. 94, box 7, LC, NSA.

11. Quote from Tracey Eaton, "Guillermo Novo: Freedom Fighter or Lawbreaker?," *Along the Malecón*, June 24, 2010, alongthemalecon.blogspot.com/2010/06/guillermo-novo-freedom-fighter-or.html; FBI Washington, D.C., field office to director, December 1, 1978, Letelier (FOIA) documents produced by the FBI, vol. 78, box 6, LC, NSA; "Cuban Freedom Fighter Will Appeal Sentence," *Jersey Journal*, September 27, 1969; "The Defendants," *Washington Post*, February 15, 1979, A29; Hevia, "Guillermo Novo Sampol."

12. Kihss, "Three Castro Foes," 8.

13. Guillermo Novo, interview by De la Cova, January 1, 2005, http://www.latinamericanstudies.org/audio/Novo-Sampol-Guillermo-1-1-2005.mp3; "Gráficas de los últimos acontecimientos," *Bohemia*, June 8, 1952, 68–69, http://www.latinamericanstudies.org/1952/Bohemia-6-8-1952-68.pdf; Zach Dorfman, "Codename: CHILBOM," *Atavist Magazine* 59 (2016), magazine.atavist.com/codename-chilbom.

14. Eaton, "Guillermo Novo."

15. Blake Fleetwood, "'I Am Going to Declare War,'" *New Times*, May 13, 1977, 53.

16. Guillermo Novo, quoted in Eaton, "Guillermo Novo."

17. Landau, "Novo and Me."

18. Acting chief, Latin American Division, memo to director of central intelligence, August 23, 1978, DNSA.

19. Robin Herman, "'Highest Priority' Given by U.S. to Capture of Anti-Castro Group," *NYT*, March 3, 1980, A1; Dinges and Landau, *Assassination*, 346.

20. "Defendants."21. José Suárez, interview by De la Cova, December 19, 2005, http://www.latinamericanstudies.org/audio/Suarez-Jose-Dionisio-12-19-2005.mp3; Encinosa, *Unvanquished*, 123.

22. Jeff Stein, "Inside Omega 7," *Village Voice*, March 10, 1980, 11.

23. Quotations in FBI report, July 28, 1978, Letelier (FOIA) documents produced by the FBI, vol. 70, box 6, and FBI New York field office to director, June 8, 1978, Letelier (FOIA) documents produced by the FBI, vol. 61, box 5, both in LC, NSA; de la Maza, "Cubanos," 12.

24. FBI report, July 28, 1978; Salazar, *Contreras*, 99; Dinges and Landau, *Assassination*, 240.

25. Dinges and Landau, *Assassination*, 232, 243.

26. FBI report, August 8, 1978, Letelier (FOIA) documents produced by the FBI, vol. 70, box 6, LC, NSA.

27. Guillermo Novo, open letter, "Sobre nuestra razón de ser," 1977, latinamericanstudies.org.

28. Dinges and Landau, *Assassination*, 346.

29. Ricardo Canete statement, folder Extradition/Trial, box 21, LC, NSA.

30. Méndez, *Los cuervos*, 90.

31. Didion, *Vintage*, 32–33.

32. Miami FBI office to FBI director, December 2, 1976, folder Letelier (FOIA) documents produced by the FBI, box 19, LC, NSA.

33. John Kennedy, quoted in Didion, *Vintage*, 41.

34. Taylor Branch and George Crile III, "The Kennedy Vendetta: How the CIA Waged a Silent War against Cuba," *Harper's*, August 1975, 51.

35. Fleetwood, "'War,'" 46.

36. Kami, "Diplomacy and Human Migration," chap. 2.

37. Méndez, *Los años del terror*, 46, 48.

38. Gonzales-Pando, *Cuban Americans*, 55.
39. "Legacy of Terror," *NYT*, July 16, 1978, SM8.
40. Orlando Bosch, quoted in Fleetwood, "'War,'" 46.
41. José Miró Cardona, quoted in Kami, "Human Migration," chap. 2, p. 1.
42. Quoted in Norman Kempster, "Intrigue Grows in Murder of Chilean," *Los Angeles Times*, November 3, 1976, A8.
43. Anthony Boadle, "Bay of Pigs Fiasco Spawned Anti-Castro Plotters," CNN, April 17, 2001, www.latinamericanstudies.org/bay-of-pigs/plotters.htm.
44. Transcript of television program, "World in Action—the DINA," WNET New York, January 19, 1977, Letelier (FOIA) documents produced by the FBI, vol. 22, box 2, LC, NSA.
45. Saul Landau, "The Letelier-Moffitt Trial," January 24, 1979, folder Letelier Trial, box 21, LC, NSA.
46. Orlando Bosch, quoted in Méndez, *Los cuervos*, 81.
47. Ignacio Novo, quoted in de la Maza, "Cubanos," 15; see also Encinosa, *Unvanquished*, 113–14.
48. Juan de Onís, "Anti-Castro Extremists Tolerated, If Not Encouraged, by Some Latin American Nations," *NYT*, November 15, 1975, 10; Méndez, *Los cuervos*, 90.
49. De Onís, "Anti-Castro Extremists," 10.
50. Quoted in Méndez, *Bajo las alas*, 77; see also 7.
51. Quoted from November 1976 interview in Miami, in FBI Washington, D.C., field office director, December 1, 1978.
52. Méndez, *Bajo las alas*, 7, 2.
53. Dorfman, "Codename: CHILBOM."
54. Quoted in Pierce, "Miami's Municipal Diplomacy," 220.
55. Méndez, *Los años del terror*, 3.
56. Miami FBI office to FBI director, December 2, 1976.
57. Ignacio Novo, quoted in de la Maza, "Cubanos," 15.
58. Ignacio Novo, quoted in FBI Washington, D.C., field office to director, December 1, 1978.
59. "Legacy of Terror."
60. Dorfman, "Codename: CHILBOM."
61. Quoted in "Legacy of Terror."
62. Quoted in FBI Miami field office to director, July 5, 1979; Novo interview by De la Cova.
63. "Legacy of Terror."
64. David Vidal, "Bombings Revealed Split among Cubans in Jersey," *NYT*, April 2, 1979, B1; Prieto, *Cubans of Union City*, 18–19.
65. Carole Feldman, "Little Havana on the Hudson a Mixed City," *Hudson Dispatch* (Union City, N.J.), February 16, 1977, 32.
66. Jeff Stein, "An Army in Exile," *New York*, September 10, 1979, 45; [Saul Landau?] conversation with Larry Wack, May 24, 1979, folder 1, box 44, IPS, WHS; David Vidal, "In Union City, the Memories of the Bay of Pigs Don't Die," *NYT*, December 2, 1979, E9; Prieto, *Cubans of Union City*, 25.
67. Antonio de la Cova, email communication with author, December 13, 2018.
67. Vidal, "In Union City," E9.
68. Larry Wack, quoted in [Saul Landau?] conversation with Larry Wack.

69. Stein, "Army in Exile," 45.

70. Ignacio Novo, quoted in de la Maza, "Cubanos," 15.

71. [Saul Landau?] interview notes, undated, folder 1, box 44, IPS, WHS.

72. Luis Fernández, quoted in Feldman, "Little Havana," 32.

73. José D. Suárez, "La Bandera de la Dignidad," *El Caimán* (New Jersey), January 1975, 1.

74. [Saul Landau?] interview notes.

75. FBI document, October 29, 1993, available at cuban-exile.com/doc_001-025/doc0011.html.

76. Alvin Ross, quoted in Herman, "'Highest Priority,'" A1.

77. Stein, "Army in Exile," 46.

78. Julia Valdivia, quoted in Stein, "Inside Omega 7," 13.

79. McSherry, *Predatory States*, 160.

80. Dinges and Landau, *Assassination*, 117.

81. Jon Nordheimer, "Letelier Inquiry Sees Chilean Link to Cuban Exiles," *NYT*, April 17, 1978, A7.

82. For instance, Méndez, *Bajo las alas*, 4.

83. Felipe Rivero, quoted in Méndez, *Bajo las alas*, 8–9.

84. Townley statement, folder Letelier/Civil—Materials from Saul Landau—March 16, 1979, box 14, LC, NSA.

85. Méndez, *Bajo las alas*, 15.

86. Orlando Bosch, quoted in Fleetwood, "'War,'" 48.

87. Townley statement.

88. Transcript of proceedings, criminal case no. 78-367, January 18, 1979, Washington, D.C., box 25, LC, NSA, 1599.

89. Townley statement.

90. Quoted in Dinges and Landau, *Assassination*, 239, 240.

91. Townley statement.

92. FBI report, April 24, 1978, Letelier (FOIA) documents produced by the FBI, vol. 87, box 7, LC, NSA.

93. Quoted in FBI report, November 24, 1979, Letelier (FOIA) documents produced by the FBI, Bulky Serial—Part 2, box 7, LC, NSA.

94. Townley statement.

95. Transcript of proceedings, 1604.

96. FBI report, April 24, 1978.

97. Cockerell to Propper, London, June 14, 1978, unmarked vol., box 8, LC, NSA.

98. Dinges and Landau, *Assassination*, 99–100.

99. De la Maza, "Cubanos," 8.

100. Mariana Callejas, quoted in "La muerte emprende viaje," *La Nación* (Buenos Aires), special report, 1995, 18.

101. Stein, "Army in Exile," 44.

CHAPTER 7

1. U.S. Ambassador to Chile David Popper to secretary of state, Santiago, February 21, 1975, DOS 2015.

2. Cornick to Propper, October 8, 1976, Letelier (FOIA) documents produced by the FBI, vol. 11, box 2, LC, NSA.

3. Elizabeth Subercaseaux, "Isabel, te tengo una sorpresa," *Caras* (Santiago), [May?] 1990, 6; Freed and Landis, *Death in Washington*, 83; Dinges and Landau, *Assassination*, 170.

4. Saul Landau and Isabel Letelier, Meaning of the Letelier-Moffitt assassination, September 22, 1992, audio recording, 1531A/393, IPS, WHS.

5. Oliver to Paz Cohen, Paris, June 21, 1977, folder 34, box 38, IPS, WHS.

6. Orlando Bosch, quoted in Blake Fleetwood, "'I Am Going to Declare War,'" *New Times*, May 13, 1977, 53.

7. Méndez, *Los cuervos*, 106.

8. Fleetwood, "'War,'" 51.

9. Quoted in McSherry, *Predatory States*, 158.

10. McSherry, *Predatory States*, 158.

11. Orlando Bosch, quoted in Fleetwood, "'War,'" 53. Scholar Antonio de la Cova, who interviewed several CNM members, countered that "Letelier was never discussed at Bonao." De la Cova, email communication with author, December 13, 2018.

12. Contreras to Brazilian general, Santiago, August 28, 1975, quoted in FBI Washington, D.C., field office (Cornick) to director, February 15, 1978, Letelier (FOIA) documents produced by the FBI, vol. 44, box 4, LC, NSA.

13. Townley statement, folder Letelier/Civil—Materials from Saul Landau—March 16, 1979, box 14, LC, NSA.

14. Quoted in Dinges and Landau, *Assassination*, 179, 176, 180.

15. Salazar, *Contreras*, 129.

16. Pedro Espinoza, quoted in Dinges and Landau, *Assassination*, 182.

17. Townley statement.

18. Branch and Propper, *Labyrinth*, 539–40.

19. Mariana Callejas, quoted in Dinges and Landau, *Assassination*, 183.

20. Stern, *Reckoning with Pinochet*, 139.

21. Pia Díaz, "35% de pasaportes dados entre 1975–1977 eran falsos," *La Época*, July 5, 1990, 15.

22. George Landau, quoted in Dinges and Landau, *Assassination*, 317.

23. Landau interview, ADST.

24. Elizabeth Subercaseaux, "Contreras va a declarar, que duda cabe," *Caras* (Santiago), [May?] 1990, 5; Dinges and Landau, *Assassination*, 309.

25. Dinges and Landau, *Assassination*, 311; McSherry, *Predatory States*, 157.

26. McNeil to Vaky, August 14, 1978, DNSA.

27. Dinges and Landau, *Assassination*, 311.

28. Lagos personal statement, March 1988, DOS 2015.

29. "Mónica Lagos antes de caer en manos de la DINA," *La Época*, April 21, 1990, 15.

30. All quoted in Lagos personal statement, March 1988, DOS 2015.

31. Dinges and Landau, *Assassination*, 199, 202.

32. Lagos personal statement.

33. Dinges and Landau, *Assassination*, 203.

34. Lagos personal statement.

35. David Shribman, "Plot to Kill Letelier Said to Involve Nerve Gas," *NYT*, December 13, 1981.

36. Townley statement.
37. Branch and Propper, *Labyrinth*, 546.
38. Dinges and Landau, *Assassination*, 21.
39. Ercilla, *Caso Letelier*, 33–34; FBI Washington, D.C., field office, memo to director, October 19, 1976, Letelier (FOIA) documents produced by the FBI, vol. 14, box 2, LC, NSA.
40. Quoted in Dinges and Landau, *Assassination*, 11.
41. Cornick to Propper.
42. Isabel Letelier, quoted in Subercaseaux, "Isabel," 6.
43. Joy Billington, "'His Widow Does Not Doubt That He Died for A Cause," *Washington Star*, September 22, 1976, reproduced in www.tni.org/es/node/6407; Branch and Propper, *Labyrinth*, 550.
44. Douglas Grant Mine, "The Assassin Next Door," *Miami New Times*, November 18, 1999, www.miaminewtimes.com/news/the-assassin-next-door-6357449; Barnes memo to secretary of state, Santiago, March 12, 1987, DNSA.
45. Freed and Landis, *Death in Washington*, 10.
46. Orlando Letelier, "A Testament," *NYT*, September 27, 1976, 31.
47. Lillian Montecina, quoted in Stephen J. Lynton and Ronald Kessler, "Chilean Bomb Victim Told FBI of Threats to Life, Friends Say," *Washington Post*, September 23, 1976, A1.
48. Cornick to Propper.
49. Quoted in Lynton and Kessler, "Bomb Victim," A1.
50. Quoted in FBI New York field office to director, February 9 and 19, 1977, both in Letelier (FOIA) documents produced by the FBI, vol. 20, box 2, LC, NSA.
51. Freed and Landis, *Death in Washington*, 14.
52. Ernest Volkmar and John Cummings, "The Assassination of Orlando Letelier," *Penthouse*, July 1978, 52–59, 114–17.
53. Valdés interview.
54. David Burnham, "Mail Sent to Letelier Was Tampered with, Widow Says in Court," *NYT*, February 8, 1979, A7; Cornick to Propper.
55. Isabel Letelier, interview by J. Teunissen and A. Steenhuis, February 2, 1977, audio recording 1534A/303, IPS, WHS.
56. Quoted in FBI Washington, D.C., field office, memo to director, September 28, 1976, Letelier (FOIA) documents produced by the FBI, vol. 1, box 1, LC, NSA.
57. Lynton and Kessler, "Bomb Victim," A1.
58. Del Solar, *Orlando Letelier*, 30.
59. Quoted in Lynton and Kessler, "Bomb Victim," A1.
60. Cornick to Propper.
61. Isabel Letelier interview, IPS, WHS.
62. Cornick to Propper.
63. Orlando Letelier, quoted in "El intenso exilio de Letelier," *La Nación* (Buenos Aires), special report, 1995, 30.
64. Dinges and Landau, *Assassination*, 12. Among the Cubans who were at the meeting but participated no further was Newark physician Juan B. Pulido, who was never charged: Timothy S. Robinson, "FBI Describes Bomb Killing of Letelier," *Washington Post*, June 3, 1978, A1.
65. Quoted in Branch and Propper, *Labyrinth*, 553–54.
66. Dinges and Landau, *Assassination*, 16; Robinson, "FBI," A1.

67. Antonio de la Cova, email communication with author, December 13, 2018.
68. Dinges and Landau, *Assassination*, 17.
69. Townley testimony, April [25?], 1978, DNSA.
70. Dinges and Landau, *Assassination*, 18; Saul Landau, "Two Deaths in the Morning," *Mother Jones*, December 1976, 22.
71. Townley statement.
72. Branch and Propper, *Labyrinth*, 563.
73. Kenneth Bredemeier, "Agent Details Letelier's Death," *Washington Post*, January 19, 1979, A1.
74. Branch and Propper, *Labyrinth*, 565.
75. Dinges and Landau, *Assassination*, 19.
76. Rosalind Andrews [probation officer], postsentence report on Michael Townley, May 29, 1979, DNSA.
77. Dinges and Landau, *Assassination*, 22.
78. Townley statement.
79. Dinges and Landau, *Assassination*, 24.
80. Orlando Letelier, quoted in Varas and Orrego, *El caso Letelier*, 17.
81. *Ercilla, Caso Letelier*, 43–44; Mine, "Assassin Next Door"; Branch and Propper, *Labyrinth*, 570.
82. Lagos personal statement.
83. Dinges and Landau, *Assassination*, 221.
84. Mariana Callejas, quoted in Cockerell to Propper, London, June 14, 1978, unmarked vol., box 8, LC, NSA.
85. Townley statement.

CHAPTER 8

1. David Binder, "Opponent of Chilean Junta Slain in Washington by Bomb in His Auto," *NYT*, September 22, 1976, 1.
2. "Terror in Washington" [editorial], *NYT*, September 22, 1976, 33.
3. Jeremiah O'Leary, "Left Is Also Suspect in Slaying of Letelier," *Washington Star*, October 8, 1977, A1.
4. Defense Intelligence Agency memo, September 28, 1976, folder 11, box 24, IPS, WHS.
5. Stephen J. Lynton and Ronald Kessler, "Chilean Bomb Victim Told FBI of Threats to Life, Friends Say," *Washington Post*, September 23, 1976, A1.
6. Quoted in Zach Dorfman, "Codename: CHILBOM," *Atavist Magazine* 59 (2016), magazine.atavist.com/codename-chilbom.
7. "Murder Mystery," *Newsweek*, October 11, 1976.
8. Memo, October 8, 1976, folder 30, box 38, IPS, WHS. Activist Tom Hayden accused CIA Director George Bush of authorizing a disinformation campaign blaming left-wingers for killing Letelier: Tom Hayden, "An Exiled Son of Santiago," *Nation*, April 4, 2005, www.thenation.com/article/exiled-son-santiago/.
9. David Binder, "Cuban Exiles Are Reported Linked to Slayings of Chilean in Washington," *NYT*, October 12, 1976.
10. Earl Silbert, quoted in Dinges and Landau, *Assassination*, 217.
11. Branch and Propper, *Labyrinth*, 57, 79, 56, 38–39, 55; Dinges and Landau, *Assassination*, 229.

12. Eugene Propper, quoted in Dorfman, "Codename: CHILBOM."
13. Taylor Branch, "The Letelier Investigation: The Venezuelan Connection," *NYT*, July 16, 1978, SM7; Branch and Propper, *Labyrinth*, 57; Timothy S. Robinson, "The Letelier Prosecutor: An Unlikely Celebrity in Santiago," *Washington Post*, August 3, 1978, A14.
14. Philip Taubman, "Perils of Being the Prosecution Team," *NYT*, February 28, 1983.
15. Dinges and Landau, *Assassination*, 197, 254; Branch and Propper, *Labyrinth*, 92.
16. Branch, "Letelier Investigation."
17. Isabel Letelier, interview by the author.
18. Dinges and Landau, *Assassination*, 237; Mary McGrory, "A G-Man the Left Can Love," *Washington Post*, September 24, 1989, B1.
19. McGrory, "G-Man," B1; Dinges, *Condor Years*, 90.
20. Isabel Letelier, interview by the author.
21. Branch and Propper, *Labyrinth*, 77.
22. Buenos Aires to FBI director, September 28, 1976, Letelier (FOIA) Branneman notes and memos, box 20, LC, NSA.
23. McNamara to secretary of state, Quebec City, September 27, 1976, DNSA.
24. Dorfman, "Codename: CHILBOM."
25. Dinges and Landau, *Assassination*, 242.
26. Special assistant to the director of central intelligence memo to director of central intelligence, c. September 23, 1976, DNSA.
27. Joanne Omang, "Terrorist Plot by Rightist Cuban Exiles Seen," *Washington Post*, November 3, 1976, A17.
28. "'The Bus Has Left with the Dogs': How They Blew Up the Cuban Plane," *New Times*, May 13, 1977, 52.
29. Phillips, "Terrorism and Security in the Caribbean," 209–19; FBI Caracas to director, October 7, 1976, DNSA; Freed and Landis, *Death in Washington*, 19.
30. Omang, "Terrorist Plot," A17.
31. FBI Caracas to director.
32. Dinges and Landau, *Assassination*, 271.
33. Norman Kempster, "Chilean Exile's Murder: Tale of Intrigue," *Los Angeles Times*, June 12, 1977, A1.
34. Blake Fleetwood, "'I Am Going to Declare War,'" *New Times*, May 13, 1977, 45.
35. "Prepared Statement of Mr. Blake Fleetwood, Freelance Journalist," November 15, 2007, in U.S. Congress, House Committee on Foreign Affairs, 110th Cong., 1st sess., *"Diplomatic Assurances" on Torture: A Case Study of Why Some Are Accepted and Others Rejected*, Serial no. 110-138 (Washington: GPO, 2008), 16.
36. Scherrer to director, Buenos Aires, December 16, 1976, documents produced by the FBI, additional releases, box 10, LC, NSA.
37. "Statement of Mr. Blake Fleetwood," 15.
38. Buenos Aires to FBI director, October 1, 1976, Letelier (FOIA) Branneman notes and memos, box 20, LC, NSA.
39. Binder, "Cuban Exiles."
40. Orlando Bosch, quoted in FBI Caracas to director, October 22, 1976, DNSA.
41. FBI Newark office to Propper, November 15, 1976, Letelier (FOIA) documents produced by the FBI, vol. 8, box 1, LC, NSA.
42. Dinges and Landau, *Assassination*, 253; FBI Miami field office to director,

November 1, 1976, Letelier (FOIA) documents produced by the FBI, vol. 5, box 1, LC, NSA.

43. Branch and Propper, *Labyrinth*, 111.

44. Baltimore field office to FBI director, October 5, 1976, Letelier (FOIA) documents produced by the FBI, vol. 1, box 1, LC, NSA.

45. Branch and Propper, *Labyrinth*, 92–97, 120; Dinges and Landau, *Assassination*, 253; Norman Kempster, "Intrigue Grows in Murder of Chilean," *Los Angeles Times*, November 3, 1976, A1, A8.

46. U.S. District Court, Washington, D.C., February 7, 1977, DNSA.

47. Kempster, "Chilean Exile's Murder," A1; "Cuban Exile Jailed for Refusing to Testify in Murder of Letelier," *NYT*, April 21, 1977, 7; Timothy S. Robinson and Stephen J. Lynton, "Evidence Links Letelier Death to Anti-Castro Unit," *Washington Post*, February 1, 1977, A1, A8; FBI Washington, D.C., field office to director, February 1, 1977, documents produced by FBI, additional releases, box 10, LC, NSA; Jack Anderson and Les Whitten, "Ten Key Suspects in Letelier Killing," *Washington Post*, March 27, 1977, B11.

48. Kempster, "Chilean Exile's Murder," A1.

49. FBI Miami special agent in charge to director, February 3, 1977, Letelier (FOIA) documents produced by the FBI, vol. 21, box 2, LC, NSA.

50. Dinges and Landau, *Assassination*, 213, 221.

51. Timothy Robinson, "Arrest of Missing Parolee Is Ordered," *Washington Post*, June 7, 1977, C3.

52. Branch, "Letelier Investigation."

53. Manuel Contreras, quoted in Dinges and Landau, *Assassination*, 277, 168.

54. Bob Woodward, "Ex-CIA Aide, Three Cuban Exiles Focus of Letelier Inquiry," *Washington Post*, April 12, 1977, A1.

55. Quoted in Jeremiah O'Leary, "Chilean Exile's Murder: Many Mysteries, Many Clues," *Washington Star*, April 1, 1977, E16. See also Anthony Marro, "Letelier's Murder Still Baffles U.S.," *NYT*, April 13, 1977, 4.

56. FBI New York field office to director, May 11, 1977, Letelier (FOIA) documents produced by the FBI, vol. 27, box 3, LC, NSA.

57. FBI New York field office to director, May 9, 1977, folder Letelier (FOIA), documents produced by the FBI, box 19, LC, NSA.

58. FBI New York field office to director, May 11, 1977.

59. Quoted in Dinges and Landau, *Assassination*, 254, 289–90, 292, 290–91, 294; FBI Newark field office to director, July 8, 1977, Letelier (FOIA) documents produced by the FBI, vol. 32, box 3, LC, NSA.

60. Ricardo Canete statement, folder Extradition/Trial, box 21, LC, NSA.

61. Quoted in "CHILBOMB summary," July 18, 1977, and FBI Washington, D.C., field office to director, July 12, 1977, both Letelier (FOIA) documents produced by the FBI, vol. 32, box 3, LC, NSA.

62. Dinges and Landau, *Assassination*, 296–300, 275.

63. "EE.UU. pidió a Pinochet que investigara a agentes anticastristas del regimen," *ABC* (Spain), 5 August 2012, www.abc.es/20120805/internacional/abci-eeuu-pinochet-investigara-anticastristas-201208041342.html.

64. Propper to Pastor, August 31, 1977, DNSA.

65. FBI Newark field office report, February 13, 1978, Letelier (FOIA) documents

produced by the FBI, vol. 42, box 4, LC, NSA; Jack Anderson and Les Whitten, "Tracking the Killers of Letelier," *Washington Post*, September 8, 1977, DC11.

66. Townley statement, folder Letelier/Civil - Materials from Saul Landau - March 16, 1979, box 14, LC, NSA.

CHAPTER 9

1. Jimmy Carter, quoted in Freed and Landis, *Death in Washington*, 171.
2. Renouard, *Human Rights*, 94.
3. Steven interview, ADST.
4. Quoted in Ambassador Thomas Boyatt interview, ADST.
5. Dinges and Landau, *Assassination*, 278.
6. David Binder, "Opponent of Chilean Junta Slain in Washington by Bomb in His Auto," *NYT*, September 22, 1976, 1; Branch and Propper, *Labyrinth*, 84.
7. Quoted in Dinges, *Condor Years*, 192.
8. Robert Steven, quoted in Zach Dorfman, "Codename: CHILBOM," *Atavist Magazine* 59 (2016), magazine.atavist.com/codename-chilbom.
9. Dinges, *Condor Years*, 192.
10. Bushnell interview, ADST.
11. Steven interview, ADST.
12. Grover interview, ADST.
13. Cavallo, Salazar, and Sepúlveda, *La historia oculta*, 132.
14. Cornick to Propper, October 8, 1976, Letelier (FOIA) documents produced by the FBI, vol. 11, box 2, LC, NSA.
15. Quoted in "Es irresponsable culpar a Chile del atentado contra Orlando Letelier," *La Tercera*, September 23, 1976, 19.
16. "El brazo terrorista" [editorial], *La Tercera*, September 22, 1976, 3.
17. Manuel Trucco, quoted in Robinson to U.S. delegation, Washington, D.C., September 22, 1976, DNSA, and in Dinges and Landau, *Assassination*, 223.
18. Peña and Tobar, "Manuel Contreras," 33.
19. Stedman to U.S. Ambassador to Venezuela, Washington, D.C., July 25, 1977, DOS 2016.
20. Vial, *Pinochet*, 250; Stephen J. Lynton and Timothy S. Robinson, "Letelier's Friends Keep Working," *Washington Post*, September 21, 1977, A11.
21. Quoted in Dinges and Landau, *Assassination*, 341.
22. Quoted in John Dinges, "Chile's Murder, Inc.," *Inquiry*, January 8–22, 1979, 18.
23. Dinges and Landau, *Assassination*, 341.
24. Michael Moffitt, quoted in Jeffrey Stein, "The Letelier-Moffitt Mystery," *Progressive*, November 1977.
25. Steven interview, ADST.
26. Daniel Patrick Moynihan, "On U.S. Support for the World-Bank Loan to Chile," *NYT*, January 4, 1977, L27.
27. U.S. Ambassador to Chile David Popper to secretary of state, Santiago, September 23, 1976, DNSA.
28. Dinges and Landau, *Assassination*, 198; Juan de Onís, "Chilean Court Investigates Death of Diplomat Tied to Letelier Case," *NYT*, March 8, 1978, A7.
29. Political section to Landau, March [17?], 1978, DNSA.

30. William R. Long and Roberto Brauning, "Caso Letelier amenaza a ex jefe policial chileno," *Miami Herald*, May 15, 1978.

31. Political section to Landau; John Dinges, "Pinochet against the Wall in Letelier Investigation," Latinamerica Press, March 16, 1978, 7.

32. This story was told to me on background.

33. Saul Landau, "Letelier Probe Threatens Pinochet Rule," *In These Times*, April 19–25, 1978, reproduced in www.tni.org/es/node/11719.

34. C. M., "Extrañas muertes," *Ercilla*, May 26, 1995, 22.

35. Dominique Dhombres, "L'enquête sur l'assassinat d'Orlando Letelier met en évidence les responsabilités des dirigeants chiliens," *Le Monde* (Paris), April 28, 1978, 4.

36. Political section to Landau.

37. Unnamed author, CIA memo, February 23, 1978, DNSA.

38. Judith Miller, "U.S. Granting $38 Million Credit to Chilean Farmers: Amnesty Decision Is Quoted," *NYT*, May 5, 1978, A7.

39. "To Keep the Pressure on Chile" [editorial], *NYT*, May 13, 1978, 22.

40. FBI Washington, D.C., field office, memo to director, February 8, 1978, Letelier (FOIA) documents produced by the FBI, vol. 42, box 4, LC, NSA.

41. Taylor Branch, "The Letelier Investigation: The Venezuelan Connection," *NYT*, July 16, 1978, SM7.

42. Stern, *Battling for Hearts and Minds*, 145.

43. Timothy S. Robinson, "U.S. Asks Chile to Produce Two for Probe of Slayings," *Washington Post*, February 22, 1978, A1; "Two Named in Killing of Former Envoy to U.S. Cannot Be Found in Chile," *NYT*, February 26, 1978, 13.

CHAPTER 10

1. Kornbluh, *Pinochet File*, 344.

2. "Pistas en las calles de Union City," *La Nación* (Buenos Aires), special report, 1995, 39; Isabel Letelier, interview by the author.

3. Francisco Letelier interview.

4. "Pistas en las calles," 39.

5. Chile Legislative Center, flyer, September 22, 1976, Binder Letelier-Moffitt Investigation U.S. and Foreign Press Originals, box 23, LC, NSA.

6. "Murders: Made in D.C." [editorial], *Daily World*, September 23, 1976.

7. Landau, "Two Deaths," 23.

8. Dinges and Landau, *Assassination*, 224.

9. Freed and Landis, *Death in Washington*, 18; Tim Wheeler, "Five Thousand in D.C. March Mourn Letelier," *Daily World*, September 28, 1976, 1; Alexander Cockburn and James Ridgeway, "Why Chile's Secret Police Killed Orlando Letelier," *Village Voice*, October 4, 1976, 11; Landau, "Two Deaths," 23; announcement for memorial procession, September 26, 1976, box 171, TI, IISH.

10. Wheeler, "Five Thousand," 1.

11. "Pistas en las calles," 39.

12. "Twenty-Five Hundred Honor Murdered Chilean," *NYT*, September 27, 1976, 12; Wheeler, "Five Thousand," 12.

13. Wheeler, "Five Thousand," 1.

14. George McGovern, quoted in Del Solar, *Orlando Letelier*, 55.

15. Michael Moffitt speech at memorial, September 26, 1976, folder 7, box 48, IPS, WHS.

16. Dinges and Landau, *Assassination*, 226.

17. Scranton to secretary of state, U.S. mission at United Nations, September 23, 1976, and McNamara to secretary of state, Quebec City, September 27, 1976, both in DNSA.

18. "Ecumenical Service for Letelier, Slain Chilean, Is Set for Sunday," *NYT*, October 8, 1976, 94. The organizations were the Ecumenical Committee of Concern for Chile, the Council on Hemispheric Affairs, the National Coordinating Center in Solidarity with Chile, and Chile Democrático.

19. Heck memo of conversation, October 6, 1976, DNSA.

20. Isabel Letelier, quoted in Joy Billington, "'His Widow Does Not Doubt That He Died for A Cause," *Washington Star*, September 22, 1976, reproduced in www.tni.org/es/node/6407.

21. Valdés interview. Juan Gabriel Valdés made the phone call to Venezuela.

22. Isabel Letelier, interview by the author.

23. "Letelier Is Buried in Caracas," *NYT*, September 30, 1976, 5; Elizabeth Subercaseaux, "Isabel, te tengo una sorpresa," *Caras* (Santiago), [May?] 1990, 7.

24. Isabel Letelier, quoted in Joy Billington, "Letelier's Widow Convinced the Truth Is Emerging," *Washington Star*, October 24, 1976, C2.

25. Saul Landau, quoted in Tom Hayden, "An Exiled Son of Santiago," *Nation*, April 4, 2005, www.thenation.com/article/exiled-son-santiago/.

26. Branch and Propper, *Labyrinth*, 34; an example of a message of condolence is Schneider to Barnet and Raskin, September 22, 1976, folder 12, box 13, IPS, WHS.

27. Dinges and Landau, *Assassination*, 219. See also Patrick Symmes, "The Man Who Would Not Disappear," *Washington City Paper*, September 22, 1995, www.washingtoncitypaper.com/news/article/13006608/the-man-who-would-not-disappear.

28. Dinges and Landau, *Assassination*, 218.

29. Branch and Propper, *Labyrinth*, 34–35, 47–49.

30. Quoted in Hayden, "Exiled Son."

31. Carter Cornick, quoted in Symmes, "Man."

32. Quoted in Dinges and Landau, *Assassination*, 219–20.

33. Branch and Propper, *Labyrinth*, 34–35, 47–49.

34. [Saul Landau?] meeting with Juan Gabriel [Valdés?], May 20, 1977, folder 37, box 38, IPS, WHS.

35. "The Karpens," [August?] 1991, DOS 2015.

36. Hilda Karpen affidavit, July 25, 1991, DOS 2015.

37. Paul Loeb, "Death: Bringing It All Back Home," *San José Mercury News*, September 27, 1987, box 348, TI, IISH.

38. "Ronni Moffitt Killed by An Assassin's Bomb," *Washington Jewish Week*, September 30, 1976.

39. "Karpens."

40. Hilda Karpen affidavit.

41. Rosalind Andrews [probation officer], postsentence report on Michael Townley, May 29, 1979, DNSA.

42. Hilda Karpen affidavit.

43. Cornick to Propper, October 8, 1976, Letelier (FOIA) documents produced by the FBI, vol. 11, box 2, LC, NSA.

44. Michael Moffitt affidavit, July 16, 1991, DOS 2015.

45. Michael Moffitt, quoted in Dinges and Landau, *Assassination*; see also 272.
46. Letelier and Moffitt, *International Economic Order*.
47. Isabel Letelier, quoted in Dinges and Landau, *Assassination*, 270.
48. Billington, "'His Widow."
49. Isabel Letelier, quoted in Terrence Downs, "City of Exiles: Those Who Can't Go Home Again," *Washington Post Magazine*, July 23, 1989, 12.
50. Quoted in James Gordon, psychiatric evaluation of Isabel Morel Letelier, August 2, 1991, DOS 2015.
51. Isabel Letelier, quoted in Subercaseaux, "Isabel," 7.
52. Gordon evaluation.
53. Isabel Letelier, quoted in Subercaseaux, "Isabel," 7.
54. Isabel Letelier affidavit, August 2, 1991, DOS 2015.
55. Gordon evaluation.
56. Letelier, "I Think I Have Struggled," 51.
57. Isabel Letelier affidavit.
58. Quoted in Dinges and Landau, *Assassination*, 227.
59. Gordon evaluation.
60. Stephen J. Lynton and Timothy S. Robinson, "Letelier's Friends Keep Working," *Washington Post*, September 21, 1977, A11.
61. Saul Landau, quoted in Hayden, "Exiled Son."
62. Gordon evaluation.
63. Francisco Letelier interview.
64. Cristián Letelier interview.
65. Christian [Cristián] Letelier affidavit, July 25, 1991, DOS 2015.
66. José I. O. Letelier affidavit, July 26, 1991, DOS 2015.
67. Francisco Letelier affidavit, July 22, 1991, DOS 2015.
68. Francisco Letelier interview.
69. Francisco Letelier affidavit.
70. David Montgomery, "A Car Bomb Killed Orlando Letelier on Embassy Row 40 Years Ago. A Mural by His Son Marks the Tragedy and the Progress It Inspired," *Washington Post*, September 18, 2016, www.washingtonpost.com/news/arts-and-entertainment/wp/2016/09/18/a-car-bomb-killed-orlando-letelier-on-embassy-row-40-years-ago-a-mural-by-his-son-marks-the-tragedy-and-the-progress-it-inspired/?postshare=3681474227603641&tid=ss_mail.
71. Francisco Letelier affidavit.
72. Hayden, "Exiled Son."
73. Juan Pablo Letelier affidavit, August 2, 1991, DOS 2015.
74. Francisco Letelier affidavit.
75. Isabel Letelier, quoted in Christy Macy, "Award Brings Home Human Rights," *In These Times*, October 4–10, 1978, 6.
76. Isabel Letelier affidavit.
77. Borosage to Seely, February 8, 1978, Washington, D.C., folder 11, box 24, IPS, WHS.
78. Francisco Letelier interview; Isabel Letelier, interview by the author.
79. Isabel Letelier, interview by the author.
80. Isabel Letelier CV up to 1986, folder 34, box 46, IPS, WHS; Isabel Letelier and Michael Moffitt, "Human Rights, Economic Aid and Private Banks: The Case of Chile," April 1978, box 170, TI, IISH.

81. Francisco Letelier interview.
82. David Binder, "Exile Is Often Worse than Going Home," *NYT*, July 30, 1978, E2.
83. Isabel Letelier quoted in Downs, "City of Exiles," 12.
84. Isabel Letelier speech, U.N. Commission on Human Rights, December 1976, folder 37, box 52, IPS, WHS.
85. Isabel Letelier to Jimmy Carter, Washington, D.C., June 17, 1977, folder Letelier-Moffitt, Misc., 1977–1979, box 28, LC, NSA.
86. Isabel Letelier, interview by the author.
87. Michael Moffitt, Isabel Letelier, and Martha Graff to Board of Trustees, Washington, D.C., October 21, 1977, folder 18, box 48, IPS, WHS; Isabel Letelier, interview by the author.
88. Saul Landau report, June 1977, box 303, TI, IISH.
89. Dinges and Landau, *Assassination*, 273.
90. Institute for Policy Studies, "The Investigation of the Assassination of Orlando Letelier and Ronni Karpen Moffitt: Incompetency and Cover-up," [July?] 1977, folder Letelier/Civil—Background IPS Cover-up Study, box 14, LC, NSA.
91. FBI Washington, D.C., field office to director, January 18, 1978, Letelier (FOIA) documents produced by the FBI, vol. 41, box 4, LC, NSA.
92. Isabel Letelier affidavit.
93. Gordon evaluation.
94. Rowland Evans and Robert Novak, "Contents of Chilean's Briefcase," *Washington Post*, no date (after February 18, 1977), no page. See also O'Leary, "Chilean Exile's Murder," E16.
95. Jack Anderson and Les Whitten, "Letelier's 'Havana Connection,'" *Washington Post*, December 20, 1976, C7.
96. Quoted in Freed and Landis, *Death in Washington*, 156.
97. "Action on the Letelier-Moffitt Assassinations" [flyer], [September?] 1977, folder 46, box 38, IPS, WHS.
98. Quoted in "U.S. Tried to Hide Truth in Death of Envoy, Widow Says," *Grand Rapids Press*, February 10, 1978, 1.
99. Timothy S. Robinson and Stephen J. Lynton, "Evidence Links Letelier Death to Anti-Castro Unit," *Washington Post*, February 1, 1977, A1, A8.
100. "Cover-up Grows: Press Slanders Letelier," *Chile Newsletter*, June/July 1977, 2; Freed and Landis, *Death in Washington*, 152.
101. Rowland Evans and Robert Novak, "Letelier's Political Fund," *Washington Post*, February 16, 1977, A21. See also Rowland Evans and Robert Novak, "Letelier Letters Show 'Liberals' Being Used," *Baltimore Evening Sun*, February 16, 1977.
102. Jeffrey Hart, "Letelier Led Double Life," *Baltimore News-American*, April 19, 1977.
103. "Cover-up Grows."
104. Ronald Reagan, transcript of radio program, "Letelier II," folder Transcripts 1978 (2/2), box 2, Ronald Reagan Radio Commentary, Hoover.
105. Lee Lescaze, "Letelier Briefcase Opened to Press," *Washington Post*, February 17, 1977, A3.
106. Saul Landau, "'A Campaign to Smear Letelier,'" *Washington Post*, February 18, 1977, A19. See also Saul Landau, "Letelier Probe Threatens Pinochet Rule," *In These Times*, April 19–25, 1978, reproduced in www.tni.org/es/node/11719.
107. Isabel Letelier, "Letelier's Widow Speaks for Him" [letter to editor], *Washington*

Star, April 23, 1977. See also Beatriz Allende, "Letelier: What 'Strange Double Life'?" *Washington Post*, April 30, 1977, A12.

108. Eugene Propper, quoted in Landau, "Two Deaths," 23.
109. Carter Cornick, quoted in Dinges and Landau, *Assassination*, 233.
110. Memo of conversation between Isabel Letelier and Eugene Propper, October 21, 1976, box 305, TI, IISH.
111. Isabel Letelier, quoted in Billington, "Letelier's Widow," C2.
112. Branch and Propper, *Labyrinth*, 210.
113. Memo of conversation between Isabel Letelier and Eugene Propper.
114. Eugene Propper, quoted in Dinges and Landau, *Assassination*, 271.
115. Thornburgh to Bell, Washington, D.C., February 3, 1977, and Bell to Isabel Letelier, Washington, D.C., [February?] 1977, both in folder George W. Landau The Letelier Case (Chile) (2 of 2) 1976–2006, box 3, LP, Hoover.
116. Griffin Bell, quoted in Branch and Propper, *Labyrinth*, 210.
117. Isabel Letelier and Michael Moffitt to Carter, August 26, 1977, DNSA.
118. Brzezinski to Carter, August [26?], 1977, DNSA.
119. Longhand memo attached to Pastor to Brzezinski, September 20, 1977, DNSA.
120. Brzezinski to Isabel Letelier and Michael Moffitt, Washington, D.C., October 11, 1977, DNSA.
121. Isabel Letelier, interview by the author.
122. Saul Landau, "Report on the Murder Investigation," Institute for Policy Studies, September 19, 1977, Letelier (FOIA) documents produced by the FBI, vol. 39, box 3, LC, NSA.
123. "Action on the Letelier-Moffitt Assassinations."
124. Isabel Letelier speech, DePaul University, September 10, 1977, folder 37, box 52, IPS, WHS.
125. Michael Moffitt and Isabel Letelier to Harman, September 14, 1977, Washington, D.C., folder 14, box 45, IPS, WHS. See also "Action on the Letelier-Moffitt Assassinations."
126. Saul Landau and Susan Berner, "To All Members of the Transnational Institute," October 28, 1976, box 45, Planning Board Correspondence 1976, TI, IISH.
127. Moffitt, Letelier, and Graff to Board of Trustees.
128. Isabel Letelier, quoted in David Moberg, "'I've Had No Time to Be a Sad Widow,'" *In These Times*, September 21, 1977, 9.
129. Quoted in Symmes, "Man."
130. Timothy S. Robinson, "Eight Indicted in Letelier Slaying," *Washington Post*, August 2, 1978, A1.
131. Ingram to Moore, March 3, 1978, Letelier (FOIA) documents produced by the FBI, vol. 44, box 4, LC, NSA.
132. Isabel Letelier, quoted in "La veuve d'Orlando Letelier: 'Gare à l'amnistie de Pinochet,'" *Le Matin* (Paris), April 27, 1978. See also Nicholas M. Horrock, "U.S. Said to Weigh Move against Chile over Murder Case," *NYT*, March 4, 1978, 45.

CHAPTER 11

1. Dinges and Landau, *Assassination*, 322.
2. Steven interview, ADST.

3. "A Chilean Paper Says Suspect in Killing of Ex-Allende Aide Is North American," *NYT*, March 6, 1978, A10.

4. Quoted in Branch and Propper, *Labyrinth*, 424.

5. Jeremiah O'Leary, "Letelier Suspect Is U.S. Citizen, Pro-Junta Chilean Paper Says," *Washington Star*, March 6, 1978.

6. Cornick to FBI director, March 12, 1978, Letelier (FOIA) documents produced by the FBI, vol. 44, box 4, LC, NSA; Zach Dorfman, "Codename: CHILBOM," *Atavist Magazine* 59 (2016), magazine.atavist.com/codename-chilbom.

7. Jeremiah O'Leary, "Letelier Slaying Suspect Identified by Woman in U.S. as Her Brother," *Washington Star*, March 13, 1978.

8. Cornick to FBI director.

9. Dinges and Landau, *Assassination*, 329.

10. "Pursuing the Letelier Killers," *NYT*, March 11, 1978, 22.

11. Jeremiah O'Leary, "Chilean Slaying Suspect American, Marine Says," *Washington Star*, March 8, 1978.

12. "Chile Paid Cuban Exiles $1 Million to Murder Letelier, Magazine Says," *Washington Star*, March 9, 1978.

13. Augusto Pinochet, quoted in U.S. embassy in Santiago to secretary of state, March 10, 1978, Letelier (FOIA) document produced by the Department of State, February 6, 1980, vol. 1, box 8, LC, NSA.

14. Kornbluh, *Pinochet File*, 397; Landau to secretary of state, March 11, 1978, DNSA.

15. Callejas, *Siembra vientos*, 9, 11.

16. Manuel Contreras, quoted in Dinges and Landau, *Assassination*, 324.

17. Townley statement, folder Letelier/Civil - Materials from Saul Landau - March 16, 1979, box 14, LC, NSA.

18. Michael Townley, quoted in Dinges and Landau, *Assassination*, 324.

19. Townley statement.

20. Dinges and Landau, *Assassination*, 324.

21. Townley statement.

22. Dinges and Landau, *Assassination*, 332.

23. Quoted in Callejas, *Siembra vientos*, 20–21.

24. Dinges and Landau, *Assassination*, 325.

25. "'Mi marido no ha salido de Chile, está en el sur,'" *La Tercera*, March 9, 1978, 2.

26. Mariana Callejas, quoted in "Michael no se ha fugado y declarará ante la Justicia," *La Tercera*, March 25, 1978, 9.

27. Nicholas M. Horrock, "F.B.I. Said to Link Townley and Cubans in Chilean's Killing," *NYT*, April 20, 1978.

28. Branch and Propper, *Labyrinth*, 434.

29. George Landau, quoted in Dinges and Landau, *Assassination*, 333.

30. Todman to Christopher, April 6, 1978, DNSA.

31. Branch and Propper, *Labyrinth*, 460. See also unauthored CIA report, March 23, 1978, DNSA.

32. CIA, "Latin America Weekly Review," March 23, 1978, DNSA.

33. Quoted in Kornbluh, *Pinochet File*, 172.

34. Unauthored CIA report, March 23, 1978, DNSA.

35. Mena to Pinochet, March 23, 1978, DOS 2015.

36. Dinges and Landau, *Assassination*, 334.
37. George Landau, quoted in Branch and Propper, *Labyrinth*, 462, 467; John Dinges, "U.S. Chileans Agree on Access in Letelier Case," *Washington Post*, March 24, 1978; Dinges and Landau, *Assassination*, 335–36.
38. "Maratónica declaración de Townley ante fiscal militar," *La Tercera*, March 30, 1978, 5.
39. Author redacted to FBI, March 31, 1978, Letelier (FOIA) documents produced by the FBI, vol. 47, box 4, LC, NSA.
40. Todman to Christopher; U.S. embassy in Santiago to director of FBI, April 4, 1978, Letelier (FOIA) documents produced by the FBI, vol. 48, box 4, LC, NSA.
41. Landau interview, ADST.
42. Juan de Onís, "Two in Chile Said to Deny Slaying Link," *NYT*, April 5, 1978, A10.
43. Augusto Pinochet, quoted in Juan de Onís, "Chile Pledges Cooperation with U.S. Inquiry into Letelier's Slaying," *NYT*, April 6, 1978, A11.
44. Augusto Pinochet, quoted in Cavallo, Salazar, and Sepúlveda, *La historia oculta*, 172.
45. Dinges and Landau, *Assassination*, 337.
46. Quoted in Callejas, *Siembra vientos*, 117; Cavallo, Salazar, and Sepúlveda, *La historia oculta*, 173.
47. Quoted in Dinges and Landau, *Assassination*, 340, 341.
48. Mignosa to Moore, Washington, D.C., April 10, 1978, Letelier (FOIA) documents produced by the FBI, vol. 49, box 4, LC, NSA.
49. "New Evidence Links Cubans to Letelier," *NYT*, April 16, 1978, 9; FBI Newark field office to director, April 19, 1978, Letelier (FOIA) documents produced by the FBI, vol. 51, box 4, and FBI report, April 25, 1978, Letelier (FOIA) documents produced by the FBI, vol. 57, box 5, both in LC, NSA.
50. Author redacted, FBI arrest report, April 26, 1978, Letelier (FOIA) documents produced by the FBI, vol. 57, box 5, LC, NSA; Branch and Propper, *Labyrinth*, 519–20, 525–31.
51. "Two Connected to Letelier Arrested by Miami F.B.I.," *NYT*, April 16, 1978, 8.
52. Carter Cornick, quoted in Branch and Propper, *Labyrinth*, 533, 532.
53. FBI Washington, D.C., field office to director, April 15, 1978, Letelier (FOIA) documents produced by the FBI, vol. 51, box 4, LC, NSA.
54. Quoted in Callejas, *Siembra vientos*, 133.
55. Carter Cornick, quoted in Dorfman, "Codename: CHILBOM."
56. Nicholas M. Horrock, "American Charged in Letelier Slaying," *NYT*, April 27, 1978, NJ23.
57. Carter Cornick, quoted in "'La DINA financió a Suárez,'" *La Nación* (Santiago), April 22, 1990, 15–16.
58. "Carta de Townley al 'Estimado Don Manuel,'" *El Mercurio*, June 4, 1995, D4; Townley to Pinochet, July 1978, DNSA.
59. Public statement by Michael Townley, reproduced in Vance to U.S. embassy in Santiago, April 27, 1978, Documents produced by the State Department, additional releases, box 10, LC, NSA; see also FBI Washington, D.C., field office to director, April 14, 1978, Letelier (FOIA) documents produced by the FBI, vol. 50, box 4, LC, NSA.
60. Mignosa to Moore, May 4, 1978, Letelier (FOIA) documents produced by the FBI, vol. 59, box 5, and FBI New York field office to director, May 1, 1978, Letelier (FOIA) documents produced by the FBI, vol. 53, box 4, both in LC, NSA.

61. Quoted in Timothy S. Robinson, "Three More Linked to Letelier Plot," *Washington Post*, May 6, 1978, A1; Newark office to FBI director, May 5, 1978, Letelier (FOIA) documents produced by the FBI, vol. 54, box 5, LC, NSA.

62. "F.B.I. Offers Reward for Two Cubans Wanted in Murder of Letelier," *NYT*, July 5, 1976, A4.

63. FBI director to deputy attorney general, December 7, 1978, Letelier (FOIA) documents produced by the FBI, box 19, LC, NSA.

64. FBI report, April 21, 1978, Letelier (FOIA) documents produced by the FBI, vol. 57, box 5, LC, NSA.

65. FBI Washington, D.C., field office to director, April 16, 1978, Letelier (FOIA) documents produced by the FBI, vol. 51, box 4, LC, NSA.

66. FBI director to Washington, D.C., field office, indictment, August 1, 1978, Letelier (FOIA) documents produced by the FBI, vol. 68, box 5, LC, NSA.

67. Méndez, *Los cuervos*, 46.

68. Michael Moffitt, quoted in Nicholas Horrock, "Seven Indicted in U.S. Murder of Chilean Aide," *NYT*, August 2, 1978, A1, A4.

69. William F. Buckley Jr., "How Chile's Pinochet Might Atone for the Murders," *Washington Star*, August 6, 1978, D4.

70. Lawrence Meyer, "Some Letelier Witnesses Given Federal Protection," *Washington Post*, October 18, 1978, A12.

71. Fabiola Letelier, quoted in Héctor Olave Vallejos, "Cubanos anticastristas dicen que fueron traicionados por la CIA, EE.UU., y Chile," *La Tercera*, January 10, 1979, 115.

72. David Burnham, "Three Cuban Exiles Go on Trial in the Murder of a Former Chilean Envoy: Chileans Are Indicted," *NYT*, January 10, 1979, A6.

73. Héctor Olave Vallejos, "Perros rastrean bombas en la sala del caso Letelier," *La Tercera*, January 9, 1979, 2; "Defensa pidió cambio de Tribunal acusó a FBI en el 'caso Letelier,'" *La Tercera*, January 10, 1979, 14; Kenneth Bredemeier, "Tight Security Set for Trial of Three in Murder of Chilean Here," *Washington Post*, January 7, 1979, A18.

74. David Burnham, "Old Conflicts Are Bared at the Letelier Slaying Trial: A Clash of Ideologies," *NYT*, January 29, 1979, A10.

75. Quoted in Olave, "Cubanos anticastristas," 14–15.

76. Quoted in Jeff Stein, "An Army in Exile," *New York*, September 10, 1979, 46.

77. Héctor Olave Vallejos, "Ignacio Novo Sampol: Le vamos a ganar. Todo es falso. Todo es mentiro," *La Tercera*, January 10, 1979, 15; Dinges and Landau, *Assassination*, 347.

78. Freed and Landis, *Death in Washington*, 24.

79. Burnham, "Three Cuban Exiles," A6.

80. Héctor Olave Vallejos, "Con lupa seleccionan a los miembros del 'Gran Jurado,'" *La Tercera*, January 13, 1979, 4–5; Héctor Olave Vallejos, "Desde Watergate nunca demoró tanto selección de un Jurado,'" *La Tercera*, January 14, 1979, 7; Abraham Santibáñez, "Primera semana del juicio," *Hoy*, January 17–23, 1979, 12–13.

81. David Burnham, "American Testifies Chilean Officer Instructed Him to Murder Letelier," *NYT*, A3; Kenneth Bredemeier, "Agent Details Letelier's Death," *Washington Post*, January 19, 1979, A1; Héctor Olave Vallejos, "Película de terror repitió Michael Townley en la Corte," *La Tercera*, January 19, 1979, 2; Saul Landau, "The Letelier-Moffitt Trial," January 24, 1979, folder Letelier Trial, box 21, LC, NSA.

82. Dinges and Landau, *Assassination*, 368–69, 350, 351.

83. Branch and Propper, *Labyrinth*, 588.

84. Héctor Olave Vallejos, "Revelan presunto acuerdo en la entrega de Townley a EE.UU.," *La Tercera*, January 25, 1979, 5.

85. Bredemeier, "Agent Details," A1.

86. Michael Townley, quoted in David Burnham, "American Testifies He Has No Regrets about Assassinating Letelier," *NYT*, January 23, 1979, A10.

87. Michael Townley, quoted in Kenneth Bredemeier, "Townley Says He Acted as 'Soldier,' Has No Regrets About Killing Letelier," *Washington Post*, January 23, 1979, A5.

88. Michael Townley, quoted in Kenneth Bredemeier, "Townley Sentenced to Terms of Deal," *Washington Post*, May 12, 1979, A10.

89. Kenneth Bredemeier, "Letelier Trial Told Exile Boasted He Made Bomb," *Washington Post*, January 31, 1979, A4.

90. Transcript of proceedings, criminal case no. 78-367, February 1–2, 1979, Washington, D.C., box 24, LC, NSA, 3813.

91. Héctor Olave Vallejos, "Fiscal Propper alteró sus planes: No llamará a declarar a Mariana Callejas," *La Tercera*, January 30, 1979, 2.

92. Alvin Ross, quoted in transcript of proceedings, criminal case no. 78-367, February 5–6, 1979, Washington, D.C., box 24, LC, NSA, 4375.

93. FBI Washington, D.C., field office to director, February 6, 1979, Letelier (FOIA) documents produced by the FBI, vol. 85, box 6, LC, NSA.

94. FBI director to Scherrer, Washington, D.C., January 23, 1979, Letelier (FOIA) documents produced by the FBI, vol. 83, box 6, LC, NSA.

95. Reproduced in FBI Washington, D.C., field office to director, August 15, 1978, Letelier (FOIA) documents produced by the FBI, vol. 70, box 6, LC, NSA.

96. Quoted in Branch and Propper, *Labyrinth*, 582.

97. Saul Landau, "The Letelier-Moffitt Trial," January 24, 1979, folder Letelier Trial, box 21, LC, NSA.

98. FBI Washington, D.C., field office to director, February 9, 1979, folder Letelier (FOIA) documents produced by the FBI, box 19, LC, NSA; David Burnham, "Chile Tape Barred in Letelier Case," *NYT*, February 10, 1979, 5.

99. Quoted in Kenneth Bredemeier, "Cuban Exiles Guilty in Letelier Death," *Washington Post*, February 15, 1979, A1.

100. Transcript of proceedings, criminal case no. 78-367, February 14, 1979, Washington, D.C., box 25, LC, NSA.

101. Quoted in Freed and Landis, *Death in Washington*, 26.

102. Quoted in FBI director to Scherrer, February 15, 1979, Letelier (FOIA) documents produced by the FBI, vol. 85, box 6, LC, NSA. See also David Burnham, "Two Cubans Guilty in Bomb Killing of Chilean Exile," *NYT*, February 15, 1979, A1.

103. Guillermo Novo statement before Judge Parker, Washington, D.C., March 23, 1979, latinamericanstudies.org; transcript of proceedings, criminal case no. 78-367, March 23, 1979, Washington, D.C., box 24, LC, NSA, 17, 18–19, 21.

104. Transcript of proceedings, criminal case no. 78-367, March 23, 1979, Washington, D.C., box 24, LC, NSA, 52, 66, 69, 75; "Two Sentenced to Life for Murder of Letelier," *NYT*, March 24, 1979, A4.

105. Peter Kihss, "Two Castro Foes Are Sought in Bombing," *NYT*, March 27, 1979, B7.

106. Walter Waggoner, "Anti-Castro Cubans in Jersey Say Officials Ignore Terrorists' Threats," *NYT*, March 28, 1979, folder 1, box 43, IPS, WHS; "Omega 7 Uses Bombs for a Cause," *NYT*, April 2, 1979, B4.

107. Quoted in David Vidal, "Bombings Revealed Split Among Cuban in Jersey," *NYT*, April 2, 1979, B1.

108. Les Ledbetter, "Explosion Damages Cuban Mission to U.N.; Three Persons Hurt Slightly," *NYT*, October 28, 1979, 1.

109. Robert D. McFadden, "Cuban Refugee Leader Slain in Union City," *NYT*, November 26, 1979, B2.

110. David Vidal, "In Union City, the Memories of the Bay of Pigs Don't Die," *NYT*, December 2, 1979, E9.

111. David A. Andelman, "Police Got Warning of Bomb at Mission," *NYT*, December 9, 1979, 31; Robert McG. Thomas Jr., "Bomb Damages Russian Mission on East 67th St.," *NYT*, December 12, 1979, A1; Jeff Stein, "Inside Omega 7," *Village Voice*, March 10, 1980, 13.

112. Quoted in Robin Herman, "'Highest Priority' Given by U.S. to Capture of Anti-Castro Group," *NYT*, March 3, 1980, A1.

113. Elizabeth Schneider for the New Jersey Civil Liberties Union and New Jersey Council of Churches, "The Basis of and Need for Coordinated Federal and State Investigation and Prosecution of Cuban Exile Terrorists: A Factual and Legal Memorandum," [1980?], no box noted, LC, NSA.

CHAPTER 12

1. John Dinges and Kenneth Bredemeier, "The Assassin," *Washington Post*, January 22, 1979, A1.

2. Michael Townley affidavit, July 27, 1981, DNSA.

3. Jeremiah O'Leary, "Townley's Wife Knew of Plot to Kill Letelier," *Washington Star*, June 11, 1978, A1; Townley to Etchepare, Washington, D.C., June 24 and November 20, 1978, both in DNSA; Patrick E. Tyler, "Letters Say Chile Aided Letelier Murder Figure," *Washington Post*, February 23, 1981, A1; Townley to Mena, October 2, 1979, DNSA.

4. Callejas, *Siembra vientos*, 129; Townley to Pantoja, Washington, D.C., July [24?], 1978, DNSA.

5. Rosalind Andrews [probation officer], postsentence report on Michael Townley, May 29, 1979, DNSA.

6. Callejas, *Siembra vientos*, 137, 146.

7. Townley to Etchepare, May 29, 1979, DNSA.

8. Callejas, *Siembra vientos*, 146–47, 149.

9. Townley to Etchepare, June 11, 1979, Letelier Investigation, box 16, LC, NSA.

10. Callejas, *Siembra vientos*, 142.

11. Mariana Callejas, quoted in Mauricio Carvallo, "Mariana Callejas y su 'larga noche,'" *Hoy*, April 8–14, 1981, 11.

12. Mariana Callejas, quoted in Jeremiah O'Leary, "Assassin's Wife to Go to Chile," *Washington Star*, February 22, 1979; and in Cecilia Domeyko, "La última version de Mariana Callejas," *Hoy*, March 7–13, 1979, 9.

13. Meeting notes, June 8, 1982, folder Letelier-Moffitt Investigation Chilean Press (photocopies), box 21, LC, NSA.

14. IPS press release, Washington, D.C., July 28, 1983, folder unmarked, box 21, LC, NSA.

15. Callejas, *Siembra vientos*, 150, 158.

16. David Binder, "Exile Is Often Worse than Going Home," *NYT*, July 30, 1978, E2.

17. Isabel Letelier, letter to Sam [Buffone?], December 5, 1978, folder 16, box 45, IPS, WHS.
18. Quoted in "Llegó Viuda de Letelier," *El Mercurio*, November 25, 1978, C1.
19. Quoted in *La Tercera de la Hora*, November 25, 1978, 32.
20. "Isabel Morel Viuda de Letelier: 'Esta semana quedará presentado recurso ante los tribunales,'" *El Mercurio*, November 28, 1978; M. Angélica Bulnes, "Isabel de Letelier: 'Orlando Encabezaba la Resistencia Chilena," *Qué Pasa*, November 30–December 6, 1978, 16–17.
21. Letelier to [Buffone?].
22. Quoted in Landau to secretary of state, Santiago, November 29, 1978, unmarked volume, box 8, LC, NSA.
23. FBI Washington, D.C., field office to director, November 30, 1978, Letelier (FOIA) documents produced by the FBI, vol. 78, box 6, LC, NSA.
24. Landau to secretary of state.
25. FBI Washington, D.C., field office to director.
26. "Caso Orlando Letelier: En la Corte Suprema recurso de reclamación," *El Mercurio*, December 1, 1978.
27. Isabel Letelier to Sam [Buffone?].
28. FBI Washington, D.C., field office to director.
29. Michael Moffitt affidavit, July 16, 1991, DOS 2015; Andrews postsentence report.
30. Moffitt affidavit.
31. Borosage to all IPS employees, February 15, 1979, Washington, D.C., folder 11, box 24, IPS, WHS.
32. Isabel Letelier affidavit, August 2, 1991, DOS 2015.
33. James Gordon, psychiatric evaluation of Isabel Morel Letelier, August 2, 1991, DOS 2015.
34. Isabel Letelier, "The Revival of 'Old Lies' about Orlando Letelier" [letter to editor], *NYT*, November 8, 1980, 22.
35. Quoted in "Letelier Monument," *Human Events*, October 3, 1981, folder 11, box 24, IPS, WHS. See also Kornbluh to Bob, Saul, John, Michael, Isabel, October 21, 1980, Washington, D.C., folder 11, box 24, IPS, WHS.
36. Isabel Letelier to Anita, October 30, 1980, folder 21, box 45, IPS, WHS.
37. Tigar to Turner, undated, folder 4, box 53, IPS, WHS.
38. Stephen Labaton, "For Defense Lawyer in Bomb Case, Latest in a Line of Unpopular Clients," *NYT*, June 9, 1995, B9.
39. Patrick Symmes, "The Man Who Would Not Disappear," *Washington City Paper*, September 22, 1995, www.washingtoncitypaper.com/news/article/13006608/the-man-who-would-not-disappear.
40. Quoted in Jeremiah O'Leary, "Two Families Sue Chile for Damages in Letelier Case," *Washington Star*, August 8, 1978.
41. Isabel Letelier, quoted in "Margarita Isabel de Letelier," *El Socialista* (Madrid), November 12, 1978.
42. Sam Buffone, quoted in Symmes, "Man."
43. Megan McDonough, "Samuel J. Buffone, D.C. Lawyer in Major Cases, Dies at 68," *Washington Post*, April 11, 2015, www.washingtonpost.com/local/obituaries/samuel-j-buffone-dc-lawyer-in-major-cases-dies-at-68/2015/04/11/985911a0-de33-11e4-a1b8-2ed88bc190d2_story.html?utm_term=.198f5e9a3aac.

44. "Letelier, Moffitt Survivors File Suit Here against Chile," *Washington Post*, August 9, 1978, A19.

45. Hansell to [Christopher?], August 16, 1978, unmarked volume, box 11, LC, NSA.

46. Landau to secretary of state, Santiago, October 16, 1978, unmarked volume, box 8, LC, NSA.

47. Bernabei to Callahan, Washington, D.C., October 9, 1979, unmarked folder, box 21, LC, NSA.

48. Sam Buffone, quoted in Symmes, "Man."

49. Joyce Green, quoted in Isabel Letelier to Wexler, June 9, 1980, folder 21, box 45, IPS, WHS.

50. Joyce Green, quoted in Laura A. Kiernan, "Judge Says Chile Can Be Sued for Bombing Death Damages," *Washington Post*, March 12, 1980, B5.

51. Michael Moffitt, quoted in Letelier/Moffitt staff to All Institute People, Washington, D.C., March 12, 1980, folder 4, box 53, IPS, WHS.

52. Isabel Letelier to Wexler, June 9, 1980, folder 21, box 45, IPS, WHS.

53. "Se inició demanda por caso Letelier," *El Mercurio*, June 21, 1980, A16.

54. Isabel Letelier, interview by the author.

55. L/M Fund to Key Contacts, Washington, D.C., November 5, 1980, folder 4, box 53, IPS, WHS.

56. "Survivors in Letelier Case Are Awarded $5 Million," *NYT*, November 5, 1980, A14.

57. L/M Fund to key contacts, Washington, D.C., November 5, 1980, folder 4, box 53, IPS, WHS.

58. Michael Moffitt, quoted in Laura A. Kiernan, "Bomb Blast Victim's Kin Awarded $4 Million," *Washington Post*, November 6, 1980, A4.

59. L/M Fund to key contacts.

60. Michael Tigar, quoted in Kiernan, "Bomb Blast," A4.

61. Townley testimony, April [25?], 1978, DNSA.

62. Landau to secretary of state, Santiago, July 27, 1978, DNSA.

63. U.S. Congress, House Committee on Government Operations, "Alleged Violations of U.S. Aviation Laws and Regulations by LAN Chile Airlines," 96th Cong., 2nd sess., report no. 96-1157 (July 8, 1980): 1–13; Jack Anderson, "Chilean Airline Tied to Smuggling," *Washington Post*, September 27, 1979, D37; and Burton to Pearce, Washington, D.C., November 30, 1979, Rauh and Barcella to Robinson, Washington, D.C., November 30, 1979, FBI report, "Lineas Aereas Nacional Chilena," January 25, 1980, and Lally to Achenbach, May 30, 1980, all in DNSA.

64. Burton to Bond, Washington, D.C., November 14, 1979, DNSA.

65. "LAN desmiente," *Ultimas Noticias* (Santiago), June 20, 1980, 16; "LAN no ha transportado materiales explosivos," *El Mercurio*, June 20, 1980.

66. "¿Nuevas represalias?" *Hoy*, May 28–June 3, 1980, 9–12.

67. Patricia Verdugo, "En pistas chilenas," *Hoy*, May 28–June 3, 1980, 12–13.

68. U.S. Congress, "Alleged Violations," 8.

69. Lally to CIA deputy director for operations, July 21, 1980, DNSA; Achenbach to Lally, September 9, 1980, DNSA; Cohen to Lally, September 22, 1980, DNSA.

70. Lally to Burton, March [10?], 1981, in U.S. Congress, "Alleged Violations," 8; Wallig and Williams to director, Bureau of Compliance and Consumer Protection, May 21, 1981, DNSA.

71. Blank, March 20, 1981, DNSA.

72. Atwood to Burton, January [21?], 1981, DNSA.
73. Martin Walker, "The Fight for Bread and Roses," *Guardian*, March 3, 1981.
74. Scott Armstrong, "Chilean Plane Leaves, Defying Letelier Judgment," *Washington Post*, March 19, 1983, A1.
75. Tamar Lewin, "U.S. Judge Threatens Chilean Airline," *NYT*, December 20, 1983, D4.
76. "Chile Airline Compliance Set," *NYT*, December 24, 1983, 40.
77. Isabel Letelier, quoted in Domeyko, "Buscando en LAN," *Hoy*, January 17, 1984, n.p.
78. Privitera to Borosage, April 10, 1984, Washington, D.C., folder 10, box 24, IPS, WHS.
79. U.S. Court of Appeals for the Second Circuit, November 20, 1984, folder 9, box 53, IPS, WHS.
80. Privitera to Moffitt and Letelier, February 4, 1985, Washington, D.C., folder 10, box 24, IPS, WHS.
81. Privitera memo, Washington, D.C., June 20, 1985, folder 10, box 24, IPS, WHS.
82. Francisco Letelier interview.
83. Rep. Howard Berman, quoted in U.S. Congress, 100th Cong., 2nd sess., *Congressional Record* 134, no. 117 (August 8, 1988): H6484; Buffone and Privitera, "Chronology of Events: Letelier-Moffitt Assassination, 1976–August 1990," August 1990, DNSA.
84. "U.S. Court Upsets Conviction of Three in Letelier Slaying," *NYT*, September 16, 1980, A9.
85. "Justice and the Letelier Bombers" [editorial], *NYT*, September 30, 1980, A26.
86. Larry Barcella, quoted in Laura A. Kiernan, "Letelier Convictions Overturned by Court," *Washington Post*, September 16, 1980, A1.
87. Laura Kiernan, "Two Letelier Case Figures Ordered Free on Bond," *Washington Post*, April 9, 1981, A2.
88. Transcript of proceedings, criminal case no. 78-367, May 13, 1981, Washington, D.C., box 26, LC, NSA.
89. Laura A. Kiernan, "Townley Repeats Story of Letelier Slaying in Retrial," *Washington Post*, May 15, 1981, A17.
90. Lawrence Dubin, quoted in Laura A. Kiernan, "New Tactics Led to Acquittal in Letelier Case," *Washington Post*, June 1, 1981, B1.
91. Laura A. Kiernan, "Townley Admits Lying to Chilean Questioners," *Washington Post*, May 17, 1981, A10.
92. Paul Goldberger, quoted in Buffone and Privitera, "Chronology."
93. Paul Goldberger, quoted in Laura A. Kiernan, "Two Acquitted in Letelier Murder Case," *Washington Post*, May 31, 1981, A1.
94. Kiernan, "New Tactics," B1.
95. Saul Landau, "Guillermo Novo and Me," *Counterpunch*, September 19, 2003, www.counterpunch.org/2003/09/19/guillermo-novo-and-me/.
96. "U.S. Judge Jails Cuban Exile for Perjury in Letelier Case," *NYT*, June 27, 1981, 5.
97. "Affidavit of Alvin Ross Diaz," October 1981, and "Affidavit of Guillerno Novo Sampol," October 8, 1981, both in Letelier investigation, box 16, LC, NSA.
98. "Supplemental Affidavit of Alvin Ross Diaz," November 5, 1981, Letelier Investigation, box 16, LC, NSA.
99. "Released by Mixup, Convict Back in Jail," *Ottawa Citizen*, October 22, 1981, 52.
100. Isabel Letelier, quoted in Kiernan, "Two Acquitted," A1.
101. Letelier to Baez, June 1, 1981, folder 23, box 45, IPS, WHS.

CHAPTER 13

1. Quoted in "La Hora de Contreras," *Qué Pasa*, February 27, 1993, 10; "Aficionado a novelas," *La Tercera* (Santiago), June 1, 1995, 11.
2. Landau memo of conversation with Cubillos, to Vance, April 26, 1979, folder George W. Landau The Letelier Case (Chile) (1 of 2) 1976–2006, box 3, LP, Hoover.
3. Quoted in Juan de Onís, "U.S. Agents Expect Indictment of Three Chilean Officers in Letelier Case," *NYT*, May 23, 1978, A3.
4. Salazar, *Contreras*, 8.
5. Gillespie interview, ADST.
6. Landau to secretary of state, February 23, 1978, DOS 2015.
7. Quoted in Charles A. Krause, "Chile Arrests Three Named in Letelier Indictment," *Washington Post*, August 2, 1978, A10.
8. Landau to secretary of state, Santiago, April 18, 1978, unmarked volume, box 8, LC, NSA.
9. De Onís, "U.S. Agents," A3.
10. Quoted in transcript of interview with Fernández, attached to Shultz to American consul in Rio, Washington, D.C., January 22, 1987, DOS 2015.
11. Armando Fernández, quoted in George Lardner Jr., "Pinochet Linked to Murder Cover-Up," *Washington Post*, February 5, 1987, A12.
12. Quoted in transcript of interview with Fernández, attached to Shultz to American consul in Rio.
13. Quoted in Kornbluh, *Pinochet File*, 400.
14. Barnes to U.S. embassy in Buenos Aires, Santiago, January 15, 1987, DOS 2015.
15. DiGenova press release, February 4, 1987, DNSA. See also transcript of court proceedings, criminal case no. 78-0367, Washington, D.C., February 4, 1987, DNSA.
16. Quoted in transcript of interview with Fernández, attached to Shultz to American consul in Rio.
17. Quoted in Cavallo, Salazar, and Sepúlveda, *La historia oculta*, 133.
18. Vaky to [Christopher?], Washington, D.C., August 14, 1978, DOS 2016.
19. CIA, "Pinochet's Role in the Letelier Assassination and Subsequent Coverup," May 1, 1987, DOS 2016.
20. Unauthored CIA report, May 24, 1978, DNSA; Shirley Christian, no title, *NYT*, August 14, 1978, 21; Landau to secretary of state, Santiago, November 13, 1978, unmarked volume, box 8, LC, NSA; Department of Defense report, January [10?], 1989, DNSA.
21. CIA, "Pinochet's Role."
22. Cavallo, Salazar, and Sepúlveda, *La historia oculta*, 251.
23. Larry Barcella, quoted in Carla Hall, "Life after Letelier," *Washington Post*, September 21, 1981, B1.
24. Timothy S. Robinson, "The Letelier Prosecutor: An Unlikely Celebrity in Santiago," *Washington Post*, August 3, 1978, A14; "La visita de Propper y el FBI" [editorial], *La Tercera*, May 25, 1978, 3.
25. Juan de Onís, "Chilean Right Voices Bitterness at U.S.," *NYT*, May 30, 1978, A10.
26. Branch and Propper, *Labyrinth*, 576.
27. Luis Cordero B., "Contra el imperialismo norteamericano," *La Tercera*, May 26, 1978, 3.
28. Pablo Rodriguez Grez, "Ofensiva contra Chile," *La Tercera*, May 29, 1978, 3.

29. Hernán Millas, "Esquina peligrosa," *Hoy*, May 31–June 6, 1978, 10–11. See also Charles A. Krause and Timothy Robinson, "Chile Told Three Key Agents Face Charges in Letelier Slaying," *Washington Post*, June 9, 1978, A1.

30. Pastor to Brzezinski, June 28, 1978, DNSA.

31. Bushnell to [Christopher?], June 21, 1978, DOS 2015.

32. George Landau, quoted in Kornbluh, *Pinochet File*, 398.

33. Quoted in Branch and Propper, *Labyrinth*, 576–77.

34. Landau interview, ADST.

35. Quoted in John M. Goshko and Timothy S. Robinson, "Envoy to Chile Recalled over Letelier Probe," *Washington Post*, June 24, 1978, A1.

36. Bushnell to Christopher, June 27, 1978, DNSA.

37. Goshko and Robinson, "Envoy to Chile," A1.

38. Vance to Carter, June 30, 1978, DNSA.

39. Juan de Onís, "Paraguayan Links Chilean General to Letelier Case," *NYT*, July 20, 1978, A3.

40. FBI director to Washington, D.C., field office, February 22, 1979, Documents produced by FBI, additional releases, box 10, LC, NSA.

41. DiGenova press release.

42. Grover to secretary of state, Santiago, August 24, 1978, DNSA.

43. Christopher to U.S. embassy in Chile, Washington, D.C., August 24, 1978, DNSA.

44. Sergio Miranda Carrington, quoted in "La esperanza de Contreras," *Qué Pasa*, September 11, 1993, 24.

45. Krause, "Chile Arrests Three," A10.

46. Sergio Miranda Carrington, quoted in "La esperanza," 24.

47. Quoted in Branch and Propper, *Labyrinth*.

48. Francis McNeil, quoted in Kornbluh, *Pinochet File*, 403.

49. Nena Terrell, "Pinochet Stalked by Domestic Foes, U.S. Investigators," *In These Times*, September 13–19, 1978, 9.

50. Salazar, *Contreras*, 138.

51. Cavallo, Salazar, and Sepúlveda, *La historia oculta*, 206, 252.

52. Cavallo, Salazar, and Sepúlveda, *La historia oculta*, 173.

53. Michael Moffitt, quoted in Shirley Christian, "Chile Orders Three Held for Letelier Killing," *Asheville Times*, August 2, 1978, 25.

54. Quoted in Saul Landau, "Letelier Probe Threatens Pinochet Rule," *In These Times*, April 19–25, 1978, reproduced in www.tni.org/es/node/11719.

55. Isabel Letelier speech, September 1978, folder 36, box 52, IPS, WHS.

56. Landau to secretary of state, August 2, 1978, unmarked volume, box 8, LC, NSA.

57. Stern, *Battling for Hearts and Minds*, 146.

58. Quoted in Landau to secretary of state, Santiago, August 3, 1978, unmarked volume, box 8, LC, NSA.

59. CIA report, August 17, 1978, DNSA.

60. CIA, "Pinochet's Role."

61. John Dinges, "Chile's Murder, Inc.," *Inquiry*, January 8–22, 1979, 20.

62. "Judge Closes Hearings on Chilean Extradition," *Washington Post*, September 24, 1978, A30.

63. Charles A. Krause, "U.S. Shows Unease over Chile's Handling of Letelier Case," *Washington Post*, September 28, 1978, A21.

64. John Dinges, "Chief Defendant in Letelier Slaying Obtains U.S. Evidence Given Chile," *Sacramento Bee*, October 12, 1978.
65. Landau to secretary of state, Santiago, October 11, 1978, DOS 2015.
66. DiGenova press release.
67. Landau to secretary of state, Santiago, October 18, 1978, unmarked volume, box 8, LC, NSA.
68. Testimony of Espinoza to Bórquez, October 19, 1978, and testimony of Contreras to Bórquez, October 24, 1978, both forwarded by Department of State, box 10, LC, NSA.
69. Landau to secretary of state, Santiago, October 24, 1978, unmarked volume, box 8, LC, NSA.
70. Quoted in Landau to secretary of state, Santiago, October 25, 1978, unmarked volume, box 8, LC, NSA.
71. Branch and Propper, *Labyrinth*, 586.
72. FBI director to Washington, D.C., field office, February 22, 1979, Documents produced by FBI, additional releases, box 10, LC, NSA.
73. Landau to secretary of state, Santiago, January 8, 1979, unmarked volume, box 8, LC, NSA; Juan de Onís, "U.S. Gives Chile New Evidence in Seeking Extradition of Three in Slaying," *NYT*, January 9, 1979, A4.
74. Eugene Propper, quoted in Kenneth Bredemeier, "Cuban Exiles Guilty in Letelier Death," *Washington Post*, February 15, 1979, A1.
75. Charles A. Krause, "Letelier Verdict, Amply Covered in Chile, Has Little Impact," *Washington Post*, February 16, 1979, A36.
76. Landau to secretary of state, Santiago, April 30, 1979, DOS 2015.
77. Charles A. Krause, "Chilean Minister Says Extradition Unlikely for Three Secret Agents," *Washington Post*, February 9, 1979, A12.
78. Grover to secretary of state, Santiago, April 3, 1979, DOS 2015.
79. Timothy S. Robinson, "Extradition Deal for Chilean Bomb-Murder Suspect Said Rejected by the U.S.," *Washington Post*, October 23, 1979, A12.
80. Quoted in "No conceder extradición no significa sea inocente," *La Tercera*, May 8, 1987, 6.
81. Landau to secretary of state, Santiago, May 14, 1979, DOS 2015.
82. Manuel Contreras, quoted in "La justicia chilena es professional y da confianza," *La Tercera*, May 15, 1979, 4.
83. Alfredo Etcheberry, quoted in "Estoy desilusionado, pero no desalentado," *La Tercera*, May 15, 1979, 5; Charles A. Krause, "Chilean Judge Bars Extradition in Letelier Case," *Washington Post*, May 15, 1979.
84. "U.S. Recalling Envoy over Chile's Refusal to Extradite Three: A Diplomatic Warning Four Men Convicted," *NYT*, May 16, 1979, A8.
85. State Department untitled document, May 21, 1979, DOS 2015.
86. Juan de Onís, "Chile Bans an Opposition Magazine: Minister Ratifies Edict Extradition Decision Criticized," *NYT*, June 26, 1979, A12.
87. Israel Bórquez, quoted in "Chilean Aide Ridicules Letelier Jury," *Washington Star*, May 28, 1979, A4.
88. Isabel Letelier press release, Washington, D.C., May [29?], 1979, folder 18, box 48, IPS, WHS.
89. Propper to Isabel Letelier, Washington, D.C., July 27, 1979, unmarked folder, box 21, LC, NSA.

90. Landau to secretary of state, Santiago, July 13, 1979, unmarked volume, box 11, LC, NSA.

91. Alfredo Etcheberry, quoted in Juan de Onís, "U.S. Completes Appeal in Chile For the Extradition of Three in Killing," *NYT*, July 25, 1979, A3.

92. CIA, "Pinochet's Role."

93. Landau to secretary of state, Santiago, October 1, 1979, Documents produced by the State Department, additional releases, box 10, LC, NSA.

94. Alfredo Etcheberry, quoted in Charles A. Krause, "Chile's High Court Rejects U.S. Plea in Letelier Case," *Washington Post*, October 2, 1979, A1.

95. Larry Barcella, quoted in María Cristina Jurado, "'El pueblo norteamericano se siente disilusionado,'" *Ultimas Noticias* (Santiago), October 2, 1979.

96. Augusto Pinochet, quoted in Juan de Onís, "Top Chilean Court Won't Yield 3 Army Officers Wanted by U.S.," *NYT*, October 2, 1979, A4.

97. Cubillos to Digen-Diplan, United Nations, October 3, 1979, folder memos, correspondence, clippings, 1978–1979, box 19, Cubillos, Hoover.

98. Cubillos to acting minister, United Nations, October 3, 1979, folder memos, correspondence, clippings, 1978–1979, box 19, Cubillos, Hoover.

99. William R. Long and Roberto Brauning, "Caso Letelier amenaza a ex jefe policial chileno," *Miami Herald*, May 15, 1978; Cavallo, Salazar, and Sepúlveda, *La historia oculta*, 206.

CHAPTER 14

1. Grover interview, ADST.

2. Karen DeYoung and John Dinges, "Chile Takes Steps to Liberalize Rule," *Washington Post*, April 17, 1978, A1.

3. Quoted in Charles A. Krause, "Dramatic Political Change Caused by Pressures on Chile," *Washington Post*, June 11, 1978, A31.

4. Juan de Onís, "U.S. Letelier Inquiry Troublesome to Chilean Leader," *NYT*, March 26, 1978, 3; Dinges and Landau, *Assassination*, 331.

5. Unsigned CIA memo, April 17, 1978, DNSA.

6. Quoted in CIA report, "Chile: Implications of the Letelier Case," May 1978, DNSA; CIA report, August 17, 1978, DNSA.

7. Juan de Onís, "Pinochet's Tightening Grip," *NYT*, July 29, 1978, 5.

8. Jeremiah O'Leary, "Fall of Pinochet Seen as Key Chile Generals Desert Junta Regime," *Washington Star*, July 26, 1978, A1.

9. Situation room to Brzezinski, July 24, 1978, DNSA.

10. CIA, area brief, July 25, 1978, DNSA.

11. John B. Oakes, "Pinochet in No Rush," *NYT*, May 3, 1979, A23.

12. Augusto Pinochet, quoted in Juan de Onís, "Pinochet, Marking Six Years in Power, Rejects Calls for Civil Rule in Chile," *NYT*, September 12, 1979, A12.

13. Quoted in U.S. Congress, 95th Cong., 2nd sess., *Congressional Record* 124, part 18 (August 2, 1978): 23915.

14. John M. Goshko, "Halt in Arms for Chile Is Passed and Reversed," *Washington Post*, August 3, 1978, A1.

15. Ralph Cox, quoted in Juan de Onís, "Chile Attracts U.S. Business," *NYT*, October 4, 1979, A7.

16. Robert Steven, quoted in Morley and McGillion, *Reagan and Pinochet*, 11.

17. Kennedy and Church to Carter, Washington, D.C., May 14, 1979, DNSA.

18. Tom Harkin, "Extradite!," *NYT*, June 28, 1979, A19.

19. Examples include National Chile Center to Chile Committees and Key Contacts and Chile Legislative Center to Chile Committees and Key Contacts, both June 4, 1979, folder L/M case—Extradition-memos, statements, etc., box 21, LC, NSA.

20. Stuart Auerbach and Charles A. Krause, "U.S. Ambassador to Chile Recalled in Protest Move," *Washington Post*, May 16, 1979, A22.

21. Christopher to Carter, October 2, 1979, DNSA.

22. Quoted in "U.S. Assails Chile Court's Refusal to Extradite Three in Letelier Case: Accused of Planning Murder," *NYT*, October 3, 1979, A4.

23. Derian to Vance, October 12, 1979; see also Pastor to Brzezinski, October 11, 1979, both in DNSA.

24. State Department press release, November 30, 1979, DNSA. See also Brzezinski to Vance, Washington, D.C., November 27, 1979, and Vance to Carter, Washington, D.C., October 19, 1979, both in DNSA.

25. Tom Harkin press release, Washington, D.C., November 30, 1979, DNSA.

26. Edward Kennedy, quoted in Edward C. Burks, "Kennedy Assails Carter's Actions on Chile as Weak: 'An Act of Terrorism,'" *NYT*, December 1, 1979, 39.

27. "Chile soportará estas presiones porque está políticamente firme y militarmente seguro," *La Tercera*, December 1, 1979, 5.

28. Landau memo of conversation with Cubillos, to Vance, April 26, 1979, folder George W. Landau The Letelier Case (Chile) (1 of 2) 1976–2006, box 3, LP, Hoover.

29. Quoted in Charles A. Krause, "U.S. Bluff in Letelier Case Bolsters Pinochet in Chile," *Washington Post*, January 2, 1980, A1.

30. Landau to Vance, March 18, 1980, DNSA.

31. Landau interview, ADST.

32. Juan de Onís, "U.S. Envoy Resumes His Duties in Chile," *NYT*, December 6, 1979, A13; Secretary of state to U.S. embassies worldwide, April 15, 1980, DNSA.

33. George Landau, quoted in Morley and McGillion, *Reagan and Pinochet*, 12.

34. Reagan reprint of radio program, "Letelier II," folder Transcripts 1978 (2/2), box 2, Ronald Reagan Radio Commentary, Hoover; quoted in Anthony Lewis, "The Real Reagan," *NYT*, October 24, 1983, A19.

35. "Triunfo de Reagan es favorable para Chile," *La Tercera*, November 6, 1980, 4.

36. Kornbluh, *Pinochet File*, 409.

37. Jeane Kirkpatrick, quoted in "La 'tía Jeane' y Chile," *Hoy*, September 2–8, 1981, n. p.

38. Barbara Crossette, "Senate Approves '82 Foreign Assistance Bill, 40–33," *NYT*, October 23, 1981, A9.

39. John M. Goshko, "Administration Reviews Plan to Renew Chile Aid," *Washington Post*, March 5, 1982.

40. Ted Kennedy, quoted in Edward Schumacher, "Chile Votes on Charter That Tightens Pinochet's Grip," *NYT*, September 11, 1980, A2.

41. Edward Schumacher, "Chilean Leader, Winner of Vote, Attacks the U.S.," *NYT*, September 13, 1980, 2.

42. Pollack, *New Right*, 78.

43. Oppenheim, *Politics in Chile*, 120.

44. Dodson to Clift, Washington, D.C., October 23, 1980, DNSA.

45. Ronald Reagan, quoted in Peter R. Kornbluh, "So, Chile's Two Murders Are Now Forgiven?" *NYT*, March 3, 1981, A19.
46. Alexander Haig, quoted in Morley and McGillion, *Reagan and Pinochet*, 41.
47. Theberge to secretary of state, March 16, 1982, DOS 2015.
48. Mary McGrory, "The Ghost Who Haunts Our Chile Policy," *Washington Post*, March 28, 1982, C1.
49. Larry Barcella, quoted in Kornbluh, *Pinochet File*, 411.
50. Elliott Abrams, quoted in Morley and McGillion, *Reagan and Pinochet*, 96–97.
51. Steven, citing Abrams, quoted in Zach Dorfman, "Codename: CHILBOM," *Atavist Magazine* 59 (2016), magazine.atavist.com/codename-chilbom.
52. George Shultz, quoted in Morley and McGillion, *Reagan and Pinochet*, 96–97, 191.
53. George Shultz, quoted in Kornbluh, *Pinochet File*, 419.
54. Isabel Letelier, quoted in David Shipler, "Chilean Exiles Hurt and Angry," *NYT*, July 18, 1986, A8.
55. Phyllis Oakley, quoted in "U.S. Accuses Chile of Inaction," *NYT*, July 3, 1987, A4.
56. "The Right Message on Chile" [editorial], *NYT*, August 2, 1986, 22; Kennedy statement, March 10, 1986, DNSA.
57. Betsey Barnes, "About My Husband and the General, Part I," *American Diplomacy*, March 2015, www.unc.edu/depts/diplomat/item/2015/0106/fs/barnes_husband_p1.html.
58. Naftali, *Blind Spot*, 14–101, quotation on 97.
59. Abrams to U.S. embassy in Santiago, Washington, D.C., February 5, 1988, DNSA.
60. CIA Directorate of Intelligence, "Pinochet's Role in the Letelier Assassination and Subsequent Coverup," May 1, 1987, nsarchive.gwu.edu/NSAEBB/NSAEBB560-CIA-report-concludes-Pinochet-behind-Letelier-Moffit-bombing-in-1976-and-calls-it-act-of-state-terrorism/Document%201%20-%20CIA%20assessment.pdf.
61. Shultz to Reagan, Washington, D.C., October 6, 1987, nsarchive.gwu.edu/NSAEBB/NSAEBB532-The-Letelier-Moffitt-Assassination-Papers/letelierdocument.pdf.
62. Baker to U.S. embassy in Santiago, Washington, D.C., February 28, 1990, DNSA.

CHAPTER 15

1. Quoted in George Lardner Jr., "Bomb Suspect Returned to Clear Name," *Washington Post*, February 6, 1987, A1; and "Las revelaciones de Fernández Larios," *Hoy*, February 9–15, 1987, 13–14.
2. Quoted in transcript of interview with Fernández, attached to Shultz to American consul in Rio, Washington, D.C., January 22, 1987, DOS 2015.
3. "El ex capitán nació en Washington, Estados Unidos,'" *La Tercera*, February 6, 1987, 8.
4. "El ultimo bar de un hombre rudo," *La Época*, May 6, 1987, 9.
5. Francisco Letelier interview.
6. Fiona Dove interview.
7. Letelier, "I Think I Have Struggled," 52.
8. Francisco Letelier interview.
9. Letelier, "I Think I Have Struggled," 52, 51–55.
10. "The 'Evenhanded' Test in Chile," *NYT*, September 26, 1981, 22.
11. Isabel Letelier, quoted in Raymond Bonner, "Exile of Lawyer Tied to End of Letelier Case," *NYT*, September 24, 1981, A12.

12. Quoted in "Letelier Case Reversal," *Washington Post*, January 16, 1982, D1.
13. "Escarban la verdad en el caso Letelier," *Ultimas Noticias* (Santiago), January 16, 1982, 14.
14. U.S. Senate, 99th Cong., 1st sess., *Congressional Record* 131, part 17 (September 12, 1985): 23647.
15. Theberge to secretary of state, Santiago, June 12, 1983, DOS 2015.
16. Armando Fernández, quoted in John Dinges and Saul Landau, "Derailing Pinochet," *Nation*, March 7, 1987, 280.
17. Armando Fernández, quoted in "Las revelaciones," 14.
18. Armando Fernández, quoted in Lardner, "Bomb Suspect," A1.
19. Zach Dorfman, "Codename: CHILBOM," *Atavist Magazine* 59 (2016), magazine.atavist.com/codename-chilbom.
20. Jones interview, ADST.
21. Quoted in Durkee to Abrams, April 14, 1986; Abrams to Armacost, Washington, D.C., June 5, 1986, both in DOS 2015.
22. Jones interview, ADST.
23. Barnes telegram to secretary of state, Santiago, November 10, 1986, DOS 2015.
24. Dorfman, "Codename: CHILBOM."
25. State Department, "Results of Interview with Indicted Letelier Conspirator," ca. January 26, 1987, DNSA.
26. Barnes to U.S. embassy in Buenos Aires, Santiago, January 15, 1987, DOS 2015.
27. State Department, "Results of Interview."
28. Barnes to secretary of state, Santiago, January 17, 1987, DOS 2015.
29. Barnes telegram to secretary of state, Santiago, December 23, 1986, and Armacost to U.S. embassy in Santiago, January 10, 1987, both in DOS 2015; Jones interview, ADST.
30. Barnes to secretary of state, January 17, 1987.
31. Armando Fernández, quoted in Lardner, "Bomb Suspect," A1.
32. Armando Fernández, quoted in Dinges and Landau, "Derailing Pinochet," 280; Isabel Letelier interview.
33. Jones interview, ADST.
34. Barnes to secretary of state, January 17, 1987.
35. John Dinges and Saul Landau, "The Letelier Case Continues," [February?] 1987, folder 21, box 39, IPS, WHS.
36. Armando Fernández, quoted in Lardner, "Bomb Suspect," A1; "Fernández viajó en avión del FBI," *La Época*, February 6, 1987, 1; "El ex capitán," 8.
37. Armando Fernández, quoted in Philip Shenon, "Chilean, in Remorse, Admits Role in Letelier Slaying in '76," *NYT*, February 5, 1987, A1; Lardner, "Bomb Suspect," A1.
38. Armando Fernández, quoted in Lardner, "Bomb Suspect," A1.
39. "El ex capitán," 8.
40. Dinges and Landau, "Derailing Pinochet," 280.
41. Isabel Letelier, quoted in Valdés interview.
42. Isabel Letelier, interview by the author.
43. Armando Fernández, quoted in Nancy Lewis, "Chilean Given Up to 7 Years in Letelier Slaying," *Washington Post*, May 7, 1978, A19.
44. Armando Fernández, quoted in "Juez Parker: 'Fernandez no pudo demostrar evidencia creíble," *La Tercera*, May 7, 1987, 5.

45. "No respetaron ninguno de los acuerdos con Fernández Larios," *La Tercera*, May 9, 1987, 6; Patricia Escalona, "Abogado: 'Fernández Larios fue amenazado de muerte,'" *La Tercera*, May 10, 1987, 7; "Chilean Imprisoned in Killing of Letelier Is Set Free by Judge," *NYT*, September 11, 1987, A6; Douglas Grant Mine, "The Assassin Next Door," *Miami New Times*, November 18, 1999, www.miaminewtimes.com/news/the-assassin-next-door-6357449; Barnes memo to secretary of state, Santiago, March 12, 1987, DNSA.

46. Isabel Letelier, quoted in "Quedó libre el ex mayor Armando Fernández Larios," *La Tercera*, September 11, 1987, 16.

47. Isabel Letelier, quoted in George Lardner Jr., "Pinochet Linked to Murder Cover-Up," *Washington Post*, February 5, 1987, A12. See also Patricia Escalona, "Fernández Larios condenado a una pena mínima de 27 meses de cárcel," *La Tercera*, May 7, 1987, 4.

48. Isabel Letelier, quoted in "Habla viuda del ex canciller," *La Tercera*, February 6, 1987, 7.

49. Quoted in "Ministro García: 'Imagen de Chile es distorsionada,'" *La Tercera*, February 6, 1987, 7.

50. Augusto Pinochet, quoted in "Pinochet Calls Army Officer a Deserter after Testimony," *Globe and Mail*, February 11, 1987.

51. Errázuriz to acting minister of foreign relations, secret cable 196-206, Washington, D.C., February 13, 1987, Archivo General Histórico, Ministerio de Relaciones Exteriores, Santiago.

52. CIA Directorate of Intelligence, "Chile: Pinochet and the Military [Redacted]," April 1987, DNSA.

53. Gelbard to Barnes, March 13, 1987, DOS 2015.

54. Barnes to secretary of state, May 22, 1987, DOS 2015; John M. Goshko, "U.S. Asks Chile to Arrest and Expel Two Officers Wanted in Letelier Murder," *Washington Post*, May 27, 1987, A16.

55. William Claiborne, "Chilean Sought by U.S. Was Serving in S. Africa," *Washington Post*, December 18, 1987, A36.

56. "Chile no aceptó expulsar a EE.UU. a Gral. Contreras y Pedro Espinoza," *La Tercera*, June 18, 1987, 7.

57. Juan Pablo Letelier, quoted in Jones to secretary of state, Santiago, July 10, 1987, DOS 2015.

58. Bradley Graham, "U.S. Hope of Exposing Letelier's Killers Dims," *Washington Post*, May 7, 1988, A17.

59. Quoted in Shirley Christian, "Chilean Official Links a General, Long Suspect, to Letelier Killing," *NYT*, January 26, 1989, A1.

60. José Miguel Barros, quoted in "Ex embajador Barros ratificó el contenido del exhorto acusador," *La Tercera*, January 28, 1989, 4.

61. Buffone and Privitera, "Chronology of Events: Letelier-Moffitt Assassination, 1976–August 1990," August 1990, DNSA.

62. Fabiola Letelier, quoted in Greg San Miguel, "Arrest a U.S.-Chilean Dilemma," *Sydney Morning Herald*, June 16, 1989, 9.

63. James F. Smith, "U.S., Slain Chilean's Kin Launch Initiatives: Chile Pressured to Reopen Letelier Case," *Los Angeles Times*, May 14, 1989, A12.

64. Nancy Lewis, "Letelier Case Suspect Pleads Not Guilty," *Washington Post*, April 19, 1990, A24.

65. Elizabeth Góngora, quoted in Bill McAllister, "Suspect Arrested in Letelier Slaying," *Washington Post*, April 12, 1990, A4; "Cayó cubano buscado por muerte de Letelier," *La Tercera*, April 12, 1990, 5.

66. "Diez cargos contra el cubano Suárez," *La Tercera*, April 19, 1990, 5.

67. "Detención permitirá reabrir investigación," *La Tercera*, April 12, 1990, 4.

68. Isabel Letelier, quoted in "Viuda del ex canciller: 'El caso no está cerrado," *La Tercera*, April 13, 1990, 7.

69. Isabel Letelier, quoted in "Viuda de Letelier: Crimen se aclarará," *La Tercera*, April 14, 1990, 7 and in "'Suárez es cerebro de peligrosa banda terrorista internacional,'" *La Época*, April 14, 1990, 4.

70. "Diez cargos," 5.

71. Kaye Fair, "Bombing Suspect's Wife Says He's Innocent," UPI, May 2, 1990.

72. Pia Díaz, "Dionisio Suárez solicitó urgente ayuda económica para afrontar gastos del juicio," *La Época*, April 17, 1990, 17.

73. Author unknown (Landau?), notes of pretrial hearing, May 14, 1990, folder L-M Suárez, box 28, LC, NSA; Martin McReynolds, "Long-Dormant Letelier Case Suddenly Revived," *Miami Herald*, May 30, 1990, 4A; Dorfman, "Codename: CHILBOM."

74. Pia Díaz, "Elizabeth Góngora: 'Los mismos que le pidieron ayuda ahora le dan la espalda,'" *La Época*, April 14, 1990, 16.

75. Paul Goldberger, quoted in Tracy Thompson, "Suspect Pleads Guilty in Car Bombing Plot," *Washington Post*, September 11, 1990, D4.

76. Sharon LaFraniere, "Suspect in '76 Bombing Is Arrested by FBI in Florida," *Washington Post*, April 24, 1991, A2.

77. Lawrie Mifflin, "Officials Try to Save TV Crime Show," *NYT*, September 7, 1996, 8.

78. Sam Buffone, quoted in Patrick Symmes, "The Man Who Would Not Disappear," *Washington City Paper*, September 22, 1995, www.washingtoncitypaper.com/news/article/13006608/the-man-who-would-not-disappear.

79. Francisco Letelier interview.

80. "Suspect in Envoy's '76 Death Held," *Chicago Tribune*, April 24, 1991, NW6.

81. Sherry Owens and Clint Johnson, quoted in Tim Golden, "Cuban Exile Is Arrested in Florida in 1976 Slaying of Chilean Envoy," *NYT*, April 24, 1991, A1.

82. Quoted in Dorfman, "Codename: CHILBOM."

83. Quoted in "Estudian acciones en asesinato de Letelier," *La Tercera*, April 15, 1991, 8.

84. William Gavin, quoted in "Suspect in Envoy's '76 Death," NW6.

85. "Transfer for Bomb Suspect," *NYT*, April 28, 1991, 26; "Suspect in '76 Killing of Envoy Denies Guilt," *NYT*, May 3, 1991, A32; Tracy Thompson, "Man Implicated in Letelier Murder Pleads Guilty," *Washington Post*, July 31, 1991, A22.

86. Quoted in "Twelve-Year Term for Assassin of Chilean Envoy," *NYT*, September 13, 1991, 16. See also "Doce años de cárcel para el cubano Virgilio Paz," *La Tercera*, September 13, 1991, 11.

87. Juan Pablo Letelier, quoted in "'Principal fugitivo sigue en libertad,'" *La Tercera*, April 24, 1991, 11.

88. Michael Moffitt, quoted in Robert Pear, "Cuban Exile Pleads Guilty in the 1976 Bomb Slaying of Chilean Ambassador," *NYT*, July 31, 1991, A14.

CHAPTER 16

1. Isabel Letelier, quoted in Martin Walker, "The Fight for Bread and Roses," *Guardian*, March 3, 1981; Rep. George Miller, quoted in Carla Hall, "Life after Letelier," *Washington Post*, September 21, 1981, B1.
2. Isabel Letelier, quoted in Rosa Cisneros, "Está probado que la CIA mató a Letelier," *El Diario* (Lima), July 11, 1982, 4.
3. Quoted in Joshua Muravchik, "The Think Tank of the Left," *NYT*, April 26, 1981, SM19.
4. Saul Landau, quoted in Hall, "Life."
5. Isabel Letelier, quoted in Barbara Gamarekian, "Chilean's Widow Pursues His Cause," *NYT*, March 11, 1982, B12.
6. Isabel Letelier, quoted in Hall, "Life."
7. Juan Pablo Letelier, quoted in Suzanne R. Spring, "Pablo Letelier, Twenty, Carries No Hate, But Will Join Fight," *Washington Post*, July 6, 1981, B1.
8. Juan Pablo Letelier to "Galo," Washington, D.C., [September?] 1980, folder 72, box 47, IPS, WHS.
9. Juan Pablo Letelier, quoted in Spring, "Pablo Letelier," B1.
10. Isabel Letelier to undisclosed, late April 1981, folder 72, box 47, IPS, WHS.
11. Isabel Letelier, quoted in Hall, "Life."
12. "Autorizado regreso del jet set de exiliados," *La Tercera*, June 22, 1983, 1.
13. Isabel Letelier, quoted in Odette Magnet, "Isabel Margarita Morel: 'Con la justicia no se transa,'" *Hoy*, July 20–26, 1983, 19.
14. Isabel Letelier to Wexler, September 26, 1983, folder 28, box 45, IPS, WHS.
15. Isabel Letelier and Borosage report, 1985, box 251, TI, IISH.
16. Juan Pablo Letelier to Loveluck, April 1983, folder 72, box 47, IPS, WHS.
17. Isabel Letelier to Wexler, September 26, 1983, folder 28, box 45, IPS, WHS.
18. Stephen Kinzer, "Chilean Lawyer Says He'll Press the Letelier Case," *NYT*, September 17, 1983, 2.
19. "Habla viuda del ex canciller," *La Tercera*, February 6, 1987, 7.
20. "Familia de Letelier pedirá reabrir el proceso en Chile," *La Tercera*, February 7, 1987, 4; Shirley Christian, "Hopes Rise for Chilean Trial in Letelier Case," *NYT*, March 26, 1987, A6.
21. Juan Pablo Letelier affidavit, August 2, 1991, DOS 2015.
22. Shirley Christian, "Why the Laughter in Chile? Because Democracy is 'Fun,'" *NYT*, December 18, 1989, A12.
23. Isabel Letelier, interview by the author.
24. Francisco Letelier interview.
25. Paul Knox, "Report Condemns Junta's Atrocities," *Globe and Mail*, March 5, 1991.
26. Soderberg to Kennedy, March 5, 1991, DNSA.
27. Gillespie interview, ADST.
28. Murray Karpen, quoted in Olson to Kozak and Verville, September 17, 1986, DOS 2015.
29. Michael Moffitt affidavit, July 16, 1991, DOS 2015.
30. Quoted in Olson to Kozak and Verville, September 17, 1986, DOS 2015.
31. Secretary of state to U.S. embassy in Santiago, Washington, D.C., July 30, 1987, DNSA.

32. Colson to Sofaer, Washington, D.C., May 16, 1988, DOS 2015.
33. Michael Kozak, quoted in Kornbluh, *Pinochet File*, 465.
34. Patrick Symmes, "The Man Who Would Not Disappear," *Washington City Paper*, September 22, 1995, www.washingtoncitypaper.com/news/article/13006608/the-man-who-would-not-disappear; Robert Pear, "U.S. Bills Chile in Killing of Letelier," *NYT*, October 13, 1988.
35. Soderberg to Kennedy, January 31, 1990, DNSA.
36. Mónica González, "EE.UU. insiste en indemnización para familias de las víctimas," *La Nación* (Santiago), April 20, 1990, 6; Robert Pear, "Chile Agrees to Pay Reparations to U.S. in Slaying of Envoy," *NYT*, May 13, 1990, 1.
37. U.S.-Chile memorandum of understanding, March 2, 1990, folder Letelier Claim, 1/12/89 Dip. Note, box 131, Abraham D. Sofaer Papers, Hoover; Soderberg to Kennedy, May 2, 1990, DNSA.
38. Sam Buffone, quoted in Anne Kornhauser, "Isabel Letelier's Quest for Justice," *Legal Times*, June 11, 1990.
39. Quoted in Pear, "Chile Agrees," 1.
40. Juan Pablo Letelier, quoted in Paul Knox, "Chile Nears Action on 1976 Killing," *Globe and Mail*, September 12, 1990.
41. State Department, quoted in Kornbluh, *Pinochet File*, 466; Peay to Williamson, Washington, D.C., September 27, 1990, DNSA.
42. K. L. Stevens, "Kennedy-Harkin Amendment Sanctions—Justification for Presidential Certification," October 30, 1990, DNSA; Gillespie to secretary of state and White House, November 21, 1990, DNSA.
43. Claudia Riquelme, "Un millón 600 mil dólares para Isabel Morel e hijos," *La Tercera*, January 13, 1992, 7.
44. Ted Kennedy, quoted in Barbara Crossette, "$2.6 Million Awarded Families in Letelier Case," *NYT*, January 13, 1992, A11.
45. Gillespie interview, ADST; embassy of Chile communiqué, April 10, 1992, DNSA.
46. Juan Pablo Letelier, quoted in Patricia Andrade, "'Lo que nos importa es justicia,'" *La Tercera*, January 14, 1992, 6.
47. Fabiola Letelier, quoted in "'Compensación fue un arreglo,'" *La Tercera*, January 15, 1992, 5.
48. Quoted in Kornhauser, "Quest for Justice."
49. José I. O. Letelier affidavit, July 26, 1991, DOS 2015.
50. "Rehabilitan nacionalidad a Letelier," *La Tercera*, May 13, 1990, 6.
51. "Todo listo para funerales de Orlando Letelier," *La Tercera*, November 1, 1992, 12; "Masivo funeral de Letelier," *La Tercera*, November 5, 1992, 6; Malcolm Coad, "Letelier's Body Comes Home to Rest as Chile Awaits Murder Inquiry Result," *Guardian*, November 5, 1991, 10.
52. Quoted in José Ale, "Lápida de mármol negro identifica tumba definitiva," *La Tercera*, November 3, 1992, 8.

CHAPTER 17

1. Manuel Contreras, quoted in "Contreras rompió su silencio," *Ercilla*, March 27, 1991, 5; "El 'efecto Contreras,'" *Ercilla*, April 3, 1991, 10.
2. Manuel Contreras, quoted in "Contreras rompió," 5.

3. "Showdown in Chile," *Journal of Commerce*, June 22, 1995, 6A.
4. Cath Collins, "The Politics of Prosecutions," in Collins, Hite, and Joignant, *Politics of Memory*, 65.
5. Manuel Contreras Jr. and Contreras, quoted in Peña and Tobar, "Manuel Contreras," 20, 22, see also 41; Salazar, *Contreras*, 141.
6. Manuel Contreras, quoted in Pilar Molina Armas, "¡Ay de los vencidos!" *El Mercurio*, June 4, 1995, D10.
7. Quoted in Salazar, *Contreras*, 145.
8. Molina, "¡Ay de los vencidos!" D10; William R. Long, "Hated Symbol of Chilean Repression Prospers," *Los Angeles Times*, June 23, 1991, VYA8; Jaime Valdés Concha, "El sur: Último refugio de la DINA," *La Nación* (Santiago), September 29, 1991, 2–3; "La Ira de Contreras," *Qué Pasa*, August 21, 1993, 21; Katherine Ellison, "Pinochet Henchman Vows He'll Avoid Jail," *Toronto Star*, January 2, 1994, E8.
9. "Showdown in Chile," 6A.
10. Katherine Hite, Cath Collins, and Alfredo Joignant, "The Politics of Memory in Chile," 8, and Collins, "Politics of Prosecutions," 69, both in Collins, Hite, and Joignant, *Politics of Memory*.
11. Pollack, *New Right*, 144.
12. Augusto Pinochet, quoted in Greathead, "The Long Road to Justice: A Report on the Letelier-Moffitt Case," September 1991, folder Letelier-Moffitt (1991), box 28, LC, NSA.
13. Gabriel Escobar, "In Chile, Army Bows to Civil Justice," *Washington Post*, June 1, 1995, A16.
14. Rosenberg, "Force Is Forever," *New York Times Sunday Magazine*, September 24, 1995, 44–46, 49.
15. Oppenheim, *Politics in Chile*, 221; Claudio Fuentes interview.
16. Independent Democratic Union, quoted in Pollack, *New Right*, 145.
17. *Report of the Chilean National Commission*, 802.
18. Pollack, *New Right*, 144.
19. Oppenheim, *Politics in Chile*, 218.
20. Landau to Barcella, February 12, 1980, DOS 2015.
21. Transcript of interview with Fernández, attached to Shultz to American consul in Rio, Washington, D.C., January 22, 1987, DOS 2015.
22. Scherrer to Ingram, May 23, 1978, Letelier (FOIA) documents produced by the FBI, vol. 57, box 5, LC, NSA.
23. FBI Washington, D.C., field office to director, July 27, 1978, Letelier (FOIA) documents produced by the FBI, vol. 67, box 5, LC, NSA.
24. "Nadie sabe quién es Liliana Walker Martínez," *La Tercera*, August 3, 1978, 4.
25. Landau to secretary of state, August 4, 1978, DNSA; Washington, D.C., field office to FBI director, August 9, 1978, DNSA; Grover to secretary of state, Santiago, August 24, 1978, DNSA; Grover to secretary of state, Santiago, March 9, 1979, unmarked volume, box 11, LC, NSA; Crigler to U.S. embassy in Santiago, Bogotá, September 8, 1980, DOS 2015; Vance to U.S. embassy in Caracas, Washington, D.C., January 29, 1979, DNSA.
26. Gillespie to secretary of state, Santiago, March 29, 1989, DOS 2015.
27. "Liliana Walker: ¿Un misterio aclarado?" *La Tercera*, April 19, 1990, 5.
28. Mariana Callejas, quoted in "Mariana Callejas: 'Demanda judicial de esposa de Letelier es primer paso político," *La Tercera*, August 10, 1978, 5.

29. "Existen casi cincuenta identidades de la mujer," *La Tercera*, April 19, 1990, 7.
30. Landau to Barcella, September 17, 1980, DOS 2015.
31. Barnes to secretary of state, June 15, 1988, DOS 2015.
32. Buffone and Privitera, "Chronology of Events: Letelier-Moffitt Assassination, 1976–August 1990," August 1990, DNSA.
33. Mónica Lagos, quoted in "Ex agente acusa a jefes de la DINA," *La Época*, April 20, 1990, 1.
34. Lagos personal statement, March 1988, DOS 2015.
35. Mónica Lagos, quoted in Manuel Salazar, "Mónica Lagos narra toda su pesadilla," *La Época*, April 20, 1990, 16.
36. Lagos personal statement.
37. "Familia Lagos-Aguirre está de nuevo en casa," *La Época*, April 20, 1990, 17.
38. "Diario íntimo de 'Liliana' sería una bomba de tiempo," *La Tercera*, April 19, 1990, 5.
39. "El padre de la joven pidió comprensión," *La Tercera*, April 20, 1990, 4.
40. Lagos personal statement.
41. "Yo soy Liliana Walker," *La Época*, April 17, 1990, 1, 15.
42. "El hallazgo de Liliana Walker Martínez," *La Época*, April 30, 1990, 13.
43. Quoted in Salazar, *Contreras*, 150–52.
44. Mónica Lagos, quoted in "Ex agente," 1.
45. Armando Fernández, quoted in "¿Un misterio aclarado?" 5.
46. "Protección policial para Luisa Mónica Lagos," *La Tercera*, April 20, 1990, 4; "Existen casi cincuenta," 7.
47. Isabel Letelier, quoted in McReynolds, "Long-Dormant Letelier Case Suddenly Revived," *Miami Herald*, May 30, 1990, 4A.
48. "Fabiola Letelier prepara escritos para solicitar reapertura del caso," *La Tercera*, April 20, 1990, 6.
49. Isabel Letelier, quoted in "Ya era hora que se activara esta causa," *La Tercera*, April 25, 1990, 5.
50. Fabiola Letelier, quoted in "Familia Letelier quiere llevar a los responsables a proceso," *La Tercera*, April 26, 1990, 5.
51. "Con custodia permanente día y noche está la ex agente Dina," *La Tercera*, April 30, 1990, 4; Shirley Christian, "Obstacles Delay Chilean Inquiry into '76 Slaying," *NYT*, May 31, 1990, A5.
52. "Nuestra protesta," *La Época*, May 4, 1990, 1.
53. "'Se intenta ocultar misión que realizó Liliana Walker,'" *La Tercera*, May 30, 1990, 6.
54. Christian, "Obstacles," A5.
55. "Pedirán que Corte Suprema nombre ministro en visita," *La Tercera*, May 31, 1990, 10.
56. Fabiola Letelier, quoted in "Rechazan petición de ministro," *La Tercera*, June 6, 1990, 13; "Chilean High Court Rejects Inquiry into Envoy's Killing," *NYT*, June 6, 1990.
57. Buffone to Arena, Washington, D.C., April 23, 1991, folder Letelier-Moffitt (1991), box 28, LC, NSA; Weeks, *Military and Politics*, 79.
58. U.S. House of Representatives letter to Bush, June [?], 1991, DNSA.
59. Greathead, "The Long Road to Justice: A Report on the Letelier-Moffitt Case," September 1991, Folder Letelier-Moffitt (1991), box 28, LC, NSA.
60. Pear, Robert Pear, "Cuban Exile Pleads Guilty in the 1976 Bomb Slaying of Chilean Ambassador," *NYT*, July 31, 1991, A14.

61. Quoted in Patricia Bravo, "Ministro Bañados: Un juez silencioso," *La Tercera*, May 31, 1995, 37.

62. Quoted in Greathead, "Long Road to Justice."

63. Alejandra Matus, "Ministro Bañados reabrió proceso por crimen de Orlando Letelier," *La Época*, August 1, 1991, 17.

64. Manuel Contreras, quoted in Molina, "¡Ay de los vencidos!" D10.

65. "Así lo notificaron," *La Tercera*, September 24, 1991, 4.

66. Fabiola Letelier, quoted in Malcolm Coad, "Chilean Reopens Case of Exile's Murder," *Guardian*, August 2, 1991.

67. Isabel Letelier, interview by the author.

68. Manuel Contreras Jr., quoted in "Hijo de 'Mamo' acusa de persecución política," *La Tercera*, September 24, 1991, 7.

69. Patricia Andrade, "Contreras se negó a ratificar declaración," *La Tercera*, September 25, 1991, 8.

70. Juan Pablo Letelier, quoted in Raquel Correa, "'Ahora estoy en paz,'" *El Mercurio*, June 4, 1995, D2.

71. Juan Pablo and Fabiola Letelier, quoted in "Juan P. Letelier: 'Se rompe mito Contreras,'" *La Tercera*, September 24, 1991, 7.

72. Sergio Baeza, quoted in Nathaniel C. Nash, "Letelier Case at Critical Stage as Chile's Top Court Takes Over," *NYT*, November 8, 1991, A11.

73. Fabiola Letelier, quoted in Sara Isaac, "Old Murder Case Tests Chile Justice," *Orlando Sentinel*, November 10, 1991, articles.orlandosentinel.com/1991-11-10/news/9111100168_1_letelier-espinoza-contreras.

74. Jaime Castillo, "Emoción familiar," *La Nación* (Santiago), November 19, 1991, 7.

75. Irene Strodthoff, "Michael Moffitt: 'EE.UU. debe pedir plena justicia,'" *La Tercera*, November 20, 1991, 6.

76. Adolfo Bañados, quoted in José Ale, "Confirman encargatorias de reo a Contreras y Espinoza," *La Tercera*, November 19, 1991, 6.

77. Jaime Castillo, "General Contreras no pudo ser prontuariado," *La Nación* (Santiago), November 28, 1991, 3.

78. Jaime Castillo, "Segunda negativa de Contreras al fichaje," *La Nación* (Santiago), November 29, 1991, p. 3.

79. "Protección policial para abogados de Contreras," *La Tercera*, January 11, 1992, 4.

80. Malcolm Coad, "Chile Wants to Question Bush over Letelier Killing," *Guardian*, January 29, 1992, 8; F. P., "Pasaportes a un homicidio," *Ercilla*, May 26, 1995, 20–22.

81. José Ale, "Bajo fuerte seguridad, parten interrogatories en caso Letelier," *La Tercera*, February 18, 1993, 4.

82. Fabiola Letelier, quoted in José Ale, "¡Amenazado de muerte el general (R) Contreras!" *La Tercera*, February 20, 1993, 9.

83. Manuel Contreras, quoted in "'No me arrepiento de nada,'" *La Tercera*, February 26, 1993, 4.

84. "'Contretras daba las órdenes,'" *La Tercera*, February 4, 1993, 4–5.

85. Manuel Contreras, quoted in María Eugenia Oyarzún, "'General Pinochet jamás me dió órden de asesinar a nadie,'" *La Tercera*, August 22, 1993, 6–8.

86. Quoted in William R. Long, "Missing Chilean Scientist Raises Ghost of Military Rule," *Los Angeles Times*, June 19, 1993, VYA1.

87. Nathaniel C. Nash, "Spy Network Inflaming Uruguay-Chile Tension," *NYT*, July 20, 1993, A7; Long, "Missing Chilean Scientist," VYA1.

88. Quoted in Nash, "Spy Network," A7.

89. Long, "Missing Chilean Scientist," VYA1.

90. Fabiola Letelier, quoted in Nash, "Spy Network," A7.

91. Fabiola Letelier, quoted in Long, "Missing Chilean Scientist," VYA1.

92. "Chile: condenan a los asesinos del 'químico' de Pinochet," *El Comercio*, August 12, 2015, https://elcomercio.pe/mundo/latinoamerica/chile-condenan-asesinos-quimico-pinochet-194154.

93. Huneeus, *Chile, un país dividido*, 185.

94. Fabiola Letelier, quoted in Nathaniel C. Nash, "Chile Refuses to Forget Crimes of Past," *NYT*, September 26, 1993, E3.

95. Alejandra Matus, "Contreras y Espinoza, culpables de homicidio," *La Época*, November 13, 1993, 12.

96. Fabiola Letelier, quoted in Don Podesta, "Two Generals Convicted in Killing of Letelier," *Washington Post*, November 13, 1993, A19.

97. Malcolm Coad, "Eyewitness: Terror Chief Scorns Risk of Serving Time," *Guardian*, November 18, 1993, 15.

98. Manuel Contreras, quoted in William R. Long, "Jail Sentences May Not Spell End of Chile's Letelier Case," *Los Angeles Times*, November 19, 1993, A1.

CHAPTER 18

1. "Caso Letelier: Ampliado el período de relación privada," *El Mercurio*, January 12, 1995, C9.

2. "Comienza hoy en C. Suprema alegatos por el caso Letelier," *El Mercurio*, January 25, 1995, C1, C6.

3. "El historial de los jueces de Contreras," *Qué Pasa*, February 11, 1995, 14–17.

4. E. G., "Año nuevo en caso Letelier," *Ercilla*, January 6, 1995, 14–15.

5. Quoted in "Querellante solicita nueva suspension de Caso Letelier," *El Mercurio*, January 5, 1995, C1.

6. "TVN y Chilevisión transmitirán en directo alegatos del caso Letelier," *El Mercurio*, January 24, 1995, C11.

7. Kornbluh interview.

8. "Caso Letelier: Comenzó la relación pública," *El Mercurio*, January 24, 1995, C5.

9. E. G., "Alegatos en vivo," *Ercilla*, January 27, 1995, 16.

10. "Alegatos en vivo," 18.

11. Juan Bustos, quoted in "Los alegatos del Caso Letelier," *La Nación* (Santiago), January 26–28, 1995.

12. Quoted in Jorge Piña and Eugenio González, "Fallo 'a presión,'" *Ercilla*, April 28, 1995, 16.

13. Soledad Alvear, quoted in "Aburto rechaza presiones a la Corte Suprema," *El Mercurio*, April 28, 1995, A1, A16.

14. "PS: Campaña no se debe estimar ataque a FF.AA.," *El Mercurio*, April 28, 1995, C2.

15. "Horas difíciles," *El Mercurio*, April 30, 1995, D1, D4.

16. Quoted in "Comandantes militares regresaron a unidades para mantener normalidad," *El Mercurio*, April 28, 1995, C3.

17. Bitar interview.
18. Huneeus, *Chile, un país dividido*, 185.
19. Raúl Rojas, "Ejército acatará la sentencia," *La Tercera*, May 25, 1995, 5.
20. "Cardenal reiteró llamado a acatar fallo," *El Mercurio*, May 28, 1995, C1.
21. Eduardo Frei, quoted in María José Errázuriz, "Frei estima que situación del país es de total orden," *El Mercurio*, May 25, 1995, C1, C4.
22. "Cardenal reiteró," C1.
23. Fabiola Letelier, quoted in José Ale, "'Sus palabras son muy graves y constituyen una provocación y un llamado a la violencia," *La Tercera*, May 29, 1995, 6.
24. Natalia Pinilla and Hernán García, "Comandos en fundo de Contreras," *La Tercera*, May 29, 1995, 4; "Grupo especial castrense viajó a fundo de Contreras," *El Mercurio*, May 29, 1995, A1.
25. Quoted in O'Shaughnessy, *Politics of Torture*, 153.
26. "C. Suprema da a conocer fallo en caso Letelier," *El Mercurio*, May 30, 1995, A1.
27. Alexandra Gallegos, "... Y punto final," *Ercilla*, June 2, 1995, 10.
28. Quoted in José Ale, "Cuarta Sala confirmó el dictamen," *La Tercera*, May 31, 1995, 18.
29. Eduardo Frei, quoted in Gabriel Escobar, "Chilean Court Upholds Key Convictions; Generals in Letelier Case Now Face Prison Terms," *Washington Post*, May 31, 1995, A21.
30. Juan Pablo Letelier, quoted in Pamela Gutiérrez and Paola Sais, "La emoción de una familia," *La Tercera*, May 31, 1995, 22.
31. José Letelier, quoted in Gabriel Escobar, "In Chile, Army Bows to Civil Justice," *Washington Post*, June 1, 1995, A16.
32. Isabel Letelier, interview by the author.
33. Fabiola Letelier, quoted in Gallegos, "Y punto final," 11.
34. Quoted in Calvin Sims, "Two in Chile Get Jail Terms in U.S. Killing," *NYT*, May 31, 1995, A13.
35. "Suprema ratificó condena contra Gral. (R) Contreras," *El Mercurio*, May 31, 1995, A1, A11; "'Ahora tengo una tristeza perfecta,'" *La Tercera*, June 1, 1995, 15.
36. Lucía Pinochet, quoted in "'Lo hieren lo que más quiere,'" *La Tercera*, June 2, 1995, 4.
37. "Cerrando viejas heridas" [editorial], *La Tercera*, June 1, 1995, 3.
38. Quoted in Eugenio González Z., "La obstinación de Contreras," *Ercilla*, June 2, 1995, 15.
39. Sergio Miranda, quoted in Gallegos, "Y punto final," 11.
40. Manuel Contreras, quoted in Escobar, "Chilean Court," A21.
41. Quoted in "'No voy a ir a ninguna cárcel,'" *El Mercurio*, May 31, 1995, A1, A11; "Gobierno hará cumplir fallo en caso Letelier," *El Mercurio*, June 1, 1995, A1.
42. Quoted in "Gobierno no descarta que se utilice la fuerza," *El Mercurio*, June 1, 1995, C3; "Allamand: 'Fallo de la Suprema debe ser acatado en plenitud,'" *El Mercurio*, June 1, 1995, C4. See also "Según dirigentes, Contreras debe acatar la sentencia," *El Mercurio*, June 1, 1995, C4.
43. Manuel Contreras, quoted in Eduardo Roseel and Samuel Mena, "Contreras quema todos sus cartuchos," *La Tercera*, June 1, 1995, 4.
44. Manuel Contreras, quoted in Calvin Sims, "Chilean Vows to Avoid Prison in Letelier Case," *NYT*, June 1, 1995, A9.
45. Editorial cartoon, *El Mercurio*, June 3, 1995, A3; De la Barra, editorial cartoon, *La Tercera*, June 3, 1995, 4.
46. Augusto Pinochet, quoted in Salazar, *Contreras*, 9, 10.

47. Juan Pablo Letelier, quoted in Raquel Correa, "'Ahora estoy en paz,'" *El Mercurio*, June 4, 1995, D2.

48. Rodolfo Arenas R. and Patricia Bravo, "Caso Letelier: Para los historiadores del futuro," *La Tercera*, June 4, 1995, 8–9.

49. Calvin Sims, "Justice Sought for Killings by Chile Army," *NYT*, June 4, 1995, 9.

50. Noll Scott, "Court Upholds Sentence on Chilean Torture Chief," *Guardian Weekly*, June 11, 1995, 3.

51. Gabriel Escobar, "Chilean Vigil for Arrest of an Ex-General," *Washington Post*, June 13, 1995, A16.

52. Fabiola Letelier, quoted in "Fabiola Letelier pide igualdad ante la ley," *La Tercera*, June 10, 1995, 7.

53. Juan Pablo Letelier, quoted in "'Ningún chileno cree que está enfermo,'" *La Tercera*, June 14, 1995, 14.

54. His words were *darme la baja*, which typically means "fire me." But since Contreras was already retired, he may have meant "arrest me" or "kill me." Contreras appeal to Corte Suprema Chile, December 23, 1997, folder Contreras: Apelación de Sentencia, box 28, LC, NSA. See also "'Salí del fundo para evitar enfrentamiento,'" *La Tercera*, June 12, 1995, 6.

55. Raúl Rojas, "La trastienda del 'cúmplase,'" *La Tercera*, June 13, 1995, 18.

56. Manuel Contreras Jr., quoted in "'Hubo más de 100 disparos,'" *La Tercera*, June 12, 1995, 7.

57. "El martes negro del gobierno," *Qué Pasa*, June 17, 1995, 16–20; Eduardo Sepulveda, "Adiós a Fresia," *El Mercurio*, June 18, 1995, D1; Salazar, *Contreras*, 11.

58. "El martes negro," 16–20; John Kavanagh, "Army Flexes Muscles on Sentence for Murder of Key Pinochet Associate," *Irish Times*, June 17, 1995, 9.

59. Gabriel Escobar, "Chile's Civilian Rule Continues Six-Day Standoff with Pinochet-Led Military," *Washington Post*, June 19, 1995, A12.

60. Augusto Pinochet, quoted in Maria Eugenia Oyarzún, "Pinochet: 'Proceso fue injusto,'" *La Tercera*, June 15, 1995, 4; "Pinochet Calls Court 'Unjust,'" *NYT*, June 16, 1995, A11.

61. Mauricio Carvallo Avaria, "Los días nerviosos," *El Mercurio*, June 18, 1995, D2.

62. Fuentes interview.

63. Carvallo, "Los días nerviosos," D2.

64. Quoted in Jonathan Friedland, "Pinochet's Comments Start Alarm Bells Ringing in Chile," *Globe and Mail*, June 20, 1995.

65. Paul Walder, "Nuestra Guerra del Golfo," *Hoy*, June 19–25, 1995, 18.

66. Pedro Espinoza, quoted in "Espinoza decidió no ir a la cárcel," *La Tercera*, June 19, 1995, 4.

67. Juan Pablo Letelier, quoted in "Chilean Officer Reports to Prison," *St. Petersburg Times*, June 21, 1995, 2A.

68. "Primeros informes médicos establecen posibilidad de intervención a Contreras," *El Mercurio*, June 22, 1995, C14.

69. "Postergan traslado final de General (R) Contreras," *El Mercurio*, July 8, 1995, C1, C12.

70. Huneeus, *Chile, un país dividido*, 185, 187.

71. Esther Schrader, "Demon Lurks in Chile: The Once-Brutal Military Remains a Powerful Influence," *San José Mercury News*, August 22, 1995, 1A; Stern, *Reckoning with Pinochet*, 155.

72. Augusto Pinochet, quoted in Tina Rosenberg, "Force Is Forever," *New York Times Sunday Magazine*, September 24, 1995, 44–46, 49.

73. "Construirán cárcel especial para militares," *El Mercurio*, January 6, 1995, A1, A16.

74. Roberto Muñoz Barra, "Punta Peuco," *La Tercera*, June 21, 1995, 3.

75. "Encontradas reacciones por cárcel especial," *El Mercurio*, January 6, 1995, A16; "Recintos para militares hay en todo en mundo," *El Mercurio*, January 7, 1995, A1, A16.

76. Eduardo Gallardo, "General in Solitary as Chile Debates Imprisoning Pinochet's Henchmen," *Los Angeles Times*, September 17, 1995.

77. Paulina Calleja N., "Así es la celde que ocupa el ex brigadier Espinoza," *La Tercera*, June 21, 1995, 7.

78. "Gendarmería garantiza seguridad de presidio," *El Mercurio*, June 21, 1995, C2.

79. Rodrigo Eitel, quoted in Eduardo Gallardo, "Latin America Keeping General in New Jail Costly Business for Chileans," *Globe and Mail*, August 22, 1995.

80. Rosenberg, "Force Is Forever," 44–46, 49.

81. Weeks, *Military and Politics*, 105–6.

82. Juan Andrés Guzman, "Primeros minutos de Contreras en prisión," *La Tercera*, June 21, 1995, 9. See also "El ultimo operativo," *Qué Pasa*, October 28, 1995, 21–22.

83. Eduardo Frei, quoted in William R. Long, "Chile Jails Former Chief of Secret Police," *Los Angeles Times*, October 22, 1995, A8.

84. "El episodio del año," *Ercilla*, January 1, 1996, 21.

85. Quoted in Maria Cristina Prudant, "'Nos sentimos contentos y en paz,'" *La Tercera*, June 22, 1995, 6.

86. Juan Pablo and Fabiola Letelier, quoted in José Ale, "Abogados: Alegría y desencanto," *La Tercera*, June 22, 1995, 14.

EPILOGUE

1. Quoted in Verónica Torres, "Punta Peuco IV: Las historias no contadas de familiares y presos," CIPER, February 5, 2012, ciperchile.cl/2012/05/02/punta-peuco-iv-las-historias-no-contadas-de-familiares-y-presos/.

2. Eugenio González Z., "Más sobresaltos para Contreras," *Ercilla*, May 12, 1995, 18–19; E. G., "Disparos en Roma llegan a Chile," *Ercilla*, February 17, 1995, 18–19; Kevin G. Hall, "Top Pinochet General Held, May Be Extradited to Italy," *Contra Costa Times*, March 15, 2000, A14.

3. Stern, *Reckoning with Pinochet*, 256.

4. "No Amnesty for Ex-Spy Chief," *Toronto Star*, November 18, 2004, A15; Kornbluh, *Pinochet File*, 482.

5. Bitar interview; Fuentes interview.

6. Collins, "Human Rights Trials," 75.

7. Quoted in "La DINA tras las rejas," *La Nación* (Santiago), January 29, 2005.

8. Dinges, *Condor Years*, 259.

9. "Juan Cristóbal Peña desentraña vida de 'El Mamo' marcada por su infancia, Pinochet, Dios y la DINA," *El Mostrador* (Santiago), August 8, 2015, www.elmostrador.cl/noticias/pais/2015/08/08/juan-cristobal-pena-desentrana-vida-de-el-mamo-marcada-por-su-infancia-pinochet-dios-y-la-dina/.

10. Stern, *Reckoning with Pinochet*, 334.

11. "Chile: Ex-Secret Police Chief Guilty in Disappearance," *Washington Post*, April 18, 2008, A23.

12. "Condenan al 'Mamo' Contreras a otros 15 años de cárcel efectiva," *La Nación* (Santiago), October 7, 2011; Claudio Leiva Cortés, "General (R) Contreras está sentenciado a 239 años de cárcel," *La Nación* (Santiago), March 23, 2011.

13. Quoted in Peña and Tobar, "Manuel Contreras," 47.

14. Manuel Contreras, quoted in Luis Andres Henao, "Led Pinochet's Secret Police in Chile," *Washington Post*, August 9, 2015, C08.

15. "Juan Cristóbal Peña desentraña."

16. Manuel Contreras Jr., quoted in Peña and Tobar, "Manuel Contreras," 54, 53, and 55; "La boda más glamorosa el año: Mamo Contreras se casó con su ex secretaria de la DINA," *The Clinic*, September 8, 2010, www.theclinic.cl/2010/09/08/la-boda-mas-glamorosa-el-ano-mamo-contreras-se-caso-con-la-que-era-su-secretaria-en-la-dina/.

17. Bonnefoy, "Manuel Contreras," 21.

18. Quoted in "Chile Ex-Spymaster, Manuel Contreras, Dies at 86," BBC, August 8, 2015.

19. "Chile Celebrates Death of Ex-Spy Chief Manuel Contreras," *Latin Correspondent*, 10 August 2015.

20. "Hijo de Manuel Contreras: 'Mi padre se fue protegido por su ejército,'" *Soy Chile*, August 14, 2015, www.soychile.cl/Santiago/Sociedad/2015/08/14/340243/Hijo-de-Manuel-Contreras-Mi-padre-se-fue-protegido-por-su-Ejercito.aspx; "Chileans Cheer, Lament Death of Pinochet's Hated Secret Police Boss Manuel Contreras," ABC Australia, August 8, 2015, www.abc.net.au/news/2015-08-09/chileans-cheer-lament-death-of-secret-police-chief-contreras/6683548.

21. Pascale Bonnefoy, "Two Sentenced in Murders in Chile Coup," *NYT*, January 28, 2015, A8.

22. Douglas Grant Mine, "The Assassin Next Door," *Miami New Times*, November 18, 1999, www.miaminewtimes.com/news/the-assassin-next-door-6357449; Barnes memo to secretary of state, Santiago, March 12, 1987, DNSA.

23. "Fernández Larios enfrenta impasible el juicio," *La Nación* (Santiago), September 24, 2003.

24. "Fernández Larios: 'Fui sólo un joven teniente,'" *La Nación* (Santiago), October 4, 2003.

25. "Fernández Larios condenado en EE.UU.," *La Nación* (Santiago), October 16, 2003.

26. Center for Justice and Accountability, "Cabello v. Fernandez Larios," no date, www.cja.org/section.php?id=32 (accessed November 27, 2018).

27. Valdés interview.

28. "Argentina Seeking Murderer of Letelier in Another Killing," *NYT*, April 19, 1983, A10; Stuart Taylor Jr., "Justice Dept. Aids Argentina in Bid to Extradite Assassin," *NYT*, May 19, 1983.

29. "U.S. Won't Extradite Figure in Letelier Case," *NYT*, July 26, 1983, A11.

30. Joseph Lelyvelds, "Swedes Seek Palme Case Clue in '76 Assassination in U.S.," *NYT*, June 9, 1986, A10.

31. Barnes to secretary of state, Santiago, June 24, 1988, DOS 2015.

32. Mariana Callejas to Barnes, Santiago, September 12, 1988, DOS 2015.

33. Callejas, *Siembra vientos*, 159, 168.

34. Jack Chang, "Downstairs from Her Glittering Chilean Salon, There Was a Torture

Chamber," McClatchydc.com, August 3, 2008, www.mcclatchydc.com/news/nation-world/world/article24494053.html.

35. Manuel Hevia Frasquieri, "Guillermo Novo Sampol: ¡Yo no soy un terrorista!" *La Jiribilla*, April 12–22, 2005, www.latinamericanstudies.org/belligerence/bill.htm.

36. Ileana Ros-Lehtinen, quoted in Tristram Korten and Kirk Nielsen, "The Coddled 'Terrorists' of South Florida," Salon.com, January 14, 2008, www.salon.com/2008/01/14/cuba_2/.

37. Zach Dorfman, "Codename: CHILBOM," *Atavist Magazine* 59 (2016), magazine.atavist.com/codename-chilbom.

38. Virgilio Paz, quoted in Alex Vega, "Cuban Exile Apologizes for '76 Car Bombing," *Miami Herald Tribune*, August 2, 2001, 6B.

39. Quoted in Dorfman, "Codename: CHILBOM."

40. See the interviews with Guillermo Novo, José Suárez, and Virgilio Paz on latinamericanstudies.org.

41. José Suárez, quoted in "INS Frees Second Cuban Exile Convicted in Fatal 1976 D.C. Bombing," *Naples Daily News*, August 16, 2001, www.latinamericanstudies.org/belligerence/dionisio-free.htm.

42. "Conspirator in '76 Letelier Assassination Released," *Washington Post*, August 16, 2001, A13; "INS Frees 2nd Cuban Exile."

43. Janine Zeitlin, "Cuban Painters and Fugitives," *Miami New Times*, November 1, 2007, www.miaminewtimes.com/news/cuban-painters-and-fugitives-6333356.

44. Guillermo Novo, quoted in Tracey Eaton, "Guillermo Novo: Freedom Fighter or Lawbreaker?" *Along the Malecón*, June 24, 2010, alongthemalecon.blogspot.com/2010/06/guillermo-novo-freedom-fighter-or.html.

45. McSherry, *Predatory States*, 161.

46. Glenn Kessler, "U.S. Denies Role in Cuban Exiles' Pardon; Panama Frees Four Convicted in Plot to Kill Castro," *Washington Post*, August 27, 2004, A18.

47. Méndez, *Bajo las alas*, 106.

48. "'La DINA financió a Suárez,'" *La Nación* (Santiago), April 22, 1990, 14.

49. Mary McGrory, "A G-Man the Left Can Love," *Washington Post*, September 24, 1989, B1.

50. Robert Scherrer, quoted in Adela Gooch, "Ex-Agent Vows Justice in Letelier Case," *Washington Post*, September 26, 1989, A16.

51. Dennis Hevesi, "E. Lawrence Barcella, Prosecutor of Terrorism Cases, Dies at 65," *NYT*, November 17, 2010, www.nytimes.com/2010/11/18/us/18barcella.html.

52. Augusto Pinochet, quoted in Katherine Ellison, "Pinochet Ends Rule over Chilean Army," *Philadelphia Inquirer*, March 11, 1998, A02; Linda Diebel, "Clinging to Power," *Toronto Star*, February 10, 1998, A16.

53. Quoted in Dinges, *Condor Years*, 35–36.

54. Murray Karpen, quoted in David Adams, "For Pinochet's Victims, Closure Far from Certain," *St. Petersburg Times*, October 21, 1998, 1A.

55. Francisco Letelier, "Now the World Will Know the Truth," *Los Angeles Times*, October 21, 1998, articles.latimes.com/1998/oct/21/local/me-34692.

56. Katherine Ellison, "Pinochet Continues to Polarize Chile," *Gazette* (Montreal), November 26, 1998, B1.

57. E. Lawrence Barcella Jr., "A Look at . . . Pursuing Pinochet; The Case We Made,

22 Years Ago," *Washington Post*, December 6, 1998, C03; George Miller, "U.S. Should Investigate Gen. Pinochet's Role in U.S. Assassination," U.S. Congress, 105th Cong., 2nd sess., *Congressional Record* 144, part 7 (May 22, 1998): 10720.

58. Quoted in Saul Landau, introduction for TNI/IPS booklet, undated, box 249, TI, IISH. See also "'La DINA financió a Suárez,'" 14; and Isabel Letelier speech, Algeria, January 1978, folder 37, box 52, IPS, WHS.

59. Quoted in Barcella, "A Look At," C03.

60. Manuel Contreras Jr., quoted in Eduardo Olivares, "Ally Accuses Pinochet in Murder Case," *Guardian Weekly*, March 15, 1998, 13.

61. Augusto Pinochet, quoted in Dominic Lawson, "An Audience with the General," *Sydney Morning Herald*, August 14, 1999, 44.

62. Al Goodman, "Judge Lays Out Pinochet Case in Full Detail," *NYT*, December 11, 1998, A11.

63. Fabiola Letelier, quoted in Duncan Campbell, "Coup Ghosts Await Pinochet's Return," *Observer*, January 23, 2000, 23.

64. Quoted in Kornbluh, *Pinochet File*, 462.

65. Officials and FBI's Carey, quoted in Vernon Loeb and David A. Vise, "U.S. Probe of Pinochet Reopened," *Washington Post*, March 23, 2000, A01.

66. Jan McGirk, "U.S. Pursues Pinochet for Plot to Murder Diplomat," *Independent* (London), March 24, 2000, 17.

67. Vernon Loeb, "Documents Link Chile's Pinochet to Letelier Murder," *Washington Post*, November 14, 2000, A16.

68. Vernon Loeb and David A. Vise, "Pinochet Probers Tout New Evidence," *Washington Post*, May 28, 2000, A01; Larry Rohter, "Chile Seeks U.S. Files on 1976 Assassination," *NYT*, September 21, 2006, A6; Kevin G. Hall, "Relatives Don't Rest after Death of Pinochet," *Contra Costa Times*, December 12, 2006, F4.

69. Clifford Kraus, "Chilean Military Faced Reckoning for Its Dark Past," *NYT*, October 3, 1999.

70. Alexander Wilde, "A Season of Memory: Human Rights in Chile's Long Transition," 34, 44, and Elizabeth Lira and Brian Loveman, "Torture as Public Policy: 1810–2010," 118, both in Collins, Hite, and Joignant, *Politics of Memory*.

71. Dinges, *Condor Years*, 256.

72. Cath Collins, "The Politics of Prosecutions," in Collins, Hite, and Joignant, *Politics of Memory*, 61.

73. Carlos Huneeus and Sebastián Ibarra, "The Memory of the Pinochet Regime in Public Opinion," in Collins, Hite, and Joignant, *Politics of Memory*, 204; Kathleen Day and Pascale Bonnefoy, "New Spotlight on Pinochet," *Washington Post*, August 26, 2004, E01; Larry Rohter, "Pinochet Entangled in Web of Inquiries," *NYT*, February 7, 2005, A7.

74. IPS Program Director Sarah Anderson interview.

75. Timothy L. O'Brien and Larry Rohter, "The Pinochet Money Trail," *NYT*, December 12, 2004, sec. 3, col. 5, 1.

76. Manuel Contreras, quoted in "Duelo histórico en Lo Curro," *La Nación* (Santiago), November 20, 2005.

77. Manuel Contreras, quoted in Hector Tobar and Eva Vergara, "Chile's Ex-Spy Chief Details 580 Political Killings," *Los Angeles Times*, May 14, 2005.

78. Larry Rohter, "Former Aide Says Pinochet and a Son Dealt in Drugs," *NYT*, July 11, 2006, A3.

79. Manuel Contreras, quoted in "La última traición del 'Mamo,'" *La Nación* (Santiago), December 2, 2007.
80. Isabel Letelier, quoted in Childress, *Pinochet's Chile*, 141.
81. Anderson interview.
82. Augusto Pinochet, quoted in Monte Reel and J. Y. Smith, "A Chilean Dictator's Dark Legacy," *Washington Post*, December 11, 2006, A01.
83. Kevin G. Hall, "Relatives Don't Rest," F4.
84. Augusto Pinochet, quoted in Lawson, "Audience with the General," 44.
85. Murray Karpen, "A State Terrorist, Still at Large," *Washington Post*, January 12, 2002, A21.
86. Michael A. Karpen, "The Searing Pain of Chile's Past," *NYT*, January 15, 2000, A16.
87. "Chile: Court Orders Inquiry into 1976 Killing of American," *NYT*, June 20, 2012, A6.
88. This story was told to me on background.
89. An example is Francisco Letelier to Obama, December 5, 2014, reproduced in "Son of Victim of Terrorism Asks Obama to Free the Cuban 5," *CubaSí*, December 3, 2014.
90. Tom Hayden, "An Exiled Son of Santiago," *Nation*, April 4, 2005, www.thenation.com/article/exiled-son-santiago/; Elisa Fernández, "Hay que llevar el arte a los abandonados," *La Nación* (Santiago), August 11, 2006.
91. David Montgomery, "A Car Bomb Killed Orlando Letelier on Embassy Row 40 Years Ago. A Mural by His Son Marks the Tragedy and the Progress It Inspired," *Washington Post*, September 18, 2016, www.washingtonpost.com/news/arts-and-entertainment/wp/2016/09/18/a-car-bomb-killed-orlando-letelier-on-embassy-row-40-years-ago-a-mural-by-his-son-marks-the-tragedy-and-the-progress-it-inspired/?postshare=3681474227603641andtid=ss_mail.
92. Hayden, "Exiled Son."
93. Susan Ferriss, "Pinochet Misses Clinton's Address; President Praises Democratic Reforms," *Atlanta Journal and Constitution*, April 18, 1998, 01B.
94. Larry Rohter, "World Briefing: Americas: Chile: Lawmaker Detained," *NYT*, May 23, 2003, www.nytimes.com/2003/05/23/world/world-briefing-americas-chile-lawmaker-detained.html; Francisco Letelier interview.
95. Francisco Letelier, quoted in Michael Laris, "A Chilean and American Monument to Pinochet Bombing Victims Rises in Washington," *Washington Post*, February 25, 2018, www.washingtonpost.com/local/a-chilean-and-american-monument-to-pinochet-bombing-victims-rises-in-washington/2018/02/25/145462da-1a4c-11e8-9de1-147dd2df3829_story.html?utm_term=.ac93259841db.
96. John Dinges, quoted in Dorfman, "Codename: CHILBOM."
97. Collins, "Chile a más de dos décadas," 82; Collins, "Human Rights Defense," 133.
98. Collins, "Human Rights Trials," 74.
99. Valdés interview.
100. Isabel Letelier, interview by the author.
101. Francisco Letelier interview.
102. U.S. Second Circuit Court of Appeals, quoted in Doyle, "Creative Justice," 12.
103. Eugene Propper and Carter Cornick, quoted in De Young et al., "'This Was Not an Accident. This Was a Bomb,'" *Washington Post*, September 20, 2016, www.washingtonpost.com/sf/national/2016/09/20/this-was-not-an-accident-this-was-a-bomb/?utm_term=.57984422ebde.
104. L. Carter Cornick, "Chilbom," *The Grapevine*, August 2016, 11–16, https://cdn

.ymaws.com/www.socxfbi.org/resource/resmgr/history_committee_articles/Chilbom.pdf.

105. Carter Cornick, quoted in "'La DINA financió a Suárez,'" 16.

106. John Hanrahan, "The New Import: Terror," *Chicago Tribune*, July 3, 1977, "Perspective" section, 1.

107. Anti-Terrorism and Effective Death Penalty Act, Pub. L. 104-132, 110 Stat. 1214, sec. 221(a)(1)(A).

108. Bitar interview.

109. Steven interview, ADST.

BIBLIOGRAPHY

ARCHIVES

Chile
    Archivo de la Administración, Santiago
        Fondo Orlando Letelier
    Archivo General Histórico, Ministerio de Relaciones Exteriores, Santiago

Netherlands
    International Institute of Social History, Amsterdam
        Records of the Transnational Institute

United States
    Hoover Institution Archives, Stanford, California
        Papers of Hernán Cubillos Sallato
        George W. Landau Papers
        Ronald Reagan Radio Commentary
        Abraham D. Sofaer Papers
    National Security Archive, Washington, D.C.
        Letelier Collection
    Wisconsin Historical Society, Madison, Wisconsin
        Institute for Policy Studies Records

DIGITAL COLLECTIONS AND PUBLISHED GOVERNMENT RECORDS

Congressional Record
Department of State, Additional Release: Chile Declassification Project, 2015
Department of State, Additional Release: Chile Declassification Project, 2016
Digital National Security Archive Collection, Chile and the United States: U.S. Policy toward Democracy, Dictatorship, and Human Rights, 1970–1990, National Security Archive, Washington, D.C.
Latinamericanstudies.org

ORAL HISTORIES BY THE AUTHOR

Anderson, Sarah, Washington, D.C., June 19, 2017
Bitar, Sergio, Santiago, Chile, July 18, 2017
Cavanaugh, John, Washington, D.C., June 19, 2017
De la Cova, Antonio, email communication, December 13, 2018
Dove, Fiona, Amsterdam, Netherlands, January 17, 2017
Fuentes, Claudio, Santiago, Chile, July 27, 2017

Kornbluh, Peter, Washington, D.C., September 22, 2015
Letelier, Cristián, Venice, California, May 8, 2017
Letelier, Francisco, Venice, California, May 8, 2017
Letelier, Isabel, Santiago, Chile, July 19, 2017
Teunissen, Jan Joost, email communication, May 2, 2017
Valdés, Ambassador Juan Gabriel, Washington, D.C., June 13, 2017

ORAL HISTORIES BY THE ASSOCIATION FOR
DIPLOMATIC STUDIES AND TRAINING

Boyatt, Ambassador Thomas D., interviewed by Charles Stuart Kennedy, March 8, 1990
Bushnell, John, interviewed by John Harter, December 19, 1997
Crimmins, Ambassador John Hugh, interviewed by Ashley C. Hewitt Jr., May 10, 1979
Gillespie, Ambassador Charles Anthony Jr., interviewed by Charles Stuart Kennedy, September 19, 1995
Grover, Charles W., interviewed by Henry Ryan, November 2, 1990
Jones, George F., interviewed by Charles Stuart Kennedy, August 6, 1996
Landau, Ambassador George W., interviewed by Arthur Day, March 11, 1991
Ryan, Ambassador Hewson, interviewed by Richard Nethercut, April 27, 1988
Steven, Robert, interviewed by Charles Stuart Kennedy, August 3, 2001

ORAL HISTORIES BY ANTONIO DE LA COVA

All oral histories available at latinamericanstudies.org.
Novo Sampol, Guillermo, January 1, 2005, December 23, 2006, and July 11, 2010
Paz, Virgilio, December 28, 2004
Suárez, José Dionisio, December 19, 2005 and December 26, 2006

MEDIA OUTLETS

ABC (Spain)
ABC Australia
Along the Malecón
American Diplomacy
Areíto
Asheville Times
Associated Press
Atavist Magazine
Atlanta Journal and Constitution
Baltimore Evening Sun
Baltimore News-American
BBC
Caras (Santiago)
Chicago Tribune
Chile Newsletter
CIPER (Centro de Investigación e Información Periodística)
The Clinic
CNN
Contra Costa Times
Counterpunch
CubaSí
Daily World
El Caimán (New Jersey)
El Diario (Lima)
El Mercurio (Santiago)
El Mostrador (Santiago)
El Socialista (Madrid)
Ercilla (Santiago)
Gazette (Montreal)
Globe and Mail (Toronto)
Grand Rapids Press
Grapevine
Guardian (London)

Guardian Weekly
Hamilton Spectator
Harper's
Hoy (Santiago)
Hudson Dispatch (Union City, N.J.)
Independent (London)
Inquiry
In These Times
Irish Times
Jersey Journal
Jewish Telegraphic Agency
Journal of Commerce
La Época (Santiago)
La Jiribilla (Havana)
La Nación (Buenos Aires)
La Nación (Santiago)
La Segunda (Santiago)
La Tercera / La Tercera de
 la Hora (Santiago)
Latin Correspondent
Latinamerica Press (Lima)
Legal Times
Le Matin (Paris)
Le Monde (Paris)
Los Angeles Times
McClatchydc.com
Miami Herald / Miami Herald Tribune
Miami New Times
Monthly Review
Mother Jones
Naples Daily News
Nation
Newsweek
New Times
New York
New York Times
New York Times Sunday Magazine
Observer
Orlando Sentinel
Ottawa Citizen
Penthouse
Philadelphia Inquirer
Playboy
Progressive
Qué Pasa (Chile)
Revista Paloma (Chile)
Sacramento Bee
Salon.com
San José Mercury News
Soy Chile
States News Service
St. Petersburg Times
Sydney Morning Herald
Toronto Star
Ultimas Noticias (Santiago)
UPI
Village Voice
Washington City Paper
Washington Jewish Week
Washington Post
Washington Post Magazine
Washington Star / Washington Star-News

BOOKS, JOURNAL ARTICLES, AND DISSERTATIONS

Andrew, Christopher, and Vasili Mitrokhin. *The World Was Going Our Way: The KGB and the Battle for the Third World*. New York: Basic Books, 2005.

Bitar, Sergio. *Dawson Isla 10*. 13th ed. Santiago: Pehuén, 2011; orig. 1987.

Branch, Taylor, and Eugene M. Propper. *Labyrinth*. New York: Penguin, 1982.

Briones, Alvaro. *Ideología del fascismo dependiente*. Mexico: Editorial Edicol, 1978.

Callejas, Mariana. *Siembra vientos: Memorias*. Santiago: Ediciones ChileAmérica CESOC, 1995.

Cavallo, Ascanio, Manuel Salazar Saldo, and Oscar Sepúlveda Pacheco. *La historia oculta del regimen militar: Chile 1973–1988*. Santiago: Grijalbo, 1997.

Childress, Diana. *Augusto Pinochet's Chile*. Minneapolis, Minn.: Twenty-First Century Books, 2009.

Cmiel, Kenneth. "The Emergence of Human Rights Politics in the United States." *Journal of American History* 86, no. 3 (December 1999): 1231–50.

Collins, Cath. "Chile a más de dos décadas de justicia de transición." *Revista de Ciencia Política* 51, no. 2 (2013): 79–113.

"Human Rights Defense in and through the Courts in (Post) Pinochet Chile." *Radical History Review* 2016, no. 124 (January 2016): 129–40.

———. "Human Rights Trials in Chile during and after the 'Pinochet Years.'" *International Journal of Transitional Justice* 4, no. 1 (March 2010): 67–86.

Collins, Cath, Katherine Hite, and Alfredo Joignant, eds. *The Politics of Memory in Chile: From Pinochet to Bachelet*. Boulder, Colo.: First Forum Press, 2013.

Committee on Government Operations, U.S. House of Representatives. *Alleged Violations of U.S. Aviation Laws and Regulations by LAN Chile Airlines*. House Report 720. Washington, D.C.: U.S. Government Printing Office, 1980.

Contreras Sepúlveda, Manuel. *La verdad histórica: El ejército guerrillero*. Santiago: Ediciones Encina, 2000.

Del Solar, Edmundo. *Orlando Letelier: Biographical Notes and Comments*. Translated by Caridad Inda and Maria del Solar. New York: Vantage Press, 1978.

Díaz Nieva, José. *Patria y Libertad: La vanguardia juvenil contra Allende*. Madrid: Ediciones Barbarroja, 2013.

Didion, Joan. *Vintage Didion*. New York: Vintage Books, 2004.

Dinges, John. *The Condor Years: How Pinochet and His Allies Brought Terrorism to Three Continents*. New York: New Press, 2004.

Dinges, John, and Saul Landau. *Assassination on Embassy Row*. New York: Pantheon Books, 1980.

Dos Santos, Theotonio. *Socialismo o fascismo: El nuevo carácter de la dependencia y el dilema latinoamericano*. Santiago: Editorial Edicol, 1978.

Doyle, Kate. "Creative Justice." *NACLA Report on the Americas* 49, no. 1 (2017): 11–14.

Encinosa, Enrique. *Unvanquished: Cuba's Resistance to Fidel Castro*. Los Angeles: Pureplay Press, 2004.

Ercilla. *Caso Letelier: El crimen que estremeció al mundo*. Santiago: Ercilla, 1991.

Etchepare, Jaime Antonio, and Hamish I. Stewart. "Nazism in Chile: A Particular Type of Fascism in South America." *Journal of Contemporary History* 30, no. 4 (October 1995): 577–605.

Freed, Donald, and Fred Simon Landis. *Death in Washington: The Murder of Orlando Letelier*. Westport, Conn.: Lawrence Hill, 1980.

Fuentes Wendling, Manuel. *Memorias secretas de Patria y Libertad y algunas confesiones sobre la Guerra Fría en Chile*. Santiago: Editorial Grijalbo, 1999.

Gonzales-Pando, Miguel. *The Cuban Americans*. Westport, Conn.: Greenwood Press, 1998.

Harmer, Tanya. *Allende's Chile and the Inter-American Cold War*. Chapel Hill: University of North Carolina Press, 2011.

Huneeus, Carlos. *Chile, un país dividido: La actualidad del pasado*. Santiago: Catalonia, 2003.

Kami, Hideaki. "Diplomacy and Human Migration: A History of U.S. Relations with Cuba during the Late Cold War." Ph.D. diss., Ohio State University, 2015.

Kelly, Patrick William. *Sovereign Emergencies: Latin America and the Making of Global Human Rights Politics*. Cambridge: Cambridge University Press, 2018.

Keys, Barbara. *Reclaiming American Virtue: The Human Rights Revolution of the 1970s*. Cambridge, Mass.: Harvard University Press, 2014.

Kornbluh, Peter. *The Pinochet File: A Declassified Dossier on Atrocity and Accountability.* New York: New Press, 2003.

Letelier, Fabiola. "I Think I Have Struggled in People's Real Interests. So I Am Content, Even If I Don't Live to See the Final Victory." *NACLA Report on the Americas* 20, no. 5 (September–December 1986): 51–55.

Letelier, Orlando. *Chile: Economic "Freedom" and Political Repression.* London: Institute of Race Relations, 1976.

Letelier, Orlando, and Michael Moffitt. *The International Economic Order.* Washington, D.C.: Transnational Institute, 1977.

McSherry, Patrice. *Predatory States: Operation Condor and Covert War in Latin America.* Lanham, Md.: Rowman and Littlefield, 2005.

———. "Tracking the Origins of a State Terror Network: Operation Condor." *Latin American Perspectives* 29 (January 2002): 38–60.

Méndez, José Luis. *Bajo las alas del CONDOR.* Buenos Aries: Cartago ediciones, 2006.

———. *Los años del terror (1974–1976): Una historia no revelada.* Habana: Editorial de Ciencias Sociales, 2006.

———. *Los cuervos del imperio: Terrorismo desde Estados Unidos contra Cuba.* La Habana: Editora Política, 2003.

Morley, Morris H., and Chris McGillion. *Reagan and Pinochet: The Struggle over U.S. Policy toward Chile.* New York: Cambridge University Press, 2015.

Mount, Graeme S. *Chile and the Nazis: From Hitler to Pinochet.* Montreal: Black Rose Books, 2002.

Naftali, Timothy. *Blind Spot: The Secret History of American Counterterrorism.* New York: Basic Books, 2005.

Oppenheim, Lois Hecht. *Politics in Chile: Democracy, Authoritarianism, and the Search for Development.* Boulder, Colo.: Westview Press, 1993.

O'Shaughnessy, Hugh. *Pinochet: The Politics of Torture.* New York: New York University Press, 2000.

Oyarzún, María Eugenia. *Augusto Pinochet: Diálogos con su historia. Conversaciones inéditas.* Santiago: Ediciones Sudamericana, 1999.

Peña, Juan Cristóbal, and Miguel Ángel Tobar. "Manuel Contreras, 'El Mamo.'" In *Los malos*, edited by Guerriero, Leila, 17–55. Santiago: Universidad Diego Portales, 2015.

Phillips, Dion E. "Terrorism and Security in the Caribbean: The 1976 Cubana Disaster off Barbados." *Studies in Conflict and Terrorism* 14, no. 4 (1991): 209–19.

Pierce, Andrew Bell. "Miami's Municipal Diplomacy: Applying an Evaluation Model to the Foreign Affairs Activities of a Transnational City." Ph.D. diss., University of Miami, 2004.

Pollack, Marcelo. *The New Right in Chile, 1973–97.* New York: St. Martin's Press, 1999.

Prieto, Yolanda. *The Cubans of Union City: Immigrants and Exiles in a New Jersey Community.* Philadelphia: Temple University Press, 2009.

Renouard, Joe. *Human Rights in American Foreign Policy: From the 1960s to the Soviet Collapse.* Philadelphia: University of Pennsylvania Press, 2016.

Report of the Chilean National Commission on Truth and Reconciliation (Rettig Report). Notre Dame, Ind.: University of Notre Dame Press, 1993.

Rodríguez Castañeda, Rafael. *El asesinato de Orlando Letelier.* México: Proceso, 1979.

Salazar Salvo, Manuel. *Contreras: Historia de un intocable.* Santiago: Grijalbo, 1995.

———. *Roberto Thieme: El rebelde de Patria y Libertad*. Santiago: Editorial Mare Nostrum, 2007.
Schoultz, Lars. *Human Rights and United States Policy toward Latin America*. Princeton, N.J.: Princeton University Press, 1981.
Sikkink, Kathryn. *Mixed Signals: U.S. Human Rights Policy and Latin America*. Ithaca, N.Y.: Cornell University Press, 2004.
Stern, Steve J. *Battling for Hearts and Minds: Memory Struggles in Pinochet's Chile, 1973–1988*. Durham, N.C.: Duke University Press, 2006.
———. *Reckoning with Pinochet: The Memory Question in Democratic Chile, 1989–2006*. Durham, N.C.: Duke University Press, 2010.
Talbot, David. *The Devil's Chessboard: Allen Dulles, the CIA, and the Rise of America's Secret Government*. New York: HarperCollins, 2015.
Varas, Florencia, and Claudio Orrego. *El caso Letelier*. Santiago: Editorial Aconcagua Colección Lautaro, 1979.
Vial, Gonzalo. *Pinochet: La biografía*. Santiago: El Mercurio, 2002.
Viñas, David. *Qué es el fascismo en Latinoamérica*. Barcelona: La Gaya Ciencia, 1977.
Volk, Steven S. "The Politics of Memory and the Memory of Politics." *NACLA Report on the Americas* 46, no. 3 (2013): 18–22.
Weeks, Greg. *The Military and Politics in Postauthoritarian Chile*. Tuscaloosa: University of Alabama Press, 2003.
Weld, Kirsten. "The Spanish Civil War and the Construction of a Counterrevolutionary Historical Consciousness in Pinochet's Chile." Paper presented at the American Historical Association conference, Denver, Colo., January 7, 2017.

INDEX

Page numbers in italics refer to photographs.

ABC, 125
Abourezk, James, 41, 62, 66, 105, 148
Abrams, Elliott, 221, 229, 245
"Abscam" case, 107
Accuracy in Media, 187
Action Committee on the Letelier-Moffitt Assassinations, 160
Acuña, Manuel, 167
Adam Metal Supply, 73
AFL-CIO, 203
Air Force Academy (Santiago), 41
Alfa Omega, 250
Algonquin Hotel, 95
Alien Tort Statute, 295
Allende, Beatrice "Tati," 159–60
Allende, Hortensia, *139*, 148–49
Allende, Salvador, 1, 29, 32, 51, 57, 63, 66, 122, 203, 227–28, 282; coup against, 35–40, 62, 89, 251; presidency of, 45, 50, 87, 153
Alpha 66, 77
Alvear, Soledad, 269
American Airlines, 46, 111
American Chemists Association, 75
American-Chilean Council, 64
American Civil Liberties Union, 62
American University, 66, 69, 293
America's Most Wanted, 237–38
Amnesty International, 41, 61, 63
Amnesty Law of 1978, 252, 259, 275, 282, 294
Anaconda Copper Mining Company, 217
Anderson, Jack, 159
Andrews Air Force Base, 232
Angola, 88
Anschluss of Austria, 24
anticommunism, 25, 47, 48, 50, 88, 107, 159, 219

anti-Pinochet forces, 150
anti-Semitism, 25, 59, 85
Archbishop of Santiago, 270
Argentina, 221, 275; bombings by CORU in, 88; Chile's border dispute with, 215–16; democracy in, 220; "the disappeareds," 108; FBI in, 253
Arica, Chile, 26
Arria, Diego, 42–43, 70, *131*
Ashbrook, John, 105
Asner, Edward, 61
Association for the Disappeared and Detained, 272
Asunción, Paraguay, 90
Atacama Desert, 23
Avedon, Richard, 69
Avery Fisher Hall, bombing of, 179
Aylwin, Patricio, 224, 260; Amnesty Law and, 252; appointees to Supreme Court, 267; ascension of, 243, 248, 251, 258; attends Orlando's burial at Central Cemetery, 248; Chilean military and, 249; petitions Chilean Supreme Court to appoint special prosecuting justice, 260; reaction to indictments of Contreras and Espinoza, 262; response to Rettig Report, 243–44; writes private letter of assurance to George H. W. Bush, 246
Aylwin doctrine, 252
Aylwin government, agrees to compensation in principle, 246

Bachelet, Michelle, 290
Baez, Joan, 61, 69, 95–96, *137*, 147, 149, 159, 196
Badenstein (ship), 202
Balaguer, Joaquín, 87

Bañados, Adolfo, 260–64, 265, 267, 271, 275, 276
Barcella, Lawrence, 107, 164–65, 194, 203, 211, 213, 221, 229, 288, 289
Barnes, Betsey, 222
Barnes, Harry, 222, 230, 231, 233–34, 259–60
Barnet, Ann, 6
Barnet, Richard, 65, 67–68, 150
Barros, José Miguel, 235–36
Bay of Pigs, 76–78
BBC, 85
Beagle Channel, 215–16, 219
Bell, Griffin, 114, 123, 162
Bergenline Avenue, 80–81, 177
Berman, Howard, 245
Berríos, Eugenio, 264–65, 291
bin Laden, Osama, 8
Bitar, Sergio, 39, 270, 296
"Black Tuesday," 276–78
Bolivia, 23, 216, 220
Bonao, Dominican Republic, 87–88
Borosage, Robert, 150, 186
Bórquez, Israel, 208–13, 216
Bosch, Orlando, 78, 83–84, 87–88, 109, 110
Bottom of the Barrel restaurant, Union City, 95
Brademas, John, 148
Brazil, 27, 61, 220, 264
Brieant, Charles, 192–93
Brigade 2506 Association, 77
Bryan, William Jennings, 246
Bryan Commission, 246–47
Brzezinski, Zbigniew, 162, 215, 218
Buckley, William F., 64, 160, 176
Buenos Aires, Argentina, 108
Buffone, Sam, 163, 188–93, 238, 244–46, 272, 292
Burton, John, 192
Bush, George H. W., 91, 109, 245, 246–47, 259–60, 263
Bush, George W., 287–88, 292
Bush, Jeb, 287
Bush (George H. W.) administration, 224
Bustos, Juan, 261, 268–69

Cabello, Winston, 284, 285
Cabello-Barrueto, Zita, 284

California College of Arts and Crafts, 156
Callejas, Inés. *See* Callejas de Townley, Mariana (Inés)
Callejas de Townley, Mariana (Inés), 46, 51–53, 56, 59, 83–85, 89–90, 99–101, 132, 166–67, 173, 253; Allan Earnest and, 49; as Chilean "Tokyo Rose," 54; death of, 286; DINA and, 57–59; Fatherland and Freedom movement and, 54; first marriage of, 48; held at gunpoint by Cuban exiles, 84; indicted for Soria murder, 286; Jews and, 59; literary salons and, 58; not called as a witness at trial, 178; the press and, 167; under protection of U.S. marshals, 176; returns to Chile, 183–84; sentenced for Prats murder, 286; Townley and, 48–49, 57, 59, 170–71, 184; Vietnam War protests and, 50; in Witness Protection Program, 182; year on kibbutz, 49
Canada, 158
Canete, Ricardo, 114–16
Carabineros, 35
Caracas, 17, 42–43, 49, 67–68, 70, 77, 83, 110–11, 149–50, 154, 161, 253
Caravan of Death, 34, 88, 284, 285
Carlitos, 276
Carter, Jimmy, 62, 117–20, 148, 158, 162, 163, 213, 214, 294; excludes Chile from Unitas 21 exercises, 219; failure to follow through on threats, 219; sanctions Chile, 218, 219; signs Presidential Security Memorandum 30, 223; U.S.-Chilean relations and, 217–18
Carter, Rosalynn, 162
Carter administration, 216; Pinochet regime and, 220–21
Carvajal, Patricio, 123, 124, 168–69
case 192–78. *See* passports-homicide case
Castillo, Jaime, 228, 235, 237, 242, 260
Castro, Fidel, 27, 73, 77, 81, 88, 114, 160, 286, 287
Castro, René, 156
Castro government, 181
Castro Revolution, 75–76
Catholic Church, 220, 227
Catholicism, 25

366   Index

Cauas, Jorge, 123, 124, 125, 165
CBS, 125
Cemetery del Este, 150
Center for Constitutional Rights, 295
Center for Justice and Accountability, 284, 295
Central Intelligence Agency (CIA), 27, 87–88, 91, 106, 117–18, 159–61, 168, 187, 206, 208–9, 215; accused by Pinochet of orchestrating protests, 234–35; accused of assassinating Letelier, 178, 185, 202, 263–64, 273; under Bush (George H. W.), 109–10; Bush (George H. W.) and, 263; collaboration with Chilean right, 109; Contreras, Manuel, and, 245; Cuban exiles and, 74, 76–78, 84; Fernández and, 229; human rights violations and, 118; identifies anti-American campaign in Chile, 203; Letelier investigation and, 295; Operation Condor and, 45–46; "Pinochet's Role in the Letelier Assassination and Subsequent Coverup," 223–24; subpoena and, 161–62; terrorism and, 75, 222; Townley and, 52–53; training, 75–76; Western Hemisphere division, 46
Chase Manhattan Bank, 217
Chateau Renaissance motel, North Bergen, N.J., 98
Chavez, Cesar, 50, 187
CHILBOM team, 110
Chile, 1, 8, 23, 32, 62, 88, 114; accepts ruling of Bryan Commission, 247; anti-American campaign in, 203; arms sales to, 244; assets in the U.S., 190–91; civil liberties in, 214–15; civil suit against Chile, 187–89; coup in, 66; cover-up by, 199–213, 231; curfew in, 242; democracy in, 272–73, 277; economy of, 21, 25, 45, 57, 68, 220, 251; end of cover-up by, 225–39; excluded from Unitas 21, 219; far right Germans in, 24; fascism in, 25; Fernández's defection and, 233–34; former Nazi officers in, 24; German population of, 24; human rights groups in, 69, 153, 158, 275; human rights violations and, 122, 205, 219, 223, 240, 252, 262; justice system of, 200, 210–11, 236 (*see also* Chilean Supreme Court); Letelier legal case in, 225–39, 251–67, 267–80 (*see also* passports-homicide case); Letelier-Moffitt civil case against, 245–47, 295; Letelier-Moffitt families' demands from, 245–47; Letelier-Moffitt legal case in, 245–47, 295; Ministry of Defense, 35, 169, 205; Ministry of Foreign Relations, 119, 259; Ministry of Justice, 185, 199; named as responsible party for assassination of Letelier and Moffitt, 190, 193; national security doctrine, 27; Nazis in, 23–28; open to compensating Letelier-Moffitt families, 245–47; Pinochet dictatorship in, 251–53; political prisoners in, 118, 220; protests in, 146, 214–15; public opinion in, 203; "reconciliation" in, 248; records in, 116; refuses to cooperate in Letelier-Moffitt case, 203–5; rejects expulsion request, 235; repression in, 240; resistance to extradition, 199–213; responsibility for car bomb, 246, 252; Rettig Report and, 243; return of democracy in, 248; second truth commission in, 290; September 11, 1973, coup, 83; torture in, 220; U.S. aid to, 205, 245–46 (*see also* U.S.-Chilean relations); U.S. policy toward, 214–24 (*see also* U.S.-Chilean relations); women in, 158. *See also* Pinochet regime
Chilean Congress, 243, 246–47, 249
Chilean Constitution, Article 24, 234
Chilean military, 84; appeal of Contreras and Espinoza and, 270–71, 272; Aylwin and, 249; "Black Tuesday" and, 276–78; Contreras's defiance and, 274; Pinochet and, 249; Punta Peuco and, 281; receives eight seats in Chilean Senate, 249. *See also specific officers*
Chilean military academies, 26
Chilean press, 165–67, 185–86, 203, 208–10, 212. *See also specific publications*
Chileans, German, 12, 23–25, 30
Chilean secret police, 106. *See also* National Intelligence Directorate; National Information Center

Index   367

Chilean Senate, 249
Chilean Socialist Party, 159, 187, 241, 269
Chilean Supreme Court, 146, 185, 211, 234, 258; appeal of Contreras and Espinoza, 266, 267, 268; appeals hearing in, 212–13; appoints *ministro instructor*, 260; "Black Tuesday" and, 277; bomb scare at, 270; Callejas de Townley and, 286; denial of extradition by, 216, 217–19, 223, 226; passports-homicide case and, 200, 258; pretrial hearing in, 262; questions submitted to, 235–36; rejects calls for *ministro en visita*, 259; rejects closing of Letelier-Moffitt case, 260; rejects Contreras's final appeal, 280; reopens Letelier-Moffitt case, 260–61; request for extradition and, 208–13; response to Fabiola Letelier's appeal, 228; rules that Amnesty Law no longer applies to cases of disappeared, 284–85; sentences for Contreras, 283; shortens sentences of Contreras and Espinoza, 275; stacking of, 260; trial of Contreras and Espinoza, 260–66, 267–75; upholds sentences of Contreras and Espinoza, 271–72
Chile Chico, 18, 19, 20, 72, 97
Chile Committee for Human Rights, 69, 153, 158
Chile Legislative Center, 147
Chile-Peru treaty, 216
Christian Democratic Party, 69, 227, 228, 274
Christopher, Warren, 123–25, 204, 205, 206
Church, Frank, 217
Citibank, 217
civil liability, human rights violations and, 295
Clinton, Bill, 293
Cmiel, Kenneth, 61, 62
CNI. *See* National Information Center
CNM. *See* Cuban Nationalist Movement
CNN Chile, 283
CODELCO, 90, 201
Cold War, 7, 8, 47, 117, 224, 293–94
Collins, Cath, 294
Colombian drug cartels, 83
Colonia (2015 film), 25

Colony of Dignity, 25, 33, 53
"Committee of 75," 181
Committees for Assistance to the Defense of Manuel Contreras, 207
Communism, 21, 32, 50, 83, 85, 176, 184, 206
Communist Party, 148, 268
compensation, 189–90, 243–48, 252, 290
Concertación political alliance, 270
Concutelli, Pier Luigi, 281
Congressional Record, 159
conservatives, appeal of Contreras and Espinoza and, 272
conspiracy theories, 85, 114, 178–79
Contreras, Manuel. *See* Contreras Sepúlveda, Juan Manuel Guillermo
Contreras, Manuel, Jr. (Manolito), 28, 32–33, 249–50, 261, 270, 276, 283
Contreras, Maruja. *See* Valdebenito, María Teresa
Contreras Sepúlveda, Juan Manuel Guillermo, 26–35, 45–46, 58–59, 88–91, 94, 108, 115–17, 145, 168, 196, 352n54; accuses CIA of involvement in assassinations, 263–64, 273; appeal to the Supreme Court, 266, 267–75; arrest of, 199; asks for passports for Williams and Romeral, 205; attempts to blackmail U.S. government, 245; barred from leaving the country, 261; "Black Tuesday" and, 276–77; childhood of, 25; CIA and, 206, 245; on CNN Chile, 283; Committees for Assistance to the Defense of Manuel Contreras, 207; death of, 283–84; defiance of, 249–51, 253, 260, 261–66, 273–76, 282; delaying tactics by, 263; detainment of, 280, 281; DINA and, 32, 83, 119–21, 236, 249; failed extradition request against, 214, 233, 234, 254; feels untouchable, 249–51; Fernández and, 201–2, 209, 225; forced resignation of, 206–7; freed from Santiago Military Hospital, 213; under house arrest in daughter's home, 282; implicates Pinochet, 201–2, 291–92; imprisonment of, 294; indicted for assassination of Prats and his wife, 282; indictment of, 175, 199, 261–62; insurance

policy crafted by, 202–3; Lagos and, 254, 258; at large, 239; Letelier-Moffitt families' demands from Chile and, 245–46; loss of DINA post and, 250; memoirs published by, 282; mother of, 26; named as coconspirator by Townley, 174; Nazis and, 33; no bail set for, 210; obsession with his legal standing and legacy, 282–83; on the outs, 168; in Penal Cordillera, 283; Pinochet and, 168, 169, 189, 201, 202, 206–7, 223, 262, 270, 291–92, 307n5; Prats murder and, 286; pretrial hearing and, 262; Punta Peuco and, 279–80, 281, 282, 283; reaction to losing appeal, 273–74; request for extradition of, 199–213; resistance to extradition, 199–213; response to Pinochet's death, 292; role in cover-up, 231; at Santiago Military Hospital, 209, 210; satisfaction with extradition decision, 211; Scherrer interviews, 113; sentence of, 265; stupidity of, 296; testimony of, 210; threatens to blackmail U.S. government, 206; Townley and, 166–67, 173, 174, 182; trial of, 263–64, 265; U.S. asks Chile to arrest and expel Contreras and Espinoza, 234–35; U.S. assets frozen, 189; U.S. bank accounts held by, 191; in Washington, 163; under watch at Santiago Military Hospital, 205; wins request to dismiss passport investigation, 228

Coordinator of United Revolutionary Organizations (CORU), 88

Copiapó, Chile, 285

Coquimbo, Chile, 48

Cornick, Carter, 112–13, 151, 161, 163, 168–69, 171, 173, 174, 211, 288, 295; co-founds Counter Terrorism Consultants, 289; FBI Bomb Unit Terrorist Section, 108

counterterrorism, 223, 231, 286, 295, 296

Counter Terrorism Consultants, Inc., 288

Cox, Ralph, 217

Cuba, 79, 158, 181; idea of invading, 77; normalization of relations with, 78; trade embargo and, 78. *See also* Cuban exiles

Cubana Airlines Flight 455, bombing of, 109–10

Cuban Action, 77

Cuban American National Foundation, 286, 287

Cuban Americans, 78, 123; Letelier-Moffitt case and, 286–88; testimony of, 260; at trial, 176–77. *See also* Cuban exiles; *specific Cuban exiles*

Cuban Consulate in New York, 74

Cuban counterrevolution, globalization of, 79

Cuban exiles, 73–86, 90, 114, 119, 161, 165, 168, 178–79, 236–39; aggressiveness of, 180–81; arrest of, 172–73; car bombs and, 80; overturned convictions of, 194; DINA and, 85; indictments of, 175; named as coconspirators by Townley, 174; retrial of, 194–95; role in Orlando Letelier bombing, 99–100; subpoena of, 112; terrorism and, 78, 79, 80, 179–82; trained by CIA, 78; trial of, 178, 186, 210, 232; verdict against, 178, 186. *See also specific Cuban exiles*

Cuban Mission to the United Nations, bombing of, 179, 181

Cuban Nationalist Movement (CNM), 77, 84–86, 88, 98, 116, 167–68, 179, 180, 238; assassination conspiracy and, 114; bombings by, 179–81; extortion and, 82; Griffin Bell and, 114; hitting targets outside of Cuba, 79–81; members in Chile, 116; Novo brothers and, 80. *See also specific members*

Cuban National Liberation Front, 77

"Cuba Uber Alles" (Cuba before all), 78, 81

Cubillos, Hernán, 204, 209, 213, 218–19

Cumplido, Francisco, 259

"Cumplido Laws," 259, 260

Cuthbert, Sofia, car bombing of, 59

Dade County, 77

Daily World, 147

Dartmouth University, 107

Davis, Angela, 69

Dawson Island, 36, 38–40, 99, 154, 227

Days of National Protest, 220, 242

de-Chilenization, 24

Defense Intelligence Agency, 105

Defense Ministry, 35, 116
Delle Chiaie, Stefano, 44, 59
democracy, 8, 82, 96, 208, 218, 234; in Chile, 22, 68, 222, 234, 241, 243, 248, 251, 269–70, 272–73, 277–78; "democracy promotion," 221; Townley and Callejas on, 54–55; "protected," 220
Democracy in Chile Act, 222
De Paul University, 163
Derian, Patricia, 62, 218
"The Dialogue," 181
Diario de la Marina, 75, 77
Didion, Joan, 74, 77
Diego Portales building, 121, 170
DINA. *See* National Intelligence Directorate
Dinges, John, 32, 89, 208, 294
diplomats, bombing investigation and, 117–24
"the disappeared," 147, 158, 241, 264; Amnesty Law and, 284–85; families of, 262, 268; investigation of in Chile, 252
District of Columbia police, 108–9
Dominican Republic, 87, 227
Dow Chemical, 217
Dupont Circle, anti-Pinochet rally at, 147–48

Earnest, Allan, 49, 59
Ecuador, 31
Ecuadoriana Airlines, 171
El Caimán, 82
El Ché. *See* Guevara, Ché
El Cronista, 208
Eleventh World Festival of Youth and Studies in Cuba, 156
Elizabeth II (queen), 216
El Mamo. *See* Contreras Sepúlveda, Juan Manuel Guillermo
El Mercurio, 119, 164–65, 203
El Nacional, 110–11
El Nacionalista, 80
El Salvador, 62
Enyart, Kenneth. *See* Townley, Michael
Ercilla (magazine), 280
Errázuriz, Hernán Felipe, 234
Espinoza Bravo, Pedro, 34–35, 57, 83, 88–90, 93, 100–101, 115, *145*, 196, 225, 249, 260; appeal to the Supreme Court, 266, 267–75; barred from leaving the country, 261; "Black Tuesday" and, 277–78; confession of, 201; Contreras and, 264; delaying tactics by, 263; Fernández and, 200–201; imprisonment of, 294; indictment of, 175, 199, 261–62; Lagos and, 252–55; Letelier-Moffitt families' demands from Chile and, 245–46; named as coconspirator by Townley, 174; no bail set for, 210; in Penal Cordillera, 284; pretrial hearing and, 262; public statement by, 273; Punta Peuco and, 279, 281, 283, 284; request for extradition of, 200–213, 214, 233, 234, 254; role in cover-up, 231; at Santiago Military Hospital, 205, 213; sentences of, 265, 284; testimony of, 209–10; trial of, 263–64; U.S. asks Chile to arrest and expel Contreras and Espinoza, 234–35
"espousal," 245
Etcheberry, Alfredo, 200, 209, 210, 211, 212, 213, 229, 230
Evans-Novak "revelation," 161
Export-Import Bank, 218
"extrajudicial killing," 296
Exxon, 217

Falconbridge, 217
Fatherland and Freedom movement, 52–56, 81, 83, 203
Federal Aviation Administration (FAA), 192
Federal Bureau of Investigation (FBI), 74, 76–77, 81, 84, 97, 185, 205, 211, 223, 288, 293; in Argentina, 253; Cuban exiles and, 112, 116, 181; FBI Academy, 173; Fernández and, 231, 232; human rights violations and, 294; investigation of Townley, 167–68; IPS and, 150; Isabel Letelier and, 161; photo of mystery men leaked by, 164; Letelier-Moffitt case and, 2, 6, 8, 105–16, 117, 152, 158, 160–65, 167–69, 176, 179–80, 191, 295; New York Bomb and Terrorism Squad, 108; New York Division, 107–8; Novo and, 172–73; Paz and, 175, 180, 238–39; Propper leading investigation

by, 106–16, 119–20, 123–25, 158–59, 161–65, 168–75 (*see also* Letelier-Moffitt case); Suárez and, 175, 180; surveillance of Chilean embassy, 45; terrorism and, 79, 295; Townley and, 59, 191
Felt Forum, Madison Square Garden, 96
Fernández, Alfredo, 225, 232
Fernández, Rose Marie, 165
Fernández Larios, Armando, 34, 88, 90–95, 165, 166, 167, 168, 196, 201–2, 211, 225–26; after release from prison, 284; charged with kidnapping, 285, 290; Chile refuses to let U.S. interview, 203–5; Chile's request for extradition of, 285; civil lawsuit against, 284, 285; confession and interrogation of, 230–31; Contreras and, 201–2, 209; conveys remorse to Isabel Letelier, 233; defection of, 229–32, 255; denies involvement in Letelier assassination, 169; goes to DINA headquarters after Letelier killing, 200–201; indictments of, 175, 199, 285; Lagos and, 252–54, 257; on LAN-Chile plane, 191; meets with Pinochet, 205–6; named as coconspirator by Townley, 174; in Paraguay, 201; passport obtained by, 165, 290; penance of, 233; pleads guilty to acting as accessory after the fact, 232; potential of, to flip, 211; request for extradition of, 200–213, 254–55; at Santiago Military Hospital, 205, 213; testimony of, 209, 242
Fervic Corp., 284
Fisher, Beverly, 65
Fisk, Robert, 114
Fleetwood, Blake, 110
Florida, 46, 56, 77, 80, 101, 108, 168, 236, 238, 258, 259, 286–87, 295
Foggy Bottom, 118, 217, 218
Fonda, Jane, 61
Ford, Gerald, 62, 117–18, 120, 149
Fordham University Law School, 108
Ford Motor Company, 46, 54
Foreign Service, 91, 231
Foreign Service Institute, 18
Foreign Sovereign Immunities Act (FSIA), 188–89, 193, 245, 296

Forestier, Carlos, 121–22
forgetting, politics of, 252
Fort Belvoir, Virginia, 26
Fort Benning, Georgia, 26, 27
Fourth National Day of Protest, 242
Franco, Francisco, 45, 53, 81
Fraser, Don, 62
Frei, Eduardo, 267, 270, 271–72, 277, 280, 288
Fresno, Ana, 44–46
Friedman, Milton, 32, 123
Fuentes, Manuel, 54

García, Orlando, 78
Garzón, Baltasar, 289
Gavin, William, 239
Gawler's Funeral Home, 148
Geneson, David, 232
Germany, 24, 25, 60, 82
Gillespie, Charles, 247
Góngora, Elizabeth, 236–37
Goodyear, 217
Gordon, James, 153
Great Britain: arrest of Pinochet in, 288–90; bombings by Cuban exiles in, 79
Greathead, Scott, 260
Green, Joyce, 189–90, 193
gremialismo ("guildism"), 52
Guatemala, human rights violations in, 240
Guevara, Ché, 27, 73–74, 81
Guirado, Guido, 176–77
Gutiérrez, Nélida, 250, 276, 283
Guzmán, Juan, 285, 290

Haig, Alexander, 221
Haiti, 220, 240
Harkin, Tom, 62, 148, 216, 217, 218
Harkin Amendment to the Foreign Assistance Act, 63, 68
Harrington, Michael, 62, 160
Hart, Jeffrey, 160
Helms, Jesse, 159, 220
hijackings, 223
Hiriart, María Lucía, 31, 119
Hitler, Adolf, 24–25, 34, 78, 81
Holland, 69, 158
Hoover, J. Edgar, 45, 107

Horman, Charles, 240, 284
House Investigating Committee, 150
Hoy, 212
human rights, 8, 232, 296; in the Letelier case, 220–21, 294; transnational power of, 294–95. *See also* human rights movement
Human Rights Mobile Education Project, 158
human rights movement, 62–72, 137, 142, 259–60, 268, 275; impact of Letelier-Moffitt case on, 220–21, 294. *See also* human rights violations; *specific people and groups*
human rights violations, 240; in Chile, 252; CIA veto on reporting of, 118; civil liability and, 295; Cold War and, 293–94; downplayed in Chile as part of hierarchy, 251; FBI and, 294; in Guatemala, 240; justice for, 246, 252, 265, 293–94; by Pinochet regime, 205, 240, 243, 249, 251, 262, 283, 284; United States and, 240. *See also specific victims and perpetrators*
Human Rights Watch, 61
Humphrey, Hubert, 69, 105

Immigration and Naturalization Service, 287
Independent Democratic Union, 251
Institute for Policy Studies (IPS), 65, 68, 78, 87, 100–101, 106, 150, 153, 157–58, 161, 186, 212; Chilean exiles at, 151; fear of retaliation and, 186; Human Rights Project, 240; Letelier-Moffitt Special Recognition Award, 288; on obtaining Chilean government assets, 190; press conference after civil suit victory, 190; Sheridan Circle bombing and, 1–2, 5
Insurrectional Movement for Revolutionary Recovery, 77
Inter-American Development Bank, 16, 42, 69
International Commission of Jurists, 41
international law, 245, 247
International League for Human Rights, 259–60
International Red Cross, 40–41
international terrorism, 8, 190, 196, 207, 220, 222–24, 295–96

Iran, 27, 295–96
Iran-Contra scandal, Reagan administration and, 234
Irvine, Reed, 187
Ivan Shepetkov (ship), bombing of, 76

Jara, Víctor, 295
JM/WAVE, 77–78
John Paul II (pope), 234–35
Johnson, Lyndon, administration of, 222–23
Jones, David, 288
Jones, George, 229, 230, 231–32, 235
justice: human rights violations and, 220–21, 293–94; quest for, 187–96, 240–48, 252–66, 267–80; terrorism and, 293; tyrants and, 293

Kaminsky, Sherman, 194
Karpen, Harry, 152
Karpen, Hilda, 6, 64–65, 151–52
Karpen, Michael, 292
Karpen, Murray, 64–66, 151–52, 234, 244, 247, 289, 292
Karpen, Ronni. *See* Moffitt, Ronni Karpen
Karpen family, 252, 292
KCIA, 295–96
Kennedy, Edward, 62–63, 68, 78, 87, 105, 123, 142, 203, 217, 218, 220, 222, 245–47
Kennedy, John F., 77. *See also* Bay of Pigs
Kennedy administration, 65, 78, 222–23
Kennedy-Harkin amendment, repeal of, 220
Kennedy International Airport, 94, 111; bombing at, 180; LAN-Chile planes at, 190–91
Kennedy Library, 80
Kent State, 65
Keys, Barbara, 61
King Solomon's cemetery, Clifton, N.J., 151–52
Kingston, Jamaica, bombings by Cuban exiles in, 79
Kirkpatrick, Jeane, 219, 228
Kissinger, Henry, 42, 46, 54, 62–63, 78, 93, 117, 213
Kleiboemer, Axel, 229, 231, 232
Kornbluh, Peter, 187, 268

Kozak, Michael, 245
Ku Klux Klan, Chilean branch of, 25

Lafourcade, Enrique, 48
Lagos, Mónica. *See* Lagos Aguirre, Luisa Mónica
Lagos, Ricardo, 290
Lagos Aguirre, Diana, 93
Lagos Aguirre, Luisa Mónica, 92–95, 101, 144, 252–59, 261
Lally, Richard, 192
LAN-Chile, 87, 94, 99, 190–93, 244
Landau, George, 91, 120, 123, *136*, 150–51, 161, 168–69, 171, 199–200, 202, 204–5, 217–19; on Bórquez decision, 211; request for extradition of Contreras, Fernández, and Espinoza and, 208–9
Landau, Rebecca, 150
Landau, Saul, 68, 78, 87, 89, 150, 155, 158, 161–62, 178, 195, 240, 292
Lane and Edson, 212
La Segunda, 204
Las Señoras de Dawson, 41
Lasker, Morris, 192–93
La Tercera, 119, 203, 273
"legat" (legal attaché), 108
Leigh Guzmán, Gustavo, 36–37, 215
Leighton, Bernardo, 44–46, 69, 85–86, 89, 97, 188, 281, 286
Leigner, Beverly Ann, 313n78
Leiva, Fernando, 227
Lennox Islands, 215–16
lesa humanidad (crimes against humanity), 282
Letelier, Cecilia, 7
Letelier, Cristián, 7, *146*, 155, 247, 267, 292–93
Letelier, Francisco "Pancho," 7, 29, 42, 70, *146*, 153, 155–57, 226–27, 238, 240–42, 292–93; appeal of Contreras and Espinoza and, 267; Letelier-Moffitt Human Rights Award and, 294; reaction to Pinochet's arrest, 289; receives compensation from Chile, 247; on reversal in civil suit, 193
Letelier, Isabel, 83, 99, 108, 113, 117–18, *139*, *142*, 199, 228, 234, 238, 290, 293; advocates sanctions against Chile, 217; after

Orlando's assassination, 147–50, 153–63; after the coup, 35–38; during Allende presidency, 16–22; appeal of Contreras and Espinoza and, 267, 272; attends trial, 177–78; barred from Chile, 240; Chilean exiles and, 157; Chilean journalists and, 185–86; civil suit and, 244; with commemorative plaque, *141*; as director of Third World Women's Project, 157; in exile in Venezuela, 43; fear of retaliation and, 186; and Fernández, 233; files for restoration of Orlando's nationality, 184–85; follows extradition saga in Chile, 207; haunted by Orlando's murder, 240–41; IPS and, 157, 240; as judgment creditor, 190, 193; on LAN-Chile trial, 193; Letelier-Moffitt Human Rights Award and, 294; life in exile before bombing, 68–70; meeting with FBI, 161; meets with subsecretary of Ministry of Justice, 185; Novo-Ross trial and, 177–78, 186; on Orlando's Chilean citizenship stripped, 95–97; patience of, 240; Paz and, 287; post-traumatic stress disorder and, 186–87; press coverage of visit to Chile, 185–86; quest for justice and, 158, 187–96, 240–48, 296; reaction to Bórquez's racial slurs, 212; receives compensation from Chile, 247; reopening of passports-homicide case and, 258; requests banning of private loans, 218; response to acquittals of Cubans, 196; response to Pinochet's death, 292; retires to Santiago, 243; return of nationality to Orlando and, 248; returns to Chile, 184–86, 242–43; right-wing propagandists and, 187; Rojas and, 222; Scherrer and, 288; shaming power over U.S. government, 294; Sheridan Circle bombing and, 1–2, 5–7; slander against, 186–87; smear campaign against, 159; speech on extradition issue, 207–8; Suárez's arrest and, 237; survivor's guilt and, 186–87; takes the stand at trial, 178; Ted Kennedy and, 245–46; testimony of, 194; travels in U.S., 158; views of Pinochet, 29–30; while Orlando in prison, 40–42

Index 373

Letelier, José Ignacio, 155, 240, 241, 293; appeal of Contreras and Espinoza and, 267, 272; receives compensation from Chile, 247; return of democracy in Chile and, 248

Letelier, Juan Pablo, 7, 37–38, 41, 68, 70, 146, 156, 235, 239–40, 246, 248, 269; accused of bribery, 293; appeal of Contreras and Espinoza and, 267, 272; arrest in Chile, 241, 242; "Black Tuesday" and, 278; calls for *ministro en visita*, 259; in Chilean senate, 293; Contreras's defiance and, 274–75; reaction to indictments of Contreras and Espinoza, 261; receives compensation from Chile, 247; returns to Chile, 241, 242–43; runs for seat in Chilean legislature, 243; speaks to media, 242–43

Letelier, Nicolette, 146

Letelier, Orlando. *See* Letelier del Solar, Marco Orlando

Letelier, Orlando (grandson of Orlando), 241

Letelier del Solar, Fabiola, 41–42, 145, 154, 226–28, 235–37, 242, 247, 258–59, 263, 270, 280, 293; appeal of Contreras and Espinoza and, 267, 272; arrest of Pinochet and, 289–90; on Berríos's disappearance, 264–65; calls for *ministro en visita*, 259; comes to U.S. for trial, 176; Contreras's defiance and, 275; decries "total impunity" of Pinochet regime, 262; quest for justice and, 265; reaction to indictments of Contreras and Espinoza, 261, 262

Letelier del Solar, Marco Orlando, 34–39, 44–46, 64–67, 83, 85–88, 93, 98–99, 111, 147–48, 151, 153; affairs of, 70, 313n78; during Allende presidency, 16–22; as ambassador to U.S., 129; appointment as Allende's Minister of Defense, 29; arrest of, 130; Beatrice Allende and, 159, 160; briefcase found in car, 159–61; burial of in Venezuela, 149; Chevelle (car) and, 110; childhood of, 11; Chilean exiles and, 69; commemorative plaque, 141, 187; courtship of, 14–16; in Cuba, 128; Cuban exiles and, 98; declared victim of terrorism by DINA, 243; dedication of statue to, 146; diplomacy of, 117–24; exile in Venezuela, 43, 131; expulsion from Chile, 43; funeral for, 148; H4 visa and, 69; in Holland, 69; imprisoned by Pinochet, 40–42; IPS and, 68; justice for, 180; Lagos and, 252; legacy of, 222; letter to *New York Times*, 96; life in exile before bombing, 68–70; loss of Chilean citizenship, 95–96, 101, 119; marriage to Isabel, 16, 127; memorial for, 139; mural honoring, 293; nationality restoration and, 184–85; reinterment in Central Cemetery, Santiago, 248; released from prison, 42–43; return of nationality to, 248; smear campaign against, 159–61; speech at benefit concert, 137; statue honoring, 293; surveillance of, 99, 144; targeting of, 87–101; threats against, 96–97; youth of, 13–14, 126. *See also* Letelier-Moffitt case

Letelier diplomacy, 117–25

Letelier family, 156–57, 161, 260; appeal of Contreras and Espinoza and, 267, 272; appeals ruling on passport investigation, 228; calls for sanctions by, 222; closure and, 248; compensation for, 189–90, 245–48, 252; continued fight for justice, 240; Contreras's defiance and, 274–75; demands from Chile, 245–47; Lagos and, 253; petitions to reopen case 192-78, 235, 236, 237; reaction to indictments of Contreras and Espinoza, 262; return of democracy in Chile and, 248; return to Chile, 248; shaming power over U.S. government, 244, 294; Suárez's arrest and, 237. *See also specific family members*

Letelier-Moffitt case, 25, 46, 61, 70, 94, 105–16, 117–20, 123, 125, 150, 158, 162, 167–68, 183; changes how U.S. deals with international terrorism, 196; CHILBOM (code word), 109; in Chile, 251–52; Chilean cover-up of, 199–213; Chilean government and, 109, 187–89, 199–213, 244–47, 295; civil suit against Chile, 187–89, 244–47, 295; costs of investigation, 245; criminal case, 175–78,

188; Cuba-Chile connection theory, 112, 162; Cuban exiles and, 75–76, 80, 90, 109, 112, 162, 286–88; defeats and reversals in, 196; "definitive stay" appealed by Fabiola Letelier, 228; denial of extradition by Chile, 216–19, 223, 226; end of, 280; FBI and, 2, 6, 8, 105–16, 117, 152, 158, 160–65, 167–69, 176, 179–80, 191, 295; first charges in, 173–74; historical legacy of, 293–94; impact on human rights movement, 220–21, 294; international implications of, 108–9; investigation of in Chile, 252; lack of cooperation from Chile, 203–5; legal action, 187–96; legal precedents set by, 294, 296; media attention and, 165–67, 176, 187–96, 208, 209, 265, 268, 270, 271; political nature of, 252; prosecution of, 252; quest for justice, 187–96, 240–48, 252–66, 267–80; reversal in civil suit, 193; Sheridan Circle bombing, 1–8, 89–90; significant victories in, 196; South American connection, 162; statute of limitations and, 260; symbolism of, 262, 268–69; terrorism and, 196, 243; threats against investigators, 111; Townley's trial, 177–80; U.S. attempts to resolve, 244; U.S.-Chilean relations and, 244, 259–60; U.S. Justice Department and, 167–68. *See also* passports-homicide case

Letelier-Moffitt Human Rights Award, 157, 294

Letelier-Moffitt Memorial Fund for Human Rights, 163, 190

Letelier-Moffitt Special Recognition Award, 288

Levi, Edward, 161

Levine, Jack, 105

Libedinsky, Marcos, 200

Liebman, Marvin, 64

Lima, Peru, bombings by Cuban exiles in, 79

Linares, Marco, 253

Lipshutz, Robert, 162, 163

Little Havana, Miami, 77

Lo Curro, 58, 89, 170, 182, 183–84, 286, 291

London, Great Britain, bombings by Cuban exiles in, 79

Los Angeles Times, 112

Madariaga, Mónica, 199

Madrid, Spain, bombings by Cuban exiles in, 79

Mapocho River, 32

Mapuche, indigenous, 23, 240

Marées, Jorge González von, 24

María Teresa (ship), bombing of, 74

Marini, Leo, 250

Martí Insurrectional Movement, 77

Marxism, 52–53, 82, 119

Marxists, 15, 161, 210, 220

Mas Canosa, Jorge, 286

Matos, Húber, 76

Max Factor & Company, 75

McCarthy, Eugene, 50, 148

McDonald, Larry, 159

McGovern, George, 62, 148

McGrory, Mary, 221

McNeil, Francis, 206

Mena, Odlanier, 168, 170–71, 210

Meneses, Carlos, 271

Mérida, Mexico, bombings by Cuban exiles in, 79

Mexico, bombings in, 79, 88

Miami, Florida: bombings in, 79, 88; Cubans in, 77, 79

Military Club in Lo Curro, 291

Military Group, 218

Military School (Santiago), 28

military tribunals, 265

Miller, George, 62, 68, 148

Miranda Carrington, Sergio, 206, 273

Miró Cardona, José, 78

Missing (film), 221, 240

Mississippi Civil Liberties Union, 62

"Miss Nazi" contest, 25

Moffett, Toby, 62, 105

Moffitt, Michael, 1–7, 8, 64–68, 98, 100–101, 113, 142, 161, 163, 185, 234; advocates sanctions against Chile, 217; after Ronni's assassination, 151–53, 157–58, 163; appeal of Contreras and Espinoza and, 272; appointed receiver to run U.S. LAN-Chile operations, 192–93; civil suit and, 244; continued fight of, 244–48; follows extradition saga in Chile, 207; "International Economic Order Project,"

66; involvement with case begins to wane, 186; IPS and, 87; as judgment creditor, 190, 192–93; knowledge of Orlando's affair, 70; at Letelier-Moffitt memorial, 139; marriage to Ronni Karpen, 67; Marxism and, 66–67; Novo-Ross trial and, 186; quest for justice and, 120, 187–96; reaction to civil case victory, 190; reaction to ruling that civil case could proceed, 189; receives compensation from Chile, 247; requests banning of private loans, 218; response to indictments in case, 175–76; during Sheridan Circle bombing, 1–8; stays away from Letelier case in the 1990s, 292; survivor's guilt and, 186; Ted Kennedy and, 245–46; television interviews, 153; testimony of, 177; trauma suffered by, 244; on trials of Paz and Suárez, 239; wife's funeral and, 148–49

Moffitt, Paul, 66

Moffitt, Ronni Karpen, 7, 64–65, 100–101, 113, 117, 133, 147, 151; commemorative plaque, 141, 187; declared victim of terrorism by DINA, 243; funeral for, 148; investigation into assassination of, 292; justice for, 180; marriage to Michael Moffitt, 67; memorial for, 139; mural honoring, 293. *See also* Letelier-Moffitt case; Sheridan Circle bombing

Moffitt-Karpen families, 161; calls for sanctions by, 222; compensation for, 189–90, 245, 252; demands of Chile, 245–47

Molotov cocktail, 54

Montecina, Lilian, 96

Montero Marx, Enrique, 236

Montero-Silbert agreement, 170

Montevideo, Uruguay, 91

Montreal, bombings by Cuban exiles in, 74–75, 79

Moon, Reverend Sun Myung, 83

Morales, Ricardo, 78

Morel family, 30

Morel Gumucio, Isabel Margarita, 11, 243; courtship and marriage to Orlando, 14–16, 127; youth of, 11–13, 126. *See also* Letelier, Isabel

Morro Castle (Santiago, Cuba), 76
Moscoso, Mireya, 287
Los Muertos No Callan (The dead are not silent), 178
Music Carry Out, 65
Mussolini, Benito, 44, 81
My Lai, 61

Naftali, Tim, 223
Nation, 68
National Days of Protest, 242
National Identity Cabinet, 116
National Information Center (CNI), 119
National Intelligence Directorate (DINA), 105, 121; American-Chilean Council and, 64; Berríos and, 264–65; Callejas and, 56–57, 59; Callejas de Townley and, 286; Contreras and, 45, 207, 236, 250, 291; Cuban exiles and, 83–84, 85, 119, 161–62; disappearances and, 282; disbanded by Pinochet, 119; dissolution of, 213, 294; documents of, 202–3; establishment of, 32–34; fascism and, 33; Fernández and, 200–201, 209–10, 225, 254–55; human rights violations by, 158, 251, 268, 295–96; implicated in plot, 202; interrogations by, 249; Lagos and, 252–54; orders LAN-Chile pilots to help in plot, 191; other activities of, 170, 173; responsibility for car bomb, 252; Rettig Report and, 243; secrecy oath of, 173; targets of, 69, 148, 151, 222; Townley and, 88–92, 95, 98, 100; U.S. knowledge of, 46; in U.S. territory, 118

National Review, 160
National Security Council, 105, 116, 218, 223; Executive Committee on Combating Terrorism, 223
National Socialist Movement of Chile, 24
National Socialist Party, 25
National Stadium, 34
Nazi Germany, 24–26
Nazis, 23, 24; in Chile, 23–28; former officers, 24; parades, 26; sarin gas and, 94
NBC, 125
Negrín, Eulalio José, 181
Neruda, Pablo, 67

Neutrality Act, 75
New Jersey, 46, 64–65, 80–83, 89, 95, 98–99, 107–8, 112, 151, 180, 194, 236–37
New Jersey Civil Liberties Union, 181
New Jersey Council of Churches, 181
New Jersey Cuban Program, 180
New Republic, 153
Newsweek, 105–6
New York, bombings by CORU in, 88; bombings by Cuban exiles in, 79
New York Academy of Music, bombing attempt at, 111
New York Times, 96, 105, 176, 194, 200, 203, 213, 217, 222
Nixon, Richard, 45, 117, 177
Nixon administration, 20–21, 45, 223
nongovernmental organizations, 217
North Bergen, New Jersey, 73–77
Novo, Guillermo, 73, 79–80, 83–85, 95, 98–99, 116–17, 168, 237, 286–87; acquittal of, 195; arrest of, 172–73; conviction overturned, 194; Fleetwood interview, 99, 111; at grand jury, 113; guilty verdict and sentencing of, 179–80; indictment of, 175, 199; named as coconspirator by Townley, 175; retrial of, 194–95; terrorist attacks by, 74–75; trial of, 175–78, 186
Novo, Ignacio, 73–75, 79–81, 83–85, 101, 114, 176, 178–79, 286–87; acquittal of, 195; arrest of, 175; conviction overturned, 194; Fleetwood interview, 110–11; and grand jury, 112; guilty verdict and sentencing of, 179–80; indictment of, 175, 199; named as coconspirator by Townley, 175; retrial of, 194–95; terrorist attacks by, 74–75, 78; threats from, 179; trial of, 175–78, 186
Novo, Ignacio, Sr. ("Pipo"), 75
Nueva, 215–16

O'Connor, Frank, 74, 75
Office of Strategic Services, 222
O'Higgins, Bernardo, 89
O'Leary, Jeremiah, 120, 161, 164, 165
Omega 7, 77, 180, 181
Onda Brava, 92
Operation Condor, 45, 46, 59, 83, 88, 90, 108, 223, 265, 294

Operation Eagle, 77
Orange Bowl, 77
Organization of American States, 62, 78, 93, 165
Orlando Letelier Muralist Brigade, 156
Orozco, Héctor, 169, 173, 201–2, 231, 235
Ortsgruppen (local Nazi lodges), 24
Osorio, Guillermo, 121, 122
Osorio, Mary Rose, 121, 122
Osorio, Renato, 121–22
Osorno, Chile, 24, 26
Otero, Rolando, 84, 115–16
Overseas Private Investment Corporation, 218

Palme, Olof, 286
Panama, bombings by CORU in, 88
Panama Canal treaties, 120, 162
Panama Canal Zone, 45–46
Panama School of the Americas, 27
Pancho. *See* Letelier, Francisco "Pancho"
Pappalardo, Conrado, 91
Paraguay, 90, 205, 240
Paris, bombings by Cuban exiles in, 79
Parker, Barrington, 177, 179, 180, 194, 195, 212, 232, 233
passports-homicide case, 200, 205, 213, 228, 235–37, 258, 260–61. *See also* Letelier-Moffitt case
Pastor, Robert, 116
Paz, Virgilio, 76–77, 83, 85–86, 95, 99–101, 116, 176, 179, 196, 238–39, 259, 286–88; indictment of, 175, 199; mugshot of, *143*; named as coconspirator by Townley, 175; sought in connection with bombing, 180
Peace Corps, 62
Peña, Juan Cristóbal, 283
Penal Cordillera, 283, 284
Penthouse magazine, 165
Pérez, Carlos Andrés, 42, 150, 263
Pérez-Soto, Sagrario, 70
Pérez Yoma, Edmundo, 274
Pérez y Pérez, Julio Cesar, 73–74
Peru, 23, 220
Peterson, Hans. *See* Townley, Michael
Philippines, 220
Picton Island, 215–16

Index 377

Pimentel, Stanley, 232
"Pinocheques" case, 251
Pinochet, Augusto. *See* Pinochet Ugarte, Augusto José Ramón
Pinochet, Augusto, Sr., 30
Pinochet, Lucía, 33, 272–73
Pinochet family, French origins of, 30
Pinochet regime, 8, 32, 34, 46, 62, 87, 89, 117–19, 147, 211, 251–53; Carter administration and, 220–21; cover-up by, 199–213; disappearances during (*see* "the disappeared"); end of, 224; human rights violations by, 223, 243, 283, 284; political crimes under, 281; pressured to cooperate, 205; Reagan and, 219–20; Reagan administration and, 219–22, 240; repression by, 62; Republican Party and, 216, 219. *See also specific branches of Chilean government*
Pinochet Ugarte, Augusto José Ramón, 1, 7, 36–39, 59, 68–69, 95–96, 118–20, 122–23, 162–63, 196, 200–201; accuses Carter of being soft on "Soviet imperialism," 216; in Allende's administration, 29–35; allies of outside South America, 45; anticommunist regime, 83; appeal of Contreras and Espinoza and, 270; appointees to Supreme Court, 267; arrested in London, 288–89; asks for Contreras's resignation, 206–7; "Black Tuesday" and, 277–78; Chilean military and, 249; Contreras and, 46, 168–69, 189, 202, 206–7, 262, 270, 274, 279, 282, 291–92, 307n; coup against Allende, 35–40, 62, 89, 251; cover-up by, 231; crash of free-market reforms, 68; death of, 291–92; declares himself senator for life, 288; defended by Chilean press, 165–67; denies Chile's involvement in Letelier assassination, 165–66; dictatorship of, 251–53; disbanding of DINA by, 119; exempts Letelier case from Amnesty Law under U.S. pressure, 252; extradition requests and, 207–8, 213, 218–19; failure of White House to confront, 293–94; Fernández and, 205–6, 225, 229, 231, 234; "Freedom Award," 80; indictment of, 289–90; lifts state of siege, 169; loses to Aylwin, 224; meets with Carter, 158; meets with Landau, 204; "No" campaign against, 243, 286; plebiscite and, 220, 245; Punta Peuco and, 279; refuses to resolve Letelier-Moffitt case, 223; returns to Chile from Great Britain, 290; role in assassinations, 90, 105, 151, 202–3, 223–24, 233, 289, 292; smear campaign against Orlando Letelier, 85; stacking of Supreme Court and, 260; statement issued on death bed, 292; stripped of immunity and indicted in Chile, 291; stupidity of, 296; threatens to bring back dictatorship, 251; torture and, 63; Townley and, 169–71, 174, 182; U.S. bank accounts held by, 290–91; U.S.-Chilean relations and, 215–16, 221, 290–91. *See also* Pinochet regime
Plan Z, 32
Polytarides, Antonio, 194
Popper, David, 117–18
Port Elizabeth, New Jersey, 76
Portugal, under Salazar, 53
Posada Carriles, Luis, 78, 110, 287
Prats, Carlos, 59, 69, 89, 184, 268, 282, 285–86
Presidential Security Memorandum 30, 223
the press, 165–67, 176, 185–86, 187–96, 203, 208–10, 212, 265, 268, 270, 271. *See also specific publications*
Prewett, Virginia, 160
Princeton University, 69
Pro-Peace Committee, 227
Propper, Eugene, 138, *138*, 203, 206, 209–12, 272, 288, 295; Cuban Nationalist Movement (CNM) conspiracy to assassinate, 114; death threats received by, 177; leads FBI investigation, 106–16, 119–20, 123–25, 158–59, 161–65, 168–75; Letelier assassination case and, 107; letters rogatory, 163; retirement of, 194; threats against, 113, 179
Puerto Arenas, hospital in, 40
Puerto Montt, Chile, 24
Puerto Rico, 240
Punta Arenas, Chile, 24, 36, 202
Punta Peuco, 279

Quayle, Dan, 224
Quebec City, 149
Qué Pasa (magazine), 85, 203

Radio Liberation, 54
Raskin, Marcus, 65–66, 150
Rauff, Walter, 24–25
Rausch, James, 148
Reagan, Ronald, 62, 160, 214; administration of, 219–20; calls Letelier "unregistered foreign agent," 219; CIA report and, 224; Iran-Contra scandal and, 234; monetary policy of, 220; Pinochet regime and, 219–20
Reagan administration: asks Pinochet to resolve Letelier-Moffitt case, 223; civil suit against Chile and, 189; Fernández's defection and, 232, 233–34; forced to "certify" Pinochet's human rights progress, 294; openly criticizes Pinochet's human rights violations, 223; Pinochet regime and, 219–22, 240; takes on claim of Letelier and Moffitt families, 245; terrorism and, 190; U.S.-Chilean relations and, 222, 223
Regan, Don, 221
Reno, Janet, 290
Renouard, Joe, 62
Renovación Nacional, 274
reparations. *See* compensation
Republican Party, Pinochet regime and, 216, 219
Rettig, Raúl, 243–44
Rettig Report, 243–44, 249, 252, 290
Revolutionary Left Movement (Chile), 69, 92, 105
Riggs National Bank, 189, 290–91
Ritoque concentration camp, 41
Rivero, Felipe, 77, 79, 83, 88
Robinson, Aubrey, 237, 239
Rock Creek Park, Washington, DC, 156
Rodríguez Grez, Pablo, 53, 55–56, 165, 203
Rojas, Rodrigo, 222, 233
Rome, 44, 97
Romeral Jara, Alejandro, 90, 109, 111, 123, 164, 167, 168, 205. *See also* Fernández Larios, Armando

Ros-Lehtinen, Ileana, 286, 288
Ross, Rosita, 176–77
Ross, Stanley, 74
Ross Díaz, Alvin, 75–77, 82, 112, 114–16, 168, 287; acquittal of, 195; arrest of, 172; conviction overturned, 194; guilty verdict and sentencing of, 179–80; indictment of, 175, 199; named as coconspirator by Townley, 175; retrial of, 194–95; trial of, 175–78, 186
Rozas, Raúl, 258, 259
Ryan, Hewson, 46
Ryden, Elizabeth, 111

Salazar, Antonio, 53
Salazar Salvo, Manuel, 34, 255–56, 259
Sandoval, Miguel Angel, 282
Santiago, Chile, 23, 25–26, 32, 52, 63, 92, 119
Santiago Military Hospital, 205, 209, 210, 213, 231
sarin gas, 94
SAVAK, 295–96
Sayago, Miguel, 243, 293
Schäfer, Paul, 25, 33, 53
Scherrer, Robert, 25, 108, 113, 116, 169, 171, 173, 195, 211, 253, 288
Schneider, Mark, 62–63, 218
School of Engineers of Tejas Verdes, 26
Schoultz, Lars, 61–62
Schulback, Helmut, 275
Secret Cuban Government, 77
Seeger, Pete, 61, 95
September 11, 2001, terrorist attacks of, 290–91
Sheridan, Philip, 2
Sheridan Circle bombing, 1–8, 75–76, 101, 125, 150, 152, 157, 161, 240–41; anniversary of, 162; Chilean regime and, 105; commemorative plaque, *141*, 187; fortieth anniversary of, 292–93; investigation of, 105–16, 117–24, 164–82; reactions to, 105; statue memorializing, 293; stupidity of, 296. *See also* Letelier-Moffitt case
Shultz, George, 189, 221–22, 224, 232
Sierra Maestra, 76
Silbert, Earl, 106, 123, 180
Sofaer, Abe, 245

Index 379

Solar, María del, 111
Solar Rosenberg, Inés de, 13, 247
Soria, Carmelo, 58, 281, 286
South American intelligence agencies, 109
Southern Cone, 45–46, 88. *See also specific countries*
South Korea, 27, 295–96
Soviet Mission, bombing of, 181
Soviet Union, 27, 61, 119
Spacek, Sissy, 240
Spain, 22, 25, 53, 60, 75, 76, 271
Spanish Civil War, 53
Stark, Peter, 148, 216
state-sponsored assassination, 8, 292
Stavins, Ralph, 158
Steven, Robert, 117, 118, 120, 164, 217, 296
Stevin Group, 69
St. Joe Minerals, 217
St. Matthew's Roman Catholic Cathedral, 148, 153
St. Paul the Apostle, Church of (New York City), 149
Stroessner, Alfredo, 90, 91
Suárez, José Dionisio, 76, 77, 82–84, 95, 100, 135, 196, 239, 286–88; arrest of, 236–37, 258; attempt to bomb New York Academy of Music, 111; building car bomb, 99; indictment of, 175, 199; named as coconspirator by Townley, 175; offered immunity, 112; sought in connection with bombing, 180; tied to bombing of Russian ship, 111; trial of, 237
Superior Oil, 217
Swastika (magazine), 25
Sweden, 158, 286

Tegualda, 250
terrorism, 8, 190, 196, 207, 222–23, 229, 232, 247, 295; CIA and, 75, 222; counterterrorism, 223, 231, 286, 295, 296; Cuban exiles and, 79, 80, 179–82; domestic vs. international, 295–96; FBI and, 79, 108, 295; Foreign Sovereign Immunities Act and, 245; international, 196, 207; justice and, 293; Letelier campaign against, 247; Letelier-Moffitt case and, 196, 243; Reagan administration and, 190; threat posed by Contreras, 245; U.S. Senate investigation into funding of, 290–91
Teruggi, Frank, 284
Theberge, James, 221
Thieme, Roberto, 53
Third National Day of Protest, 242
Third World Women's Project, 157–58
Thirtieth of November Movement, 77
Tigar, Michael, 161, 162, 187–91
Tigar & Buffone, 189–90
Times Square (New York City), 73
Tohá, José, 178
Tohá, Moy, 178
Tonight Show, 61
torture, 34, 58, 63
"The Touchstone Gallery," 69
Townley, Brian, 49
Townley, Christopher, 49
Townley, Margaret, 47
Townley, Michael, 46–60, 83–86, 88–90, 93–95, 98, 101, 115–17, 132, 164–65, 168, 196; alibi of, 100; anti-Allende stance of, 52; and CIA, 52; Argentina seeks extradition of, 285–86; arrest of, 171–73; assassination attempt against Leighton and Fresno, 45; car bombings and, 45, 59, 75, 99–100; charged with conspiracy, 173–74; childhood of, 47; children of, 49; Contreras and, 166–67, 173, 174, 182; credibility of, 212, 268; defense strategy of, 178–79; denies involvement in Letelier assassination, 169; DINA and, 57–58, 88–92, 95, 98, 100; education of, 47–48; Espinoza and, 264; explosives and, 55; expulsion of, 169–71, 174–75, 200, 207; fake passport, 91; FBI investigation of, 167–68; at Federal Correctional Institution, Englewood, 183–84; Fernández and, 201–2, 204, 209, 211, 225; handed over by Pinochet, 215; held at gunpoint by Cuban exiles, 84; imprisonment of, 182–84, 196; Lagos and, 252–53; on LAN-Chile plane, 191; marriage to Callejas, 48, 49, 57, 59; move to Miami, 50; passport obtained by, 165, 290; penance of, 233; personality

problems of, 48; photo of, *140*, 214; Pinochet and, 174, 182; pleads guilty, 173; possible assassination of Allende, 54–55; Prats murder and, 286; the press and, 167; probation hearings of, 182–83, 184; protected from extradition, 173; under protection of U.S. marshals, 176; questioned by U.S. government, 169; remorse of, 177, 178; sarin gas, 94; smuggling bomb parts into U.S., 94; split with Callejas, 184; stupidity of, 296; taped threatening judge, 179, 194; testimony of, 173–75, 177, 178, 180, 191, 194, 201, 281; threats against, 179; trial of, 232; U.S. Justice Department and, 167–68; visa cancelled, 91; in Witness Protection Program, 182, 286

Townley, Vernon Jay, 46, 47, 48, 183

Transnational Institute (Amsterdam), 66, 68

Treaty for the Settlement of Disputes That May Occur between the United States and Chile, 246

Trinquero, Victor, 172

Trucco, Manuel, 118–19, 147

Ugarte, Avelina, 30–31

Unification Church, 83

Union City, New Jersey, 75, 81, 116, 177, 195, 287

Unitas 21, 219

United Nations, 149; attack on building, 73–74; Commission on Human Rights, 39, 214; condemns Chile for human rights violations, 219; Convention against Torture, 287; General Assembly, 73, 119, 122; Secretariat, 73; targeting of, *134*

United States, 27; aid to Chile, 205, 245–46; asks Chile to arrest and expel Contreras and Espinoza, 234–35; human rights violations and, 240; Letelier-Moffitt case and, 294–95; policy toward Chile, 214–24, 222–23; relationship with Chile, 117, 214–24; request for extradition of Contreras, Fernández, and Espinoza, 206–13

The United States of America v. Manuel Contreras et al., 175

University of California, Berkeley, 62, 155

University of Chicago, 32

University of Chile, 24, 31

University of Maryland, 65, 155

University of Miami, 50, 77

University of Minnesota, 106

University of Virginia, 108

Uruguay, 220, 264, 265

U.S. Army Intelligence, 91

U.S. Army School of the Americas, 35

U.S. Attorney for New York, 114

U.S. Attorney's Office, 107

U.S. business community, U.S.-Chilean relations and, 217

U.S.-Chilean relations, 8, 169, 205–13, 214–24, 246–47, 259–60, 293–94

U.S. Code 1116(a), 123

U.S. Commission on Human Rights, 158

U.S. Congress, 62–63, 289; cuts off aid to Chile, 205; forced to "certify" Pinochet's human rights progress, 294; Foreign Sovereign Immunities Act and, 245; Iran-Contra scandal and, 234; Letelier-Moffitt case and, 247; U.S.-Chilean relations and, 216, 217, 218, 222. *See also* U.S. House of Representatives; U.S. Senate

U.S. Defense Department, 34, 205, 206, 218, 222, 244

U.S. Department of Agriculture, 122

U.S. District Court for the District of Columbia, 112

U.S. embassy, Buenos Aires, 108

U.S. embassy, Caracas, 110

U.S. embassy, Santiago, 41, 229, 272

U.S. House of Representatives: Foreign Affairs Committee, 286; FSIA and, 193, 245; House Government Activities and Transportation Subcommittee, 191–92; House Judiciary Committee, 193; H.R. 3763, 193; U.S.-Chilean relations and, 259–60

U.S. Justice Department, 106–7, 117–18, 125, 159, 163, 167–68, 191, 201, 221, 289, 293; Cuban exiles and, 111–13, 181; Fernández and, 229, 231; Major Crimes Division, 107; quest for justice and, 196; grand jury investigation into Pinochet, 290; shuts down American-Chilean Council, 64; suspicion of DINA, 162; Townley and, 167–68, 172, 174–75, 285; U.S.-Chilean relations and, 216. *See also* Federal Bureau of Investigation; Letelier-Moffitt case

U.S. Navy, 108

U.S. Senate: Foreign Sovereign Immunities Act and, 245; investigation into terrorist funding, 290–91

U.S. State Department, 2, 69, 118, 149, 161, 165, 196, 247, 289; accused of harboring political objectives, 208; advanced knowledge of possible assassinations, 46; American Republics Bureau, 206; on Bórquez decision, 211–12; civil suit against Chile and, 189, 244; Contreras and, 206; Fernández and, 231; Foreign Sovereign Immunities Act and, 245; human rights and, 62, 220; Iran-Contra scandal and, 234; LAN-Chile and, 192; Letelier-Moffitt families' demands from Chile and, 245–46; recalls Landau, 204–5, 212; U.S.-Chilean relations and, 205, 217, 218, 222, 223; use of word "terrorists," 218; Williams-Romeral fake passports and, 111

U.S. Supreme Court: Bush v. Gore, 287; Letelier-Moffitt case and, 193

U.S. Treasury: denies loans to Chile, 219

U.S. War Department, 46. *See also* U.S. Defense Department

Valdebenito, María Teresa, 26–27, 250
Valdés, Juan Gabriel, 69, 151, 294
Valdés Puga, Enrique, 121
Valdivia, Julia, 83
Valech Report of 2003–4, 290
Valparaiso, Chile, 23
Vance, Cyrus, 123, 213, 218
Vanderbilt Law School, 107
Vatican City, 44
Venezuelan secret police, 110
Videla, Eugenio, 271

Viejo Roble, 250, 270, 273, 275, 276
Vietnam War, 52, 61–62, 65, 106
Villa Grimaldi, 214

Wack, Lawrence, 107–8, 111, 112–15
Walker, Charly, 92
Walker, Liliana, 144, 191, 230, 235, 252–59. *See also* Lagos Aguirre, Luisa Mónica
Walker, Patricio ("Pato"), 92, 93, 101
Walsh, Philip, 74
Walters, Vernon, 91, 109, 209
War Academy in Santiago, 26
War of the Pacific, 23, 26
Warren, Ray, 46
Washington Office on Latin America, 69
Washington Post, 113, 116, 125, 161, 178, 203, 204, 213, 275, 292
Washington Star, 113, 125, 161, 164
Watergate, 62, 78, 113, 116
Whitten, Les, 159
Wiley, Alyce, 5
Williams-Romeral fake passports, 120, 121, 125. *See also* passports-homicide case; Romeral Jara, Alejandro; Williams Rose, Juan
Williams Rose, Juan, 90, 109, 111, 115–16, 123, 164–65, 167, 168, 205. *See also* Townley, Michael
Willoughby, Federico, 211, 229, 230
"Willoughby gambit," 211
Wilson, Edwin P., 113
Witness Protection Program, 182, 233
Woodward, Bob, 113
World Bank, 69, 120
World War I, 30
World War II, 24, 25, 35, 73, 91, 206

Yeshiva Central, 106
Young Cuba, 77

Zone I (Cuba), 80
Zone II (New Jersey), 80
Zone III (Miami), 80

www.ingramcontent.com/pod-product-compliance
Lightning Source LLC
Chambersburg PA
CBHW030517230426
43665CB00010B/650